Forever on the Mountain

Forever on the Mountain

THE TRUTH BEHIND ONE OF MOUNTAINEERING'S MOST CONTROVERSIAL AND MYSTERIOUS DISASTERS

James M. Tabor

W. W. NORTON & COMPANY

New York   London

Maps of Alaska & Mt. McKinley / Denali (pages 8–9) and 1967 Tragedy Area: Camp VII
to Summit (page 233) by Paul J. Pugliese. Map of Mount McKinley, Alaska / Route of the
Wilcox Expedition (pages 84–85) reproduced courtesy of Joseph Wilcox.

Excerpts from *Guide to the Muldrow Glacier Route* by Bradford Washburn and from Washburn's
correspondence (contained in the Washburn Collection at the Gottlieb Archive, Boston University,
and the Washburn Collection at the University of Alaska) reproduced by permission of Barbara
and Bradford Washburn. Excerpts from *White Winds* (1983) and *A Reader's Guide to the Hall of
the Mountain King* (1981) are reprinted by permission of Joseph Wilcox. Excerpts from *The Hall of
the Mountain King* by Howard Snyder (1973) and Snyder's expedition records and correspondence
reproduced by permission of Howard Snyder.

For information about permission to reproduce selections from this book, write to Permissions,
W. W. Norton & Company, Inc., 500 Fifth Avenue, New York, NY 10110

Manufacturing by Quebecor World Fairfield
Book design by Chris Welch
Production manager: Anna Oler

Library of Congress Cataloging-in-Publication Data

Tabor, James M.
Forever on the mountain : the truth behind one of mountaineering's most controversial
and mysterious disasters / James M. Tabor. — 1st ed.
p. cm.
Includes bibliographical references and index.
ISBN 978-0-393-06174-1 (hardcover)
1. Mountaineering accidents—Alaska—McKinley, Mount.
2. Mountaineering—Alaska—McKinley, Mount. I. Title.
GV199.42.A42M3273 2007
796.52209798—dc22

2007013711

W. W. Norton & Company. Inc., 500 Fifth Avenue, New York, N.Y. 10110
www.wwnorton.com

W. W. Norton & Company Ltd., Castle House, 75/76 Wells Street
London W1T 3QT

2 3 4 5 6 7 8 9 0

This book is dedicated to my family.

Contents

PART THREE

Accident

PART FOUR

Aftermath

Maps

Acknowledgments

This book would never have been written but for the faith and hard work of three people: my wife, Liz, who, more than anyone or anything else, made it happen; my intrepid literary agent, Ethan Ellenberg, the first publishing industry professional who recognized the book's value and then made it better; and W. W. Norton's marvelous editor Erik Johnson, who took the ball from Ethan and ran with it. If he is not Maxwell Perkins incarnate, I will eat my galley proofs.

It would be nice to say good things about the other W. W. Nortonians who helped create the book, but I cannot. I can only say *great* things about each and every one. Norton people are, quite simply, the kind that current conventional wisdom claims have disappeared from book publishing. *I* say, bosh. At Norton, they are utterly committed to excellence, generous to a fault with their time, endlessly patient, and exquisitely skilled at what they do.

Nancy Palmquist, managing editor; Don Rifkin, associate managing editor; and Barbara Feller-Roth, copy editor, did not blink when I turned in a 140,000-word manuscript, though the contract called for 85,000. They not only ensured the book's accuracy but also artfully polished its sometimes-rough writing.

If clothes make a person, design and production make a book. Chris Welch, interior designer, gave this one lovely elegance. Debra Morton Hoyt, art director, and the DesignWorks Group jacket design studio captured McKinley's beauty *and* menace. Anna Oler, production manager, made sure that everything kept flowing despite deadlines that seemed to approach at light speed.

A book that nobody knows about is like that proverbial falling tree in the forest. Publicist Adele McCarthy-Beauvais made sure that *Forever on the Mountain* came out with a bang. A book that nobody buys is every writer's nightmare, which Sales Director Bill Rusin made certain I would not have to endure. Finally, Felice Mello, U.S. subsidiary rights director, ensured that the book will find expression in so many other media that I have lost track of all of them—but not of my debt to her.

Special thanks must go to several other authors who gave their time to read early versions of the book and their wisdom to make it better. David Roberts I have thanked elsewhere. David Baron, the award-winning science journalist and author of *The Beast in the Garden*, provided far too much invaluable advice to list here, but I am deeply in his debt, as I am to the superb mountaineering writer and photographer Gordon Wiltsie, author most recently of *To the Ends of the Earth*.

Wallis Anne Wheeler, and my sons, Damon and Jack, read early versions and critiqued them wisely. Tasha Wallis and Missy Siner Shea's early encouragement helped greatly.

Many dedicated National Park Service (NPS) employees aided my research, including Stacey Chadwick, Kim Fister, mountaineering ranger Gordy Kito, Missy Smothers, and Stacey Walker. Denali National Park and Preserve's current South District ranger, Daryl Miller, and Chief Climbing Ranger Roger Robinson, deserve special mention. Both consummate climbers and search-and-rescue experts, they shed priceless light on Denali's terrain, weather, rescues, and characters. Denali National Park historian Frank Norris supplied important information about the 1967 tragedy's impact on park service policies and practices.

The University of Alaska's (UA) William Schneider, curator of Oral History, presides over the Jukebox Oral History Series, surely one of the world's finest such collections. Very helpful work on my behalf was performed by UA archivists Peggy Asbury, Robyn Russell, Arlene Schulman, Caroline Atuk-Derrick, and Elizabeth Keech.

Though in their nineties, Brad and Barbara Washburn granted a number of interviews. They also gave permission to quote from materials contained in the Washburn Collection at the Howard Gottlieb Archival Research Center at Boston University, the Washburn Collection in the

Rasmussen Library at the University of Alaska Fairbanks, and the Washburn Collection at the American Alpine Club's (AAC) library in Golden, Colorado. Boston University Archivist JC Johnson and AAC library director Bridget Burke made my visits to their archives as enjoyable as they were fruitful. Betty Howlett of the Waitsfield Public Library was more helpful than I can express. Kim Woblaver transcribed many hours of taped interviews with estimable speed and accuracy.

Dr. Charles Houston, member of the legendary 1953 American K2 Expedition and paterfamilias of high-altitude research, was the single most important source of information about altitude's effect on humans. He and another American K2 veteran, the writer, cartographer, and artist Dee Molenaar, also helped me better understand ties that bind together brothers of the rope.

David Roberts shared his limitless knowledge of mountaineering history, helping me avoid the embarrassment of errors made by one less expert.

Weather was a key player in this tragedy, and a number of meteorologists unraveled mysteries of the epic storms of July 1967. These included forensic meteorologist Dr. Greg MacMaster; the Alaska Climate Research Center's Dr. Martha Shulski; and National Weather Service meteorologists Ted Fathauer and Scott Whittier. Meteorologists Matthew Sturm and Keith Heidorn were also helpful.

Forensic expertise came from a number of sources. Dr. Ruth Holmes, nationally known certified document examiner, analyzed handwriting samples from expedition members. Mark Wisniowski performed forensic examination and reconstruction of key photographs. Dr. Charles Perrow, author of the groundbreaking *Normal Accidents*, shed light on how complex systems such as mountain climbing expeditions fail. Dr. William Bass, founder of the legendary Body Farm at the University of Tennessee, helped me understand the esoterica of body decomposition. Psychologist Gail Rosenbaum illuminated the effects of altitude on intellect and personality.

Bill Romberg, vice chair of the Alaska Mountain Rescue Group (AMRG), dug bravely through his organization's dusty archives to locate long-lost documents of value to me.

Former NPS seasonal ranger Gordon Haber recollected events during and after the July 1967 tragedy that were most helpful, as were McKinley veteran Norm Benton's memories of Mark McLaughlin and other expedition members. I was, sadly, unable to locate the MCA's Gary Hansen.

Craig Medred, outdoor columnist for the *Anchorage Daily News*, provided insights into the history and current state of Denali climbing.

Roberta Sheldon, widow of the incomparable pilot Don Sheldon, graciously shared her knowledge of Alaskan aviation and aviators.

Cheryl Kehr Cleveland spoke openly and movingly about her 1967 marriage to Joe Wilcox.

The famed climber and internationally acclaimed search-and-rescue expert Wayne Merry was Mount McKinley National Park's only mountaineering ranger in 1967, and as such played a pivotal role in the events of that July. His help with my research was no less pivotal. Now in his seventies, Wayne has an appetite for adventure that remains almost as sharp as his memory. I will never be able to thank him fully for his endless patience and tireless efforts to help me excavate details from beneath the accumulated weight of forty years.

Led by Bill Babcock, the Mountaineering Club of Alaska Expedition's heroic attempt to rescue the seven men trapped by the July 1967 storm has sadly been overshadowed by the tragedy itself. This book tries to provide at least some of their long overdue recognition. Bill and Jeff Babcock, Gayle Nienheuser, and John Ireton shared their journals, photographs, maps, and memories without reservation. I was unable to locate Chet Hackney, the fifth member of that inestimable team, but have tried to portray his contribution to the MCA effort.

THE TRAGEDY PRODUCED seven victims and five survivors. Without the limitless cooperation of Jerry Lewis, Anshel Schiff, Howard Snyder, Joe Wilcox, and Paul Schlichter, this book would have died aborning. Among many other things, without their trust and memories, I could never have come to know victims Jerry Clark, Hank Janes, Dennis Luchterhand, Mark McLaughlin, John Russell, Steve Taylor, and Walt Taylor. Jerry Lewis, Anshel, Howard, Joe, and Paul willingly reexplored a horribly traumatic period, at considerable cost in time, labor, and pain to themselves, with no reward other than helping an unfamiliar author look for truth. Joe and Robin Wilcox, Jerry and Louisa Lewis, Paul and Beverly Schlichter, and Howard Snyder welcomed me into their lives as well as their archives.

More than that an author cannot hope for.

Introduction

In July 1967, seven young Americans died on Alaska's Mount McKinley, the highest mountain in North America and one of the most dangerous mountains on Earth. It was one of the worst tragedies in
mountaineering history up to that time. It is still the worst expeditionary
mountaineering disaster in North American history. It is also, according
to no less an authority than acclaimed climber and mountaineering
writer Jonathan Waterman, "the most tragic and bitterly contested controversy in Denali history." Denali (the mountain's Native American
name) and Everest are the world's two truly iconic peaks, so that is saying something.

Proper investigation would have done much to prevent such tragic
and bitter controversy. In 1949, when thirteen young Smokejumpers
died in Montana's Mann Gulch (by fire rather than ice), a formal government inquiry convened the world's top forest fire experts, who spent
weeks investigating the tragedy and issued formal reports hundreds of
pages long.

There was no such lengthy, formal investigation into why and how the
seven men died on McKinley in 1967. What passed for an investigation
lasted a day and a half, was held in a posh Anchorage hotel, and included
neither testimony from nor appearances by any of the five survivors. As
it turned out, the survivors' testimony wasn't really needed, because the
conclusions were foregone before the meeting began.

There was press coverage of the tragedy, of course. Newspaper articles
appeared, as did an article in *Time* magazine. But this was 1967, remem-

ber. The United States was deep in Vietnam's quagmire, our inner cities were exploding, college campuses were erupting, and a presidency was self-destructing. Seven deaths on a remote mountain, although terrible, had to vie with such tectonic disruptions for column inches.

The July 1967 tragedy did hold center stage for North America's close-knit mountaineering community. *Summit Magazine,* then one of the world's premier climbing publications, ran a lengthy article about the event. The American Alpine Club (AAC), then and now perhaps the world's preeminent mountaineering organization, published an analysis of the disaster. Two expedition members wrote books. But *Time's* account was flawed, as was—uncharacteristically—the AAC's analysis. Both books were *mea non culpas,* which rendered them suspect. Rescuers eventually found three bodies, but lethal weather prevented their recovery. The rescuers did not find cameras or diaries, both of which could have shed light on what happened. Thus post-expedition writings only thickened, rather than dissipated, the fog of disaster.

For all these reasons, as Jonathan Waterman noted, the 1967 Mount McKinley disaster remains the most mysterious, controversial, and bitterly debated event of its kind in North American mountaineering history. I would take that one step further, and suggest that it may well be the most controversial, bitterly contested, and mysterious tragedy of its kind, period. Some mountaineers, and knowledgeable laypeople, may object that the mystery of Mallory and Irvine on Everest takes precedence. It's not an unreasonable reflex, given the vastly greater attention paid to the two valiant Englishmen who perished high on Everest in 1924. But the mystery of Mallory and Irvine remains just that, a mystery, which Webster tells us "is not fully understood or . . . baffles or eludes the understanding." There has simply never been enough information about Mallory and Irvine's fate on Everest, and more specifically about whether or not they reached the summit, to generate the divided, warring camps of opinion required for true controversy, which is, after all, debate marked by dispute, quarrel, and strife. Thus over decades consensus has devolved to a frustrated but noncombative "wait and see" impasse not relieved even by the discovery of Mallory's body by Conrad Anker on May 1, 1999.

Other people may object still further, holding up the 1996 debacle on Everest brilliantly depicted in Jon Krakauer's *Into Thin Air*. Although it was certainly tragic, and ignited a firestorm of outrage and grief, neither mystery nor true controversy attended that disaster's sad denouement. Its genesis, conduct, and aftermath were thoroughly documented: One victim, Rob Hall, spoke to his wife by satellite phone while he lay dying at 28,500 feet; parts of the story appeared in a blockbuster IMAX film; and Jon Krakauer's book took up residence on the summit of the *New York Times* best-seller list. Finally, there was no real argument over that tragedy's prime mover. When all the superficials were stripped away, it became clear that money—marginally experienced clients paying $60,000 fees to guides—was the root of the problem.

But still — twelve men went up a dangerous mountain, there was a storm, five came down. End of story, right? No. As Norman Maclean demonstrated in his book *Young Men and Fire* about the 1949 Mann Gulch disaster, all stories—and tragedies most of all—contain other stories. Sometimes these other stories are obvious; sometimes they need help to tell themselves. Maclean put it this way: "often the best we can do with catastrophes, even our own, is to find out exactly what happened and restore some of the missing parts—hopefully, even the arch to the sky."

After the Mann Gulch fire had burned every living thing there was to burn, including roots of trees deep in the soil, a wealth of explanatory evidence remained. On August 6, the day after the fire, searchers recovered all thirteen bodies right where they had fallen as the fire sprinted faster than they could. Investigators photographed everything and took statements from the three survivors, from pilots and supervisors and dispatchers, from everyone connected in any way to what happened. The government convened not one but two official inquiries and issued two official reports. And even with all of that, for Maclean the story was still missing far too many of its parts, and far too many questions remained unanswered. The most terrible one was whether Wag Dodge, the leader of the Smokejumper crew who survived, caused the deaths of the thirteen men who did not.

INVESTIGATORS RECOVERED NO bodies after the 1967 McKinley tragedy, took no forensic photographs, convened no official inquiries. Thus this story had even more missing parts and more unanswered questions. One thing, however, was clear: The young men who died on McKinley in 1967 were very good men indeed, capable climbers and exemplars of the best and brightest that the United States was then capable of producing. The youngest was twenty-two, the oldest thirty-one. Seven of the twelve had been Eagle Scouts and, later, Scout leaders. Two had been star athletes in high school and college. Between them they held six bachelor's degrees, four master's degrees, and a PhD. One man, Walt Taylor, was enrolled in an elite program leading simultaneously to an MD and a master's degree in philosophy. The men had won many scholarships and awards, including a Danforth Fellowship. One had completed a meritorious tour of military service. Another had just graduated with honors from the U.S. Air Force Academy, and would go on to fly three hundred combat missions in Vietnam. One was planning to embark on a South American mission for his church when he returned from McKinley. Another—a white man—taught school in one of Portland, Oregon's, worst inner city neighborhoods; his principal called him "a blossoming young teacher of great potential . . . who commanded such appreciation and respect." If you had scoured this country seeking All-American boys suitable for the covers of *Life* or *Time,* you would have been hard-pressed to outshine this group.

When villains and evildoers die, it's usually enough to know that they're gone, and good riddance. The manner of their departure is less important than their welcome absence. It is different when good young men, such as the 1967 McKinley climbers, die mysteriously and tragically. It does not much matter whether they die by fire in a gulch or by ice on a mountain, but what happens after their deaths *does* matter for many reasons. The most obvious is that they are no longer able to speak for themselves, to explain why this very bad thing happened to these very good people, and to make sure that any investigation of the quick and the dead does justice to both.

The "quick"—those who get out of a tragedy alive—are usually thought the lucky ones. Survivors of the McKinley tragedy escaped with their lives, but many suffered severe and lasting damage. Twenty-seven years after the expedition, an interviewer, Jonathan Waterman, found that "Howard Snyder is still haunted by the expedition. He dreams of all but one of the missing men walking back down to him . . ."

One of the other survivors wept when viewing thirty-nine-year-old photographs of the expedition. Grief killed one victim's mother, who died from a heart attack not long after learning of her son's death. Another victim's younger brother, already suffering from depression, was driven to suicide by his sibling's death on McKinley. One climbing ranger, devastated by the abortive rescue attempt's failure to save a single life, abandoned a promising ten-year career with the National Park Service in disgust. Fourteen years after the event, he told expedition organizer and leader Joe Wilcox that "your tragedy has profoundly affected my life also." Today, forty years later, one rescue party member still weeps when viewing photographs of the expedition. As he told me, "Even today, when I look at the slides of our climb, I often find myself breaking down in tears at the sadness of this tragedy." Another said of his experience on McKinley, "That was a reference point for my life." And he, remember, was a *rescuer*.

Of all the survivors, though, Joe Wilcox unquestionably suffered the longest and hardest. The McKinley tragedy undermined Joe's marriage to his first love, Cheryl Kehr. Whereas some survivors of a tragedy find redemption in its aftermath, thirteen years after this one, Joe had not: "Although some people seem religiously strengthened by surviving an ordeal against immense odds, I was not. I did not feel that my life had been spared for some great or noble purpose." If there is a fate worse than death, it surely must be surviving a tragedy while men under your care and direction did not—regardless of how well you thought you led them. Finally, public pronouncements by the world's leading Mount McKinley expert, echoes of those pronouncements through the mountaineering community, and a book, *The Hall of the Mountain King*, by fellow climber Howard Snyder all suggested that Joe's flawed leadership contributed to the tragedy. In 1983, Joe published *White Winds*, attempting to refute those accusations, but his critics had already taken and held the high ground. Thus as late as 1998, Jonathan Waterman would write in his book *In the Shadow of Denali,* "Ask any Denali devo-

tee why the [1967] tragedy happened and they will answer: because of
Wilcox." If that long, sad list needed a coda, it was provided by my visit
to Joe in 2005, thirty-eight years after the disaster on McKinley. I got to
know Joe Wilcox well during that extended visit and the years it took to
write this book. But no one knows Joe as well as his current wife, Robin.
During one private moment she confided, "I do not think Joe has ever
really faced his demons."

While I was writing this book, many people asked the logical question: Why resurrect the July 1967 McKinley tragedy after all these years?
One reason was to perform the first objective, unbiased investigation of
the disaster, in the hope of revealing what actually happened to the victims, and why. In addition, I wanted to clarify Joe Wilcox's role once and
for all. For nearly four decades he had lived under a shadow. Was he vil-
lain, victim, or something else altogether? But the question's best answer
may well have come from Craig Medred, the superb outdoor writer for
the *Anchorage Daily News* and himself an accomplished mountaineer
who has done his own hard time on McKinley: "I'd love to talk about the
Wilcox Expedition," Craig told me, "because a lot of people are living
under the illusion it couldn't happen again."

Cast of Characters

The 1967 Joseph F. Wilcox Mount McKinley Expedition

Joe Wilcox, leader
Jerry Clark, deputy leader
Hank Janes
Dennis Luchterhand
Mark McLaughlin
John Russell
Anshel Schiff
Steve Taylor (Joe Wilcox's only close friend on the team)
Walt Taylor

The 1967 Colorado Mount McKinley Expedition

Howard Snyder, leader
Jerry Lewis
Paul Schlichter

Mount McKinley National Park Personnel

George Hall, superintendent
Gordon Haber, seasonal ranger
Arthur Hayes, chief ranger
Wayne Merry, climbing ranger
Bradford Washburn, consultant

Mountaineering Club of Alaska (MCA) 1967 Mount McKinley Expedition

Bill Babcock, leader
Jeff Babcock
Chet Hackney
John Ireton
Gayle Nienheuser
Grace Jansen-Hoeman

Alaska Rescue Group

Gary Hansen, chairman, Alaska Rescue Group
Don Sheldon, search and rescue pilot

Forever on the Mountain

Sharp End of the Dream

*I*t is 3:00 p.m. on Monday, July 17, 1967. In Camp VII at 17,900 feet, six members of the Joseph Wilcox Mount McKinley Expedition are making final preparations for their attempt on the mountain's summit—2,420 vertical feet higher and two miles distant. They are expedition deputy leader Jerry Clark and climbers Hank Janes, Dennis Luchterhand, Mark McLaughlin, John Russell, and Walt Taylor. A seventh man, Steve Taylor (unrelated to Walt), is suffering from altitude and will stay in his tent while the others climb.

They all have endured the agonies of hell for this one shot at McKinley's summit, but they take plenty of time to make sure that Steve has everything he will need while they're gone. Many climbers would be shattered by failing to reach the top after having invested so much money, time, and pain to reach that one small white spot, no bigger than a tabletop, at 20,320 feet. But Steve is a gentle, playful twenty-two year old, and a devout Mormon, and that helps him accept fate with grace unusual in one so young.

Their bodies, journals, and cameras are still somewhere on McKinley, but before the expedition they wrote autobiographies and many letters. After it people who knew them well wrote many things about them, and the expedition's five other men remember them well. In addition, all expeditions making ready for their summit bids go through similar rituals, so I can see them piling more snow around Steve's orange tent, giving him an extra sleeping pad, chocolate, Logan bread. Tall Mark McLaughlin, team jester, may toss in an extra roll of toilet paper—because you're so full of it! Hank

3

Janes, the small, quiet teacher who has turned out to be utterly capable up here, might melt extra snow for Steve's water.

Their leader, now that Joe Wilcox and four others have descended to a lower camp, is freckle-faced Jerry Clark, thirty-one, a good man to be with on a bad mountain: affable, unflappable, quick to smile and slow to snap. It's rare to find him not grinning about something, but just now it bothers him that National Park Service rangers down below have provided no weather forecast. He has spent years in high mountains as far away as Antarctica and can read signs such as backing wind and puffy altocumulus clouds clustering up like fat boys at a dance, and, especially, thin, high cirrus clouds that look like white scratches in the polished blue sky. The signs he can't see are the ones that concern him.

It's not idle worry, because McKinley is like no other place on Earth, and Jerry knows it. The highest point in North America, McKinley is 2,400 miles and 35 degrees of latitude farther north than Everest, which one expert calls "tropical" by comparison. Earth's atmosphere is thickest near the equator and grows thinner nearing the poles; McKinley's proximity to the North Pole makes its 20,320-foot altitude equal to 23,000 feet or more in the Himalaya. Finally, this mountain is not far from the Bering Sea, which sends monstrous storms whirling east with frightening regularity. McKinley, due east, is like a rock sticking up into a river's violent whitewater.

Jerry understands all this. He knows, too, that McKinley is one of those mountains big enough to brew up its own bad weather, which can go from blue sky to wild blizzard in an hour or less, bringing storms such as the white squalls that kill big ships on the open ocean.

By now the men have had three hours of clear sky, stable temperatures, and light winds, and Jerry knows that on a mountain like this there are no guarantees—hopes, probabilities, possibilities, but never guarantees. So at some point, after all the signs are read and permutations calculated, you have to commit and go. It's like the V1 takeoff "point of no return" for aircraft—once you reach that speed, stopping is no longer an option. You just have to aim for the sky and have faith.

Jerry takes one final look at the men in their puffy parkas the colors of autumn leaves. Making up the first rope are handsome, indefatigable Walt Taylor, strongman John Russell, and fireplug Hank Janes. Jerry Clark, lanky Dennis Luchterhand, and good-humored, steady Mark McLaughlin are the second rope. At about half past three, Jerry shouts something like,

Hey, you mothahs—we gung ho and good to go?

They shout back, but one man at least is not feeling so gung ho. Two days before, John Russell, the expedition's Incredible Hulk, gave out suddenly, astonishing himself as much as his rope mates, on the grueling carry from Camp VI, at 15,000 feet, to Camp VII, at 17,900 feet. The next day was a storm day, which allowed him some rest. He feels better today than when he crept into camp so sick he could barely see after that horrible haul. But he does not feel good, and it is the first time in his life that John's iron-muscled body has betrayed him.

One of the hard lessons they've all learned during this, their first excursion above 14,000 feet, is that altitude sucks. Literally. It sucks energy from muscles and thoughts from brains and joy clean out of dreams. If you're a woman with children, imagine your worst hangover on top of first-trimester morning sickness combined with the flu. If you're a male, combine the hangover and flu with running sprints.

Altitude is not only debilitating—it's fickle beyond imagining. Every human reacts differently, so the hundreds of training miles you ran, those endless sickening wind sprints, the fast hikes under hundred-pound packs may count for absolutely nothing up high. During the first ascent of Mount McKinley in 1913, the party leader, Archdeacon Hudson Stuck, suffered cruelly from altitude and saw how differently others on his team responded: "Karstens, who smoked continually, and Walter, who had never smoked in his life, had the best wind of the party." Up here all suffer, a few thrive, and some just sit down and die, as did a climber on June 29, 2006, while descending the Headwall of the West Buttress route at about 15,500 feet. At 5:30 p.m., the man simply sat down and never stood up again, despite teammates' frantic CPR and rescue efforts.

Thus stocky Walt Taylor, the twenty-four-year-old wunderkind enrolled in an elite MD/MA program, has never been above 14,000 feet but is the strongest of them all up here. Face painted clownlike with white zinc oxide, head crowned with his orange wool fez, he has the lead spot on the first rope. That's like being an infantry squad's point man, working harder, taking the big risks: first to fall in a crevasse, first to be eaten by an avalanche, first to crack a cornice and take a 7,000-foot plunge.

Walt is perfect for point work—muscular and tough and with the genetic blessing of acclimatizing well. He's also funny, in a wry Indiana way, and humor is a huge help on an expedition, especially in somebody leading the pack. In the autobiography he wrote as part of his climbing permit application, Walt stated: "I was born in Indiana, went to high school in Indiana, attended college in Indiana, have a burial plot reserved in Indiana, but I plan to die elsewhere." About a month before the expedition, he also wrote this in a letter to his good friend Jerry: "Perhaps our party is a lot weaker than I've guessed."

Back in camp, Steve Taylor stands alone watching his friends climb the easy slope to Denali Pass. Steve started this expedition at 150 pounds. By this, the twenty-ninth day, he's lost more than fifteen pounds, so his red parka and pants are hanging on his bony, six-feet-two frame. His scraggly beard and weather-battered face make him look ten years older.

Jerry Clark is not the kind of man—none of them are—who will abandon a sick companion high up, summit or no summit, if he thinks doing so will endanger him. But Steve is eating and drinking, urinating and defecating, making sense when he talks, and staying upright when he walks. His lungs are clear, and his brain, though fogged like all the others', is still ticking over. He has enough food and fuel to sustain him here for days, and the weather looks stable. So he urged the others on, knowing how much they have sacrificed for this, and he is genuinely happy as he watches them climb right to left across the silver arc of Denali Pass, heading toward the black rocks at its southern end, their silhouettes, a half mile distant, etched into the cobalt sky as they climb to the sharp end of their dream.

PART ONE

APPROACH

The mountains one gazes at, reads about, dreams of and desires are not the mountains one climbs.

—Robert Macfarlane
Mountains of the Mind

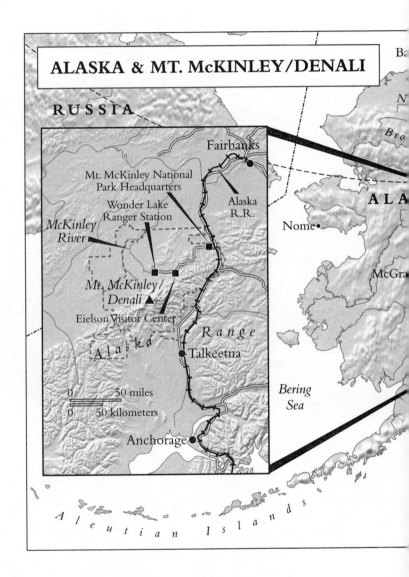

ALASKA & MT. McKINLEY/DENALI

RUSSIA

Fairbanks

Mt. McKinley National
Park Headquarters

Wonder Lake
Ranger Station

*McKinley
River*

Alaska
R.R.

Nome•

*Mt. McKinley/
Denali* ▲

Eielson Visitor Center

A l a s k a

R a n g e

•Talkeetna

0   50 miles

0   50 kilometers

*Bering
Sea*

Anchorage•

A l e u t i a n   I s l a n d s

Ba

N

Bro

A L A

McGra

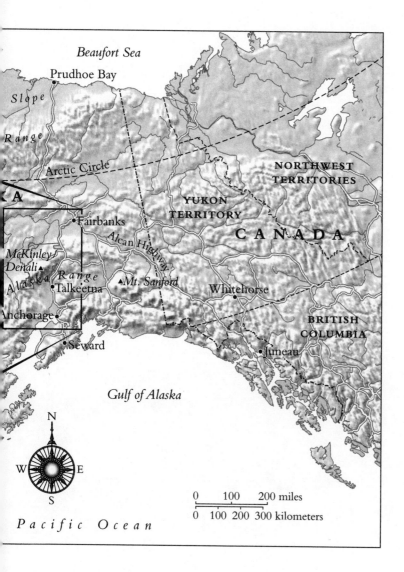

Beaufort Sea

Prudhoe Bay

Slope

Range

Arctic Circle

NORTHWEST
TERRITORIES

YUKON
TERRITORY

C A N A D A

A

Fairbanks

Alcan Highway

McKinley
Denali

Range

Ala ska

Talkeetna

Mt. Sanford

Whitehorse

Anchorage

BRITISH
COLUMBIA

Seward

Juneau

Gulf of Alaska

N

W   E

S

0   100   200 miles

0   100 200 300 kilometers

Pacific   Ocean

Realms of Myth

You might legitimately ask why anyone would want to climb a mountain such as McKinley anyway, especially if you know that legendary climber George Leigh Mallory's classic comment "because it's there" was meant to shoo off a pest reporter rather than formulate a sincere answer. Mallory's reasons were far more complex, and darker, than that verbal flip-off suggests. We'll examine his reasons in due course for the light they shed on the 1967 tragedy, but for the moment let's talk about the mountain where it happened. First, a word about names. The mountain is known now by its Native American name, Denali, which translates roughly as "The Great One." In 1967, the era of our concern, it was almost universally called McKinley.

McKinley is not, to this eye anyway, a beautiful place, as are, say, Vermont mountains in autumn or coral reefs in the Caribbean. Until someone's blood reddens white snow, there are no inherent colors on McKinley—only black, white, and shades of gray, so visually it is famished rather than a feast for the eye.

McKinley is striking rather than beautiful, a place of jagged and unpredictable immensities that are more like vast static than music. Beauty draws us in, makes us want more of it, soothes and softens. McKinley does not do that. McKinley strikes hard at senses and spirit. And like certain other iconic places—great deserts, polar wastes, open ocean—McKinley reduces existence to its two essentials: living and dying.

An opportunity to enter the realm of myth and icon is one reason why climbers climb. McKinley enjoys iconic status that may be shared only by Everest in the Himalaya. In *Imperial Ascent: Mountaineering, Masculinity, and Empire*, Peter L. Bayers finds that these two mountains tower above all others in the global psyche:

> Everest and Denali offered modern nations symbolic potential far beyond just any unexplored space or mountain, something akin to the value placed on the space of the North and South Poles. In their distinctiveness as the highest mountain on earth and the highest mountain in North America, respectively, Everest and Denali became powerful imperial and national icons.

In North America, McKinley's iconic potency is unchallenged not only because it is the continent's highest mountain but because it embodies many other superlatives. Bradford Washburn, the great McKinley expert and a man familiar with Everest as well, has written: "I know of no spot where wind and temperature can be more powerfully combined than McKinley's upper reaches—and I am referring to the summer months."

In addition to the attributes cited by Washburn, McKinley has the highest base-to-summit elevation of any mountain on Earth, rising 18,000 feet from the surrounding tundra, thus exceeding Everest's base-to-summit elevation by more than a vertical mile. (Everest's summit is only 12,000 feet from its base.) McKinley's sixty-mile circumference may make it the world's largest massif; experts are still debating this one. These two factors—base-to-summit rise and mass—help account for McKinley's infamous localized storms. The mountain makes its own weather—disturbances that, having no distance to travel, can brew up in an hour or less. These are not the only storms that attack McKinley, however. To complicate matters even further, McKinley sits east of the Bering Sea and north of the Gulf of Alaska, both of which generate horrendous storms with 150 mile-per-hour winds, prodigious snowfall, and summit temperatures of minus 40 degrees—in summer. This unique meeting of atmospheric phenomena and geographic features brings storms that are often longer, colder, windier, and snowier than any encountered in the Himalaya.

As if maniacal weather were not enough, the scale of things on McKinley is so shocking, even by Himalayan standards, that just the sight of it puts back on their heels many who see it for the first time. The place can give you a kind of vertigo, an urge to put your hands out to steady yourself while your brain tries to adjust. I did something like that when the plane dropped me and my partner onto the Kahiltna Glacier for our attempt on the mountain. Originally intending to climb another, lower peak, which proved inaccessible, we decided at the last hour, in an Anchorage bar (the first mistake of many), to give McKinley a toss. Its Talkeetna Ranger Station was just a few hours drive away. What could go wrong?

What, indeed. Ill-equipped mentally and physically, short of food, fuel, and toilet paper, we got no higher than Windy Corner, something like 14,000 feet. That, as one wag chided when we slunk back into Kahiltna Base, barely amounted to stubbing our toes on the mountain. Whiskey, McKinley, and hubris were a bad blend.

McKinley's size is not all that matters. You could think of McKinley as a battlefield, rich with threat from every conceivable direction, as military battlefields are. The aforementioned world-class climber, Everest summiter, and contemporary dean of high-altitude research, Peter Hackett, MD, believes that of all things that can be compared to big-mountain climbing, "Perhaps the closest is war. Where there's constant anxiety of a mortar shell. Worrying about a mortar shell coming into your camp may be similar to worrying about an avalanche coming into your camp. And in war, there's sleep deprivation and problems with eating and drinking properly." But even war, Hackett believes, may not be quite as extreme, because "you don't get the hypoxia. You can get the cold certainly, in cold climates, but not the hypoxia. So there really is nothing that's quite like climbing an extreme altitude mountain."

On McKinley, threat is also constantly underfoot because of thinly bridged crevasses. Snowfall disguises them more perfectly than the most ingenious human booby trap or improvised explosive device. Crevasse falls killed three of the first four men to die on McKinley, and they were all expert climbers.

As Hackett notes, threat of "aerial attack" is very real, in the form of cornices and avalanches, many of which could bury a village and not leave a steeple peeking through. Climbers have described avalanches roaring a half mile down the Muldrow Glacier (where the July 1967 expedition climbed) from the Harper Icefall, spitting house-size blocks of ice as they went. The sunlight that fuels life on Earth will blind your unshaded eyes in minutes and, if this is not carrying the military metaphor too far, there is even the threat of a particularly invidious kind of gas attack. Life-giving air itself, stripped of oxygen, becomes, in a sense, poisonous. Going into thin air can cause your lungs to drown in their own fluid and your brain to suffer strokelike derangement. Climbers up high have reported walking with ghosts, hearing cello music, and meeting Yetis. At 16,000 feet on Mount Sanford in Alaska's Wrangell-Saint Elias Wilderness, I smelled hamburgers frying, an olfactory hallucination so real that it made me salivate. Thin air has blinded climbers, paralyzed them, wracked them with convulsions. Occasionally, hypoxic climbers have become so violent that companions had to truss them up in climbing ropes and haul them like dead bodies down to lower altitudes where, resurrected but amnesiac, they often vehemently denied their fits.

For all these reasons, McKinley first-timers become (or at least this one did) like children made hypervigilant by abuse, never sure where or when the next blow will fall, knowing only that it *will* come. You can't escape even when you try to sleep, either because you can't sleep, which is usually the case, or because when you do your dreams vibrate with anxiety. Above 15,000 feet, hypoxia can also induce in many people a uniquely unpleasant condition called Cheyne-Stokes respiration, wherein while sound asleep you simply stop breathing for a while. Then you lurch awake in a gasping panic, feeling as though you are suffocating, which in fact you are. The result of all this is that at some point on virtually every serious mountaineering expedition, climbers decide that the mountain they are on is a monstrous, damnable place best viewed as a quickly receding image in a rearview mirror.

Though we now sing the praises of high places, "beautiful mountains" was oxymoronic until about 250 years ago. Psychologist, author, and mountaineer James Lester, seeking to understand climbing's genesis, found that during "the theology-dominated Middle Ages mountains were seen as a curse on humankind." Before the 1700s, people appreciated land almost purely for the uses to which it could be put: growing crops, building houses, forging roadways, creating castles, and, yes, burying the dead. Because mountains could not be plowed, sowed, reaped, built upon, or inhabited by the living or the dead, they were not only useless but disturbing. In *Mountains of the Mind*, a brilliant meditation on climbing, Robert Macfarlane cites references in 1600s literature to mountains as "boils," "warts, wens," and *"Nature's pudenda."* [Italics in the original]

Mountains were thought to be as dangerous as they were ugly. Just as mariners and cartographers peopled their quaint maps with leviathans and giant snakes, so did earlier generations fear that malign gods, evil spirits, and terrifying monsters inhabited unreachable peaks. The earliest climbers, suffering altitude sickness they could not otherwise explain, put it down to the deadly breath of invisible dragons.

All that began to change in the eighteenth century. Like most epochal shifts, this one began not with a single event but with a coinciding series of them. Emerging interest in geology (in its nascent form, little more than bespatted, elegant gentlemen sauntering around beaches or poking shaley cliffs with their silver-handled canes) kindled a new interest in mountains as objects worthy of scientific investigation.

At the same time, a few people began considering mountains in ways that cast them not as the homes of devils and monsters but as things "sublime." When we hear the word *sublime* now, we associate it with experiences of nature, a connection established by the Romantic painters and by the poets Byron, Shelley, and especially Samuel Taylor Coleridge. James Lester has written about this connection between romanticism and modern climbing:

> The fact that alpinism arose in the context of European culture just when romanticism was permeating it, and that climbing for its own sake was simply nonexistent in other cultures of the world until it spread there as part of the spread of Western modernity, seems to me a highly persuasive argument.

Coleridge was the first true adrenaline junkie (or at least the first one who wrote beautifully about his habit) and put himself in harm's way many times on mountains in search of Altered States. I'm indebted to Robert Macfarlane for pointing out that Coleridge may have completed

the first real rock climb of which we have a record. In an 1802 letter to
a friend, Coleridge described what was not only the first but almost his
Last Climb (he loved to capitalize certain words, in the Germanic style),
after finding himself trapped alone and unroped on a rock ledge in dis-
integrating weather above a sheer face:

> Oh God I exclaimed aloud, how calm, how blessed am I now, I
> know not how to proceed, how to return, but I am calm and fear-
> less and confident. If this reality were a dream, what agonies had I
> suffered! What screams! When the Reason and the Will are away,
> what remain to us but Darkness and Dimness and a bewildering
> Shame and Pain that is utterly lord over us, or fantastic Pleasure,
> that draws the soul along swimming through the air in many
> shapes, even as a flight of Starlings in a wind.

Souls and starlings aside, Coleridge was lucky to find another way
down the mountain that did not kill him, and thus lived to wax lyrical
about the experience, remaking it into one of those "spontaneous over-
flow of powerful feelings recalled in moments of quiet repose" things.

Poetry and painting may have inspired early alpinists such as the
hardy Swiss pair Jacques Balmat and Michel Paccard, who first ascended
Mont Blanc in 1786, or Englishman Edward Whymper, conqueror of the
Matterhorn in 1865. Nationalism was part of the mix when Frenchmen
Maurice Herzog and Louis Lachenal made the first ascent of an 8,000-
plus-meter peak, Annapurna (at 26,545 feet/8,091 meters, the world's
tenth-highest mountain), in 1950. What we can say for sure is that by
the mid-nineteenth century mountaineering had evolved to the point
that humans were happily scrambling up and falling off peaks all over
the world.

Including McKinley in Alaska. Four hearty Alaskans, known forever
after as "the Sourdoughs," made the first ascent of McKinley's 19,470-
foot North Peak in 1910. Without one day of mountaineering experience, they were inspired to attempt the mountain not by poetry but by a
Fairbanks barroom challenge. Their accomplishment was, according to
no less an authority than famed mountaineer and author Fred Beckey,

"simply phenomenal, one of the most noteworthy expeditions of all time." As such, it deserves a digression here.

It all began in 1909. Prospector Tom Lloyd was getting whiskeyed up in Bill McPhee's Fairbanks saloon when the bar owner announced his conviction that no "living man could make the ascent" of Mount McKinley. Bolstered by barleycorn, Tom Lloyd disagreed and said *he* could do it. Because Lloyd was more than fifty years old, flabby, and had never climbed anything more challenging than a bar stool, McPhee doubtless felt safe in calling Lloyd's bluff and laying down a substantial wager. The amount varies from $1,000 to $5,000, depending on whose history you're reading. Even at the low end, it was a tremendous amount for that time and place: $1,000 in 1909 would be about $21,000 today.

Money was not the only incentive. McKinley's unclimbed summit was one of the world's most coveted. None of the chauvinistic Alaskans wanted the first ascent of their continent's highest peak (and that hefty prize) to be snatched by "furriners" or, perhaps worse, *easterners*. So to pick up the gauntlet that McPhee had thrown, Tom Lloyd assembled his team: Billy Taylor, twenty-three, a miner; Pete "Swede" Anderson, forty-three, also a miner; and Charlie McGonagall, forty, a prospector and dogsled mail carrier. Two other recruits dropped out early on.

The final four were a tough bunch and proved it right out of the gate. For starters, the Sourdoughs traveled 150 miles from Fairbanks to Kantishna, near McKinley, by dogsled in January, when daylight lasted just three hours and temperatures routinely hit 50 below zero. After occupying a series of camps from the McKinley River to what became known as McGonagall Pass, they arrived at the Muldrow Glacier on March 13. From there they began to encounter crevasses, about which Lloyd wrote in his diary, "You can look down in them for distances stretching from 100 feet to Hades or China."

To make a short story even shorter, Pete Anderson and Billy Taylor climbed onto McKinley's 19,470-foot North Peak at 3:25 p.m. Not least amazing of the Sourdoughs' accomplishments was that they dragged behind them a spruce pole, fourteen feet long and as big around as a fist, almost all the way up. There was a method to this apparent madness: a flagppole, visible from afar, would verify their ascent. While Anderson and Taylor trod the summit, Charlie McGonagall remained at a clump of rocks at 18,700 feet, securing their flagpole, which did, in fact, verify their climb when detractors voiced doubts. The ascent from 10,900 feet to the North Peak summit took just twelve hours. Expeditions today usually require several days, and not unusually a week. Even more amazing—and here is where their achievement begins to border on the surreal—the Sourdoughs had to negotiate an icy, 2,200-foot-long, 55-degree couloir to reach the North Peak's summit ridge. This obstacle would present a daunting challenge to most expert modern climbers with cutting-edge equipment. The Sourdoughs climbed it unroped, without ice axes or proper crampons, using homemade instep "creepers" fashioned from sheet metal. Then, on their return trip, they *downclimbed* the same terrain—much more difficult, dangerous, and frightening than ascending. When you ponder the fact that in going up and down that unforgiving couloir, just one stumble or misstep out of many thousands meant certain, and very unpleasant, death, their achievement passes from unlikely to unimaginable. Subsequent controversy over their claim to have made the summit was eventually quelled when another party spotted their flagpole right where they said it was. The couloir now bears their name—Sourdough Gully—and they justly wear the title of legends.

Even legends can err, however. In the entirety of their climb into history, the Sourdoughs made just one mistake, but it was a big one: they climbed the wrong peak. McKinley's South Peak, at 20,320 feet, is the mountain's true summit. But from Wonder Lake most of the way up the Muldrow Glacier route, the North Peak actually appears higher than the South Peak. In addition, their prospector friends in Kantishna could see only the North Peak and, as one Sourdough later said, they wanted those others to "know damned well that we'd been there."

The final ascent into the heavens to scale McKinley's true summit was made, appropriately enough, by a man of God in 1913. His name was Hudson Stuck, and he was Episcopal archdeacon of the Yukon—a position that might have been punishment or reward, when you consider how many devout Episcopalians were running around the Yukon back then. That aside, everything fell into place with such nearly miraculous ease for Stuck and his team that one could be forgiven for suspecting a bit of divine intervention.

Stuck's "boss" may indeed have lent a hand, but the good archdeacon, then forty-nine, was no *cheechako,* as Native Americans and white Alaskans alike referred to tenderfoot newcomers. Rather, he was an experienced mountaineer who had cut his climbing teeth in Scotland, the American Rocky Mountains, and the Pacific Northwest, including Mount Rainier. Stuck's eye had been fixed on McKinley for some time. "I would rather climb that mountain than discover the richest gold mine in Alaska," he stated before his expedition.

Stuck was a meticulous man. In one expedition photo, he looks as though he stepped out of a vintage L.L.Bean catalog: beard neatly trimmed, jacket spotless and unwrinkled, wearing a luxurious Cossack fur hat and mitts. But the most striking things in the photo are his boots, perfectly laced, knee-high shoepacs with thirty-six eyelets each. Just imagining him every morning patiently stringing up those monstrosities, and reversing the process each evening, makes my head hurt.

Stuck's attempt was seemingly blessed from the beginning, and he knew it, writing: "As so often happens when everything unpropitious is guarded against, nothing unpropitious occurs." Instead of climbing west up to Denali Pass, then turning left, or south, toward the summit—today's *voie normale*—they "took a straight course up the great snow ramp directly south of our camp and then around the peak into which it rises; quickly told but slowly and most laboriously done." This placed them atop the ridge, at about 18,700 feet, that leads to the mountain's summit.

Although it may have been without bad luck, their climb was not without pain, especially acute at this altitude, in a savage north wind, and with the temperature just above 0 degrees Fahrenheit. The forty-nine-year-old Stuck was worst off: "the writer's shortness of breath became more and more distressing. At times everything would turn black before his eyes and he would choke and gasp and seem unable to get breath at all."

Indomitable Walter Harper led Stuck's team all the way from their high camp to the summit, and, appropriately, late on Friday afternoon, native Alaskan half-breed Walter Harper became the first person to set foot on McKinley's true summit. They had unlocked one of the world's great peaks, brightening the future of mountaineering considerably.

Not so, tragically, Walter Harper's future. With Hudson Stuck's help,

Walter prepared for and was accepted by a lower 48 medical school. While he and his wife were en route, their ship, the *Princess Sophia*, struck a barrier reef off the coast of Juneau and sank. The Harpers and about three hundred other souls perished in the Gulf of Alaska's black water.

Those early McKinley pioneers wrote about their exploits, and Hudson Stuck's classic *The Ascent of Denali* is one of the great mountaineering books of all time. But these were men of their age, strong and silent, whose code of honor led them, even if unconsciously, to gloss over hardship and their own suffering. Thus even in Stuck's book, you have to read between many of the lines to gain a full understanding of just how much misery expeditions such as those on McKinley can inflict. Every foot of gain exacts a substantial price in pain, even without serious accidents.

Thus we come full circle to Coleridge's discovery that it is one thing to romanticize mountains and love them from afar and quite another to get on their backs and climb them. It would be an interesting exercise, in fact, to tabulate the accounts of climbs that begin with, "This was my chance to complete a great climb, in the best style, with a stellar partner. I was ready," and end with, "I was suffering like never before, mentally and physically shattered, just wanting to get off this mountain."

Those are real before-and-after quotes taken from Steven Koch's article "Light Traveler," his account of climbing on McKinley in the 2002 *American Alpine Journal*. Koch and his partner, Marko Prezeli, did pioneer new McKinley routes in mountaineering's latest envelope-busting extension of style, "single push" climbing, while managing to get off the mountain with fingers, toes, and brains intact. Amazingly enough, at least to most people who don't climb and even some who do, a month later Koch and others of similar bent might do it all over again on some peak equally terrible or worse. This proves two things. One is the human brain's blessed—or maybe cursed, depending on how you look at it—ability to quickly forget intolerable pain. The other is that dreams, like viruses, have an unpleasant habit of attacking, and not infrequently destroying, their hosts.

2

For Want of a Wrist

G rand tragedies require a singular confluence of time, fate, circumstance, will, and mishap. Think *Titanic*, Johnstown Flood, Kennedy assassination, *Challenger* explosion. The July 1967 disaster on Mount McKinley was such a tragedy. Readers may recall that, at one point during Carlos Castaneda's sorcerer's apprenticeship, the Yaqui shaman Don Juan revealed a grid of glowing lines that circumscribe the Earth and help determine destinies. I found this image helpful in trying to envision what happened in July 1967 on McKinley, when lines of time, fate, ego, will, ignorance, and mischance converged there fatally.

One of these lines, that of mischance, begins bending toward McKinley in June 1967 when Jerry Lewis's youngest brother, Steve, and a friend are celebrating the end of exams at the University of Colorado. They borrow middle brother Brian Lewis's green Alfa Romeo convertible for a spin up toward Estes Park. For some reason, probably to be a good fellow and in the celebratory spirit of the evening, Steve Lewis lets his friend drive. How often, after all, does life give you the chance to end a semester by piloting an Alfa Romeo convertible along a road like a rally course? Not often, obviously, but the friend's zeal outstrips his skill. He takes a corner too fast, runs off the road, and crashes into South Saint Vrain Canyon.

Jerry Lewis and Howard Snyder are packing food for their imminent Mount McKinley Expedition when the call comes. It's a short conversation, from which Jerry returns ashen faced. There has been an accident—

a serious accident—and the Alfa is destroyed. Steve's friend is alive but badly hurt. Steve survived, but his nose and left wrist are broken.

This is one of those instances in which horrors pile on one another faster than the brain can adequately register them. Howard and Jerry gape, torn between concern for the injured men and a dawning awareness that, with a broken wrist, Steve is out of the expedition for which they are scheduled to leave in seven hours. Both men no doubt have that sick feeling you get when fate kicks you squarely in the gut.

Howard remembers the moment vividly. "We were grateful Steve wasn't seriously injured, saddened that his friend *was* badly injured (we learned upon return from Alaska that he was permanently paralyzed), and dismayed that our Mount McKinley climb was in jeopardy for the second year in a row. The supplies were purchased, the food packed, the equipment ready to go. We had intended to start for Alaska in seven hours. . . ."

Howard dreamed of climbing McKinley since he was twelve. He had spent the last four years organizing and preparing to lead a McKinley expedition. He invested thousands of hours and dollars in pursuit of this life goal. It would be hard to blame him had he begun smashing gear, inflamed by the same kind of rage that drove Lear to his great line about gods tormenting us for sport, like mean little boys pulling the wings off flies.

In his book *The Hall of the Mountain King,* published after the expedition, Howard wrote, "our expedition's independence snapped along with the bone in Steve's hand. We had fallen below the minimum four-man expedition requirement set by the National Park Service. After two years of painstaking and expensive planning and preparation, our expedition was ground to a halt."

Howard reaches for the telephone, not unlike a drowning man might grab for the last hunk of jetsam.

Wʜᴇɴ ᴛʜᴇ ᴘʜᴏɴᴇ rings in the home of Cheryl Kehr Wilcox's parents in Puyallup, Washington, her husband, Joe Wilcox, sprints for it. He has been waiting most of the day for some word from Walt Taylor, who is supposed to join Joe and the rest of the 1967 Joseph F. Wilcox Mount McKinley Expedition here at the Kehrs, the staging point for their own imminent jump-off to Alaska. But it's not Walt Taylor who's calling. Rather, it is another young expedition leader like Joe himself, drowning in disappointment, clutching for a final straw before his dream goes under for the second and probably last time.

Howard Snyder is on the other end of the line. The two men had corresponded about McKinley earlier, but Joe is surprised that Howard is calling him here. When Howard explains the catastrophic accident, however, Joe knows what's coming next. Howard asks if he and his two remaining friends can become part of Joe's team.

The National Park Service (NPS) strictly controlled access to McKinley in those days. You could not climb without a permit, and you could not get a permit if your party had fewer than four members. In truth, even the minimum four made the NPS nervous, so earlier they suggested to Howard that he and his team consider some kind of unofficial cooperation with Joe's group on the mountain. The NPS left the climbers to figure out for themselves exactly how it would work. Joe and Howard had batted around various ideas and finally settled on something Joe would call a "semi-merger." The loosely defined arrangement called for the men to share radios, fixed rope, certain expenses, and—maybe—camps.

But now things have changed. Either the Coloradoans climb as part of Joe's team, under Joe's leadership, or they don't climb at all. In those days, a leader in Joe's position, knowing NPS regulations and cognizant of the "more is better" philosophy underlying them, would probably have been happy to get a phone call such as this one from Howard. But Joe is not happy. No one in his team wants to climb with strangers. Most of them strongly opposed the idea and expressed that in angry pre-trip letters to one another and to Joe. Given this background, Howard's call puts Joe in a tough spot.

Joe cradles the receiver, thinking hard. Joe and Howard have talked on the phone and exchanged letters but never met. Howard's letters have impressed Joe, for the mountaineering experience they reflect and for their appearance. Howard writes on custom-designed stationery with mountaineers in various poses of ascent climbing up the edges. All of his letters are typed, and there has not been one single error, erasure, or overstrike in any of them. The letters are *perfect*.

Joe is something of a perfectionist himself, focused on details by nature and because he's experienced enough to know that on a mountain such as McKinley, death is in the details. But something else is a bit troubling. On the phone with Howard, Joe has detected a certain distance—"a coldness I couldn't explain," he will call it later.

Joe also knows how resistant his own team members have been even to climbing loosely joined with the Coloradoans, let alone embracing them as part of their team. But to lose the Coloradoans means sacrificing money they have agreed to pool for ropes, radios, and other supplies, and Joe's expedition is painfully short of funds. The Coloradoans' removal will also shrink the expedition by 25 percent. In the linear park service calculus of that day—which Joe has no reason to question yet—that shrinkage will increase his own team's risk factor by 25 percent.

Then Joe flashes on a solution. Howard mentioned at some point that if they didn't climb McKinley, he and his friends would probably head to British Columbia to climb there. Joe had scheduled a preexpedition warmup and crevasse rescue practice on Mount Rainier, and Rainier is on the way to British Columbia. The two teams could meet, get to know each other, albeit quickly, and have face-to-face discussions about the idea of adding three total strangers to Joe's group. It seems to him, if not an ideal solution, the best they are going to salvage.

When Joe explains the new development to his own group, "there were varied reactions and a lot of deep thinking." All of the men except Steve and quiet Hank had opposed even a loose collaboration, let alone a formal union. Now, instead of divesting, it appears they may be joining more closely than ever—literally tied together, in fact, when they rope up for the real climbing. This is no casual conjoining. As many mountaineering writers, including Howard Snyder and Joe Wilcox, have observed, when you tie into a rope with a climbing partner, you are literally putting your life on the line.

3

Fool's Gold

Joe Wilcox and his team and the Coloradoans are following a path to McKinley well worn even then by mountaineers looking for ultimate challenges. After cutting teeth, and steps, up the snow and ice of the Rockies, serious climbers usually did (and still do) their graduate work on Mount Rainier, the lower 48's closest approximation to McKinley. To cite just one example, the 1963 American Mount Everest Expedition, which made Jim Whittaker the first American to summit Everest and put four other Americans on top as well, trained on Rainier for their Himalayan epic.

Rainier, one of the world's most massive volcanoes, is 14,410 feet tall and laced with a network of glaciers not unlike those surrounding McKinley. It is also battered by tremendous storms ripping in off the Pacific that can bring hundred-mile-per-hour winds, prodigious snowfall, and the same milk-thick whiteouts that bedevil McKinley climbers. Though more than a mile lower than McKinley, Rainier is a serious mountain, one that has claimed in excess of three hundred lives since the creation of the national park more than a century ago. Almost half of those were aboard a plane that crashed there in 1946, but the remainder were climbers who came to grief.

MOUNTAINEERS SAY THAT the best summit is one they haven't climbed yet. Then and now, McKinley is the logical, and emotional, follow-up to Rainier, and Joe had spent years getting ready for The Great One. He started exploring mountains in Colorado with the Boy Scouts at age fourteen, spent a number of summers in the Sangre de Cristos as a Philmont ranger, and began working for the National Park Service as an assistant engineer on Mount Rainier in 1963. By 1966 he was an accomplished mountaineer, having summited a number of the toughest Northwest peaks and led many climbs on Mount Rainier. During the summer of 1966, he hired on as a surveyor for the National Forest Service in southeastern Alaska. In all his time there, he never saw the great mountain, but few serious climbers could spend months in Alaska and not contract McKinley fever. Returning to Washington at the end of his surveying stint, Joe had already decided that, come next summer, he would climb Mount McKinley.

In his book *White Winds*, written after he endured years of criticism for many alleged sins of omission and commission on the mountain, Joe takes great pains to demonstrate that his decision

> to climb a major mountain was not impulsive, but evolved from many contributing factors: mountaineering knowledge and experience, the wisdom and judgment to make crucial decisions, physical stamina and the ability to acclimatize to the thin air of high elevations, the financial resources to support the trip, and the ever-present motivation and desire.

In short, he was ready for a big mountain, but he could not afford a Himalayan expedition. He *could* afford McKinley, and that's where he set his sights.

WHEN JOE AND Cheryl arrive in Provo, Utah, in the late summer of 1966, to take up residence as students at Brigham Young University (BYU), Joe finds few skilled winter mountaineers but lots of good rock climbers who want to *become* all-around mountaineers. With his considerable Rainier and leadership experience, Joe is just the man to help them do that. A number of the area's serious climbers naturally gravitate toward the six-feet-one, hard-muscled, drop-dead-handsome young man with high Cherokee-ancestor cheekbones and, surprising in their contrast, sharp blue eyes. He looks and moves like the athlete he is, having played football (on full scholarship) at Kansas State College and, before that, captaining one of the best high school teams in Kansas, a state that takes football very seriously.

In September 1966, he and Cheryl are young, flushed with the joy of first love and marriage, optimistic about their future as only those who have lived just two decades can be. Cheryl has lustrous dark hair cut cheekbone length, serious eyes, and a disposition to match her sweet smile. She isn't a serious climber but loves to go hiking with Joe. She understands that climbing the highest mountain in North America is important to Joe, and that's good enough. When the expedition gathers momentum, she quickly becomes its secretary. She helps Joe put the whole thing together, managing correspondence and finances, food and equipment lists and purchases, and much else.

First, though, Joe needs partners to climb a mountain as big as McKinley—lots of partners in fact. He begins the search with sterling expectations:

> The best possible combination is a group that has climbed together for years, with an understanding of each other's moods, feelings, and thoughts. Few and fortunate are the expeditions that exhibit a composition of long-time friends, and even this does not guarantee social serenity. High stakes in a naturally stressful environment have brought the best of friends to blows.

It's a lovely ideal to shoot for, but expeditions in final form rarely are lovely or ideal, and Joe's is no exception. Four calls soon reveal that his closest climbing friends can't go, for a depressing slew of personal reasons. Next he calls Steve Taylor, a BYU senior whom Joe met in a physics class. Steve, twenty-two, actually whoops with joy at Joe's invitation. He is devout about God, a girl he plans to marry, and mountains. Steve is six feet two and 155 pounds—"What you would call *skinny!*" he writes in his climbing application. He combs his hair straight back from an expansive forehead and smiles so much, and so contagiously, that it seems to be radiating from some inner light. It may well be, given the intensity of his faith and his ancestry: Brigham Young is his great-great grandfather.

Joe has climbed with Steve often, respects his skills on rock and especially on ice, and has seen firsthand the value of Steve's easygoing nature and cool head in a crisis. Most impressive, perhaps, was a dangerous mountain rescue the two worked on, when an injured climber had to be helicoptered off a treacherous rock face. Joe had been impressed as Steve performed flawlessly "among falling rocks and whirling chopper blades."

In spite of all this, though, Steve does lack serious expeditionary mountaineering experience, which will make the National Park Service nervous and cause them to initially refuse him a climbing permit. Displaying the consistent inconsistency that seemed to characterize its dealing with mountaineers at the time, the NPS at McKinley also refuses a permit for a later addition, John Russell, even though his experience is clearly sufficient to qualify him for a McKinley climb. Incensed, Joe goes to bat for both with a supporting letter on April 18, 1967:

> John Russell's application is quite brief. . . . I have requested him to complete another application. . . .
>
> Steve is mature for his age and I know I can count on him under the severest conditions. It is my opinion that Steve is not the least qualified member of the expedition. In selecting the expedition members, I have considered experience an important factor, however, I have considered general attitude and safe climbing even more important.

Joe's reassurances prompt the NPS to reconsider, and on May 10 the agency issues an expedition permit that includes all his climbers. With anxieties not fully allayed, however, the NPS imposes certain conditions. The team will be required to carry a radio, must not split into groups that place all less experienced men in one, and must conduct preexpedition training on Rainier. The requirements, although sensible, are largely redundant. Joe had already planned for his group to have at least two, and possibly three, radios. He never intended, once on the mountain, to divide into such imbalanced teams. And the practice on Rainier had been part of his plan almost from the beginning.

The NPS letter, authored by Chief Ranger Arthur Hayes, contains one more important statement: "We congratulate you on a fine job of planning and organization."

It's important to put in the proper context this back-and-forth about Steve Taylor, John Russell, and climbing permits. Today, anyone who can post a $200 "Mountaineering Special Use Fee" can get a permit to climb McKinley, whereas in 1967, NPS regulations required detailed applications, medical examinations, climbing resumes, and equipment checks, in addition to the minimum of four climbers per team. For reasons that will soon be apparent, the 1966 NPS isn't comfortable even with four-man teams. Regardless of the experience of a team's individual members, the NPS urges such smaller and, in its estimation, weaker groups to join forces with larger and, in its estimation, stronger ones. The NPS philosophy then was seemingly as linear and rigid as a line on a graph: more is better. Eight are twice as safe as four, twelve are three times as safe. Even if the mathematics wasn't quite that precise, it was still bureaucratic policy based on conventional wisdom. But mountaineering isn't just about numbers, and mountains don't much care about policy.

Three things are apparent about those NPS policies. One is that the service's intention—protecting climbers and potential rescuers—was laudable. Another is that self-protection was part of the mix, because the polices grew out of experience almost as painful for the bureaucracy as it was for the climbers involved. In 1960, on the "easy" West Buttress route, a catastrophic accident struck the John Day Expedition, which included some of America's best climbers: Lou Whittaker, Jim Whittaker (who would become the first American to summit Everest), Pete Schoening, and leader John Day. The accident occurred when, descending the steep west face beneath Denali Pass, Jim Whittaker slipped and pulled his three rope mates off as well. They crashed down 400 feet, and when they slid to a stop both Whittakers were unconscious, Day had a badly broken leg, and Schoening was disoriented by a possible concussion. The subsequent rescue effort remains the most complex and expensive ever mounted on McKinley, and also the one most fraught with mishap and embarrassment.

Radio messages to Anchorage kicked off the massive rescue, which ultimately involved multiple military and civilian aircraft and more than fifty army and civilian personnel. The effort received huge media attention. The injured men were indeed saved, but the rescue became a near debacle. Would-be rescuer Helga Bading came down with pulmonary edema and required evacuation. Only incredible flying—and courage— by glacier pilot Don Sheldon saved her from certain death. In a separate incident, a helicopter pilot, confused by whiteout, crash-landed and nearly killed his two rescuer passengers. In a third separate incident, a fixed-wing aircraft transporting sightseers crashed, killing the pilot and a passenger. If there is one thing that bureaucracy hates more than change, it is the spotlight. Thus, as Fred Beckey wrote in *Mount McKinley: Icy Crown of North America,* "The rescue effort, in addition to the loss of life and equipment, brought wide repercussions," including increased scrutiny and regulation of climbers.

The third thing that can be said about the NPS in 1967 is that its good intention—applying climbing rules and regulations to protect climbers, potential rescuers, and itself—was undermined by a dearth of consistency and logic. In 1963, the agency allowed seven Harvard undergraduates to attempt the unclimbed, indescribably hazardous Wickersham Wall. Not one of the climbers had ever been on a major expedition, and only one had even visited Alaska. They had nothing to recommend them for such an audacious attempt except Brad Washburn's urging that they should try it. That aside, in one of the great—and most overlooked— accomplishments of modern mountaineering, one that ranks with the Sourdoughs' achievement, those magnificent seven young men, one of whom was acclaimed writer David Roberts, did complete their climb, via a route so lethal that it has not been repeated in forty years. But their astonishing, against-all-odds victory should not obscure the fact that, in allowing them on the mountain at all, the NPS was wildly violating its own policy.

The 1963 Harvard Wickersham Wall Expedition was not the only notable policy deviation. In 1967, when the NPS initially refused a permit to John Russell (whose climbing resume was impressive) for the July climb, it permitted a total tyro named Ray Genet to climb the mountain in *winter.* Finally, the agency rigidly insisted that one party of twelve men would be safer than two separate groups of nine and three members, regardless of the many other factors involved, thus forcing the Snyder and Wilcox groups together. This unthinking allegiance to the more-is-better theory ignored an important fact about mountains—namely that they are a kind of looking-glass world where light can blind you, and the air can kill you, and more can be actually, dangerously, less.

With STEVE TAYLOR on board, Joe is off to a good start at creating his idealized climbing team. But by the end of September 1966, he is still two climbers short of a permit. Though his proposed expedition launch is still ten months away, the deadline for recruiting is *now*, because it will take any new additions that long to prepare. He is about ready to postpone his expedition when he gets a letter, handwritten in big, blocky capitals, from a Northwest climber named Mark McLaughlin, who heard about the climb from a mutual friend, Norm Benton. Norm summited with a successful 1964 expedition to McKinley, so he knows what climbing the mountain will require. Norm tells Joe that Mark is "well qualified and [has] what it takes to make good on an expedition." He continues that "Mark has led some routes on Rainier, and is a really nice fellow, easy to like and easy to get along with."

Like Steve Taylor, Mark enjoys a joke. Once, before a Rainier climb's required equipment check, he gave the NPS ranger a trick ice ax that he'd rigged up with a balsa-wood shaft. Tapped on a rock, it promptly snapped, and they both had a laugh. Mark, a good-looking guy, almost always smiling, is tall and fit with neatly barbered dark hair, a big square jaw, and Clark Kent glasses. He is on the board of directors of the Obsidians, a top Oregon outdoor and climbing organization, for which he also serves as chair of the Climbing Committee and the Search and Rescue Committee. Norm Benton believes that Mark, had he not died on McKinley, would have been the Obsidians' next president.

Norm is still alive, living in Oregon after a life of impressive adventuring all over the world. Nothing has changed his esteem for Mark McLaughlin, or his opinion that Mark had the experience and expertise to tackle McKinley. Critics will later malign Joe Wilcox for taking a crew of inexperienced tyros to McKinley. Mark, obviously, was not one.

Nor was the next recruit. Learning that the ranks are still thin, Mark recommends his friend Jerry Clark, thirty-one, who has even more serious mountaineering experience, including two scientific Antarctic excursions and the ascent of an unnamed peak there. Jerry is single and has been climbing for twelve years, with wide experience on rock, ice, snow, and big mountains. In 1963 he helped organize and was approved as coleader of another McKinley expedition that died aborning. Jerry writes seeking a spot on Joe's team.

Jerry Clark's climbing resume is impressive. It includes the first ascent of that nameless Antarctic mountain, Mount Rainier via the Nisqually Icefall route and others, and climbs in New Zealand, Oregon, Colorado, and the Tetons. Jerry is also a radio communications expert and a master of wilderness navigation, thanks to his Antarctic experience. He holds a BS in electrical engineering and a Master of Science in engineering geophysics, and is working on a PhD in clinical psychology.

Jerry spent those two Antarctic seasons doing glaciological and geophysical surveys that required over-snow exploration journeys totaling 2,000 miles. There's even more good news. In 1961 he was an instructor for the U.S. Antarctic Research Program climbing and ice-safety orientation. He was also recommended by the noted American Alpine Club to be an instructor for the U.S. Army's Cold Weather and Mountain Training Command. With considerable understatement, Joe writes that Jerry will be a "welcome addition" and gets him on board immediately.

A clean-shaven, smiling, bright-eyed young man with perfect teeth, Jerry has curly blond hair parted on the right. He has a big forehead, strong chin, and slightly oversized ears. In the photo he sends to Joe, he's wearing not a mountaineer's rig but a conservative blazer, fashionably slim dark tie, and white shirt with button-down collar. There is something universal about his features, and irresistibly engaging—one of those guys who looks just like a guy you used to know, and most people probably say that to him. He also looks impossibly, painfully young for his thirty-one years.

He is the tipping point for Joe's expedition and has lots of climbing friends, two of whom he quickly recommends to Joe. After examining their credentials, Joe readily agrees to their addition. Self-effacing Hank Janes, twenty-five, is a small man with a huge heart and courage to match. He teaches junior high school in one of Portland, Oregon's, worst neighborhoods. He has solid experience, with ascents of many Colorado

14,000-foot-plus peaks, and has climbed in winter temperatures down to minus 40 degrees. He is also experienced in technical ice climbing. His resume includes Mount Adams, Mount Hood, Three Fingered Jack, the East Face of Long's Peak, Crestone Needle, Mount Sneffles, Shadow Peak, Mount Saint Helens, and Mount Rainier.

At six feet four and 175 pounds, Dennis Luchterhand is Jeff to Hank's Mutt. Luchterhand is just finishing a master's degree in geology at the University of Wisconsin and has been climbing seriously for seven years. In addition to four Rainier climbs (including three as a leader), Dennis lists on his McKinley application ascents of Mount Saint Helens, Mount Jefferson, Three Fingered Jack, Mount Washington (western), Olympus and Middle Olympus, and Mount Adams. He is the Eugene unit leader for the Mountain Rescue and Safety Council of Oregon. Not least important, he is familiar with Alaskan weather, having spent the summer of 1964 there surveying and doing archaeological work.

So now there are five climbers, but the letters keep coming. Anshel Schiff, thirty, a professor of seismology engineering at Purdue and another acquaintance of Jerry's, applies next. He's light on mountaineering experience but heavy on scientific expertise. Joe, who has been seeking funding to do some scientific research on the glacier, accepts him with the understanding that he will do the science and carry loads but not go for the summit. Anshel happily agrees.

Charismatic Walt Taylor, a much more experienced climber, is in an elite MD/MA program at the University of Indiana. "I should be able to name a punctured organ or broken bone and apply a Band-Aid," he jokes after someone suggests he function as expedition doctor. Walt has been climbing since 1958, including ascents of the Middle Teton, Disappointment Peak, Capitol Peak, and Snowmass Peak. He has served as a technical climbing instructor for three summers at an Aspen mountaineering school and has extensive winter camping experience.

Last of all comes a letter from John Russell of Eugene, Oregon. He learned about the climb from a friend of Jerry Clark's, putting him four degrees of separation from the expedition leader. John has never met Jerry or any of the others, but he is one of those people who not only thinks outside the box but lives out there, too.

Joe Wilcox:

Mark McLaughlin tells me that you have an opening on your Mt.
McKinley expedition this summer, I would like to go. . . . Since I first
saw McKinley in 1960 I've wanted to climb it, I don't know why,
do you?
P.S. Play harmonica until asked not to.

John is the team's most idiosyncratic member. Raised in Canada and schooled in England, he was introduced to "riding and the 'art of etiquette' " early on. He jumped off that path before it led to campus or office. In the previous five years, he has traveled in Europe, Central America, and the United States, climbing and working variously as sheet metal journeyman, electronics assembler, adding machine repairman, and shoemaker.

John has red hair, a beard, and a temper. He is five feet nine and immensely strong—175 pounds of solid, irascible muscle. When one of the Wilcox team's trucks breaks down on the Alcan Highway, John jacks it up using a stump and a ten-foot log for a lever. He also has considerable climbing experience in Washington and Oregon, and two years working with mountain search-and-rescue (SAR) teams.

It's impossible not to note the resemblance between John and the irrepressible Ray "Pirate" Genet, who will become, with Art Davidson and Dave Johnston, an overnight legend by completing the first winter ascent of McKinley in March 1967. Both are short, stocky, curly haired, brusque, very outspoken, and unbelievably strong. In Art Davidson's classic account of the Winter Climb, *Minus 148*, Ray Genet, like John, seems always to be charging from here to there, never just speaking but always shouting or exclaiming *Yaaaarrrgh!* That's John Russell.

There *is* one difference between John and Ray Genet, however: mountaineering experience. John Russell is a far more experienced climber than Ray, as described by Art Davidson in his book: "His mountaineering background wasn't particularly impressive. He cited his youth in Switzerland's Alps, cross-country skiing, and winter hunting trips as his experience. His most notable ascent was of a squat, roundish peak only forty-five hundred feet high." Genet was such a rookie, in fact, that he could not even rope himself in, and had to be shown how by another member of the Winter Expedition.

John Russell, by contrast, has experience that's a match for his bluster. He has been at it seriously for a decade and has climbed six major Northwest peaks, including Rainier by the Emmons-Winthrop Glacier route. He has participated in six mountain rescue operations, leading one. He's an instructor of snow and ice procedures for the University of Oregon Alpine Club and is also an expert rock climber.

Although some say that the expedition's generally low level of mountaineering experience contributed to the tragedy, the evidence does not support that, or even the assertion that experience is the gold standard for survival on McKinley. Wilcox, Clark, Janes, McLaughlin, Luchterhand, and Walt Taylor were experienced in winter mountaineering, more than making up for the lighter resumes of Steve Taylor and Anshel Schiff, who, from the beginning, never intended to summit.

Indeed, McKinley's first four fatalities were experienced climbers. Number four on that list was the 1967 Winter Expedition's most experienced member, acclaimed French alpinist Jacques Batkin, who died on the expedition's first day after cavorting around unroped on the lower Kahiltna Glacier and taking a fatal crevasse fall. If experience were the main determinant, it's unlikely that Ray Genet would have made it up the mountain and back down—let alone become the expedition's hero. Genet, greenest of the green, probably saved the Winter Climb summit trio during their darkest hour by venturing from their ice cave into a winter hurricane to retrieve precious fuel from a cache.

Experts, including Jonathan Waterman, who guided and rangered on McKinley for nine years, speculate that experienced climbers may be even more likely to suffer death or injury because they take more risks on tougher routes and, with many years of climbing behind them, may get careless. Such was the case on May 21, 1992, when Mugs Stump, one of the twentieth century's greatest Alaskan mountaineers, walked too close to the edge of a visible crevasse, which collapsed and killed him.

Bob Gerhard is a career National Park Service employee who spearheaded development of the Mount McKinley climbing ranger program.

He was involved in many search-and-rescue operations in the days before helicopters came into use. Gerhard asserts that attempts to link inexperience to accidents are specious. In 2000, he told interviewer Dave Krupa: "My experience was that there wasn't a real good correlation of experience and prevention of accidents. I saw top climbers get in trouble and I saw some pretty inexperienced people go up and down without any trouble." Data analysis supports Gerhard's thesis. The park's current chief district ranger, Daryl Miller, an accomplished climber and veteran of countless search-and-rescue missions on the mountain, reviewed ninety-one fatality and about six hundred accident reports from 1932 until 2000. His conclusion: "We find that people who get into problems here, there's not a lot of correlation with experience and inexperience. Out of the ninety-one fatalities, a lot of them were very experienced people—more than half."

Miller's 1989 attempt on the West Rib with partner Mark Stasik provided even more compelling evidence. "We were coming down the West Rib. We ran into three Brits we had passed [going up] four or five hours earlier. Mark said, 'The weather's going to hell. You should come down with us.' One guy said, 'I just got off Everest and so we're going up.' They were all three dead that morning."

4

Ire of the Mountain King

L ike virtually every expedition, Joe Wilcox's is short of money. And like virtually every other expedition leader before and since, Joe knows that the promise of publicity can be bartered for equipment, food, and even cash.

To make this quid pro quo work, however, an expedition has to do something newsworthy. Making a first ascent, climbing a new route, going solo, and climbing in winter are four ways to "guarantee news coverage of some unique advertising benefit," as Joe wrote later in *White Winds*.

This was nothing new or unusual. A photo taken by Robert Scott's polar expedition photographer Herbert Ponting shows an Antarctic expedition stalwart happily spooning up Heinz baked beans. That they could be nothing but Heinz baked beans is affirmed by the clearly labeled wooden crate on which the apparently ecstatic model (beans did *that?*) has been seated. This photo was used by Sir Ranulph Fiennes in his 2004 book about polar exploration, *Race to the Pole*. In the accompanying caption, Fiennes writes, "Ponting made sure to take good custom-posed shots of Scott's men with sponsors' goods by way of quid pro quo. Nothing had changed by the 1970s, when I had to take photographs of equipment for well over a thousand sponsors against a polar backdrop."

In pursuit of support, Joe and Steve Taylor meet with Roy Gibson, news director of KCPX-TV, Salt Lake City's ABC affiliate at the time, and with the editor of the city's *Deseret News* who, serendipitously, has a reporter already in Alaska. The TV newsman and the newspaper editor tell Joe, however, that to have value for them the expedition must score some kind of "firsts." Just climbing McKinley is no longer news.

Mount McKinley has two summits, the true South Peak, at 20,320 feet, and the subordinate North Peak, at 19,470 feet. It occurs to Joe that climbing both summits simultaneously, or overnighting on both, might constitute "firsts" that could be of interest to media and sponsors. In February, Joe writes to Wayne Merry, then the mountaineering ranger and acting chief ranger at Mount McKinley National Park, asking whether anyone has summited both peaks at the same time, and whether any expeditions have overnighted on one or both. On February 27, Wayne replies that members of the Meiji University Expedition spent the night of May 14, 1960, on the summit. He adds that a well-known mountaineer named Bradford Washburn may have as well.

Following Wayne's suggestion, Joe writes to the Japanese expedition leader, Takeichi Katano. The latter's response, as cordial and friendly as Wayne Merry's, comes quickly:

> Dear Mr. Joseph Wilcox:
> I received your letter on May 22. To your 3 questions I wish to answer:
> (1) We did not bivouac we intended to establish a camp and actually did so, because we wanted to gain experience about quarity [sic] of Japanese made tents.
> (2) Secondly wanted to stay on the summit. This we did for 18 hours.
> (3) We used high camping gear:
> *Tent nylon-2 man
> *Stove Butane gas
> With best regard to you all.
> Sincerely yours
> Takeichi Katano

Joe also writes to Dr. Bradford Washburn, the other man mentioned in Wayne Merry's letter. Washburn is a fifty-seven-year-old Boston Brahmin, a Harvard graduate, and an honorary PhD recipient. He was introduced to climbing early in life, first in New Hampshire and later with top guides in the Alps. In 1927, he sold two cover stories about his climbing exploits to a then-popular magazine for young men, *Youth's Companion*:

"A Boy on the Matterhorn: A Sixteen-Year-Old Boy Tackles the Alps" and "I Climb Mont Blanc: A Seventeen-Year-Old Boy Conquers Europe's Monarch Mountain." The next year, G.P. Putnam & Sons published Washburn's first book, *Among the Alps with Bradford*, effectively establishing his reputation as a coming young climber and paving the way for his many subsequent books.

Washburn began mountaineering in Alaska in the summer of 1930, while still a Harvard undergraduate. For climbers, all routes in Alaska lead eventually to McKinley, and Washburn climbed it three times—twice by the Muldrow Glacier route in 1942 and 1947, and in 1951, pioneering the first ascent of the West Buttress route. This is still the most popular way up McKinley.

Although frail-looking, Washburn was immensely strong, with ambition to match. His early successes make "precocious" a gross understatement. He became a published book author at age eighteen, and he took over as director of Boston's New England Museum of Natural History when he was just twenty-eight. He propelled that institution to international renown as the prestigious Museum of Science, its current name.

Washburn had a long and illustrious career as director of that museum, but he also carried on a lifelong love affair with McKinley that rivaled George Leigh Mallory's obsessive attraction to Everest. A gifted photographer and skilled cartographer, by 1967 Washburn had justifiably earned the title of "Mr. McKinley" with his Ansel Adams–quality photographs, maps, and writings about North America's highest peak.

Joe Wilcox assumes that if anyone knows the answers to his questions, Washburn will, so he sends a letter in early May:

Dear Dr. Washburn:

I will be leading a nine-man expedition on Mt. McKinley this June. It appears that we will receive considerable publicity from area newspapers and TV stations to the extent that they may send men to Alaska to cover the expedition. They seem excited by the fact that we may put a camp on the summit, climb both summits simultaneously, or put a camp on each summit. According to the Park Service, some climbers spent the night on the summit in 1960. To the best of your knowledge:

   1. Has anyone else spent the night on the summit?

2. Has any group climbed both peaks simultaneously?

3. Has anyone camped on the north summit?

4. Has anyone camped on both summits simultaneously?

Your help will be greatly appreciated. I do not want my group to claim a "first" unless it is, indeed, a "first." Please reply soon, because the news media are anxious to start releases.

Sincerely,

Joseph F. Wilcox

The response from Boston is as prompt as the ones from Japan and Talkeetna, but very different indeed:

May 17, 1967

Dear Mr. Wilcox:

We have received your extraordinary letter regarding the plans for your record-breaking efforts this year on Mt. McKinley. I have answered hundreds of queries about McKinley over a long period of time, but never before have I been faced with the problem of answering one quite like this. In fact, I am amazed that the National Park Service would grant a permit for such a weird undertaking.

A Japanese party spent a very comfortable night on top of the South Peak and another party climbed both peaks of McKinley on the same day. In fact, the 1942 Army Expedition and our 1947 expedition lived comfortably for literally weeks above 15,000 feet and could easily have spent a week or more on top of either or both of the peaks if we had had the slightest inclination to do so—or any conceivable practical reason for it. After all, climbers have spent week after week on Everest, K2, Nanga Parbat, and scores of other Himalayan giants far in excess of McKinley's altitude, packing heavy loads and climbing difficult rock and ice simply for the sheer love of it—not just sleeping their way into headlines!

For your information, according to our records, McKinley has not yet been climbed blindfold [sic] or backwards, nor has any party of nine persons yet fallen simultaneously into the same crevasse. We hope that you may wish to rise to one of these compelling challenges.

Sincerely,

Bradford Washburn, Director

Joe gets this letter from Brad Washburn—legendary Mr. McKinley himself, a man venerated by many, including Joe—and simply cannot believe what he is reading. Is Dr. Washburn spoofing, pulling his leg? Joe reads it over and over. No. The letter is serious, and it hurts deeply. In *White Winds,* he would later write,

> I was completely befuddled. Washburn knew very little about our expedition. How could a man in his high position of public respect moralize on such little evidence? Besides, wasn't this the same Bradford Washburn on whose published accounts of McKinley exploits I had cut my climbing teeth? He had certainly received more publicity than any McKinley climber. With a kindled temper I wrote Washburn a searing letter and discarded the matter as unsalvageable. I felt an empty sadness at the crumbling of a child-hood idol.

Like many men great within their fields but anonymous beyond them, outside mountaineering circles Brad Washburn does not enjoy celebrity status. In 2005, photographer Kurt Markus wrote a laudatory *Outside* magazine profile of Brad at age ninety-five. Washburn's obscurity, richly undeserved in Markus's view, is one theme of the article. Markus quotes Tony Decanaes, the Boston photo dealer who sells Brad's work: "Mountaineers knew about Brad, but outside of that sphere he was almost unknown."

But within the tight world of serious mountaineering, Brad Washburn is already, by 1967, well known indeed. Men who achieve greatness—even circumscribed versions—are rarely shrinking violets. The Markus profile in *Outside* magazine summed him up as "tough, gruff, and feisty." Washburn's friend of more than forty years, acclaimed climber and writer David Roberts, told Markus, "It's instructive that he never went on an expedition led by anyone else."

Men who lead mountaineering expeditions aren't Casper Milquetoasts, either. Washburn's hot letter ignites Joe's "searing" response, launching a memorable fight that will leave the two with horns locked for decades. Thirty years later, in fact, Washburn will remain so incensed by their differences that he will call Joe Wilcox "a skunk." Joe's letter:

Dear Dr. Washburn:

*I received your letter today and am amazed that you are rather child-
ish and jealous. I have felt in previous correspondence that you have
been uncooperative—your last letter seems to clarify things.*

*As you may recall I contacted you last November concerning sup-
port for some scientific work that my group plans to do. Without
knowing anything about the group you accused us of seeking a scientific permit as a smoke screen for air support of our climbing team. For
your information, we will not be getting air support but still plan to do
the research for the sheer love of it. The expedition is entirely self-
supporting and we will be paying out of our own pockets for rent and
insurance on the instruments. . . .*

*You may be interested to know that we have generally not encour-
aged publicity—our objectives have not been changed to satisfy any
type of publicity. We have eliminated the possibility of filming a doc-
umentary because of the inconvenience it would cause us. If news
reports must be made we are concerned that they be accurate, however.*

*As a fellow purist, I'm sure you have had the same problem with
news media. I sympathize with you for the great amount of unwanted
publicity which you have received. . . . Let's not kid ourselves, you
have received more publicity from your McKinley trips than anybody
and are hardly in a position to write "for the sheer love of it" letters. I'm
quite surprised they haven't named the mountain after you. Should we
send you a royalty for climbing your mountain? . . . Good luck in your
life as a hypocrite—may you someday come face-to-face with its incon-
sistancies [sic].*

Sincerely,

Joe Wilcox

It's impossible not to imagine the hot-tempered Washburn, then
already fifty-seven, seated behind an expansive desk in his stately
Museum of Science office, opening and reading with growing, apoplec-
tic disbelief such a letter from a twenty-four-year-old unknown.

At this point, a man in Washburn's position (and men in Washburn's
position will always have to deal with upstarts) has three choices. The
first would be to roll his eyes at the hotheadedness of youth and take it

no further. The second would be to offer a conciliatory, grandfatherly reply, with well-intentioned advice about the realities of McKinley mountaineering. Washburn does neither, choosing instead to fight ire with ire.

Dear Mr. Wilcox:
I have received your letters regarding McKinley. At the time I wrote my note to you I was well aware that you might react violently and critically because of the fact that we had received much publicity for our trips in past years, however, there is in my opinion a considerable difference between making the first ascent of a big peak or a significant new route on it—and then receiving publicity for it—and deliberately seeking publicity for what appear to others to be inconsequential "firsts" as you call them.

My wife made the first ascent of McKinley by a girl [Barbara Washburn was at the time 30 years old and the mother of three children] and I am proud of it.

We worked for nearly 15 years making a fine map of McKinley and I am proud of the results of our labors.

Few people object to others getting publicity, particularly when the accomplishment involved is substantial. Frequently, substantial publicity is required to finance a substantial project—for example, the U.S. Everest Expedition. Frequently substantial publicity comes from inconsequential events—over which the person who receives it has little or no control. This is unfortunate, and a sad and inevitable part of our modern way of life.
Sincerely yours,
Bradford Washburn

Though wounded by what Brad has written, Joe takes solace from his belief that Washburn's scorn is confined to the letters and thus remains between the two of them, gentleman to gentleman. Unfortunately, Washburn does not consider the argument settled—or private. What Joe can't know is that on May 17, the same day that Brad Washburn writes to him, he also writes to a friend in the American Alpine Club, with the express intent of subjecting Joe Wilcox and his team to public ridicule:

Dear Margot,
Over the years I have received hundreds of letters asking for informa-
tion on Mt. McKinley, but the enclosed really tops it all. I thought that
you might enjoy posting it and my reply in an appropriate spot where
they can be coordinated with and enjoyed by our local AAC friends.
Ever Sincerely,
Brad Washburn

Nor does Joe suspect that Brad sends an equally scornful letter, with Joe's original attached, to George Hall, the new superintendent of Mount McKinley National Park, and possibly to other people associated with the park. This particular letter was sufficiently pungent that its impression was still fresh twenty-four years later when University of Alaska oral historian Ron Inouye interviewed Hall:

> He wrote some horrible letters, just horrible letters, I mean, the dignity of the man disappeared in those moments, I'll tell you. And so he wrote me then, and he said, "You're new, but I'm telling you, don't let those stupid asses on the mountain." What was I supposed to do?

Not the least remarkable thing about George Hall's recollection is his use of the plural "letters," indicating that there was more than one. Hall died in early 2005, before I could interview him, but he was a career government man who rose high in the bureaucracy. He knew how to parse words and would not have used the plural unless he meant to. Even more surprising is his recollection of the way Washburn, a civilian with no official NPS standing, addresses him, superciliously, as superior to subordinate.

You're *new* . . .
   I'm *telling* you . . .
   Don't let those stupid asses on the mountain.

Hall thanks Brad for his input and suggests in a June 6 letter that he may have judged Wilcox too harshly:

*Regarding your note on the Wilcox expedition, I feel that the basic let-
ter prepared by Mr. Wilcox poorly expressed his intent and subsequent
correspondence has indicated that the strong publicity accent has been
eliminated or played down. I believe their goals are now set on the
sound and serious business of the ascent itself.*

Washburn fires off yet another scorching letter, one that conspicu-
ously omits George Hall's official title and instead addresses him dismissively as

Dear Mr. Hall:
*Thank you very much for your comments about the Wilcox expedition
in your letter of June 6th with regard to the Manuscript. I am, of
course, sorry that we misinterpreted Mr. Wilcox' objectives. However,
after all, the only source which we had to evaluate these objectives was
Mr. Wilcox' letter itself—which certainly, and in the most unequivocal terms, inferred that record-breaking on the upper part of the
mountain was to be an integral part of their operation! My letter to
him was not by any means an offhand explosion, but was carefully
coordinated with two other members of the American Alpine Club
who discussed it with me. . . .*

Reading this, it's impossible not to notice how quickly Brad Washburn
becomes defensive. And it is telling that he would bother to review a letter to a nobody with *two* American Alpine Club officials or members.
   In the next paragraph, Washburn repeats something he said in his letter to Joe:

*It is very much another thing to go off record seeking as an end in
itself—particularly when expeditions like Cassin's, Everett's, and
Thayer's (not to mention ours) could easily have spent days on top of
either peak if there had been the slightest reason to do so.*

Washburn even contacts Berle Mercer, the horse packer whom Joe
and Howard have contracted to haul their supplies, and tries to dissuade
Mercer from doing business with the expedition. In a 2000 interview

with historian Jarrod Decker, Mercer recalled that Brad raised, among other things, liability issues: "He wanted to be sure that I wasn't involved in where they could accuse me of giving them false information of what they could do or might not do."

Brad Washburn will cast a long shadow over the Wilcox Expedition and its aftermath, and Joe sees more of it soon. He receives a call from Boyd Everett, a well-to-do New York securities analyst who is also one of America's boldest and most brilliant mountaineers. Tragically proving that adage about the dearth of climbers both bold and old, Everett's luck will run out two years later on Dhaulagiri. But now he is at the height of his climbing arc, famed for creating and leading big, meticulously organized siege-style expeditions. He is bringing one of his small armies (fifteen climbers in three separate teams) to climb not one but three difficult routes simultaneously, and they will be on McKinley at the same time that Joe's team will be attempting the Muldrow Glacier route. A multipronged assault such as Everett's needs much air support, and he is concerned about pilot conflicts. After an exchange of pleasantries, he gets down to the nitty-gritty, asking whether Joe intends to retain local glacier pilot Don Sheldon. Joe says that no, he can't use Sheldon, because planes can't land on the Muldrow, where he's going.

Everett thanks him, then adds that he's heard about Joe's run-in with Brad Washburn. A lot of people up here, including me, says Everett, think that Brad's the last person in the world to complain about others getting some publicity for climbing.

Joe can't believe it. Did Brad tell you directly about our conflict? he asks.

Not directly, Everett says. You know how it is up here. Word gets around fast. I think he wrote some letters to the park people and it got out.

I'd appreciate it if you'd let Brad know what you told me. About publicity, I mean.

I don't think I should do that right now. There are still a lot of climbs up here I want to do.

You mean, you think he'd try to block an expedition?

He tried it with yours, didn't he? Look, the man has a lot of influence. I don't want to take any chances.

Until that moment, Joe hasn't realized that Brad is indeed trying to torpedo his expedition. It would be nice to say that Washburn was motivated solely or even primarily by a concern for safety. But it's hard to make a strong case for that, because he doesn't know anything about the quality or experience of Joe's team. He hasn't seen their climbing resumes, autobiographies, medical exams, or permit applications, hasn't spoken with any of them, does not even know their names, and has had no contact with the expedition other than the letters from Joe. For all he knows, they could be world-class mountaineers.

Whatever the source of Washburn's feelings, the expedtion's tragic end will appear to justify the antipathy that this great expert expressed before it began. But even experts err, and appearances are most famous for their deceit.

5

Clash at Cougar Rock

J oe and his eight team members, scattered from New York to Seattle, spend the next eight months getting ready. The men finally begin assembling on Sunday, May 28, at the home of Cheryl Kehr's parents in Puyallup, Washington. August and Gloria Kehr cheerfully agree to host this confab; with limited exposure to such things, they probably envision something like an expanded weekend camping trip. Then the big, strong young men with alarming appetites and unbelievable amounts of equipment (more than a ton of food, for starters) begin arriving and just keep on coming. In short order, August and Gloria decamp and stay with friends.

On Thursday, June 1, eight of the nine climbers come together for the first time. Walt Taylor will join them in a few days. The men realize now, if they have not before, that their expedition is composed of three, rather than two, smaller groups. Steve and Joe are the Provo duo. Jerry Clark, Hank, Dennis, Mark, Anshel, and Walt are what could be called the Clark contingent. Singleton John Russell is, well, John Russell. At this point they have no way of knowing that they will soon become a four-part crew, a decision so unfortunate that only two of them will live to regret it.

For Joe, their gathering is "like meeting people for the first time with the feeling that you have always known them." It's easy to envision this meeting, which, despite a flock of worried letters in the last six weeks (some strong enough to threaten the climb's future), must have been something like first encounters between dorm mates at the beginning of

freshman year. There would have been a lot of handshaking and laughing, beneath which brewed a confusing mix of opposing feelings: enthusiasm and apprehension, tentative affection and concealed suspicion,
hope and fear, all charged with awareness that the experience of a lifetime awaits in Alaska—"sobered by moments of truth and doubt," as Joe
wrote later.

On Friday, June 9, the Wilcox team arrives at Mount Rainier National
Park for their planned practice session and first meeting with Howard
Snyder's team. But there is not a Coloradoan in sight, nor the team's last
straggler, Walt Taylor. They wait as long as they can, and then, feeling
pressed, spend the afternoon simulating crevasse escapes by dangling
from ropes beneath a nearby bridge. They treat themselves to dinner at
the park's Longmire Inn and overnight at a nearby campsite. On Saturday
morning, they drive ten miles to Paradise Visitor Center, the designated
meeting place, and wait several hours. Still no Coloradoans. Again reluctant to waste valuable time, they climb a steep nearby hill to practice
self-arrests, a technique that allows climbers to stop sliding after taking
a fall on steep terrain by driving their ice ax points into the mountain surface. Self-arrest practice is actually great fun, as Joe's description in *White
Winds* reflects: "Soon we were as excited as children on a sledding hill."

After a morning of play, they break for lunch, then start hiking toward
the Nisqually Glacier, where they will make camp in preparation for Sunday's more serious engagement with the mountain: practice at hauling
themselves and one another out of real Rainier crevasses. Along the way,
they're accosted by a man who looks like nothing so much as a lost clown
with his baggy wool pants, orange fez, dark beard, and white zinc oxide
cream smeared over his mouth and nose.

"I'm looking for Joe Wilcox," he announces. Even underneath this
getup, it's easy to see that Walt Taylor is a young man who, as Joe wrote
later, "could go to a party without a date and leave with two." Joe wel-
comes him warmly, but learns that Walt has not seen the Coloradoans
either. Their failure to show up angers Joe. He suspects that Howard and
his friends haven't much experience with glacier travel and crevasse rescue, and the Muldrow is riddled with invisible killer cracks. Crevasse
falls, in fact, have caused three of McKinley's four recorded fatalities
up to then.

Howard and his men never do show, so Joe and the others make camp for the night near a crevasse field. John Russell takes dinner-making chores upon himself, and even at this early juncture his unusual relationship with gear surfaces. "When he handled a piece of equipment, no one was quite sure whether he was operating it or effecting a forcible disassembly," Joe would write later.

Next morning, Joe and the others awake to find themselves surrounded by a host of Seattle Mountaineer Club members who have already staked claims to every suitable crevasse nearby. Faced with the ironic task of being unable to find a good crevasse just when they need one, Joe and his crew have breakfast, then eventually locate a crack big enough to gobble them all.

Here they get down to work—literally—and it is hard work indeed. When you fall into a crevasse, if you're lucky and your rope mates are alert they will arrest your fall after ten to twenty feet. Topside, your companions rig anchors in the snow and set up a rescue pulley system. Dangling thus, you will notice how quiet it is down here, and how blue the light, and, before very long at all, how cold the air.

Presently your friends will drop a line and drag your monster pack over the crevasse's lip. You're next. Today, uninjured crevasse fall victims can climb out on their own using mechanical ascenders—ingenious gadgets that incorporate spring-loaded, toothed cams, which allow the devices to slide up the rope but then bite and prevent them from sliding down.

In 1967, before mechanical ascenders came into wide use, impecunious climbers relied on knots called Prusiks, which, like ascenders, will slide up a rope when unweighted but (theoretically) not down when weighted. They are affected much more than mechanical devices by wet, icy ropes, and they are much more difficult to manipulate with bulky mittens or frozen fingers. In any case, Prusiks could get you out of crevasses, albeit later rather than sooner, in 1967.

They also helped make very popular the second way of getting out of a crevasse: just have your buddies up top do all the hauling from the get-go.

JOE KEEPS HIS team at it all day, taking turns being fallees and haulees, working on self-arrests, boot-ax belays, Prusiking, and mountain first aid. At nine thirty that night, thoroughly whipped, they wriggle into mummy bags and sleep well in camp at Mount Rainier's base.

The next day's session begins early and ends in midafternoon. While the others are packing gear into the vehicles, tall Dennis Luchterhand, normally a fount of good humor, quietly takes Joe aside. It's an extraordinary conversation, which Joe recorded verbatim in *White Winds*.

Dennis says, "I'm not going."

"Not going where?" It never enters Joe's mind that Dennis means McKinley.

"Not going on McKinley."

Joe laughs. Dennis the joke lover is putting him on. *Here we go again.*

"No, I'm not climbing McKinley." Dennis means it.

"Why on earth not?" They have just completed two days of excellent practice and, Joe feels, have begun to coalesce as a team.

"I'm not sure. I just don't feel good about it. I have a feeling that there will be problems on the climb," Dennis confides.

"Can you be specific? A particular thing, a particular person?"

"I'm not sure. I didn't feel very well on the summit during my climb with Mark last week, but mostly it's just a 'gut' feeling that something will go wrong."

This puts Joe in a tough spot. Scuba dive masters and skydiving jumpmasters are taught never to talk a reluctant diver into the water or a jumper into the air. But Joe hasn't been trained that way, and he's already begun to feel a bond with Dennis. He points out that nearly everyone living at a low elevation notices the altitude when climbing Rainier. On McKinley, they will have three weeks to acclimatize gradually.

Dennis understands that but still seems dubious, so Joe says that he respects any decision Dennis will make and just asks him to think the matter over carefully, because they will have to repack many supplies if Dennis leaves them.

Howard Snyder told me that Dennis had reservations about the makeup of his team: "It should come as no surprise that some (or all) of the expedition members should have 'second thoughts' about the venture, since that commonly takes place in such circumstances, especially with a large group containing several previously unacquainted people, none of whom had ever been involved in a major mountaineering expedition."

Joe, on the other hand, thought that Dennis's decision was prompted by different worries: "Dennis did not say exactly what was bothering him (he may have told Clark), but I always felt that it was the merger with the Colorado Group."

There's no way of knowing which man's assessment, or either of them, might be correct. Howard's suggestion seems logical enough, although Dennis had met and climbed with other members of Joe's team. Joe's thought is supported by concerns that Dennis had already raised in his letters. Joe and Howard could be correct in their estimations, or there might have been a third source entirely. But cause of the speculation may be less important than the fact that Dennis's premonition was strong enough to bring him close to going home.

T HEIR PRACTICE COMPLETE, Joe and his team go looking for Howard and his. Park rangers tell them that the Coloradoans have arrived at nearby Cougar Rock Campground, a new site that Joe, ironically, helped survey in 1963. Joe, Mark, Dennis, and Anshel drive over to find the prodigals.

As they approach the campsite, there's no mistaking the Coloradoans— they are an impressive trio indeed. Howard is the smallest at six feet two and about 175 hard-muscled pounds. But beside the other two, he actually does look small. Paul Schlichter stands six feet four and weighs a bit over 200 pounds. Rounding out their group is Jerry Lewis, six feet five and 230 pounds.

They're also good-looking. Howard has neatly trimmed hair and a Kirk Douglas cleft in his strong chin. His eyes are almost electric blue. Paul's posture and bearing have been honed to commanding perfection by four years at the Air Force Academy. Jerry is, well, *huge*. He moves and speaks softly, though, and the impression he makes is one of reticence rather than threat.

Joe and Howard come together for the first time, after so many letters and phone calls. Joe's description of their first meeting:

> As we pulled into their Cougar Rock campsite, Howard approached
> with a beaming smile. We managed a cordial, but short, greeting. I
> was more than a little disappointed that they had missed the

Rainier workout and quickly turned the discussion to serious matters. Howard said they had arrived late and did not think that they
could locate us on the glacier in the foul weather.

And Howard's:

> That afternoon, at Cougar Rock Campground, we had our first
> meeting with Joe Wilcox. He drove up to our campsite, and I
> walked to his car to greet him. I said a cheery hello, and introduced
> myself. Wilcox said nothing. He sat in his car, unsmiling, and sur-
> veyed me like a Hong Kong tailor sizing up a customer. With Wilcox
> were Mark McLaughlin, Dennis Luchterhand, and Anshel Schiff.
> McLaughlin, a friendly and outgoing sort of fellow, broke the awk-
> ward silence by bounding out of the car and introducing himself to
> us. Schiff, Luchterhand, and Wilcox followed suit rather mechani-
> cally. . . . We hardly knew what to think of our first meeting. Only
> one of their group had been friendly, and Wilcox had been nothing
> less than brusque in his manner. No one had proffered so much as
> a "thank you" for the "special delivery" snowshoes we had brought
> them. Lewis said, "If they're going to be ornery, we just won't go."
> Schlichter suggested, not wholly in jest, "We should call home and
> have Steve [despite his broken wrist] put on the first jet for Seattle."

The first meeting was clearly not what anyone had hoped for. Paul
Schlichter, forty years later, remembered it as "pretty frosty," and added,
"My thought is that when we gathered at Rainier, there was an unsettled
feeling among all the climbers. Unsettled because we were a loose team
of strangers (in many ways) who were at the jumping off point for the
'great adventure.' Rainier was pretty much the point where a go/no-go
decision was made. Once we left there and crossed the border into
Canada, we were pretty well committed."

Jerry Lewis found this first meeting even more unsettling than did
Joe, Howard, or Paul. "I was disappointed at the reception we got. There
was a very unfriendly atmosphere. I just didn't understand it." The vibes
were so negative, in fact, that "I'd have backed out then and there" but
for not wanting to abandon his two friends.

What neither Howard, Paul, nor Jerry could have known is that six of

the nine men in Joe's group have strongly opposed joining the two parties. On May 9, Jerry Clark wrote,

> Mark & I are highly skeptical of the plans to climb and camp
> together. . . . It looks like we're all asking for hard feelings, extra
> delays, and the extreme difficulty of establishing massive high
> camps. . . . I feel it is more than possible that an overly restrictive
> agreement could break down miserably on the mountain.

The original proposal was for a loose alliance on the mountain, not
much more than the two teams keeping each other in sight, and Joe's
team had resisted even that. Now they were looking at something even
more objectionable: making one team out of the two—tenting, eating,
sleeping, climbing, defecating, and everything else not just near the
strangers but with them.

Though Joe engineered the nearly consummated union, he also finds
the initial encounter unpleasant, and writes later, with considerable
understatement, "Our first meeting with the Colorado climbers had
been a little uncomfortable."

There are two more likely reasons why this initial meeting was
much more than "a little uncomfortable," and they have to do with Joe
and Howard themselves. It's clear from Joe's and Howard's accounts
and later developments that the two leaders experienced "dislike at
first sight." Most of us have had a similar experience. It happens as
infrequently as the phenomenon at the other end of the emotional
spectrum—"love at first sight"—but both can be devastatingly powerful.

Why and how does "dislike at first sight" happen? Psychologists have
devoted considerable effort to answering that question. Researchers have
discovered, as Malcolm Gladwell notes in The Tipping Point, something
called "cultural micro-rhythms." We humans are constantly sending signals that can result in "interactional synchrony"—micromovements of
eyebrows, lips, fingers, facial muscles, and more. Speech rates and
latency, the lapse between the moment one speaker stops talking and
another begins, are also part of the mix. Two people may meet with very
different conversational patterns but almost instantly find common
ground.

Or not. Transmitting is only half of communication. In his second book, *Blink*, Gladwell reports that while our conscious minds are interpreting information in ways that we're fully aware of, something else is going on in a different part of the brain, something scientists have named the *adaptive unconscious*.

> This new notion of the adaptive unconscious is thought of . . . as a kind of giant computer that quickly and quietly processes a lot of the data we need in order to keep functioning as human beings. . . . The only way humans could ever have survived as a species for as long as we have is that we've developed another kind of decision-making apparatus that's capable of making very quick judgments based on very little information.

This ability of the adaptive unconscious to process information in milliseconds is termed "thin-slicing." In the first seconds of their first meeting, Joe and Howard's adaptive unconscious thin-sliced data about each other and began to flash warning signals.

Does that alone adequately explain how such intense dislike could be sparked by a first brief encounter? It might, but something else was probably also at work. Joe and Howard's first meeting, which dictated much of what would follow, was a clash of what I've come to call super alphas. The "alpha male" phenomenon has been thoroughly documented by researchers of animal and human behavior and is commonplace in freshman psychology courses. Alpha males, whether in wolf packs, horse herds, chimpanzee groups, corporations, or mountain climbing teams, are instinctive dominators. In the animal world they assert that dominance by fang and claw. In the human world, they are hardwired to rule by a combination of strength, intelligence, courage, and will. Alpha males include Napoleon, Lincoln, Trump, Clinton (who expressed presidential ambitions while still an undergraduate), Muhammad Ali, and Reinhold Messner.

One of the best contemporary descriptions of alpha males appeared in an article by a psychiatrist/psychologist team in the 2004 *Harvard Business Review*, analyzing the correlation between alpha characteristics and those of leadership:

Alpha males represent about 70 percent of senior executives, come in many forms and professions and include physicians, lawyers, politicians and educators. Alphas are highly intelligent, good at calling the shots, confident and successful, extraordinary at producing results, and . . . impatient, critical, non-collaborative, and uninspiring in people leadership.

The qualities that make some executives top dog are the same qualities that can frustrate co-workers and limit working relationships and their own development. The more authority alpha executives achieve, the more pressure they feel and the more pronounced their shortcomings become.

WITH THE FIRST meeting between members of the Wilcox and Snyder teams having thickened rather than broken the ice, the two groups pack up and drive to the provisional "Expedition HQ," the Kehrs' home in Puyallup. There all twelve men come together for the full and final debate about whether to fold the remnant of the 1967 Colorado Mount McKinley Expedition into the 1967 Joseph F. Wilcox Mount McKinley Expedition, under Joe's leadership. When all are finally assembled in the Kehr home's backyard—Wilcox contingent on one side, Coloradoans on the other, kneecaps to kneecaps as it were—they must have been even more uncomfortable than during the earlier nastiness at Mount Rainier.

Even before debate begins, a detached observer would have noticed a difference between the two groups so strikingly obvious that it's hard to understand how it has gone so long unmentioned. We're talking about size.

And not just one kind of size, but two. Group size first. One group is big, with nine men; the other is small, with just three. A less obvious, but also relevant difference, is individual size.

The Coloradoans' average height is six feet four inches; and their average weight is 205 pounds. Joe's team averages about five feet ten inches in height and 160 pounds in weight. How important are the two groups' size differences? At sea level, on a casual camping trip, not very important. But under the stresses and strains of climbing continually at high altitude, the differences, like any dissimilarity, can become much more important. If nothing else, at least up to the point where altitude sickness comes into play, the big men, carrying approximately the same loads but with bigger muscles and frames and longer strides, will be able to hike and climb faster.

For people strolling along wooded paths and trails, this is no big deal. For men literally tied together by a climbing rope at, say, 19,000 feet, it can become a very big deal. In addition, it is easier for a big man to haul a smaller one out of a crevasse than vice versa, and McKinley has cracks aplenty. The first man to drop into one on the Muldrow Glacier will be the expedition's biggest member, Jerry Lewis, and it required the combined efforts of three rope mates—Howard, Steve Taylor, and Mark—to get him out. Finally, the fact that one party's members are physically bigger than the other's is a highly visible symbol of difference. The single most unpopular man on Robert Falcon Scott's last polar expedition was Petty Officer Edgar "Taff" Evans—who was also, by a large margin, the biggest. Many of the other men disliked Evans because he was obnoxious when sober and dangerous when drunk, but it's worth asking how different things might have been were Evans an overbearing *small* man.

A̦t the kehrs' home in Puyallup, it is a tall, whippet-slim, and decidedly not overbearing man, Steve Taylor, who speaks first, and makes no bones about his objections to joining the two teams. Given that those who knew him described Steve as quiet, gentle, and retiring, speaking out so strongly in front of such a group indicates the intensity of his feelings. Howard recollected in *The Hall of the Mountain King*:

> Steve Taylor was against our combination, and by interjecting various comments he seemed to be trying to use the occasion to gain acceptance into the group, as a mountaineer among mountaineers. . . . He brought up a number of inane situations regarding the intermixing of personnel and equipment. . . . I was taken aback by Taylor's apparent lack of basic mountaineering knowledge.

Inane is a strong word; Steve's objections must have cut deep. But in light of the expedition's actual events, having concerns about the "intermixing of personnel and equipment" turned out to be prescient rather than inane.

Jerry Clark, still unconvinced and possibly the most experienced climber in the entire group, voices a primary and insightful worry: a party of three men will inevitably be able to climb faster than a party of nine. They will have less weight to pack, less snow to melt for water, less food to prepare, only one tent to set up and break down, one kitchen to bother with, and only one rope team of three climbers.

"The main concern seemed to be that we would trip gaily up the trail with our group's lighter gear," Howard wrote, "and leave the Wilcox group laboring under their Herculean loads. We assured them that we would be perfectly happy to carry their equipment."

And so they did. But Steve Taylor's and Jerry Clark's concerns about different climbing speeds will be borne out. The Colorado team will consistently climb faster than the other men. One major reason is that they do much less of the arduous trailbreaking required of advance team leaders who are forcing the new route up-mountain. From the Muldrow Glacier moraine to McKinley's summit, the route is eighteen and a half miles long. The route-finding leads are shown below:

CLIMBER	DISTANCE	PERCENT OF TOTAL
Joe	8 miles	43%
Jerry Clark	5 miles	27%
Howard	3 miles	16%
Dennis	1.125 miles	6%
John	0.625 mile	3%
Mark	0.5 mile	2%
Paul	0.125 mile	1%
Walt	0.125 mile	1%

This is not necessarily a criticism of Howard, Paul, or Jerry Lewis. Joe doubtless felt responsible for leading the way. Jerry, as deputy leader, must have wanted to hold up his end—the front, in this case—as well. Howard's lead was a small part of the total, but this cannot be overstated: he took his rope to the summit—the longest, highest, most dangerous lead of all.

Joe could have ordered others to the fore, or directed that faster climbers slow down when roped up with slower ones. Any of the other climbers also could have demanded less speed—as Jerry Clark did at the end. So without implying that the Coloradoans were slacking, we *can* say that Steve's and Jerry's concerns were far from "inane."

Even at this late date, reservations are numerous and shared by a majority of Joe's team. But the momentum of this complex undertaking is tremendous, and it crushes objections like dinghies beneath the bow of a supertanker. After a while, questions just trail off. The nine men of Joe's group, however much they may dislike the idea of roping up with strangers, also understand that the Coloradoans' fate is theirs to decide. Howard, Paul, and Jerry Lewis have put at least as much time, money, and work into preparing for their own McKinley expedition, and Joe's men know how it would feel if they, instead of the other three, were twisting in the wind with the fate of their climb in other men's hands.

Besides, these Colorado fellows don't seem like such bad guys. Although Jerry is huge, he seems affable and friendly and almost gentle. Paul is quiet and unassuming. Howard seems decent enough, too. None of these guys are out-and-out assholes.

Things get quiet and the men sit there, looking at sky or grass or their feet, at just about anything other than one another. Joe asks if there are any more questions or comments. When none are voiced, he suggests that he and Howard go inside and draw up a written agreement. That sounds fine to Howard, who knows that if he and his friends don't climb with Joe's group they don't climb at all. Neither book describes a vote, a show of hands, or further discussion.

The agreement they draw up is detailed, but the two most important clauses are:

> 1. Members of the Colorado McKinley Expedition will now be considered members of the Wilcox-McKinley Expedition.
> 2. The Colorado group will, of course, camp with, travel with, and be under the same leadership as the rest of the Wilcox Expedition.

So now, per NPS requirements, they are a twelve-man expedition under one name and leader—on paper. But in reality they are three and nine, and a long way from Joe's original description of the ideal climbing team.

The next day they will head north to McKinley, a trip of several days. But with ink barely dry on their agreement to create one group out of two, they make this journey divided, the Wilcox and Colorado teams traveling completely apart, thereby foregoing the opportunity to spend time together in conditions far more conducive to bonding than any they will encounter on Mount McKinley.

In light of that and later events, it is impossible not to recall something Joe himself wrote in pre-trip memo M-14 to the group. His intent was admirable: urging his team members to unsparingly prepare themselves physically, mentally, and emotionally for the hardest ordeal of their lives. But today the admonition has an eerie resonance:

It has been said that when the planning and organization is complete and the expedition begins, its fate is already determined.

PART TWO

ASCENT

*Do nothing in haste, look well to each step,
and from the beginning think what may be
the end.*

— EDWARD WHYMPER
Scrambles Amongst the Alps

6

The Long Road North

From Seattle to Mount McKinley, the teams face a journey of 2,500 miles, about the same distance as a cross-country trip from Seattle to Pittsburgh. On Monday, June 12, Howard and his two friends drive first to Seattle to buy extra goggles, fuel cans, and more bug dope, then head north.

Joe and his mates don't get off until Tuesday, June 13, a day behind schedule but in high spirits, nine young men setting out on the adventure of their lives, jammed happily into Hank Janes's battered blue Dodge camper-van, the Hankmobile, and Joe's 1951 Chevrolet Carryall, the Green Bomb, with its towed, overstuffed trailer.

Before long, the overloaded Green Bomb and trailer will be *hors de combat,* which reveals not only Alcan attrition but the massive amount of supplies required by a McKinley expedition. Joe's M-2 communication to the team lists no fewer than forty-three "Required Equipment" items for every man, which brings minimum pack weights into the 50-to-60-pound range. In addition are about 650 items of group gear that have to be divided among his climbers. When the Coloradoans' gear was included, the expedition was hauling, among other things, 1,200 feet of fixed rope, two ice saws, five snow shovels, twelve pots, two kettles, two pressure cookers, seven stoves, three first-aid kits, four hundred trail-marking wands, five gallons of kerosene, and more than twice that much white gas stove fuel. We know how much all of this weighed because the packer, who charged by the pound, put it on scales before loading up his horses for the cross-tundra trek. The total came to 2,315 pounds—1,900 for Joe's team, 415 for Howard's. This does not include the roughly 50-pound packs that each of the twelve men carried across the tundra themselves, adding another 600 pounds, making a grand total of about 3,000 pounds.

Most of the Wilcox climbers by now have read Brad Washburn's insulting May 17 letter to Joe and, feeling its sting as sharply as their leader did, decide to retaliate. In the dust on both vehicles, they write in big, bold letters:

BRAD IS A NO-GOODER AND A DO-BADDER

Taking this message into Mount McKinley National Park is like walking into the Vatican wearing a T-shirt reading *The Pope Is a Putz,* which, of course, is exactly as they want it. Brad's letters were addressed to Joe, but no matter. By the time the men depart for Alaska, every member of both teams has learned about the letter suggesting that they climb the mountain backwards or all jump into a crevasse and "rise to these unusual challenges." Brad has insulted their competence and integrity. It feels like a sucker punch in the face by someone they cannot punch back.

THE TWO GROUPS' overland travel styles are predictably different but, ironically, are the reverse of the philosophies they will employ on the mountain itself. There, Howard and his team will go fast, believing that speed equals safety, where Joe and his crew adhere more to a "slow-and-steady-wins-the-race" philosophy. Conversely, on the drive up, Joe plans an all-out, 2,500-mile sprint from Puyallup to Mount McKinley, driving their two older vehicles nonstop, twenty-four hours a day, rotating shifts behind the wheel with stints of sleeping in the backseats.

This nonstop grind is intended to make the most of McKinley's short climbing season, getting men on and off the mountain before August, when the glaciers become appreciably more dangerous as the snow softens and crevasses widen. Joe has contracted with local horse packer Berle Mercer to transport most of their supplies across the tundra from the park's Wonder Lake Campground to the foot of the Muldrow Glacier. They must meet Mercer in six days, on June 19. There is no flexibility in that deadline: the horse packer, like the glacier pilots on McKinley's opposite side, has clients booked before and after.

The very next client is none other than Howard Snyder. His date with the horse packer begins three days after Joe's. This enables the three Coloradoans to drive Jerry's white-over-blue Dodge Power Wagon during the day but benefit from good food and comfortable sleep each night. Howard also believes that it makes no sense to begin a climb that will likely be the most exhausting experience of their lives already beaten up by driving twenty-four hours a day.

It's not too much of a stretch to say that the Alcan is to highways as McKinley is to mountains—"everything we had feared and more," Joe will recall. By the time Joe and his team reach Northway Junction in Alaska, still some 400 miles from Mount McKinley National Park, climbers and vehicles show the strain of 2,000 miles of hard travel. If the Alcan was a torture rack for the vehicles, their backseats and cargo bays can have been little kinder to the climbers.

The Green Bomb, Joe's Chevrolet, fails first. With the engine rattling badly, they have no choice but to pull into a gas station. There the mechanic informs them that the engine bearings are just about shot and he'll have to order new parts from Fairbanks and this could take a couple of days, and *Sorry fellas, but, well, it's a pretty big job* . . .

But there isn't time to have new parts shipped from Fairbanks, nor do they have several hundred bucks for "a pretty big job." There's no other choice: they must turn to the Coloradoans for help, so when Jerry Lewis's Power Wagon comes rolling along in perfect health that afternoon, they wave it over. Joe suggests a new plan: If the Coloradoans will tow the trailer behind Jerry's truck, all nine of Joe's team will cram into Hank's van for the remainder of the trip.

Howard doesn't refuse to haul the trailer, but he points out that its added weight will reduce their gas mileage and asks to be paid for that extra cost. Joe, already short of cash, offers to barter food for gas, and Howard agrees. In his book, Howard explains the haggling this way: "In fact, we did not need the food trade, but we felt that this agreement would cement our combination and aid us in getting acquainted with the men of the Wilcox group."

Although on paper the two teams might appear as one, this negotiation makes it impossible to forget that the Colorado team began as an independent expedition with Howard as leader and, for all intents and purposes, remains so.

Two days later, Joe begins to learn the long, hard lesson that leading an expedition involves more than making lists, writing letters, and giving orders. Walt Taylor comes over to his tent and complains that the team is disorganized and needs stronger leadership. Not long after that, Jerry Clark tells Joe that he's being *too* authoritarian and needs to loosen up. Neither complaint comes in response to a specific incident; rather, they seem to reflect a more general unease about how things are going. Joe decides to defer any response until they arrive at the park.

With the Wilcox trailer in tow, Howard and his friends roll into Mount McKinley National Park at about two in the afternoon on Saturday, June 17. When they stop at the Park Information Center to ask about weather and recent expeditions, they discover something else, as Howard relates in *The Hall of the Mountain King*: "The content of Wilcox's letter to Washburn, asking what 'firsts' his party might accomplish, was common knowledge among the Park rangers. The ranger at the Information Center told us that Wilcox made himself out to be 'God's gift to Mt. McKinley' in the letter.' "

The Coloradoans drive south eighty-five more miles to Wonder Lake Campground, the actual jumping-off point for Muldrow Glacier route expeditions. This road runs through Alaskan wilderness parallel to the Muldrow Glacier, and the name Wonder Lake proves apt; it seems to the men that they have entered a magic kingdom. They see moose, Dall sheep, and a herd of caribou so vast that it flows like a brown river over the rolling green tundra. Mostly, though, they stare at the mountain itself, because even for men who have climbed the Alps and Mexico's giant peaks and who look up every day at 14,000-plus-foot Rocky Mountains, McKinley is unlike anything they have ever seen. It registers not only in their eyes but in their guts, and it must suddenly strike them— as it cannot have before—what they've set about trying to do here. I'm going to climb *that*? When they finally arrive at Wonder Lake, the great country softens a bit, welcoming them with a sunset that drenches McKinley in soft pink light.

While Howard and his friends are making camp, Joe and his eight teammates, beaten up by having been squeezed into the Hankmobile since Moon Lake, arrive at McKinley park headquarters at nine that evening, seven hours behind Howard's team. They find, as Howard did earlier, that Washburn's derision has preceded them. "No one said anything openly; yet it was clear that some half expected to see us arrive with a press bus in tow. It would be folly to debate Washburn's prejudice here on his own turf where he was a living legend, and I didn't try," Joe later wrote in *White Winds*. With that cool welcome, they all drive to Wonder Lake, tumble out of the van, and make a hasty camp near Howard's crew.

On Sunday, June 18, District Climbing Ranger Wayne Merry comes to visit. "Wayne was a quiet, but openly personable man of genuine friendliness, somehow escaping the plastic phonyness and procedural preoccupations affecting many bureaucratic employees," Joe would write in *White Winds*. Wayne is thirty-four years old then, and one of those rare people whose name accurately describes him. He's been with the National Park Service for eight years, the last two at Mount McKinley National Park. Wayne is a natural communicator, a good-humored man with buzz-cut brown hair, kind brown eyes, and an easy smile. He is liked by everyone who meets him, with the possible exception of National Park Service bosses, who may find him a bit too . . . well, *assertive*.

But Wayne is no poser. About five feet ten and 170 pounds of solid, corded muscle—what today we might call "ripped"—he has already climbed his way into legend by participating in the epic first ascent of 3,000-foot El Capitan in Yosemite National Park. This was, at the time, the greatest feat of big-wall rock climbing ever accomplished. It required the combined efforts of eight climbers, who spent a total of forty-five days on the face, placing 675 pegs and 125 bolts.

Wayne has never climbed McKinley, but he has ascended many big northwest peaks and has run complex search-and-rescue operations in the lower 48 and on McKinley. He is far and away the most knowledgeable mountaineer on staff at McKinley National Park, and one of North America's leading mountain search-and-rescue experts.

Wayne Merry is actually the only employee here who has done any serious climbing. George Hall, the newly appointed superintendent, was more typical of that era's staffing. Despite being top man overseeing park service operations on one of the world's most dangerous and coveted mountains, Hall will later admit in a tape-recorded interview with University of Alaska oral historian Karen Brewster: "It was a tough job. I came and I also was not too competent in mountain climbing information." His second in command, Chief Ranger Arthur Hayes, had no more mountaineering experience. This is not to blame these men for not being expert, or even good amateur, mountaineers. They were National Park Service career men and, like military personnel, went where they were sent. It was part of the job description if you wanted to have a future in government. But it *is* to say that in July 1967, Mount McKinley National Park was sorely lacking in mountaineering expertise.

When I got in touch with Wayne in 2005 for this book, he was seventy-three years old and had recently destroyed a knee, ripping out the medial, anterior, and posterior collateral ligaments and cracking a tibia in the process, while backcountry skiing, by himself, in the far northern wilds of British Columbia. The leg was sufficiently bollixed that he could not ski or even walk on it. The fall he took in such a remote, wild area, and in the dead of winter, could have killed a lot of people or at least necessitated an elaborate and expensive rescue. Wayne believes in self-reliance, so he carried no cell phone. Unable to call for help, he made himself a cast out of duct tape; then, using his ski poles as crutches, he stumped out miles to the road, got in his car, and drove himself home.

"Every moose in ten square miles now knows the F-word, but I didn't have to wait for rescue," he told me. Nor did he have to wait for a doctor's appointment. Wayne lives about a hundred miles from the nearest hospital and real, $600 orthopedic knee braces, so he made his own from an old plastic Krazy Karpet snow sled and "a lot of duct tape."

WAYNE SHOWS UP at the Wonder Lake Campground at eleven in the morning and immediately perceives that the expedition is a house divided. "They were two different groups with different characteristics," he recalls. "The three Colorado guys seemed in better shape and very serious. Joe's team was much bigger and more casual." But they did not strike him as incompetent or disorganized. In fact, Wayne told Joe at the time: "On paper, you are the best organized party ever to assault this mountain."

All climbers pass the then-required equipment check with flying colors, displaying their snow shovels, ice saws, excellent tents and sleeping bags, plenty of fuel, and a virtual mountain of food. Because of McKinley's notorious ability to maim with frostbite, their footwear is perhaps the single most important item of all. Wayne gives every boot an especially close look, and finds them all acceptable.

Wayne has known for weeks about the letters that Brad wrote to Superintendent George Hall, though not of others sent to different sources. "I agree entirely that Brad really went a little berserk in his correspondence re Wilcox," he says today. "Well, maybe a lot berserk. As George Hall said, he lost a lot of his dignity at that point. I was disappointed." To be helpful, Wayne has brought with him a new copy of Brad's Muldrow Glacier route climbing guide, still in draft form as a loose-leaf folder of photographs and typescript.

Howard, Jerry Lewis, and Paul pore over this new guide that Brad has just completed and sent to the park. Howard recognizes that this book could be as important to their survival as tents or ice axes, and he takes the time to make detailed notes, no doubt wishing that he could stuff the whole thing in his pack and carry it up the mountain.

The guide that they looked at still exists, residing in Denali National Park's Talkeetna Ranger Station. Mountaineering ranger Daryl Miller let me look at it, and it is, to use a phrase that Brad Washburn himself loved, *simply marvelous*—the best guide to any climbing route on Earth that I have ever seen. Like much of Brad Washburn's work, to call it simply a "climbing guide" is to vastly understate the book's true nature, because its etched prose and exquisite photographs elevate it to the level of art.

The photographs first. There are thirty 8×10 black-and-white images, beautifully composed and razor sharp in detail, showing every step of the route from Wonder Lake to the summit. Many were taken from airplanes, others from high points on the route to which Brad lugged his forty-pound camera and all the extra gear it required. The distance shots are so rich with detail that you can see individual trees, small streams, big rock cairns, and other landmarks. Moving up-mountain, the images are just as detailed, showing, for example, the exact spot where Elton Thayer met his end on the northwestern flank of Karstens Ridge in 1954. More importantly, they show the precise locations of safe campsites and climbing lines connecting them.

The text that Brad Washburn wrote to accompany the images flows from his unbelievable intimacy with the mountain:

> At an altitude of 16,400 feet (1.8 miles from Browne Tower) the top of the Lower Icefall is reached and the second icefall comes into sight ahead. There are a number of treacherous crevasses in this upper section of Harper Glacier, just where one would expect the going to be the best. The high winds up here often form smooth but very flimsy bridges of soft snow across many of the smaller cracks. These freshly filled cracks can be easily distinguished by their unusually white appearance, in contrast to the bluish solid ice or grayish older drifted snow that has been colored by rock dust from the North Peak. Although a nuisance on the way up, when one is climbing slowly and carefully, they can be exceedingly dangerous on the descent when one has the normal tendency to be a bit more lax and carefree.

For whatever reason, Joe and his teammates seem less interested in the guide. Howard will later criticize them for ignoring the book, which he feels may have been caused by their feelings about "no-gooder" Brad. Joe will say that he and his companions couldn't get to the book because the Coloradoans "monopolized it."

That afternoon, recalling Jerry Clark and Walt Taylor's two different concerns about his leadership style, Joe convenes a meeting "to discuss the expedition's organization." He is concerned not only about the different perceptions of his role but also that the group has not yet coalesced into a team.

Looking back from a perspective of forty years, the fractious atmosphere doesn't seem surprising. The men simply have not spent enough time together, on this trip or previously, to become a smoothly working team, or for Joe to have established himself as its unequivocal leader. It takes time for the accrual of small decisions and encounters that, cumulatively, persuade a group of men to like and trust one another. And it takes as much time or more for men to learn enough about one of their number—especially one they have never before met—to trust that man with their lives.

In July 1967, Joe Wilcox is just twenty-four years old. He has led smaller groups to success in smaller endeavors, but this is not a Boy Scout troop, a football team, or even a Rainier climb. This is mountaineering's Big Show, an entirely new realm of risk and reward. His team will spend many weeks on the mountain, exposing themselves to a host of objective dangers that, read aloud, sound like the name of a nasty law firm: Avalanche, Crevasse, Altitude, Frostbite, Weather & Fall.

A leader's decisions may protect his team against risks or increase it. Mountaineering history is rife with examples of both. Maurice Herzog's summit fever–driven decision to push for Annapurna's top with partner Louis Lachenal on June 3, 1950, cost Herzog all his fingers and toes and nearly caused the death of companions who climbed to their rescue. At the other end of the spectrum is the Band of Brothers cohesion created by coleaders Bob Bates and Charles Houston during the 1953 American K2 Expedition. Beset by a seemingly endless run of bad luck and worse weather, and by the death of one member, this group nevertheless coalesced around their leaders so passionately that they would remember the trip fondly for the rest of their lives.

It wouldn't be fair, or accurate, to attribute dissension in the ranks solely to whatever negative feelings arose between Joe and Howard. Among other amazing exploits (not the least of which was sawing off sizable parts of his own fingers when doctors' more traditional frostbite treatments proved too slow for his taste), Sir Ranulph Fiennes led the first pole-to-pole circumnavigation of the Earth—his Transglobe Expedition. During that ordeal he came to the following epiphany, which Diana Preston quotes in her book *A First Rate Tragedy*:

> Human beings are not ideally designed for getting on with each other—especially in close quarters. . . . On many expeditions there

is no way out, no means of transport, so a situation of forced togetherness exists that breeds dissension and often hatred between individuals and groups.

It's a lesson that the '67 men will also learn the hard way.

There are as many different kinds of leaders as there are men and
women who undertake the challenge, but there are only two basic styles
of leadership. Psychologists have applied various names to the two, but
perhaps the most useful are these: "I-Tell" and "We-Ask" leaders. The
"I-Tell" leaders are autocratic, egocentric, absolutely certain of their abilities and the legitimacy of their power. Alexander, Napoleon (and Well-
ington, for that matter), Grant, both Roosevelts, Hitler, Captains Ahab
and Queeg, Martha Stewart, and Donald Trump come to mind. The
"We-Ask" leaders, although confident, strong, and courageous, lead by
creating consensus rather than dictating actions: Jesus, King Richard the
Lionheart, Lincoln, Robert E. Lee, Gandhi, Eisenhower, Martin Luther
King, Jr., Lech Walesa.

Joe's autobiography ran to four pages of single-spaced typescript. At
one point, he gave the other team members an honest preview of himself:

> I think that socializing is a big waste of time and am considered a
> rather uncultured person. I enjoy good movies, sports, folk music,
> and occasionally dancing, but I can't stand plays, operas, or con-
> certs. I try to get by with shaving 2 or 3 times a week, but am not a
> beat-nik type. My wife thinks I am vain and conceited. Although
> never winning a popularity contest, I can get along with almost
> anyone. . . .
>   I do not have any children. I don't get along well with them. Kids
> go out of their way to sic their dogs on me or run me down with
> their tricycles.

Describing his leadership style in the autobiography, Joe informed the
others that

> As a leader I am democratic in all areas except those concerning
> safety. I feel that everyone is entitled to have a say, however, I will

be quite strict in some cases. . . . I am always glad to receive suggestions—leading is a very lonely position—but do not appreciate
people insisting on their own way when it is not in the interest of
the group. . . . I can become irritated if pressured into fast decisions, emergencies being an exception.

Whatever else may be said, it is true that Joe made no attempt to portray
himself any way but with full honesty.

When everyone convenes around Joe this afternoon, the sun is out,
warming the damp land around them, drawing out steamy mist and
scents of spruce and pine and bog. Mount McKinley, still thirty miles
distant, must loom larger than any of them thought it was possible for
anything to be, so vast that it seems to shove the sky aside. Their eyes
doubtless keep straying to this huge, mysterious mountain as the meeting progresses.

Joe is standing up, maybe leaning against a picnic table. Despite what
he wrote, his first wife, Cheryl, says firmly that he was not "vain and con-
ceited" then. That's probably fair, but it's also true—as his honest self-
portrait reflects—that there isn't much give to him. In those days,
twenty-three years before the publication of *Iron John* and the birth of
"inner children," being a good leader meant telling people what to do and
seeing that they did it. At that time, "Pattonesque" would have been
accolade rather than deprecation.

Howard Snyder, whose note taking and memory are equally remarkable, recalled Joe's comments in *The Hall of the Mountain King*. "You
have seen how big the peak is, and now you're preoccupied with getting
your *own* gear ready instead of working for the group." He adds that they
are not out for a Sunday hike where important decisions can be cast to
the momentary whims of the majority.

Walt Taylor, no doubt wearing his fez-like orange knit hat, aviator's
sunglasses, and white nose cream, is the first to respond. He has
expressed in his letters more reservations more openly than anyone else,
and his concern continues. "The trouble is we don't move, we don't get
busy and *do* things. No one even opens cans with gusto around here."

Howard feels that this was "one of the most apt and significant statements of the trip." He also claims that he and his friends had already

become aware of this strange lassitude. "The Colorado group had already discussed this malaise on the last day's drive to the Park. I caught Schlichter's eye, and we nodded our eyelids in agreement. We were glad to see that W. Taylor was aware of the problem, too, and were hopeful that he could help cure it."

Walt Taylor, for one, is apparently not suffering from this "malaise," because he volunteers to take over the organization of supplies, which, the next day, will be loaded onto horses for the overland trek to McGonagall Pass. Walt's willingness to speak out like this, and to back up words with action, will set him apart throughout the climb.

Joe then asks whether everyone has read the expedition ground rules that he wrote and circulated, and invites comments about them. There are none. Regarding the eleven silent faces surrounding him, Joe tries a joke at his own expense: "As you can see by all the news photographers, I am climbing for publicity." He does not say whether anyone laughed, but he quickly adjourns the meeting: "With the sparsely interacting discussion, I did not feel that a great deal was accomplished."

Next, Joe and Jerry Clark drive a few miles to the Wonder Lake Ranger Station. They spend two hours talking with Wayne Merry about the mountain, and establish a protocol for radio communications. The expedition will call between seven and eight every night.

Back at the Wonder Lake camp, after dinner Steve comes to Joe with a bombshell. He feels weak and nauseous, and fears he has "caught a bug." They both know that this is one of the worst times to come down with an infection (another being high on the mountain), because the next morning Berle Mercer will be packing the Wilcox team's supplies to McGonagall Pass, and the men themselves will be hiking in.

Steve is not well enough to accompany them, so Joe proposes a change in plan. After hauling the Wilcox group's supplies, Mercer will come back to begin packing the Colorado equipage, probably three days from now. Joe suggests that Steve remain at Wonder Lake for these three days to recuperate. If his condition improves after that, he can walk in with the Colorado group. If he is still sick, Joe advises him to abandon the climb.

In *White Winds*, Joe writes, "I explained the situation to Howard and suggested that Jerry Lewis accompany the first group to operate the theodolite," referring to surveying work to measure the glacier's rate of flow, a vestige of the larger scientific project contained in their original expedition plan. Joe believes that an extra three days will give Steve enough time to at least partially recover. He has another, perhaps even more compelling motive: "This would be a good opportunity to melt the icy bubble that seemed to surround the Colorado group."

Unfortunately, bubbles of ice, with their sharp edges and frozen cores, do not succumb easily.

7

Lone Man Walking

An expedition taking the Muldrow Glacier route up Mount McKinley officially departs from the Wonder Lake Campground, but it still must cross about twenty-two miles of tundra, the McKinley River, Clearwater Creek, 5,720-foot McGonagall Pass, and several more miles of gravelly rubble before putting boot to glacier. The Wilcox Expedition will be hauling about 3,000 pounds of food and equipment. As earlier contracted, Berle Mercer will carry the bulk of their supplies to Horse Cache, two miles from McGonagall Pass.

Joe and Howard are wise to have taken advantage of Mercer's mounts. Crossing tundra is, quite simply, the ugliest walking you will ever do. The passage from Wonder Lake to McGonagall Pass has a kind of picturesque allure when you read about it meandering through fragrant spruce forests and crossing clear streams, climbing scenic and easy 3,100-foot Turtle Hill, the highest point of the hike, with every step overseen by McKinley shining like God's Taj Mahal against the green sward of tundra below.

But what terrors lurk behind that lovely face. The infamous Alaskan mosquitoes, huge and bloodthirsty, swarm over the land in clouds of uncountable billions.

Tussocks are globular grassy humps up to a foot tall that present an equally maddening aspect of tundra crossing. Many hikers call them "babies' heads." Cameron Walker, a scientist writing in the winter 2003 issue of *Wild,* the magazine of the California Academy of Sciences,

penned a fine description of tussocks after spending the better part of a
summer being tortured by them:

> Here at Toolik, a research station three hours south of Prudhoe Bay,
> people compare a tussock tromp to slogging across a sea of basket-
> balls.

ON MONDAY, JUNE 19, horse packer Berle Mercer, lean, leathery, and
friendly, arrives at Wonder Lake at about seven in the morning, two
hours late, with his twelve-year-old son, Kurt, and eight pack animals in
tow. Mercer gets about half of Joe's gear aboard his horses and starts out.
The horse packer has heard about the "misunderstanding" between
Wilcox and Washburn from Brad himself, but he opines that no one has
received more publicity for climbing McKinley than Bradford Washburn. "When Washburn is on the mountain there are helicopters and
planes flying everywhere, like an invasion."

Wayne Merry has warned the climbers that the McKinley River, two
miles from Wonder Lake, is running much higher than usual. Joe, Mark,
and John hike the two miles first, moving quickly without packs, to
assess the danger. They find the river high but passable, so by radio Joe
tells Howard, Paul, and Steve Taylor to bring the first team's packs up to
the river. Thus begins a series of interactions that will widen the deep-
ening chasm between Joe's team and the Coloradoans and will make Joe
and Howard dislike each other even more—before either has set foot
on McKinley.

Howard and Paul are champing at the bit and can't wait to get going.
Steve is sick. Howard wrote in his book, and contends to this day, that
Joe did not tell him about Steve's illness. Joe wrote in his book that he
did "explain the situation to Howard" and contends that that explanation
included mention of Steve's "bug." Neither Howard nor Paul remembers
Steve telling them that he was ill.

Howard and Paul cover the two miles between Wonder Lake and the
McKinley River "rapidly, to outrun the mosquitoes and to get to the river
in time to take pictures of the pack string making the crossing," as
Howard recalled in his book.

After delivering the other team's three fifty-pound packs, Howard, Paul, and Steve start back unburdened. Having moved quickly enough with loaded packs on their way to the river, on the way back Howard and Paul "moved along the trail at a nominal pace, stopping for drinks from cold, clear springs along the way." Even so, "S. Taylor could not keep up. He kept falling behind, walking with his shoulders slumped, his head hung down, and his feet scuffing the ground. I wrote in my logbook that day that Taylor was 'so slow, so morose.' "

In *The Hall of the Mountain King*, Howard wrote that Steve "was in a continual state of depression. It was not until weeks later that I knew the reason for S. Taylor's state of mind and body. He had so very little experience that he was terrified by the sight of this icy behemoth that he was to climb, and it was literally worrying him sick."

Joe Wilcox disagrees strongly. "I knew Steve better than anyone on the expedition, and I sincerely don't believe that he was unhappy. I can think of no comments that Steve made to me nor do I see any evidence in his functioning as an expedition member [that he was unhappy]."

Anshel Schiff has similar memories. "I have no recollection of his [Steve] being unhappy and do not think that this was the case. He was quiet and got along fine. On a long trip in confined spaces with many people who were effectively strangers tensions can come up between people, but I do not recall this ever happening with Steve."

Joe Wilcox believes, and common sense would concur, that there was another reason for the tension between Steve and the Coloradoans. Steve had voiced the strongest opposition to joining the two groups. He had made his feelings known straight-up and face-to-face in their Puyallup meeting, and this, too, militates against the conclusion that he was depressed and frightened. Depressed people have neither the energy nor the inclination to stand up and voice unpleasant opinions in front of hostile groups.

Steve's criticisms obviously incensed Howard, who was still stung six years later when he wrote so dismissively about them as "inane" in *The Hall of the Mountain King*. Jerry Lewis and Paul also must have suffered hurt feelings at the least and perhaps even sharp anger at having their long-sought expedition threatened on literally the last day by Steve's vehement objections. So Steve's physical illness aside, the three men cannot have been comfortable together. It's not surprising that Steve, as odd man out of a hike with two of them, would have preferred moving on his own and that, being sick, he would have been behind rather than in front. Finally, if Steve had been afraid of McKinley, it's logical to assume that results of his fear—depression, anxiety, lassitude—would have worsened the higher he climbed. In fact, according to Howard, just the opposite happened. "After the tundra incident, [Steve] became one of the strongest and steadiest climbers on the team."

On the morning of Thursday, June 2, again traveling as a group, the three men help Mercer load his string of horses, then hit the trail toward the McKinley River. Howard warns Steve that they must hurry to reach the river before Mercer gets there, in case the water is so deep that they'll need to ride the horses across. The three of them leave together, carrying seventy-five-pound packs, but they do not arrive together.

Having become separated from Steve by the time they reach the river, Howard and Paul start across, on foot, without him. They find the first large channel flowing high and fast from two days of hard rains. Thick rain is falling upriver, which means that the flow volume will keep increasing, perhaps rapidly. They continue without pause.

The river is flowing fast enough to knock down and almost drown one of Mercer's horses, which, according to the packer, would have washed to the Bering Sea if he had not rushed to its aid. I have ridden horses across a good many rivers myself, and any current strong enough to bowl over a healthy 1,200-pound animal with four legs, and with not even a rider on its back to unbalance it, is a current to take seriously.

As Howard and Paul get farther into the crossing, things become even worse for the two of them. "We crossed two large channels, a bit touch-and-go, with an occasional flash of anxiety that the current was going to overwhelm us." Paul later recalled that crossing the McKinley might have been the whole trip's scariest and most dangerous experience for him. At this point, as Howard notes in his book, "S. Taylor was far behind, a small red speck that never seemed to move. . . ."

Howard and Paul are sufficiently frightened by the swollen river that they let Mercer's horses bring them over the second half of the crossing. On the far bank they rest, dry their feet, and change socks. Meanwhile they see Steve cross most of the river by himself, but then one of Mercer's horses gets him through the last two deep channels. Steve then joins Howard and Paul on the far bank.

While Steve dries off and rests, Howard and Paul hike on, not wanting to lose contact with Mercer and the safety that his horses represent. After about two miles they find Mercer stopped for lunch and join him. As soon as Steve arrives, Howard and Paul start out again at what Howard describes as "a good clip." Steve, without having a chance to rest, manages to keep up for a while, but eventually he becomes separated again. Paul, interviewed in 2005, had clear memories of this trek. "I don't remember [Steve] saying anything about being sick. I know he was upset that we weren't waiting for him or we were moving too fast. . . . It just looked like he didn't feel too good."

In describing this episode, you could say that Steve kept falling behind, or that the Coloradoans kept leaving him, or simply that they got separated (my choice here). But a commandment of wilderness travel is that any party is only as fast as its slowest member. Responsibility for keeping together cannot be assigned to someone not physically capable of doing so.

They are now separated in country that "was dry and pleasant, but with considerable up-and-down stretches"—stretches, in other words, that will cause them to lose visual contact with Steve, just as the deep troughs of big ocean swells conceal ships from one another. After one period of ten minutes with no sight of Steve, Howard and Paul drop their packs and go looking for him. They finally locate him not by sight but by sound. Paul bellows Steve's name to the skies, producing "from far away a faint reply."

Steve has become lost, following a wide swath of caribou tracks up the wrong valley. Realizing his error, he retraces his steps, finds the route, and catches up with the two Coloradoans. Howard has been "shocked by this, still another indication of the experience level of Steve Taylor." Howard and Paul take off again, but not before Howard chides (and later writes in his book), "I hope you don't follow meltwater channels on the glacier. They go into crevasses."

Getting lost in tundra country is not necessarily a sign of inexperience or ineptitude. While Joe and his team are higher on the mountain, another expedition from the Mountaineering Club of Alaska, led by seasoned Alaskan climber Bill Babcock, will follow caribou tracks and get so badly lost on the same hike from Wonder Lake to McGonagall Pass that they spend two full days mucking around in the wrong valley.

At about half past eleven that night, after fourteen hours on the trail with their seventy-five-pound packs, Howard and Paul make camp. Steve doesn't show up and, according to Howard's account in *The Hall of the Mountain King*, he and Paul eat, spread out sleeping bags, and turn in for the night without looking for him. At about seven the next morning, still without Steve, they hike on, passing Horse Cache, the terminus where Mercer has to unload because snow bars his horses from further travel. Howard and Paul climb another mile, meeting Joe, Hank, and Mark coming down to pick up loads from Horse Cache. A few minutes more takes them to the McGonagall Pass camp, elevation 5,720 feet. Here they drop packs, devour a huge lunch of sausage and cheese, and have a revealing exchange with Berle Mercer's twelve-year old son, Kurt.

"Wilcox is just doing this climb for publicity," Kurt declares without prompting—another indication of how far the influence of Brad Washburn's letters has spread.

WHEN STEVE DOES show up much later, he heads straight for Joe, who wrote about the encounter in *White Winds*:

> Steve sauntered up, noticeably upset. I asked how he felt, and how he managed to get so far behind. He replied that he was still weak, but felt that he was going to be all right. He then related that Howard and Paul had forced a fast pace—goading, ridiculing, and insulting him whenever he fell behind. Finally, when he was unwilling to push himself beyond reason in his recuperating condition, they had abandoned him altogether on the previous evening.
>
> "Do you mean they haven't been in contact with you since yesterday?" I asked in amazement.
>
> "That's right," Steve said with resignation.
>
> "Did they tell you that they were going ahead without you and that you were on your own?" I asked.
>
> "No," he replied. Steve started up the hill and I began loading my pack, my temper beginning to burn. Steve had the gentle disposi-

tion of a saint; it would take a great deal for him to claim that someone had been rude to him. Perhaps Howard and Paul were trying to
get even with Steve for opposing their joining the expedition. Or
even more serious, perhaps they saw nothing wrong with leaving a
lone man simply because they were comfortable at a faster pace.
Pushing for 14 hours with 75-pound packs was no way to treat an
ill hiker, especially when such a grind was completely unnecessary.

Furious, Joe confronts Howard and Paul immediately.

Joe's and Howard's books contain detailed accounts of what happens
next. Distilled to its essence, Howard's version is that, after hearing a vivid
explanation of Steve's slowness and the relative safety of the route,
"Wilcox's indignation was somewhat tempered by our forceful 'counter-
attack' so he packed a load and started up toward the pass."

Joe's recollection is different:

> Their lack of group commitment and concern was unacceptable.
> "The only thing I'm wondering is whether or not to send you two
> back. It seems that you are still the Colorado group, just worried
> about yourselves," I said with a flushed anger that ended the con-
> versation. I started hiking, leaving Howard and Paul muttering to
> each other.

Paul does not confront Joe directly, but does ask why Steve was the
sole member of Joe's group left to hike in with him and Howard. In *White
Winds*, written fourteen years after the expedition and eight years after
Howard's book, Joe claims that he told Howard about Steve's illness back
at Wonder Lake, and reminds them of that now. In his own book, written first, Howard writes, "This was the first we had heard of this from
any source." It is one of the innumerable "he said, he said" differences in
their accounts of the expedition.

No people are perfect and no expedition progresses without mistakes.
That said, it's important to try to understand Howard and Paul's actions.
How would the trek have looked from beneath *their* packs? Both of them
are fit and highly competitive. They have been anxious to set foot on the
Muldrow Glacier, the true start of their climb, for years. Charged with

energy and anticipation, they are like Thoroughbreds in the gate. When it bangs open, metaphorically, releasing them onto the tundra, they just *go*. It's probably almost involuntary.

For his part, Steve is sick and already tired from the grinding 2,400-mile drive, so a fast pace would have been the last thing he wanted. He can't be happy paired with two men he did not want to join his own team, and he certainly knows that they harbor no fond feelings for the guy who nearly killed their chances of joining the expedition. Being ridiculed after losing his way in the tundra and following the caribou trail would have made him even angrier and more avoidant.

Fortunately for all, Steve comes through undamaged. But in some sense, a gauntlet has been thrown down between the two teams' leaders. Howard and Paul go on their way, both smarting from Joe's tongue-lashing, but Howard, the erstwhile Colorado team leader now upbraided like a greenhorn in front of his best friend, must have been feeling especially humiliated and angry. In his book, he wrote, "We had been on the trail only one day, and had already engaged in a serious argument with Wilcox. It did not seem to be a good omen."

Joe's recollection is no more optimistic. "I started hiking, leaving Howard and Paul muttering to each other. If they could abandon a man so easily on the tundra, I thought, how easy would it be for them to abandon someone else on the mountain where things could get really rough."

Ultimately, though, assigning "right" and "wrong" for this specific incident is less important than understanding that the two groups' fragile alliance has already suffered another rupture. As the men go higher, the rifts between them, like the crevasse fields they are about to enter, will only increase in number and hazard.

Muldrow Glacier

McKinley River

Mount McKinley, Alaska
Route of the Wilcox Expedition
June 19–July 31, 1967

1. Wonder Lake Ranger Station
2. National Park Service Campground: 2,200'
3. Turtle Hill: 3,104'
4. Bivouac during ascent: 2,500', June 19
5. Bivouac during descent: 2,800', July 25
6. Horse Cache: 4,500'
7. Camp 1, McGonagall Pass: 5,720'
8. Bivouac during descent: 6,100', July 24
9. Camp 2: 6,500'
10. Lower Icefall: 7,000'
11. Camp 3: 8,100'
12. Great Icefall: 9,300'
13. Camp 4: 11,000'
14. Camp 5: 12,100'
15. Camp 6: 15,000'
16. Camp 7: 17,900'
17. Archdeacon's Tower: 19,650'
18. South Peak: 20,320'
19. North Peak: 19,470'
20. Denali Pass: 18,200'
21. Wickersham Wall
22. Pioneer Ridge
23. Karstens Ridge
24. Browne Tower: 14,500'
25. The Flatiron
26. Steve Taylor's ice ax found: 17,200'
27. Steve Taylor's sleeping bag and pole
    found: 17,800'

8

Divided We Falter

The terrain over which any expedition climbs divides it into natural phases, and a Muldrow Glacier ascent breaks neatly into five distinct experiences. The first phase includes crossing the tundra and rivers from Wonder Lake to McGonagall Pass, at 5,720 feet. The second phase includes load carrying and establishing Camp II at 6,500 feet, Camp III at 8,100 feet, and Camp IV at 11,000 feet, at the base of Karstens Ridge. The third phase involves cresting Karstens Ridge, then establishing intermediate Camps V at 12,100 feet, VI at 15,000 feet, and VII at 17,900 feet. Penultimate phase four is the summit climb to 20,320 feet, and the return to Camp VII. On the Muldrow, and for any expedition, the last phase—statistically most dangerous and emotionally least pleasant—is the descent.

Their initial, laborious slogging up-glacier beyond McGonagall Pass seems to confirm one of Walt Taylor's preclimb fears, expressed in a letter to Jerry Clark, about becoming a human pack mule. The work is hard and the rewards are minimal. All (except one man, as we shall see) carry loads in the seventy-five- to eighty-five-pound range. Mighty John Russell, as he is not reluctant to tell the others, carries hundred-pound loads routinely and 115-pound loads occasionally, a Bunyanesque accomplishment here or, for that matter, anywhere.

Adding some zest, if not pure fun, to their Sisyphean toil is the fact that even at this relatively low altitude, there are plenty of ways to die, because down here McKinley is rife with pitfalls—literally.

From Friday, June 23, when men of the Wilcox Expedition first set foot on the Muldrow itself, death by crevasse may be the result not only of a wrong step, but any step. Some areas, such as campsites that have been probed and packed, are less deadly than stretches of trail over open glacier. But because the Muldrow itself, like every glacier, is always flowing, danger is always present. Jonathan Waterman, in *Surviving Denali*, describes the fate of one experienced climber killed by a single misstep. After carefully probing his whole campsite and finding it crevasse-free, the man took one step outside the circle to pee, promptly dropped into a crack, and fell 130 feet to his death.

Climbing the Muldrow's heavily crevassed miles of route just once would be dangerous and unnerving enough. The July 1967 group must pass over two, three, or even more times per mile—not unlike playing Russian roulette with several bullets, rather than one, in the revolver's chambers. Siege-style climbing works the same way for an Everest expedition with 150 porters and Sherpas as it does for a self-supporting twelve-man Muldrow attempt. First, all the expedition's supplies are amassed at a base camp. For the July 1967 team, Berle Mercer's pack animals take the 3,000-plus-pounds of supplies as far as Horse Cache, after which the load goes up to Camp I, at McGonagall Pass, on the men's backs.

The process repeats itself all the way up the mountain. First, an advance rope team of three or four men, traveling with light packs, "makes the route." They climb slowly and carefully, avoiding visible crevasses and probing with long poles for others that might lurk unseen beneath thin bridges of snow. They place wands as they go, about every 300 feet down here and about 100 feet apart above 18,000 feet. Once a safe route has been explored and marked, other rope teams follow, ferrying loads of food, fuel, and equipment. As soon as the new camp is fully stocked and occupied (or sometimes even before), another advance team begins making the route to the next higher camp. Each camp vacated during the ascent is stocked with enough supplies to enable a safe descent.

From Camp I, on June 24, an advance team of Jerry Clark, Walt, Dennis, and John, climbing with light packs, makes the four-and-a-half-mile section of route to Camp II. Their passage creates a trail, compressing the snow beneath their snowshoes, and winds safely through the crevasses they can see. To locate other crevasses, rope team leader Jerry Clark painstakingly probes the snow as they go. Any hidden crevasses are marked with warning wands. This creates a safe, visible trail that leads them back down to Camp I and that subsequent teams, ferrying loads, follow up to Camp II. Safe and visible, that is, unless glacier movement, snowmelt, wind, and the stress of frequent passages change things for the worse.

Four days pass uneventfully while various rope teams make the nine-mile round-trip from Camp I to Camp II. On Tuesday, June 27, the men's luck finally runs out. Howard is leading an advance team of Jerry Lewis, Steve, and Mark, route finding from Camp II to a cache at 7,300 feet. At the base of the Lower Icefall, Jerry Lewis, second on the rope, falls ten feet into a crevasse that Howard just walked over without incident. Jerry is saved from certain injury and possible death only by the quick reactions of rope mates Howard and Steve. The next day, while load carrying up to the Hill of Cracks, John Russell falls into crevasses three times, and Hank Janes takes the plunge once. Covering this same terrain later, Joe will put his foot through fragile bridges a number of times.

The word crevasse is derived from the Old French crever, "to break." Crevasses are just that—breaks in the surface of a glacier, which is a giant river of ice flowing downhill. Variations in flow speed or bends around natural obstacles break the crevasse's surface into cracks that on McKinley are often big enough to swallow freight trains and cathedrals.

These monsters, however, are not the most dangerous ones, because they're easily seen and avoided. The real killers are the little fellows—narrower, with fragile bridges of snow and ice connecting their two edges, concealing the drop below. That's the kind of booby trap that caused the most horrible of all McKinley deaths, in 1981. Experienced climber Chris Kerrebrock and his partner, the great mountaineer Jim Wickwire, were traversing the Peters Glacier. Their goal, as preparation for an Everest attempt the next year, was to climb McKinley's 14,000-foot Wickersham Wall. Wickwire and Kerrebrock were roped more closely together than is typical for glacier travel, and this proved their undoing.

Kerrebrock was in the lead, and a heavily loaded sled was tied between them. Kerrebrock broke through an unseen crevasse bridge and plunged headfirst about twenty-five feet, pulling the sled down on top of him and Wickwire down on top of both. Because of the short rope, everything happened too quickly for Wickwire to self-arrest with his ice ax. The pile-driver blows of sled and Wickwire drove Kerrebrock deeper still and broke Wickwire's shoulder. Kerrebrock was jammed so tightly that he could not extricate himself. Even with only one usable arm, Wickwire spent many hours trying increasingly desperate tactics to get Kerrebrock out: chopping the ice around him, cutting off his pack, rigging a pulley system from the surface. In the end, nothing worked. With mountains walling them in, their CB radio was useless.

They both acknowledged, without panic or histrionics, that there was nothing either one of them could do, and that Kerrebrock was going to die. He did die, eventually: hour after hour, freezing, squeezed so tight that breathing was painful, upside down (the crucifixion position the Romans reserved for people they were particularly displeased with), and, perhaps worst of all, conscious and knowing what was happening with every passing minute. Wickwire, able to do no more, stayed with him until the end, then climbed out of the crevasse and wandered dazedly around the Peters Glacier for six days. He was saved purely by chance when a glacier pilot spotted him from the air.

CREVASSES ARE AMONG the major characters in the Wilcox tragedy's opening act, during the expedition's long slog up the Muldrow Glacier. Even before Jerry Lewis, the biggest and heaviest of all twelve men, falls into one, they spark what will become a particularly acrimonious fight—not between Wilcox climbers and the Coloradoans but between members of Joe's own team.

It begins on the afternoon of Sunday, June 25. Returning to Camp I after hauling his load to Camp II with Jerry Clark, Mark, Hank, and Howard, John Russell, red faced and furious, storms up to Joe and demands four day's worth of food, a tube tent, and a stove. He is leaving the expedition.

Nonplussed, Joe says that of course John can have what he needs, but Joe wants to know the reason for John's abrupt decision. He doesn't need to ask a second time.

This group is leading itself a dozen different ways, John declares. The

Coloradoans are one clique. Jerry Clark, Hank, and Mark are another. Everybody else is out there in no-man's-land.

Some of these people have no respect for our ground rules, John accuses. Earlier today, he was snowshoeing, and Clark and McLaughlin were using skis, and they almost yanked him off his feet. What's more, 120 feet of rope is not enough for four people.

Howard had climbed earlier to Camp II with the day's advance team of Jerry Lewis, Paul, and Walt, and he saw the fracas between John, Jerry, and Mark. He describes in his book what happened:

> As the four men who were not on the advance team prepared to return to Camp I, Russell said, "I refuse to climb on the same rope with Jerry Clark." He was still angry with Clark because of the ski-use argument.
>
> Clark attempted to reason with Russell, but to no avail. Clark then said, "As deputy leader, I have no choice but to order you to remain here. We can't have you going unroped on the glacier."
>
> Schiff tried to talk some sense into Russell, but without success. W. Taylor's face mirrored his astonishment at the situation. "C'mon gentlemen, let's do it!" Taylor exclaimed. "I'm getting cold." Russell was adamant. Finally, Clark and Schiff went on one rope, while W. Taylor took Russell on another rope.

Joe understands that John's criticisms, though aimed at other expedition members, are also criticisms of his leadership. "I had not been vigilant in my support of the expedition regulations and on a couple of occasions had even been a party to their circumvention," Joe admits in *White Winds*. He acknowledges that John's ire is at least partly justified and agrees to call another group meeting the next day. With that, John says he will defer his decision until after the meeting. It will be the second such meeting to discuss problems with the team—problems of leadership and differences among team members.

Fittingly, the next morning a storm is threatening as all twelve men come together for the meeting that Joe describes as "the agony of a verbal ordeal." Howard Snyder will write: "This donnybrook made our confrontation with Wilcox three days earlier look mild by comparison." Joe begins by saying that they need to talk about problems that lie "smoldering under the surface." John complains angrily about Jerry Clark's and Mark's use of skis. Joe recites the pre-trip agreement language banning downhill skiing as too dangerous in crevassed areas. Mark and Jerry retort that they are more experienced than anyone else, including Joe; thus he should not presume to tell them when and how to use their skis. The discussion quickly devolves into an increasingly heated debate about whether a skier or a snowshoer can better self-arrest and hold another who has fallen into a crevasse. According to Snyder's account, John, not a man with a long fuse, "became unnecessarily belligerent toward Mark and Jerry, and stated that he wouldn't climb on a rope with skiers."

Someone else ventures that the whole discussion was pointless because no crevasses had been spotted between Camps I and II, so going roped was a waste of time. *Big* mistake. This is a direct assault on Joe's ability to make basic leadership decisions. Joe's fuse is doubtless longer than John's. But he has been laboring under the weight of primary responsibility for two weeks now, dealing with frustrations small and large, surely hearing more gripes than thanks, fully aware that considerable tension still exists between the two groups and that he is the source of some of it. Joe is not some wise old Yoda of the mountains. He is just twenty-four years old, young indeed for so much responsibility in this trying environment, and has never led a team of this size, or one so divided from the very beginning. Heartily sick of the bitching and moaning, Joe barks that *only clumsy people stumble into crevasses they can see!* He points out the obvious fact that climbers fall into crevasses they can't see. As proof, he cites the example of Jacques Batkin, the 1967 Winter Expedition climber killed by such a crevasse.

So there they all sit or stand miserably in what is by now a frigid, driving rain as the meeting, rather than resolving anything, becomes hotter by the minute. Joe remembers saying, "Before the expedition, I submitted a list of regulations, at which time I received no objections. Now it seems that some people do not respect these rules. . . . For those of you who feel that this mountain or route is not a worthy challenge, I suggest that you hike out and climb Mount Logan or some other peak."

Long silence. Longer silence. Jerry Clark and Mark, perhaps irritated with John Russell before, may now be furious at having been upbraided in front of the whole team. John is probably not much mollified, because neither Jerry nor Mark has actually agreed to give up his skis. Dennis and Hank, both of whom are Jerry's friends and recruits, are probably angry that Joe has embarrassed their friend and climbing mentor in front of the group. Anshel, without close ties to anyone, is probably bemused, but he cannot be feeling comfortable about their security on the mountain after such an exchange. Howard, worried that things are getting out of hand, tries a defusing joke: "Tell you what, Joe. You take one skier on your rope and I'll take all the rest of 'em on mine." There are, of course, just two skiers in the group.

Joe asks whether anyone wants to offer more complaints. With characteristic poise, Walt Taylor breaks the tension with a joke of his own. "I didn't have any until you called this meeting. Now I'm all wet." The men laugh, then scurry back to their tents. On the way, Walt offers some encouragement. "Leading is a lonely position," he says. "I don't like to see our two leaders not getting along." Doubtless Joe appreciates the gesture, but it's not clear whether Walt is referring to Joe and Howard, or to Joe and Jerry Clark.

In *White Winds*, Joe puts a good face on the meeting's aftermath: "For the first time we were actually a group with group identity, group expectations, and group commitments." Howard's interpretation is different. "Wilcox had by now threatened to send half of the party back to Wonder Lake, including the deputy leader. . . ."

LOOKING BACK, IT'S easy to see that by calling meetings of the entire group to resolve disputes between just a few members, all the men are exposed to the arguments and are inevitably drawn to one side or the other. Joe could instead have called aside John, and later Jerry Clark and Mark, for a private bit of team building: "Look guys, I have a challenge here, and I could really use your help. . . ." This is now standard or at least recommended practice in our somewhat more enlightened age. When approached this way, most people feel embraced rather than antagonized, and they do offer to help if they can.

But this is now and that was then. Because of the era, youth, and temperament, and doubtless also because constant fatigue, altitude, and discomfort erode patience, Joe takes a more authoritarian approach. In doing so, he is simply applying that era's standard operating procedure for leaders and managers. And to be fair to Joe, it is true that every member of his team read and agreed to the rules.

If Joe and the other members hoped that this meeting would clear the air and help the group become "a well-oiled team," as Joe puts it, they are disappointed. The dispute between John, Jerry Clark, and Mark was ugly and divisive. Before long, things will get considerably uglier.

9

Friktion

The great Prussian military thinker Carl von Clausewitz (1780–1831) identified the concept of *Friktion* in organizations. Clausewitz was concerned with an army:

> we must remember that no part of it consists of a single piece, that everything is made up of men, each of whom still has his own friction at every turn. . . . Therefore this terrible friction . . . is everywhere in contact with chance, with consequences that are impossible to calculate. . . .

Taking this a step further, Laurence Gonzales, in *Deep Survival*, writes that "an army in the field . . . is not altogether different from groups of people in the wilderness."

Just as the consequences of friction multiply in an army of thousands, so do they in an expedition of twelve, particularly when they are sharpened by the animus of Super-Alpha conflict. The effects of both become more pronounced as the men enter a region of new divides both literal and psychological: the Lower Icefall and the Hill of Cracks.

Even before they begin negotiating these huge crevasse fields, however, the evening of Tuesday, June 27, brings unexpected excitement to Camp II. After pitching his tent, Joe gets ready to cook dinner but finds the Optimus white-gas stove empty. Still inside the tent, he fills the stove with gas. Some of the volatile liquid overflows and pools on the tent floor. Joe mops it up with toilet paper and then, "priming the stove, I struck a match and with a 'whump' the floor of the tent was ablaze." Joe puts out the fire by dumping a bucket of water on it, but John Russell's shouts— "Our Fearless Leader just tried to burn down the tent!"—bring everyone else running.

Almost miraculously, the tent and Joe are undamaged. Some have used this and two other stove incidents to bolster the theory that Joe's entire team was too inexperienced to have attempted McKinley, but it's a spurious allegation. White-gas stoves are infamously tricky and have blown up in the face of mountaineers older and more experienced than Joe. What's more, Joe and all of his team had been using white-gas stoves for years in environments as bad as or worse than these lower elevations of McKinley. He was intimately familiar with their operation and with the severe hazards of white gasoline, which was not called "Blazo" without good reason.

THE NEXT MORNING, under gray clouds swollen with snow, Howard, Jerry Lewis, Steve Taylor, and Mark McLaughlin, in that order, start up. Howard's sequencing on the rope is brave *and* smart. In the lead, he's the one most likely to punch through a hidden snow bridge and fall into a crevasse. And Jerry Lewis will be right behind to arrest his fall and help haul him out.

All goes well as they cross the flat glacier above camp and enter the icefall's lower reaches. Howard's route takes them over the tips of the avalanche cones, in accordance with Washburn's logic that avalanche debris will have filled in more crevasses here close to the wall's base. At one point, Howard stops on a secure-looking ice hump to adjust a snowshoe, then moves on. Jerry Lewis, crossing the same spot moments later, breaks through the surface and drops into a crevasse. He falls about ten feet before Howard's fast ice ax belay stops him.

"Do you have me?" Jerry yells, an edge of panic in his voice. He feels as though he's dropping still farther, but it is only the rope cutting deeper into the crevasse's soft edge. Howard moves as close to the crevasse as he dares and peers down.

"Are you all right?" he calls.

"Hell, no, I'm not all right," Jerry fires back with such energy that they know he may be distraught but is uninjured. They lower a rope and haul

Jerry's pack out of the hole. Then, with a pulley rigged to his waist harness, Jerry himself is hauled back up to safety. Sitting in the snow, he regains his composure quickly enough to tell them of the crevasse's beauty: "I wish there was enough light down there to take pictures. It was all subtle shades of blue."

Beautiful it may have been, but this crevasse was the especially deadly type with walls that flare out below the surface, meaning that if your rope breaks or your belay fails, there are no converging walls beneath to slow your plunge with a snowy embrace. The cavern beneath his dangling feet, Jerry says, was big enough for a basketball game. Contemplating this, and the flimsy-looking three-eighth-inch nylon rope that just saved his life, Jerry says, "The next rope I buy is going to be an inch thick."

The next day, it's Joe's turn to lead a team up past the Lower Icefall. He's aware of Jerry's mishap but also concerned about avalanches, so he decides to try the route that Howard avoided, moving farther away from the hanging seracs and avalanche cones, closer to the Lower Icefall's crevasse field. For Joe, it's a logic-driven choice: "We were trained in pulling people out of crevasses; we were not trained in fending off tons of falling ice, rock, and snow."

Joe and his three rope mates thread their way through the icefield's crevasses without disaster, though they poke their feet into holes now and then. They reach the 7,300-foot cache that Howard had established the day before, drop their loads, then hike back down to Camp II. They arrive and, as Joe would write in *White Winds*, John Russell shouts, "Joe put up a beautiful route through the icefall! I don't know who put up that suicide route under the avalanches!"

John knows full well that Howard put up the "suicide route." His jibe may just be another example of John being John, or it may be a purposeful attempt to give back the smug Coloradoans some of their own. Regardless of his motivation, John's sarcasm does not sit well with Howard.

Only a week or so later, Bill Babcock led his team through the same terrain, and I asked him which route he chose. "Oh, the one on the right," he affirmed. "Washburn recommended it and it looked the safest." In Howard's book, clearly to support the value of his own choice, he notes that Babcock's team chose his route.

So again the question arises—who was right and who was wrong? And again, there is no easy answer. Joe and Howard had logical, articulable reasons for their decisions. Joe could point to the fact that Jerry fell into a crevasse on the route that Howard had chosen to avoid crevasses, and that he considered crevasse falls a lesser danger than burial by avalanche. Howard could cite Washburn's recommendations to support his choice. (Later, though, Steve Taylor would tell Joe he believed Howard chose the route that he did—not out of obeisance to Washburn but because the Coloradoans were not experienced in crevasse rescue.)

So, once again, "right" and "wrong" matter less than the fact that the expedition's two leaders could not agree on how to cope with a significant hazard.

THE GROWING *FRIKTION* results not only from tension between Joe and Howard, but it continues among other team members, and it surfaces in a series of particularly ugly incidents. Anshel Schiff, now seventy, is winding up a long and distinguished career as a Stanford University professor of seismology engineering. Though still an avid skier, he's hindered by eyesight problems and doesn't get out to Mammoth and Squaw as much as he would like. Because health problems would have made my presence an intrusion, I interviewed Anshel by phone and e-mail rather than in person. The first time we spoke, I began our talk the way I usually do interviews, with an open-ended question: "Just tell me what you remember about the climb."

How many memories must an expedition of this complexity and a tragedy of this magnitude generate? Probably thousands. But responding to my question, Anshel did not speak of storms, stunning views, frostbite, crevasses, tent fires, altitude, or the brotherhood of the rope. Instead, his first and strongest recollections were of being weakened by sickness and being ridiculed for it. The memories had remained clear, sharp, and painful for almost forty years. To make sure I understood his meaning, he spoke specifically of confrontations that took place in late June, during the long series of carries up the Muldrow.

The first took place shortly after Joe's team meeting on Monday, June 26, and culminated later, after days of simmering, with a meaner encounter at Camp V on Friday, July 7. After the June 26 meeting—the one in which Joe threatens to throw Jerry Clark and Mark out of the expedition—Howard gets ready to lead seven other climbers on a hard carry from Camp I, at 5,780 feet, to Camp II, at 6,500 feet. As the men are loading packs, Walt Taylor, for some reason suspecting that Anshel is not carrying his fair share, yells,

"Come back here Anshel, you rascal."

Anshel, who is already on the trail, comes back as ordered, and Walt tells him to put a full load in his pack, which Anshel does, bringing his pack weight to about seventy-five pounds.

What neither Walt nor any of the other climbers, including Joe, understand is that Anshel is sick. An intestinal infection is exacerbating a preexisting chronic digestive problem so severely that Anshel cannot eat before or during carries. He manages continual pain by gobbling a dozen antacid tablets daily. Under conditions demanding triple and even quadruple the normal daily caloric intake just to keep up, Anshel has been losing weight and growing weaker each day.

Recalling this incident and one that followed, Anshel told me, "I found when I was packing loads that I couldn't eat. I was in very good shape then. The best shape of my life. I trained by carrying hundred-pound packs up flights of stairs. But for some reason I couldn't eat except one meal a day, after I'd finished packing. I pretty much lived off the fudge that Joe had made. But because of not being able to eat, sometimes I could carry only half loads. As it turned out, I went from one seventy-five to one fifty-five pounds, losing three-quarters of a pound per day. I ended up with a twenty-eight-inch waist, which I never had before or since. And I could put my thumb and forefinger around my bicep."

On the morning of Friday, July 7, under a gray sky spitting snowflakes, an advance rope team of Joe, Dennis, Mark, and Hank sets out with light loads from Camp IV, at 11,000 feet, to make the route to Camp V, at 12,100 feet, on Karstens Ridge. Other climbers are to follow in two separate rope teams, bringing more loads from Camp IV to Camp V.

By midafternoon, Joe and his team finish making the new trail. Jerry Clark leads the second team of Howard and Anshel, supposedly carrying full loads of about sixty-five to seventy-five pounds per man, up to Camp V, which they reach in two hours. The three of them dump their loads, rerope with Howard leading, and start the descent to Camp IV. At the same time, the second load-carrying team of John, Paul, Steve, and Walt arrive. When Howard's team is about fifty feet from camp, John Russell shouts that he is calling a meeting and orders Howard back to camp. Howard lets John know that he can hear just fine right where he is, so John airs his grievance. Howard made notes of every day's occurrences in two expedition journals, one pocket-size and another much larger notebook for detailed descriptions. Thus in his book he was able to re-create a number of scenes using notes made only minutes (during a subsequent rest stop, for example) or hours (in his tent at the end of the day) after they occurred. One such example is the heated exchange among climbers that follows when John accuses,

"Anshel, there's a rumor going around that you have just been carrying half loads."

Anshel denies it. Amazingly, because this is tantamount to saying "You're a liar" to Anshel's face with others present, John then demands to know exactly what Anshel's load is today. Anshel says that he's carrying about forty-four pounds, which is about one-third less than a "full load."

Anshel, a reserved man then and now, does not respond in kind to John's angry accusation about the rumor going around. But John's phrasing, at least as remembered by Howard in his book, is revealing, suggesting that not only John but others are feeling resentful as well. The truth of this is borne out later. But first, Jerry Clark, recently excoriated by John for using skis rather than snowshoes, springs to Anshel's defense.

"John, I weigh a hundred forty-five pounds to your one-eighty. I resent the implication that I should be able to carry as much as you."

Not much mollified, John fires back, "I don't mind carrying a heavier load. It's just that I don't like people carrying lighter loads on the sly; if you're going to do it, do it openly so that everyone knows what's going on."

John's blood is up now, and his next salvo is aimed at Joe. "As Fearless Leader, you should be out in the morning, organizing ropes and assigning duties." To Jerry, he says, "As Deputy Fearless, you should be doing something too."

Now even mild Dennis Luchterhand's patience is exhausted. "No, it's not his job; it's yours and mine. We're adults, and we know what has to be done each day. It's up to us to get things rolling."

Dennis has the last word, at least for now. The men stand around,

some glaring, some staring at their snowshoes, then finally begin to shuf-
fle into motion. Reactions to the brouhaha differ. When they are alone
later, Paul Schlichter, exasperated by the bickering, will tell Howard, "I
haven't seen a leader on this climb yet." Forty years later, Paul expressed
the same sentiment to me, remaining firm in his belief that neither Joe
nor Jerry Clark ever emerged as effective leaders during the climb.

Joe would write in *White Winds* that the exchange has actually been
good for the group, a kind of necessary venting. "John's one-man show
was a non-threatening source of reprimand, causing a dissipation of anxiety. I could feel it in myself, and sense it in the others. We could almost
laugh at the situation."

Unknown to Joe, however, this latest disagreement will have a particularly unpleasant denouement that will leave no one laughing. After
Dennis's declaration brings the dispute at Camp V to a close, Howard
leads his two rope mates, Anshel and Walt, back down to Camp IV. As
soon as they arrive, Walt Taylor lights into Anshel anew. He says that he
did not want to further embarrass Anshel in front of the others but has
known that Anshel has been carrying half loads since McGonagall Pass.
Anshel again claims that this is untrue. Walt remains unconvinced, and
says so with an insult that really rises to the level of fighting words: he
calls Anshel a liar to his face, not once but twice.

"Don't lie, Anshel, I know it's true. If you can't carry the loads, that's
all right with me, but don't lie about it."

Anshel was certainly not the only man carrying lighter loads than John
Russell. Nor was he the only slow climber. Jerry Clark also preferred to
climb slowly. Mark, Dennis, and Joe also expressed, at times, the desire
or need to go slowly. Even Jerry Lewis, on Howard's "express train" rope,
often preferred a more moderate pace. Anshel was not irritating, instigat-
ing, or "belligerent" (Joe's word for some of John Russell's actions). If
anything, he was just the opposite—so agreeable and accommodating
that he rarely appeared in either book.

In response to my questions about the source of John's animosity
toward Anshel, Joe thought that it probably had as much to do with their
continuing disagreements over use of group equipment, some of which
had been modified by Anshel with careful attention to technical aspects.

"My perception is that Anshel had not been trying to conceal his lighter loads as much as conceal his compromised physical condition due to persistent heartburn," Joe wrote in an e-mail. "Anshel either thought that his condition would improve or it actually did improve. Anshel made an extra carry between camps and requested to go high on the mountain and perhaps the summit."

Howard recalls that Anshel "was held in low esteem for his physical abilities and his lack of drive. (Jerry Clark was not much stronger but was much more emotionally committed.) On the other hand, Anshel was admired, by me at least, for his intellect, his concern over mistreatment of group equipment, and his realization that he was out of his depth (or 'beyond his height'), and should descend with us from Camp VII."

Approaching a climb already fractured is like putting a cracked windowpane in place. Add stress, and those cracks are sure to worsen, and that was happening during this phase of the climb. Because this expedition's conflicts are so varied, frequent, and, at times, intense, there is a danger of sliding over into this easy conclusion: *These guys fought a lot and this conflict caused the disaster.*

There is no disputing the fact that conflict dogs their steps almost from the time they begin exchanging letters. But how and to what extent might it have contributed to the disaster? Joe Wilcox thinks it did not. He told me: "Too many people have pointed to internal conflicts" as a primary reason for the tragedy.

Joe has made peace with another explanation, one to which he devoted eight years of extensive research and an entire book—namely, that a unique storm caused the tragedy. We'll look closely at the storm later, and at the question of whether it was, or could have been, the tragedy's lone gunman, responsible for killing more than half the men. For now, it's enough to say there's no doubt it contributed to what happened. Regardless, it cannot be easy for Joe—however well he may have made peace and moved on—to admit that dissension in the ranks caused, or even significantly contributed to, all those deaths. To think so would be to admit that he, as leader, was unable to manage that conflict effectively.

But perhaps such theorizing overcomplicates the matter. The acid test here may be a short, sharp question. Did conflict help or hurt the expedition? Does conflict improve or impede the success of any endeavor, let alone a mountain climbing expedition? Is an army more likely, or less, to win a battle because of friction? The common-sense answer is obvious. Of course conflict reduces chances of success.

In fact, the longer and harder any expedition, the more conflict and *friktion* build up, significantly reducing what it takes to make one contemplate murder. Apsley Cherry-Garrard wrote about this in his famous account of polar misadventures with Scott, *The Worst Journey in the World*:

> You forget how the loss of a biscuit crumb left a sense of injury which lasted for a week; how the greatest friends were so much on each others' nerves that they did not speak for days for fear of quarrelling; how angry we felt when the cook ran short on the weekly bag.

As unpleasant as conflict is on an expedition, you can avoid it—sort of—in camp. You can crawl into your tent, igloo, or sleeping bag, make extended visits to the latrine, hide in a long book, write endless pages in your journal, count the letters on toothpaste tubes (I've done it), or just sleep. Not so on the trail when you are tied—literally—to the very climbers who may be driving you to homicidal rage with their offensive jokes, vile farts, overbearing personalities, snoring, filthy habits, snotty beards—to name only a fraction of the ways that climbers grate on one anothers' nerves.

Joe Wilcox and Howard Snyder did not agree on much during their expedition, and on much less after it. But one theme does recur in both their books, and that is how infuriating it was to climb bound to faster or slower men. The tendency to go at different speeds revealed itself during the drive to McKinley National Park. It became a problem almost immediately after the men hit the mountain, when Howard and Paul set a pace crossing the tundra that Steve could not match. Or, put the other way around, when Steve went so slowly that Howard and Paul found it impossible not to get ahead of him.

From the moment the men step onto the Muldrow Glacier, these differences in climbing speed cause trouble. Howard and Paul like to climb fast and have little patience for people who cannot match their speed, which at times challenges even their own partner, Jerry Lewis. It is not really arrogance and impatience that keep them in warp drive. The desire to climb fast derives from their fitness and Howard's *you-can't-hit-a-moving-target* philosophy. Howard and his teammates believe that the best way to avoid McKinley's objective dangers—crevasses, avalanches, wind, storms, cornices—is to spend as little time as possible exposed to them on the route.

Conversely, not one of the men in Joe's team, including Joe, likes to climb as fast as the Coloradoans, and their preference for slower ascent derives from a different but equally valid philosophy. On a mountain such as McKinley, the only sure thing is that you will have accidents, sickness, equipment malfunctions, encounters with objective dangers, and other setbacks. The best protection is always leaving yourself with a reserve of energy adequate to survive these inevitable occurrences. This basic difference in philosophy breeds irritation that builds to annoyance that flares into anger that, too often, is not left on the trail but carried simmering back to camp.

The Coloradoans' affinity for speed, and frustration with the other team's slower pace, appears first as a brief mention in Howard's book and then builds with each subsequent recurrence. The first complaint Howard noted occurs on Sunday, June 25. Howard, leading a rope with Paul, Jerry Lewis, and Walt Taylor, carries loads to Camp II, then "made the return trip almost at a run. Speed was one way to alleviate monotony, and it was made possible by our now-empty packs."

On Thursday, June 29, Howard leads Mark, Jerry Clark, and Paul on an early-morning carry from Camp II. "We started up the Hill of Cracks and McLaughlin started calling out, 'A little slower,' at intervals and finally began calling for rest stops. Short rest stops are fine, but prolonged stops were later to become a problem and potential danger on the climb."

On Saturday, July 1, Howard leads another rope team of Paul, Jerry Lewis, and Mark from Camp II to Camp III. At the base of the Hill of Cracks, his team stops behind another team led by Dennis Luchterhand, which is taking a rest after continual trailbreaking. The rest goes on too long, however, for Howard's comfort.

> Schlichter, Lewis, and I were getting painfully chilled feet, because the snow was bitterly cold, even though the sun was bright. We stomped our feet and wiggled our toes, trying to keep the circulation going. Occasional rest stops of short duration are beneficial, but after five minutes the effects of a stop are more bad than good. Long stops cause a slowing of circulation and chilling of the body, especially if a person has been perspiring; muscles cool and tighten; the will to continue sometimes diminishes; and time is lost, time which may prove to be valuable beyond any price. Later in the day Lewis and I discussed the long delay on the trail and agreed that we could not endure such lengthy delays without risking frostbitten feet.

On Monday, July 3, things come to a boil after Howard traverses

> the most tedious three and a half miles I have ever endured. Russell was leading the first rope, including Luchterhand, W. Taylor, and Lewis. I was leading the second rope, with Clark, McLaughlin, and S. Taylor. . . . McLaughlin was having trouble negotiating the steep turns with skis, but he would not switch to his snowshoes. McLaughlin took five minutes of falling and floundering to top one pitch that I had passed in ten seconds. . . .
> Clark kept telling me, "Slow down! Go slower!" while I was moving as slowly as I could without stopping. To have gone any slower I would have had to stop altogether or stand like a stork between steps, with one foot suspended in the air.

They take a forced rest stop. Even before they start up again, Jerry Clark tells Howard to go slow. Howard cannot keep himself from delivering a lecture to Jerry, who is nine years his senior and has more experience in mountains. Howard quoted the exchange in his book:
"Jerry, on this mountain, speed is safety. If you go so slowly that you get caught out in the open between camps by a bad storm, you've had it."

Jerry thinks that line of reasoning not only wrong but dangerous. "No, you run a greater danger of going too fast and burning yourself out so you can't do anything." The exchange does nothing but irritate both men. Howard records, "We plodded on up the trail, and I occupied my mind by composing letters and my school schedule for the fall semester. We took just under five hours to cover the three and a half miles between Camps II and III. . . ."

There will be instances when it is appropriate and necessary to climb as fast as you possibly can. Howard correctly cites the example of trying to outrun an approaching storm when caught between camps. Being of a scientific turn of mind, his thinking reduces to, "The less time you're on the trail, the less you will be exposed to dangers there."

True enough. But if no such threats are looming, it can be argued that climbing "within your breath," as I heard one astute veteran put it, is just as appropriate and safe. McKinley is infamous for storms that strike with little warning, so what happens if you have been climbing so fast, so close to your limits, that you cannot outrun one of those?

These examples preview arguments about pace that will continue, with increasing vehemence, all the way up the mountain and will ultimately affect the location of Camp VII, with fateful consequences. The arguments also raise, again, the inevitable question: who was right and who was wrong? The answer is, both and neither. In mountains, as in life, there is no one right way to do anything all the time. The error is insisting that one's chosen course of action is the only way, every time. But here, ongoing polarization has exacerbated the tendency to do just that.

Even with the almost daily disturbances, it would be a mistake to suggest that this climb was all fight and no fun. Indeed, in some ways it is proving to be the experience of a lifetime that all the men had envisioned. On Friday, June 30, after a two-day storm dumps three feet of new snow on them, all twelve climbers depart Camp II at 11:40 p.m. Joe leads one rope with Jerry Clark, Hank, and Anshel. Dennis leads another, with John and the two Taylors. Howard leads the third, with Paul, Jerry Lewis, and Mark.

A snow-bearing, low-pressure system has been shoved on by a following high, which treats the climbers to a sunrise like nothing they have ever seen. Howard described the ecstatic vision in his book:

> The month of July tiptoed silently up behind our backs and overtook us as we approached the Lower Icefall. It brought with it the rising sun, as the low, broken clouds on the northern horizon took on the blush of dawn. Mount McKinley loomed at the head of the glacier, a blue-white giant still sulking in the shadow of night. A look down the Muldrow Glacier revealed the northern sky growing brighter, and in the opposite direction the mountain started to take on the hint of a pink glow. . . . The sky downglacier turned orange, the peak upglacier became a brilliant, glowing pink, standing bright and clear against the dark blue sky. The color shades changed with every passing moment. . . . I watched the scene largely through the viewfinder of my camera, exclaiming, "Beautiful! Beautiful! This is what I climb mountains for!" The mountain changed from pink to gold as the sun broke above the clouds on the horizon. The flat above the Lower Icefall looked like a scene from the Arabian Nights, with a caravan of climbers crossing the undulating golden dunes of the crevassed glacier.

On July 1, Joe and his rope team find themselves "hiking through a sea of rubies and diamonds." Later, descending to camp, they find that an earlier group had broken two parallel trails. On the intervening fresh snow, Walt Taylor wrote

"DO NOT CROSS MEDIAN"

Howard's and Joe's descriptions reveal an aspect of McKinley that the giant mountain's terrors often obscure, the fact that at times being there attains the beauty of a dream. But that same evening John Russell has a real dream that is not beautiful. The fact that John, not a man given to displays of sensitivity, describes the dream in detail to Joe the next morning indicates how powerfully it affected him. Joe recalled the remarkable conversation in his book.

"I had a strange dream last night," John tells Joe on this sunny, cloudless morning.

"What was strange about it?"

"I dreamt that a large jet full of people landed here. They were going to heaven and wanted me to come along."

"What did you tell them?"

"I told them that I couldn't go now because I was climbing Mount McKinley."

10

Pictures of an Expedition

By Tuesday, July 4, the men have established Camp III at 8,100 feet, on the smooth, snowy plain between the Muldrow's Hill of Cracks and, above, the Great Icefall, which looks like a vast waterfall frozen in mid-plunge. This day dawns sunny and clear. To mark the anniversary of his country's birth, John Russell sets off a three-inch firecracker. At a backyard barbecue its cannon report would have people dumping their plates, but here in the land of giants, it's just a little pop.

Given such good weather, the men decide it's time to take group pictures. Each man has to position his camera, frame the image, focus, set the self-timer, then run back to join the group before the shutter snaps. And each man wants a backup image, or two or three, just in case.

"What began as our first real act of togetherness, a group picture, soon became a serious proof sitting," Joe wrote later. What is most remarkable about his statement is not that the endless picture taking begins to try their patience. The more sobering revelation, given that they have traveled together for three weeks since the June 11 meeting at Mount Rainier, is that this is, according to the expedition leader, "our first real act of togetherness."

Pictures of the group appear in Joe's and Howard's books, and I viewed others taken by Paul, Jerry Lewis, and Howard. All the photos are remarkably similar. They show the climbers standing shoulder to shoulder, framed by towering Steve Taylor on the left and short Walt Taylor on the right. The pictures were taken in the morning, so it's reasonable to assume that the posed climbers are facing east into the sun, and the walls of Pioneer Ridge rise behind them to the west. Joe Wilcox, immediately to Steve Taylor's right in the picture, looks serious, if not grave. Steve, Howard, Mark, Paul, Jerry Lewis, and Anshel are all smiling broadly. Dennis, Jerry Clark, Hank, John, and Walt are not smiling. John may be scowling, or just squinting; it's hard to tell which, because he has doffed his sunglasses for the photo session. Enjoying the spate of good weather, they are standing around in shirtsleeves—short ones, in Hank's case. Five of the men—Dennis, Mark, Jerry Clark, Hank, and Anshel—are wearing their climbing harnesses, suggesting a reasonably imminent departure.

I studied these black-and-white photographs in the books at great length, magnifying and sharpening each face and detail, and examined them some more when the survivors showed me their color slides. You can learn an immense amount, as police work taught me and the popular television series *CSI* has taught many others, from photographs. Sometimes, if you look long enough at a photograph, something happens that's not unlike the eerie feeling you get (I do, anyway) after staring a long while at your own eyes in a mirror. A different part of the brain engages, and epiphanies may emerge. So I pored over photos of the seven dead and five living men for hours, looking for . . . what? Some premonitory clue perhaps? Some eerie light showing through the "windows on the soul" that a camera might capture but would escape the naked eye? Well, yes, but equally I sought other, more tangible details.

One of the most interesting photographs is that taken by Dennis Luchterhand, he of the Rainier premonition. He looks down at the snow instead of toward the camera, so you can't see his face. That's an odd way for a man to pose for his own group picture. Every other man is looking squarely and knowingly into the camera lens, and therefore making direct eye contact with the viewer.

What does it mean? Maybe nothing. Maybe Dennis is simply camera shy, even when it comes to his own photography. Maybe the sun hurts his eyes, even with sunglasses on. Or maybe there's something else going on in some deep place in his mind, the same place from which the premonition came, and maybe looking at the camera somehow seems to summon it up when what he really wants to do is keep it down there.

What do we think of when we look into the eye of a camera right before the shutter snaps? In Ernest Hemingway's book about Spain and bullfighting, *Death in the Afternoon*, one telling photograph shows a group of men standing around the body of legendary matador Manuel Granero. He has just died from a terrible goring—*cornada*, as Hemingway informs us—and his corpse is arrayed on a table in the infirmary. A clean sheet covers his body to the chest, and his head is turned slightly toward the camera, eyes open, almost as though he's just waking from a nap and is still alive. But he is not alive, and if you look closely at the death-skewed eyes, you can see it. The caption, which Hemingway wrote himself, says, "Granero dead in the infirmary. Only two in the crowd are thinking about Granero. The others are all intent on how they will look in the photograph."

It's safe to say that most of us, standing in front of a camera, worry first about how we are going to look in the resulting postcard to posterity. Dennis Luchterhand appears to have been worried about something else.

SEEING ALL TWELVE climbers lined up together for much of the day will determine Joe's waking dreams this night on the mountain. "Resting sleeplessly in my sleeping bag on this brisk, near zero night I pondered the strengths and weaknesses of the group's interpersonal relationships." Jerry Clark and Mark have remained close on the mountain, their earlier friendship intact. But Mark is in better shape, and has been climbing more often with Hank and Dennis. Jerry is roping more often with the slower-moving Anshel and Steve. For no discernible reason, Mark does not rope up with Anshel or Walt, though there is no apparent animosity among them. Tall Dennis Luchterhand and small Hank Janes become good friends and rope up often. Hank also climbs with Paul Schlichter and Joe, but not with Steve, Walt, or Howard. Dennis is one of the faster climbers and, perhaps because of this, ropes rarely with Jerry Clark or Anshel. He never ties in with Howard.

Joe observes that the strongest friendship of all and perhaps the most surprising arises between John Russell and Walt Taylor. In *White Winds*, Joe writes that John "reveled in insulting Anshel's educated etiquette and goading the silent tempers of Howard Snyder and Jerry Clark." Joe recalls Walt as "the witty humorist, tactful conciliator, and lubricator of gears," which may explain why he and the abrasive John get on well. It's possible that Walt, whom all the survivors will describe as the best natural leader on the expedition, was trying to defuse John for the larger good. Or it may have been that, supremely confident, Walt was the only climber who didn't take John's bluster personally.

Joe works hard to recall John's saving grace, despite the fact that John, the "brash individualist," has insulted Anshel by upbraiding him in front of other climbers, and fought openly with Mark and Jerry Clark and refused to climb with either of them. He also publicly attacked Joe's leadership, and threatened to leave the expedition. Says Joe, "I did not think John the saboteur that others did. Behind his barroom rhetoric was a concealed devotion to the group. He often greeted a descending party with a hot meal, feigning complaint to avoid receiving compliments, and routinely packed the heaviest loads."

I did not think John the saboteur that others did. "Saboteur" is a strong word. In wartime, saboteurs are often shot. Taken at face value, this statement reveals that at least some others already disliked and distrusted John. That Joe, a careful writer, did not say "a few others" or "one or two others" indicates that the concerns about John were shared by most, if not all.

Joe has observed by July 4 that Steve and Anshel are "introverted loners," drawn more to each other's slow climbing pace than by any visible camaraderie. Joe has noted, too, that Anshel is the only climber whose conditioning has not improved much from the hard work of load carrying. Joe does not learn until later about Anshel's gastrointestinal problems. In any case, Anshel would not rope up with John, because John had excoriated him in front of the others and because Anshel was driven to distraction by John's rough equipment handling.

Steve, though remaining one of the slowest climbers, has recovered from his earlier illness and never seems to tire, as Howard noted when we met. He simply prefers to climb slowly, believing it the safest way to proceed up a mountain such as McKinley. But he ropes up uncomplainingly with the fast, the slow, and everybody else. From June 24 through July 15, he climbs with seventeen different rope teams, led variously by Joe, Howard, Jerry Clark, Dennis, and Walt.

Joe comes, inevitably, to his own relationship with the Coloradoans. Climbing with Jerry Lewis and Paul Schlichter, Joe has found that they are "quiet, yet congenial and genuinely friendly."

> Howard, however, maintained a cold veneer, an edge to his disposition that was perplexing. I knew that my perception was subjectively influenced by an emerging personality clash, but still imagined that Howard felt himself a displaced leader. He seemed bothered by many of my leadership decisions and the relative inefficiency of our larger group, and I suspected these concerns were simmering and smoldering unpredictably in silent indignation.

This has taken us afield from the July 4 photo session, but now we return to it. With the possible exceptions of Dennis and John, not a hint on any face betrayed fear or even the tension of omnipresent danger, despite the fact that one of their number had already been rescued from a crevasse, most of the others had dropped partway into other crevasses, and all have witnessed several avalanches big enough to have buried towns.

They are, after all, on a mountain that would kill seven of them and has, at last count, killed more than 130 others. Their apparent insouciance, this beaming, unwitting innocence, reminded me of the beatific faces shining out of the daguerreotypes of 1861, before those young soldiers had witnessed—to use Charles Frazier's marvelous term—"the metal face of the Age." How, I wondered, could the '67 men have appeared so blissful?

Answering that question helped uncover one of the tragedy's root causes.

11

Terras Incognitas

W hen Joe and his eleven expedition members set foot on McKinley, only four men had died in the previous fifty-four years of recorded climbs. Three had died on the Muldrow route, but that, as Walt Taylor observed in one of his preexpedition letters, did not prevent it from becoming associated more with drudgery than danger.

Today there are literally hundreds, if not thousands, of books, films, and videos about Mount McKinley. All contemporary sources are riddled with warnings about the extreme danger of even the mountain's "easier" routes. Jonathan Waterman wrote an entire book, *Surviving Denali*, "to dispel the myth of Denali as a cakewalk," as McKinley veteran and altitude guru Peter Hackett, MD, wrote in the book's preface.

In 1967, though, the literature was sparse. On November 23, 1966, Joe received a letter and ten climbing application forms from Arthur J. Hayes, the recently appointed chief ranger of Mount McKinley National Park. The package also included United States Department of the Interior form M-87, revised 12-63, *"Climbing Mount McKinley and Other High Mountains Over 10,000 feet in Mount McKinley National Park."*

This document provides an invaluable look at the rules and regulations for climbing McKinley in that time period. It also reveals a great deal about how the government was struggling to "manage" two essentially unmanageable entities: Mount McKinley, and people who wanted to climb it. One of the most noteworthy items in M-87 is its "recommended reading" list:

It is recommended that all applicants obtain and read *The Moun-tain World 1956–1957* edition (see reference material). The article on Mount McKinley contains the only published material on con-ventional or proposed ascent routes.

The only published material on conventional or proposed ascent routes. Today, an Amazon.com search for "Mt. McKinley" produces almost 6,000 results. Some books, such as Colby Coombs's *Denali's West But-tress: A Climber's Guide to Mount McKinley's Classic Route*, devote them-selves entirely to a single route up the mountain. Back then, at least according to the managers of Mount McKinley National Park—who should have been in a position to know—there was only one book, and not even a whole book but a single article within it.

That says a lot about what Joe and his people could do to arm them-selves with the most important safety tool of all—information—before the climb. It's true that Wayne Merry showed them the best Muldrow route guide ever written—Brad Washburn's. But they gained that access only the day before beginning their climb. And the Wilcox contingent's attitude toward it may have been prejudiced by Washburn's earlier attacks. That aside, the fact that this priceless collection of routes, direc-tions, camps, and hazards was still unpublished in a loose-leaf binder may be the best indication of just how much about McKinley was still terra incognita.

WHEN I TOLD Joe that I'd been able to find few pre-1967 sources of information about climbing McKinley, and none about climbing the Muldrow Glacier route, and suggested that such dearth of good data might have made it hard to gauge the mountain's hazard, he bristled by e-mail:

> *You found only two publications??? After reading your e-mail, I walked over to my bookshelf and pulled out a copy of The Mountain World 1956–57 (Swiss publication) with 27 pages on McKinley climbing. Next to it was an August 1953 National Geographic with a lengthy article on Washburn's West Buttress climb (with references to*

related articles: July 1938 and Jan 53). . . . So much for the computer (search) age?

Joe's "M-14" memo is reproduced on page 327 of *White Winds*. Under the heading "Required Reading," five sources are listed: *Frostbite*, by Bradford Washburn; *The ABC of Avalanche Safety*, by Ed LaChapelle; *The Mountain World*, 1956–57 edition (referenced in the NPS M-87); *Freedom of the Hills*, by The Mountaineers; and McKinley trip logs of the Seattle Mountaineers' 1964 expedition and the 1966 Swarthmore Denali Expedition. Under "Recommended Reading," Joe lists *Americans on Everest*, by James Ramsey Ullman; *Freedom of the Hills* (entire book); *Mountain Rescue Techniques*, by Wastl Mariner; and *Mount McKinley and the Alaska Range in Literature*. Only one of these, the last, is specific to McKinley, and it is less a climbing guide than a literary collection.

Joe's 2005 e-mail to me went on to cite fifteen written or oral sources of information about climbing McKinley; but only one, *The Mountain World*, would have been readily available to his expedition members, and even it was not specific to McKinley. None of the others on any of these three lists was easily found or focused only on McKinley.

As for the reading list itself, we know that at least one climber, John Russell, mocked it as something only tyros would require. After receiving Joe's M-14, John wrote, "Reference M-14. I was not sure whether to laugh or to cry when I saw this letter. Who the hell hasn't read Freedom of the Hills. . . . If there is such a person among us, please tell me, for I should not want to climb on his rope."

We know from Walt Taylor's letters that he minimized the Muldrow route's challenges. In one letter, he suggests that attempting Mount Logan (not as high as McKinley but much more difficult to climb by any route) might be a more fitting test of their mountaineering skills. In the scores of pre-trip letters, there is only one indication that these men thought McKinley particularly deadly. They surely anticipated a long expedition more physically demanding than any they had done before, but apparently they did not anticipate one inherently more dangerous than their earlier forays.

Deputy leader Jerry Clark, who will lead the second summit team upward on July 17, is the one notable exception. On May 23, plagued by a horde of last-minute worries, he writes an eight-page, single-spaced letter to Joe: "I feel compelled to speak my mind on several subjects." These include science, publicity, photography, summit camping, radios, outside communications—and safety. Jerry admits to being initially insulted by the National Park Service's low estimation of their group. His early response to NPS critics was, "They obviously have their heads on backwards." But after due consideration, despite the fact that "It is likely they have underestimated us," he comes to believe that "they are in a position to know the past history of the mountain and how it has treated climbers. . . ."

Prodded by this concern—and here is the crux of his letter—Jerry decided to do further research on his own. "I talked to 2 previous McKin-ley climbers. I listened to tales of 10-day storms, documented with pho-tographs. . . . Other climbers who have been there have repeatedly made the point that the mountain is big enough, and potentially bad enough, to LET climbers get up it, rather than being conquered. Caught in a week or so storm, would our split-up party fare well? . . . Shouldn't we expect a certain amount of impossible weather as a safety factor?"

All of which leads Jerry to this conclusion: "Perhaps we at times have underestimated POTENTIAL difficulty."

POST-TRAGEDY CRITICS, particularly Brad Washburn, faulted the men for underestimating McKinley, but the truth is that many other climbers, among them some of history's most notable mountaineers, also dangerously underrated this mountain. In May 1960, four of the best American climbers of their era fell prey to the same failing. John Day was leading an expedition on the (supposedly) easy West Buttress route. His team included legendary K2 veteran Pete Schoening and the Whittaker twins, Lou and Jim. "Big Jim" Whittaker would soon climb his way into the history books when, in 1963, he became the first American to stand on the summit of Mount Everest.

To launch their plan for a quick jaunt up the "trade route," on May 14 Don Sheldon flew the four to 10,200 feet, rather than the customary 7,000-foot starting point on the lower Kahiltna Glacier. Their ascent was indeed speedy, covering in just two and a half days what often takes lesser mortals two and a half weeks. They summited on May 17.

But getting up is only half the battle—and, climbers will tell you, the less dangerous half by far. Climbing down just below Denali Pass, "Big Jim" slipped on 45-degree ice and pulled the three other men off behind him. They all careened 400 feet down the face, smashing into ice and rocks and one another. The fall knocked both Whittakers unconscious, gave Schoening a concussion that disoriented him for days, and broke John Day's leg. Their calamity precipitated what remains to this day the most massive rescue operation in Mount McKinley history and demonstrates how dangerous McKinley is even for world-class climbers such as these. It also raises the disturbing question of how, given the size of the Day Expedition rescue and the speed with which it was mounted, the Wilcox Expedition rescue could be so horribly botched. The equally disturbing answer to that question will have to wait for a later chapter.

Thus far, joe and his team have been laboring up the Muldrow Glacier, but beyond 11,500 feet the impassable Harper Icefall blocks their way. The Muldrow Glacier is a mile-wide river of ice that flows all the way from Denali Pass, at 18,200 feet, down to McGonagall Pass and beyond. The Harper Icefall is a murderous jumble of giant ice blocks and crevasses similar to the better-known (and even more feared) Khumbu Icefall on Everest's South Col route. Unlike the Khumbu, the Harper Icefall can be bypassed—on its northwest side by climbing the spine of Pioneer Ridge, or on the southwest by ascending Karstens Ridge.

Pioneer Ridge and Karstens Ridge are formidable, but Karstens Ridge offers a shorter, much more direct route to McKinley's South Peak, which makes it the ridge of choice for Muldrow climbers. It is not without hazard, however. The route up the spine of Karstens Ridge gains about 3,600 vertical feet, with pitches of 45 degrees. Peter Hackett has noted that McKinley's conditions make a 35-degree slope feel like one pitched at 55 degrees. Using Dr. Hackett's scale, 45 degrees will feel like 65 degrees—steep indeed.

Karstens Ridge, in fact, claimed McKinley's third fatality, an expert mountaineer named Elton Thayer, in 1954. He had worked as a ranger in Mount McKinley National Park and had made first ascents of 16,972-foot King Peak in the Yukon Territory and Alaska's 11,940-foot Mount Hess. Thayer had just led the first successful ascent of McKinley via the South Buttress route, climbing with three friends—George Argus, Les Viereck, and Morton Wood. They reached the summit on May 15, 1954. Their plan was to traverse the mountain, then descend via the Muldrow Glacier route, which involved downclimbing Karstens Ridge. A bit below 13,000 feet on the ridge, Thayer, the last man on their rope, slipped. He pulled the other three off, and they all fell a thousand feet down the ridge's steep north face. Wood later described the accident in the 1955 *American Alpine Journal*:

> I remember tumbling end over end in the snow, now and then being pulled by the rope and always unable, because of the heavy packs, to roll over on my stomach and dig in my axe to check. It was like a bad spill while skiing in powder snow except that it seemed to last for an eternity.

When they finally stopped falling, they were on the Muldrow Glacier. Les Viereck was dazed and possibly concussed, his face cut and some teeth knocked out. George Argus suffered an agonizing dislocated hip and probably spinal injuries as well. Wood was shaken and bruised, though almost miraculously escaped serious injury. But Elton Thayer was dead. The fall broke his back, and his three friends found him dangling grotesquely by the climbing rope, which had snagged on an ice pinnacle.

Joe and his team establish their Camp IV not far below the spot where Thayer died, in the shadow of the wall that rises steeply about 800 feet to the ridge's knife-edged crest. From Camp IV, they will climb this ridge's steep flank to gain its top edge. Here, as the old saying goes, the going gets tough—*really* tough.

Joe leads the first team up to the ridge early in the morning of Wednesday, July 5. Two feet or more of fresh snow have fallen during the night, and they struggle through waist-deep drifts, taking four hours to reach the ridge crest. Once there, with the indefatigable Walt Taylor leading, they start forcing their route up the ridge, which, as Joe writes in *White Winds*, is no less harrowing now than when it killed Elton Thayer:

> Should someone slip off the ridge down a hard-packed slope prob-
> ably the only hope would be for another man on the rope team to
> jump off the other side—a "jump ridge" I called it . . . a seductive
> avalanche could easily break beneath our steps and sweep us off
> the ridge, down the 3,500-foot rock-studded wall. . . .

They spend the entire day gaining only a half mile, then retreat to Camp IV. The next day, Joe leads a rope team to a flat saddle on the ridge at 12,100 feet. This will be the site of Camp V, a bench about fifty feet long by thirty feet wide. On either side, the slope drops off steeply— about a thousand feet to the Muldrow Glacier and about four thousand feet to the Traleika Glacier. Thursday, July 6, is spent ferrying loads up to the new campsite. On this exposed ridge, they dig pits about three feet deep and pitch the tents in them.

Snow begins to fall on Thursday, July 6, and continues without a break for two days and nights, trapping the men in their tents and burying the campsite beneath three feet of fresh snow. On Saturday, July 8, with the weather finally clearing, Joe hears the sound of digging and crawls out of his tent. He shouts, and presently Dennis's head pops out of a hole. Joe asks Dennis what he's up to, and Dennis replies that he's digging a snow cave. Does Joe, by any chance, want to help?

He does, although the cave is already big enough for a group. They keep working like a couple of tunnel rats, with Joe at the cave entrance, shoving out snow that Dennis, all the way in, pushes back to him. Den- nis is working so hard that Joe asks whether he is trying to excavate a monster cave big enough for all twelve men. That's the plan, Dennis affirms, adding that they may well need it. He explains that the fiberglass poles on their Mountaineer tent snapped under high wind loading the previous night, leading Joe to conclude that "the snow cave was perhaps more than bad weather amusement."

The fact that Dennis knows the value of snow caves and how to dig them is important to remember in light of later accusations that the seven victims died because they were too inexperienced to know how to dig in.

Mckinley itself — glaciers, crevasses, peaks, and icefalls—is not the only terra that, to the climbers of that day, remains largely incognita. After July 4, the climbers face not only steeper, technical terrain, they will begin to suffer from altitude. Which presents the greater danger is an open question. One indication of altitude's increasing effect on the men may have been the multiple brouhahas over load carrying, and particularly the attacks by Walt Taylor.

That such outbursts could come from John Russell, who doesn't know what he's thinking until he says it, is not surprising. But the subsequent tongue-lashings by Walt Taylor do seem out of character. Walt, after all, is remembered very positively by Joe, Howard, Jerry Lewis, and Paul. They describe him variously as calm, disciplined, easygoing, funny, a skillful conciliator—in other words, the ideal expedition climber.

Walt's uncharacteristic aggression is indicative of an influence that, to judge from diaries, books, and interviews, the climbers did not fully appreciate, mostly because so little research on the subject had been done then. But the fact is that now something new is dogging their every step, attacking their minds and bodies, altering judgment, eroding stamina, shortening tempers—in very real terms, changing them into different people. Their new companion, a thirteenth man as it were, is named Altitude.

It's probably no coincidence that the English, who pioneered mountaineering, also gave us the first excellent account of altitude's frightening effects on the human body and mind. The discovery came, as great discoveries so often do, by accident and nearly killed the two men involved.

After the legendary French Montgolfier brothers made the first hot-air balloon ascent in 1783, ballooning spread rapidly throughout Europe. By the mid-nineteenth century, using balloons filled with hydrogen (the same stuff that blew up the *Hindenburg*) rather than hot air, the British Association for the Advancement of Science was conducting manned

balloon ascents to learn more about the Earth's upper atmosphere. Englishman James Glaisher, fifty-three, a Cambridge-educated mathematician and astronomer with impeccable scientific credentials and courage
to match, headed up the work. Between 1862 and 1866, he performed
twenty-eight balloon flights with his friend, the expert pilot and equally
intrepid Henry Coxwell.

Balloons of the day were hardly fine-tuned flying instruments; the
ground crews simply filled them with hydrogen gas, cast off the tethers,
and waved good-bye. "Pilots" such as Coxwell could slow the rate of
ascent by venting off gas, and could initiate descent by venting off a lot
of it, but that was about the extent of their control. When within a hundred feet or so of the ground, they tossed out a big grappling hook in the
hope that it would snag something—tree, ditch, cow, whatever—heavy
enough that they could haul themselves down.

Of all Glaisher and Coxwell's twenty-eight flights, their adventure of
September 5, 1862, which they survived only by the narrowest of margins, remains the most remarkable. They lost control of the balloon and
shot up more than 29,000 feet, higher than the summit of Everest, in
minutes. At the apogee of their flight, Glaisher collapsed, unconscious.
With their balloon shooting toward the stratosphere and accelerating
every second, the doughty Mr. Coxwell climbed out of the wicker basket
gondola and into the rigging above, hoping to free a stuck release valve,
with no parachute or safety harness, his own consciousness fading, hands
frozen immobile, and nothing but 29,000 feet of thin frozen air between
him and the Earth. Just before blacking out, Glaisher

> dimly saw Mr. Coxwell in the ring, and endeavoured to speak, but
> could not do so; when in an instant intense black darkness, and the
> optic nerve lost power suddenly. I was still conscious with as active
> a brain as while writing this. I thought I had been seized with
> asphyxia, and that I should experience no more, as death would
> come unless we speedily descended. . . .
>
> Whilst powerless I heard the words "temperature" and "observa-
> tion," and I knew Mr. Coxwell was in the car, speaking to me, and
> endeavouring to rouse me; and therefore consciousness and hear-

ing had returned. I then heard him speak more emphatically, but I could not speak or move.

Then I heard him say, "Do try; now do!"

Then I saw the instruments dimly, next Mr. Coxwell, and very shortly I saw clearly. I rose in my seat and looked around, as though waking from sleep, and said to Mr. Coxwell, "I have been insensible."

He said, "Yes; and I too, very nearly."

Glaisher and Coxwell's flights produced many remarkable findings. For high-altitude physiology, the most important was this: Whereas Glaisher fell unconscious and was seconds from death, Coxwell retained enough strength, coordination, and sense to climb out of the gondola, up into the rigging without tether or parachute, and yank open the balloon's exhaust valve *with his teeth*. Thus the men unwittingly discovered altitude's most confounding effect: no two people react to it the same way.

Altitude's effects were well known, though not well understood, by the time George Leigh Mallory and Andrew Irvine made their legendary (and perhaps successful; we still do not know for sure whether they got all the way) 1924 attempt on Everest. They breathed compressed oxygen, as did all other high-altitude climbers until Peter Habeler and Reinhold Messner changed the game forever, proving at 1:30 p.m. on Monday, May 8, 1978, that Everest could be climbed without it.

Habeler and Messner's climb gave the scientists a metaphoric slap across the face, challenging them to catch up and match the climbers' accomplishment. New research projects arose on mountains and in laboratories all over the world. The relatively unheralded American Medical Research Expedition to Everest carried out one of the best in the fall of 1981.

John West, a climber, medical doctor, and organizer of the expedition, chronicled its work and results in his book, *Everest: The Testing Place*. Perhaps the most important revelation from the expedition's research was new knowledge about the human hypoxic ventilatory response (HVR), the volume of air that moves into and out of the human lungs. It's different for every person, and can be measured precisely. Prior research had established two critical facts: There is tremendous variation in individuals' HVR, and HVR is genetically determined, "like eye color or hair color," as John West wrote.

The scientists on Everest in 1981 wanted to know whether there was a correlation between a person's HVR at sea level and performance higher up. They found that there is indeed such a relationship, and demonstrated it more dramatically than they could have hoped. Expedition members who had the first-, second-, and third-highest HVRs at sea level were the first, second, and third to reach the summit: Chris Kopczynski, Chris Pizzo, and Peter Hackett. The three performed a variety of scientific tests on themselves while on the summit. Pizzo took samples of air from deep within his lungs, and the results proved that his ventilation had increased sixfold.

Conversely, John Evans, an immensely strong mountaineer with a stellar record, and the expedition's actual climbing leader, had the second-lowest HVR of all eight climbers tested. As low as Camp III, at 23,800 feet, he suffered crippling headaches, nausea, and uncontrollable vomiting. He did not summit.

West concluded, "The physiological advantage of a vigorous response to low oxygen at high altitude is clear. The increased breathing raises the level of oxygen in the air in the depths of the lungs and this tends to make up for the reduction of oxygen in the inspired air." Result: high-HVR-climbers' lungs pump more oxygen into their bloodstream, which enables their minds and muscles to perform better.

The human response to altitude is not only a matter of muscles, lungs, and blood. The human brain is the single biggest oxygen gobbler in the body and is extremely sensitive to hypoxia. Of all altitude responses, the brain's remain the most mysterious. Peter Hackett, current dean of high-altitude research, has noted, "The future is in the brain . . . the brain holds the secrets to mountain sickness and cerebral edema."

Cerebral edema is perhaps the most feared of all altitude's maladies. Hackett described it this way in an interview for the PBS series *Nova*:

> The brain starts to swell and one of the primary symptoms is altered consciousness. By that, I mean definite cognitive problems. Judgment becomes impaired—a person becomes confused. They don't even know where they are as it gets worse. They don't know where

they came from, where their friends are. I've had people halluci-
nate. I had a German one time at the clinic in Pheriche who saw a
red helicopter in our front yard and had to be physically restrained.
He didn't understand why we wouldn't let him get on the helicopter. There was no helicopter—it was a hallucination. So all sorts of
mental changes can take place with altitude sickness as the brain
starts to become more and more abnormal.

Cerebral edema can cause stroke, paralysis, coma, and death, all of
which have been well documented. Hackett and other researchers admit
that they don't know why the brain reacts as it does, and therefore don't
know—yet—how to prevent such responses. But they do know that
before it kills, altitude alters consciousness and can induce personality
changes that include paranoia and other problems. Climbers can
become, quite literally, different people.

But what does all of this have to do with the Wilcox team's twelve
climbers? In short, twelve climbers mean twelve different, genetically
determined abilities to acclimatize to high altitude—and not one of them
could have understood these dramatic differences as we do today.
Howard, Walt, and Paul acclimatize well. Through no fault of their
own, Jerry Lewis, John Russell, and Steve Taylor struggle increasingly
the higher they go. The other six climbers lie closer to the bell
curve's center.

Every climber on the Wilcox Expedition is affected by altitude. The
higher they go, the more pronounced their physical symptoms: headache, fatigue, malaise, nausea, vomiting. Psychological changes are also
occurring: confusion, irritability, impaired cognitive function, and, as
Hackett put it, "altered consciousness." They shadow the climbers' every
step and complicate an endeavor already suffering from more than its
share of the "usual" challenges of a McKinley climb.

12

Summit Conference

On Tuesday, July 11, amiable Dennis Luchterhand, who has turned out to be one of the Wilcox team's powerhouses, leads the advance rope team of Mark, Paul, and Hank to the site of Camp VI, at 15,000 feet on the left side (looking up-mountain) of the Harper Glacier. From here, the surface of the Harper rises gradually to Denali Pass, at 18,200 feet. The route now, going up from Camp VI, will take the climbers diagonally, left to right, across to the far side of the Harper. There, at about 17,000 feet, they will skirt the right edge of the glacier's heavily crevassed Upper Icefall and continue up the glacier's right side. Above the Upper Icefall they will turn left and head out onto the huge, relatively level area called the Great Basin, where they intend to site Camp VII, at 18,200 feet, near the south end of Denali Pass. Brad Washburn specified this site in his climbing guide because fierce winds roar down through the pass, strafing the entire exposed upper Harper Glacier, which offers not one sheltering feature. His proposed site gains at least some shelter from the rock buttresses of the South Peak.

Various rope teams continue ferrying loads from Camp V, at 12,100 feet, to Camp VI on Wednesday and Thursday. By Friday, July 14, all twelve men have occupied Camp VI. The five tents—two orange, one blue, one red, one yellow—at Camp VI are in their usual linear, orderly fashion, each tent within reaching distance of its neighbor. The Colorado tent and a Wilcox group tent are tied off to the same ski pole.

Although not threatened by steep drop-offs on each side, as on Karstens Ridge, they are exposed to any strong winds that might blow down through Denali Pass, 3,000 feet higher. You can't run or hide from the wind here, given the absence of any rock formations or terrain convolutions. The tents of Camp VI are pitched in pits dug down about two feet, which is good; the shelter of an igloo or snow cave would offer even greater security.

Howard noted when we met in 2005 that from July 8 to 14, the team enjoyed unusually good weather—by McKinley standards, a virtual eternity. Many periods of sunshine, few whiteouts, warm temperatures, and mild winds help them forget, Howard suggested, that McKinley is schizophrenic and that the mountain's alter ego kills without qualm. Of this idyllic interlude, Howard would write later,

> As the rope from 12,100 feet arrived in camp, the solar display was especially intense, and six shutterbugs proceeded to record the event. A bright shaft of light pierced the orange-red clouds on the horizon, rising like a searchlight beam from the appearing sun. This was Mount McKinley at its kindest and most beautiful.

This extended sunshiny period is made more reassuring by the fact that, at this latitude, days are twenty-two hours long. Even the two-hour "nights" never bring full darkness.

Being at Camp VI thus brings an odd mixture of relief and anxiety to the climbers. As Joe notes in his book, they are now higher than the summits of Mount Rainier and the Matterhorn. They could make it to the top of McKinley from this camp, though that would require marathon climbing and an unusually long stretch of good weather. They're not likely to do that, but he feels immense satisfaction looking back over the thirty-seven miles of route climbed thus far, during which they have also gained three vertical miles. Gazing outward, Joe remembers that "I could almost see forever across the rivers and lakes of the distant tundra. A thousand pothole lakes stared back at me in the reflection of indirect light. A dark sunset-sunrise hung off the shoulder of Taylor Spur."

Such beauty masks new threats at this altitude and above, including two things synonymous with life itself—light and air. In addition to the ills of altitude, the thin, dry air brings on bouts of panting and gasping; the air is so dry that it inflicts sore throats and bloody noses. Ironically, you can drown up here in this waterless wasteland, and McKinley's famished air is the culprit. It can cause your lungs to fill with fluid from your own body, a condition called pulmonary edema. Even if you don't drown in your own secretions, the reflexive urge to clear your lungs can bring on rib-cracking spasms of coughing.

The eyes have it bad too. Without thicker atmosphere's filtering, the light in the land of the midnight sun will burn unshaded retinas in minutes. Jerry Lewis, even much lower down, has already had one bout of snow blindness, which is incapacitating and painful; he said it felt as though someone had thrown sand in his eyes.

It is also colder up here, a fact that the next few days of wildly uncharacteristic good weather will conceal. The rule of thumb is a loss of about two and a half to three degrees of temperature for every thousand feet of ascent. At Camp VI it will be 50 degrees subtracted from whatever the temperature is down at Wonder Lake, and it will be 60 degrees subtracted by the time they reach the summit.

Cutting wind lowers the temperature even further. The climbers have not penetrated the jet stream, as Everest climbers sometimes do, but they have moved up into a realm where air's run is interrupted by no tree, building, hill, or gully. The first thing breaking prevailing westerly winds roaring in off the Bering Sea and across 150 miles of tundra is the mountain itself.

THE MORNING OF Wednesday, July 12, is picture-perfect. Eight climbers are in Camp VI. Later in the day, Dennis will lead Hank, Paul, and Mark up on what they believe will be the final carry from Camp V. But the eight who have already made it to 15,000 feet are dragging. Not surprisingly, it is self-assured Walt Taylor (who earlier refers to Muldrow climbers as "mules") who reports the team's condition to Joe: "Your horses are really tired."

Joe himself has been suffering from an altitude-induced headache. Even so, his description of how they agree on the day's course—"We finally decided it would be unwise to continue without a day of recuperation"—indicates that there was lengthy discussion of whether to go up or stay put.

Losing such a perfect day is like a maddening itch that, without the team's consent, he cannot scratch. McKinley sees only about twelve to fifteen such days each year. Howard says it himself:

> The air temperature was in the low twenties, but the sensible temperature was pleasant enough to allow us to walk around in our shirtsleeves, thanks to the intense sunlight.

Never waste good weather. It is a commandment known to all expeditionary climbers as experienced as Joe and Howard. It must disturb them both, Joe as leader especially, to sit and watch hour after precious hour drain away. At some point, Joe must contemplate overruling the group's desire for R and R.

In the end, Joe does not, but he desperately needs something to occupy mind and body, and Howard gives him just the thing. Later that afternoon, the Coloradoan must be feeling as antsy as Joe. So with his little French snow shovel Howard begins to dig a latrine—a functional pit to pee and poop in.

Before he knows it, snow is flying just a few yards to his side. Howard looks up from his hole to see Joe digging alongside him and watches, amazed. Joe's edifice has a curved staircase, a toilet seat cover fabricated from a pad of closed-cell foam, and a little frozen-snow medicine cabinet with a mirror, hand lotion, and a flower made from a wand and plastic survey tape. Joe uses adhesive tape to write "MEN" on one plastic snowshoe and "WOMEN" on another, and sticks them into the snow to prevent any gender errors at Camp VI.

Writing about this in *The Hall of the Mountain King,* Howard recalls, "For some reason, Joe wanted two latrines. . . . He labored to produce a monument to civilization." Joe puts a fun spin on the whole thing. "'What the heck,' I thought. 'There could be no harm in two outhouses.'"

In fact, Joe's "monument to civilization" was not the first instance of grand latrine building on the 1967 climb. Walt had initiated the practice back on July 2, way down at Camp III, at 8,100 feet, which may have inspired Joe's later creative burst. Returning from a hard carry to Camp IV, Joe and his rope mates saw something that from the distance they first thought was a snow fort. Then, coming closer, they discovered to their delight that this "two-sided structure was a throne, indeed, complete with buttocks-protecting slats from a Blazo crate. Walt's creation was the subject of considerable discussion and perhaps the world's most photographed outhouse."

One of the expedition's more memorable photographs shows Walt's "throne"—six-feet-high walls, crenellated battlements, climbing-wand "banners" flying from the turrets—and Dennis Luchterhand, happily ensconced on the Blazo-slat seat, peering back over his shoulder with a magnificent grin.

With deluxe and basic model latrines complete, the men retire to their respective tents to cook supper. Walt and John are occupying one of the orange Logan tents, pitched so that its door faces the door of the neighboring Coloradoans' tent. Suddenly, Howard and Jerry Lewis hear the unmistakable "whump!" that gasoline makes as it ignites when it's not supposed to. In the same moment they see, to their horror, a flaming stove shooting out of the other tent and right at their open door.

They are very lucky. The stove bounces off an icy bump in front of their tent door and lands in the trough of the trail running through camp. If the stove had shot through their front door and landed on the tent floor, a dangerous or even fatal fire could have flashed in an instant.

BY THE EVENING of Thursday, July 13, all twelve men have occupied Camp VI. At about seven o'clock, Howard, Jerry, and Paul are eating steak dinners in their tent and talking about how much Joe seems impaired by the altitude. Joe and his team are having dinner together, all nine squeezed into one of the big blue Logan tents, talking about something else.

They are a very different bunch than the nine pale-skinned, clean-shaven, wide-eyed young buckos who strode out from the Wonder Lake Ranger Station twenty-five days earlier. Their faces now are gaunt and tan as saddle leather, creased from constant squinting even with their glacier goggles on. Every day the unrelenting labor strips away fat, leaving hard edges of bone and muscle. During his time on the mountain, Jerry Lewis will lose more than twenty-five pounds, Anshel and Joe more than twenty pounds each. It's safe to assume that everyone except Howard will have dropped ten to fifteen pounds by now.

Their thoughts and feelings are being similarly distilled. Compared to what they were accustomed to in Seattle or Colorado, this high mountain environment is elemental. There are no colors, only white snow and clouds, gray rock at lower elevations and black rock near the summit, sky so dark blue that it almost looks black. When the men stand still and listen, the cacophony of civilized life—engines, horns, televisions, radios, airplanes, crowds—is replaced by a single sound: the wind. Up here, there are not even any natural odors to play in their noses.

On this particular evening, though, their minds are filled with visions of something else—the summit. Joe's group has come together to talk about how they will get to it, and the Coloradoans are not invited. Before anything else, Joe polls all the climbers to assess their condition, and he determines that only Steve and Anshel are feeling ill from altitude. Next, he reviews the status of their food supplies and is initially reassured. Working from the bottom up, they have one day's worth cached at Camp V, at 12,100 feet; five and a half days' worth at the base of the snowy hump called the Coxcomb on Karstens Ridge, at 13,000 feet; six days' supplies with them at Camp VI; and two and a half days' worth at the highest cache they have been building, at 16,500 feet.

Joe turns to Jerry Clark for a weather report, because Jerry has been maintaining regular radio communications with Gordon Haber and George Perkins down at the Eielson Visitor Center. In *White Winds*, this important exchange is repeated as it occurred:

"What is the weather forecast?" Joe asks.

"Eielson says that the next two days will be perfect," Jerry explains.

"And after two days?"

"They only have a two-day forecast. I guess they're just getting it from a radio station."

Believing that they can count on at least two days of good weather, and with no hard reason to believe that worse weather lies beyond, Joe tells the team his conviction that they should pack five days of food, dash to 18,000 feet, and go for the summit the following day. If something halts them at 18,000 feet, there are still two and a half days of rations at 16,500 feet that conceivably could be relayed up. If trapped by storms, Joe says, they could subsist on half rations, as other expeditions have done.

What ensues is, as Joe describes it, "a strongly opinionated discussion."

Mark complains that they have been ascending too fast and need more time for acclimatization.

Dennis thinks that leaving food down at the Coxcomb cache was a mistake. With the eerie intuition that he, of all the climbers, seemed to possess before and during the expedition, he warns that if a windy storm traps them above the ridge, that food will be useless.

Others agree. But the higher they go, the more they are constrained by previous decisions and placement of caches, and their options become fewer. Bringing that food up now will take four men a full day. They can count on only two days of good weather, and though they have not received a definite forecast of worse weather beyond that, they know that McKinley's ability to manufacture its own storms could shred in minutes any assurances scavenged by Eielson from Anchorage radio stations.

Finally they work out a way to do it. The original plan assumed that Steve and Anshel, with their minimal experience, would not summit but would function as support climbers, as is often done on Himalayan expeditions. Because those two have been most affected by altitude thus far, they will stay at Camp VI another day, which will give them added time to acclimatize. They will then descend to Camp V, pick up loads, and carry them back up to Camp VI. They will be joined by two of the team's strongest climbers, John and Walt, who volunteer or are directed—it's not clear which—to go with them.

The four will haul sixty man-days of food, totaling about 160 pounds, first from the Coxcomb cache at 14,500 feet back to Camp VI at 15,000 feet, then up to Camp VII at 17,900 feet. Assuming the loads at the Coxcomb cache are divided equally, each man will carry about forty pounds of food plus twenty to thirty pounds or more of personal gear—in other words, loads in the sixty- to seventy-pound range.

The remaining eight men intend to establish Camp VII at 18,200 feet. Then on July 15, while that group is making its summit bid, John, Walt, Anshel, and Steve will make the final supply carry up to Camp VII.

It's not a perfect plan. Anshel, John, Steve, and Walt will work hard ferrying the loads from Camp V to Camp VII, and the extra labor seems certain to leave some of them depleted. But Joe and his team are trying to sort through a hugely complex set of variables, under the stress of contemplating decisions that can well result in life or death, and they're doing so after spending twenty-five days of unbelievably taxing physical labor at progressively higher altitudes.

The great American climber and 1963 Everest summiter Thomas Hornbein, MD, has spent much of his life experiencing and investigating the effects of altitude. He once observed to an interviewer that

> Probably to me the more curious thing to wonder about is what happens to the brain when the oxygen level is so low up there you're convinced that you're thinking tremendously clearly. You could do all these simple-minded calculations about how much oxygen is left in the tank. But at the same time if there were an outside observer looking down on you, they might be struck by how stupid your performance appears to be.

In other words, up high, the dumber you get, the smarter you may think you're becoming.

There is a final bit of worrisome housekeeping for Joe, which he narrates in *White Winds*. How, he asks the others, are the Coloradoans going to like this plan?

They just want to get to the top, Mark says. If they're in the first summit party, they won't give a damn what the rest of us do.

I'll go get their reaction, Joe says.

You're the leader. Don't ask their opinion. Just tell them what we plan to do, Mark concludes.

No one disagrees. Joe goes to the Colorado tent. He tells them that they will all push to Camp VII tomorrow and go for the summit the following day. There will be two summit teams. The Coloradoans will be on the first team, which will also include Joe, Dennis, Hank, Jerry Clark, and Mark. The second summit team will be Walt Taylor, John, Steve Taylor, and Anshel Schiff.

Howard is pleased by that news but disturbed that the decision has been made to divide the group into two summit teams. It is an idea he has disliked from the outset, and he is especially uncomfortable with it now, on learning that the second team will include not one of the three leaders (Joe, Jerry Clark, or himself) but will include the two least experienced men.

Howard recalls (and wrote in his book) that Joe concludes by telling them,

"Eielson says there's a storm coming in on the sixteenth."

Joe wrote, and maintains to this day, that he neither knew of nor spoke about an incoming storm.

To have mounted summit attempts knowing that a storm was approaching would have been worse than a bad attack of summit fever. On McKinley it would have been suicidal, and Brad Washburn will use that word later in describing the party's flawed decision making. This was such an important point that I questioned everyone involved about it. Jerry, Paul, and Anshel don't remember with certainty whether or not a storm warning was received. Gordon Haber, the NPS seasonal ranger who conducted many radio conversations with the expedition, thinks there might have been one but can't say for sure. This crucial point, on which Howard and Joe differ so strongly, has gone unresolved for forty years. But there is evidence that resolves the dispute conclusively, and we'll look at it in detail later.

For now, it's enough to note that the Coloradoans have been excluded from the climb's most critical meeting. Reported dialogue in the Wilcox cook tent reveals that their omission was not mere oversight. It reflected the fact that most members of Joe's team disliked the idea of teaming with the Coloradoans long before meeting them, and bluntly expressed that dislike in their preexpedition letters and again when the teams met at the Kehrs' home in Puyallup. Although until then they were expressing dislike of an idea, by the time of this summit conference on July 13, dislike of a plan has evolved into dislike of people. In fact, the two groups have become antagonists, and anyone who has teamed up with others to go in harm's way—combat, caving, mountaineering, scuba diving, police and fire service—will tell you that of all the forms that *Friktion* can take, this is the most dangerous.

13

Blowup

With McKinley's summit now in their sights, the men at Camp VI spend the evening sorting gear for the next two days' ultimate effort. Now very near the pointed top of their huge logistical pyramid, they are closer to their ultimate goal, but also to the limits of food, fuel, endurance, and determination. Still, morale is higher than at any other point on the trip. "The camp soon began buzzing with the excitement of the final push," Joe recalls. He records another seemingly unimportant but critical fact:

> John was placed in charge of sorting the food and supplies to go with the first group. To save weight and energy, only essential items would be taken: a few pots, the two best functioning stoves with full fuel tanks, two snow shovels, wands, a first aid kit, two gallons of Blazo, the five-watt radio, and various other items.

Of all the team's men, John was unquestionably the strongest physically, routinely carrying loads of a hundred pounds and more. His strength and energy served the expedition well, but they were unbridled much of the time, which made him difficult. He was roundly acknowledged to be the biggest equipment abuser, for example—tossing stoves around carelessly was a particular peeve of Anshel's. He was also the most profane, which must have grated on Steve Taylor, if not others.

The *White Winds* passage, with its passive tense, does not say who put John in charge of organizing food and supplies, including wands, for the first summit team. Joe says he does not recall, and points out that it could have been he himself, or deputy leader Jerry Clark. It's also possible that John, being John, may well have put himself in charge of these chores. It could even be that someone wanted to give John some important task so he would not feel excluded and launch into another tirade. In any case, everyone else has plenty to do.

Although John may not be as ill or tired as Anshel or Steve, he is unquestionably impaired by altitude and fatigued by twenty-five days of grinding labor. He executed the entire expedition's single longest, hardest day of trailbreaking, during which he remarkably led 1,200 vertical feet at the front of the rope. His attention has to be dulled; his ability to concentrate and discriminate is certainly impaired.

It's not hard to imagine him wandering around camp, going from tent to tent and pile to pile, trying to make good decisions. Two cans of Blazo or three? Both first aid-kits or one? All the contents, or just the pills? The pressure cookers or just the pots and pans? Five-gallon plastic water jugs or individual water bottles? Crampons, snowshoes, or both? Wands? How many shovels? Where's that damned snow saw? Air mattresses? Foam pads? Flashlights? Batteries?

Then only one chore is left, and that's to get some sleep. As Joe writes in *White Winds*, his last thoughts before dropping off are, *Just three more days, and then it will be all downhill.* Howard, if anything, is even more excited. It is like Christmas Eve when they were children: "Sleep was most difficult that night."

Waking up the next morning was decidedly easier, because in the cook tent a stove explodes. Joe is there when it happens. "With a loud 'whump!' the entire tent ceiling exploded in terrifying flames above our heads. Six panicked bodies scrambled for the two exits."

Howard sees the whole thing from his frighteningly close adjacent tent. "We saw the Logan tent burst into a ball of flame, and heard the mad scramble of people trying to get out of the burning tent. The fire had lasted three seconds, all the time it took to completely disintegrate the Logan tent."

It is one of this expedition's rare strokes of luck that no one is killed or seriously injured. In the melee to escape, somebody kicks Hank Janes in the face, cutting his eyebrow. Walt Taylor, who was closest to the exploding stove, suffers first-degree burns on one hand and singed eye-brows. A photograph taken by Joe immediately after the fire shows Anshel tenderly ministering to Walt's burned left hand, applying anti-biotic ointment and wrapping it in gauze. Given what might have happened, the team got off easily.

Not so the tent, which disappeared in a terrible but lovely golden bloom, leaving only the neoprene floor and "smoldering relics of the catastrophe." One of these relics was the other stove, which, amazingly, is still burning in the midst of charred debris. John Russell, furious, place-kicks the stove, sending it arcing through the air, trailing yellow flame, into the adjoining Logan tent, which only the Coloradoans' instant smothering action saves from its neighbor's fate.

John Russell's down sleeping bag and Walt Taylor's down parka are lumps of melted nylon and charred feathers. A photograph taken by Howard immediately after the explosion shows Walt sitting on a snow-bank holding his burned hand in the air. Mark, who was not in the tent when the stove blew up, just stands and stares a few feet behind him. After kicking the stove, John, too, gapes, unbelieving.

Mark has brought a double sleeping bag and gives John one of its two components. Anshel loans Walt an extra parka. Cooking will now be done in the men's sleeping tents. All in all, not the catastrophe this might have been. In fact, Joe concludes, "It's strange how surviving a close call can precipitate illogical elation. As the clean-up progressed and the packs were made ready for the day's climb, morale was noticeably heightened; the atmosphere was bubbly."

Perhaps Joe was feeling the altitude, or perhaps fourteen years later he felt compelled to put a better face on this accident. Even Paul Schlichter, probably the expedition's staunchest member, is shaken, confiding to Howard,

"Everyone was feeling so good, and then this happened." Forty years later, Paul's recollection of the explosion and its aftermath was still sharp. "It was a big morale factor because you are up to that 15,000 foot altitude. People are tired and have been out three or four weeks. We had enough extra equipment that it wasn't an issue other than the morale factor."

In *Hall of the Mountain King*, Howard wrote: "The fire had shaken us, and tumbled our high 'summit day' spirits." But the fire did make explicit a dispute that had been simmering between Joe's group and the Colorado group, and among members of Joe's own group, since the expedition's first day: mishandling equipment.

"You know there were some issues there," Paul said. "I think John Russell was renowned for not taking care of the equipment or keeping track of what was going on. That was upsetting some of us."

As the men sort themselves out, pack up, and make ready for the climb to Camp VII, nature adds a macabre bit of symbolism. Thick gray clouds crawl up the glacier and envelop them, so that when they finally trudge out of Camp VI they are ascending into McKinley's literal equivalent of the fog of war.

THE CLIMB FROM Camp VI to Camp VII leads diagonally left to right (looking up-mountain) across the Harper, around the Upper Icefall's lower right corner, then on up, between the icefall and the steep flanks of Pioneer Ridge. It also requires the expedition's biggest single-day elevation gain, 2,900 feet, which is a lot at sea level let alone at 17,900 feet.

Joe starts out from Camp VI first, at 11:00 a.m., leading an advance team of Mark, Dennis, and Hank. Howard follows twenty minutes later with Jerry Lewis, Paul, and Jerry Clark, in that order, behind him on their rope. The fog that shrouded them at first begins to break up and burn off by 12:30 p.m., when Howard and his team round the Upper Icefall's top right corner. There, at about 16,400 feet, they find Joe and his team seated on the snow, resting and, as it appears to Howard, wasting valuable good weather time by lazily basking in the new sunshine. In fact, though, Dennis Luchterhand is ill and they stopped to let him rest.

Jerry Clark's health is holding up, but his patience is suffering badly as, once again, he is punished by the Coloradoans' pace. He asks if any of the others want to jump on this express train. Dennis says he'll just stick with the slow freight, and there are no other takers. Another five minutes of standing around is about all Howard can handle.

How long have you guys been sitting here? he asks Hank. In his book, Howard wrote that Hank says he's not sure exactly, but too long. Twenty minutes maybe.

Patience exhausted, and aware that they still have 1,600 vertical feet to climb, Howard says to Joe, How about us going on and breaking trail?

With no objection from Joe, they move out. Jerry Clark, still tied to the express train, yells that Howard will slow down when they reach the cache and he has to start breaking trail.

But Howard does not slow down. At the 16,500-foot cache, they retrieve only their bamboo crevasse-probe pole, leaving all food there because, according to Howard, Joe told them that, "We could always come down from the high camp and get it if we need more food."

After that, Howard steams uphill at a pace that requires him to stop every thirty steps, or every two to four minutes, even given his superb condition, his pre-acclimatization in Boulder, and his earlier high Mexican climbs. So the pace must have been painful indeed for Jerry Clark. In fact, as they climb up the steeper slope to the right of the Harper Icefall, Jerry, at the end of the rope, calls repeatedly for Howard to slow down. When they come over the crest of the icefall and begin walking up the less steep glacier, Howard goes even faster and Jerry gets even madder:

About a mile a week slower! he shouts.

At that point, even the redoubtable Paul Schlichter voices concern. When will we stop to make Camp VII? he wants to know. Howard says they should go until seven o'clock. Paul's okay with that but insists that they agree "officially" on seven for the time to stop and set up camp.

Howard consents. He feels that by then they will be just below and south of Denali Pass, in the shadow of the North Peak, and that's where he wants to make camp.

Perhaps feeling that now he must cover even more ground in the short time left, Howard actually increases the pace. That finally pushes easygoing Jerry Clark over the edge, as Howard recalled in his book:

"Damn it, slow down! I can go all the way to the summit *today* if you want to, if we just go slow."

Howard understands that, when a gentle soul like Jerry Clark is moved to curse him, it is indeed time to stop. In his book, he continued:

I agreed, but insisted that we move upglacier a couple hundred feet
and establish camp near the foot of the uppermost granite buttress

of North Peak. This rock buttress was free of snow, and thus we would not be subject to the avalanche hazard posed by the snow faces further downglacier.

But then, without further explanation, the next sentence indicates that they did not make it to the lee of that rock buttress, and refers to yet another campsite:

> We moved up to 17,900 feet, and here we established Camp VII. I had hoped to put Camp VII at 18,200 feet, in the lee of the ridge that runs from Denali Pass to South Peak, but my hopes were not to be realized.

The 18,200-foot campsite that Howard refers to, near the southern end of Denali Pass, is not the one in the lee of a North Peak buttress that he describes earlier in this paragraph. It is, instead, the site that Brad Washburn recommended in his Muldrow route guide:

> Make camp about 200 yards east of the pass and slightly up the slope of the South Peak. The southern buttress of Denali Pass will then provide a certain amount of protection from the direct force of the southerly and southwesterly gales that scream almost cease-lessly over the mountain.

Washburn's site and the other location that Howard aimed for have elements of shelter to recommend them, but the men were not able to set up in either place. According to the meticulous diary kept by Bill Babcock of the Mountaineering Club of Alaska (MCA) expedition, which would soon cross paths with the remnant of Joe's, "The camp was pitched in a wind funnel of Denali Pass. Consequently, it got the full force of any storm." Babcock's diary includes a sketch indicating the location he describes. He drew a more precise locator on his actual expedition map, and that mark puts Camp VII not to the north, in the lee of the North Peak's granite buttress, or at Washburn's recommended spot, but out on the open Harper Glacier, directly in the path of any wind blasting through Denali Pass. The Camp VII site is so frighteningly exposed, in fact, that the first thing Bill and his team will do on arriving there on July 28 is to dig snow caves.

Howard and his mates are still clearing tent sites when Joe's team arrives about half an hour later, bringing with them a compelling reason for not relocating camp. Dennis is worse. He has been vomiting, is very weak, and simply cannot go on. His immediate need for rest trumps any thoughts of moving camp. What they have to do now is get a tent up and him in it, and that's exactly what they do.

Joe and the others cannot help but find Dennis's precipitous decline disturbing. Just a few days ago, he was one of the strongest, fastest men on the team, brimming with energy and enthusiasm. Even after a punishing day of breaking trail to establish Camp VI at 15,000 feet, Dennis was still exhilarated.

We're going to get this mothah! he exclaimed.

Moved by Dennis's outburst, Joe added his own: Just a few more days and we'll be on top of this mountain!

But then, strangely, Dennis's exultation faded as quickly as it came. He of the Rainier premonition turned quiet, looked at Joe and then up toward the still unseen South Peak, his face going grim.

Yeah, and then comes the damnable seventeen-day storm, he said.

14

Odd Man Up

J oe wakes in Camp VII at 17,900 feet. It's early in the morning on
Saturday, July 15, and not cold by McKinley standards at this altitude—only five degrees below zero. But the wind is blowing hard,
maybe forty miles per hour, blasting the tent and roaring like a 747. Joe
has led enough climbs on Rainier, the lower 48's closest approximation
to McKinley, to know that wind is the lord high executioner here. The
men won't be going anywhere with wind like that, so he rolls over onto
his other side, careful not to bump Dennis Luchterhand.

Joe tries to doze off, but he's too keyed up, so he lies there staring at
the stitching in the yellow ripstop nylon inches from his face. He has
dreamed about this day for much of his adult life, and now, having
climbed this far into the dream, what worries him is not so much his own
safety, or even primarily whether he will make the summit, but the men
for whom he is responsible. This is *his* expedition. They are *his* people.
Many years later and a father, Joe will say that the responsibility he
feels for his companions is similar to what he would feel for his own
children.

The climbers still have not been able to get anything like a reliable
weather report from the National Park Service. When they make radio
contact, as often as not the park service people ask *them* about the
weather, rather than the other way around.

So he keeps worrying, and the wind keeps roaring. Finally he may
manage to doze off. But even when you're exhausted, real sleep doesn't
come up here, and before long the tent's smell of white gas, farts, dirty

bodies, spilled soup, and all the other detritus of expedition life at altitude must pull him back to this harsher reality. His tent's walls tint the light a sickly urine yellow. In the sharp wind, the fabric snaps concussively like giant clapping hands. He waits.

In his own tent close by, Howard knows they won't be moving in this wind, but he wants to be ready the minute it dies. He crawls partway out of his mummy bag and begins quietly checking gear that he has already put into his smaller blue Gerry summit pack. From time to time he unzips the tent door just enough to peer out for a weather check.

Howard remains certain that if the weather gives them a chance, they'll get to the summit today. He's feeling especially strong himself. Jerry Lewis is suffering more from altitude than the other two but is still fit for the summit attempt. Paul Schlichter feels A–OK—if anything, even better than Howard. But the one thing that Paul never got enough of in four years at the Academy was sleep. So now he snuggles deeper into his bag, happy to wait out the wind.

For the next few hours, the men in camp doze and wake, doze and wake, all tormented to greater or lesser degrees by churning stomachs, throbbing heads, and burning bladders. But then sometime between nine and ten in the morning, Joe snaps fully awake, sits up, touches the flaccid tent wall.

No wind!

He scrambles out, finds blue sky, brightening sun, shredding clouds.

Who's going to the summit? he calls.

The plan that they had finally agreed to calls for all eight climbers to make the first summit attempt together, so Joe is assuming that Jerry Clark, Hank, Mark, and Dennis (if he's able) will accompany him and the Colorado trio. The other four—John, Anshel, Walt, and Steve—will be coming up from the 15,000-foot camp later today and presumably will make their summit climb tomorrow.

But Dennis is still sick. Yesterday he promptly puked almost everything he ate, collapsed into his sleeping bag last night, and doesn't want to risk breakfast this morning. He's feeling marginally better but says he'll wait to climb with the other guys tomorrow.

This doesn't surprise Joe, but he is caught off guard by Jerry Clark's reply that they're *all* going to wait to see what the weather does. It's not that Jerry's sick. His very next words—that he and Mark may give the North Peak a try, then do the summit tomorrow—indicates just the opposite. What the statement really reflects is that Jerry still thinks of his recruits as *his* men, and he will not go for the summit without them.

Early on, Jerry was out of condition and slow, but he climbed himself into better shape and has been moving—if not fast enough for Howard's taste—steadily and without illness of late. He is strong enough to summit today if he wants to, and—based on long experience with his own limits—he knows it. But if his friends don't climb today, he won't go up without them. There was also his experience on Howard's rope yesterday, finally unpleasant enough that he ended up, completely out of character, yelling and cursing at the man. He surely must not want a repeat of that to spoil his own summit day.

This decision to yet again forgo a rare window of good weather disturbs Joe, but he knows that some of the others are tired and that all want to climb with their friends. To summit or not is a decision that every man must make for himself, and the others are not novices. .

Here we must think back to the hotly disputed July 13 weather report. If Jerry Clark and his three friends had heard a weather forecast of a storm coming in on the sixteenth, would they likely have said, "Hey, Joe, I think we're all gonna wait and see what the weather does. Mark and I may give the North Peak a try and then do the summit tomorrow with the others"? Certainly not.

For Howard there is not a second of indecision. He is already standing outside his tent, and recalls asking,

Hey, Joe, are you guys ready to go?

What's the matter? Are you guys getting anxious?

You're darn right we're anxious.

When Howard learns that the other members of Joe's team aren't going up, he thinks the decision to waste this good weather is absurd. But their problems are Joe's responsibility, not his. They will not deter him and his teammates.

Well, *we're* all going, he tells Joe.

Jerry and the others' decisions not to climb today leaves Joe stuck with a Sophie's choice. Even at forty years' remove, we can imagine how he must be feeling. Standing there, he looks toward the hidden summit, then back at the tents, torn between concern for his men and the desire to consummate this climb. The pressure of planning, equipping, organizing, and struggling up the mountain's torturing flank is strong, like vast water built up behind a dam.

But still he is torn.

He looks at Howard's tent, and then Jerry's, and then up. McKinley's North Peak rears sharp and clear into the purified blue-black sky. In the absence of strong wind, the sun warms his face. No matter when he climbs, he will stay at Camp VII until everyone else has summited and is ready to go down. What difference does it make who he climbs with? McKinley doesn't give you many chances. He came to climb this mountain. He will do it today.

Looks like I'll be roping up with you guys, he tells Howard.

Even four decades later, none of the three Coloradoans has positive memories of Joe, so they could not be overjoyed about his late addition to their summit team. But there doesn't seem much choice. And it is more than a little ironic that Joe, who championed their cause against his own team's wishes, will now go to the summit with them, rather than his own group.

The four spend two more hours getting ready for their summit bid. (Later, Jerry Clark and his larger party will be roundly criticized for taking several hours to get ready.) Howard ducks back into the big Colorado group tent where he and his two friends joke and chat as each one layers up, donning (from the inside out) net underwear, a wool shirt, ski pants, a down shirt, down pants, and a windbreaker shell. They shove food, water, flags, maps, flares, cameras, film, down parkas, and mittens into their packs. Feet get special attention: six layers of protection, including (from the skin out) silk socks, heavy wool socks, down booties, felt boots, felt overboot insulation, and nylon overboots. Last of all, they strap on twelve-point crampons. Joe, the only man moving in his tent, goes through similar preparations, trying not to bump the fitfully sleeping Dennis.

At 11:30 a.m., Howard and the other two Coloradoans crawl out of their tent. Joe is outside, nearly ready to go but alarmed at how the altitude is affecting him:

Simple tasks like strapping on my crampons required great concentration and an unreasonable amount of time. The alarming revelation was that this functional slowing did not register mentally . . .
My watch seemed to be running fast!

Moments later, though, Joe discovers something much more alarming—a shortage of wands.

Do you guys have the other wands? he asks, but the Coloradoans do not. A search of the camp turns up only fifty (according to Joe) or thirty (according to Howard) of the four-foot green bamboo sticks with their little orange plastic flags. This has to be disturbing, but in his book Howard noted only that "Russell had kept most of them in Camp VI." Joe was not so sanguine.

"What a blunder!" I thought. How could John have sent us barely half the wands needed to mark the route from high camp to the summit? Perhaps he had not realized that we had to use some wands yesterday to mark the route from the 16,500 foot cache to high camp.

It's two miles to the summit. Fifty wands will allow placement of one every 211 feet, thirty wands one every 352 feet. Given that blizzard and whiteout up here can reduce visibility to zero in minutes, and that experts recommend a maximum separation of 100 feet between wands, 211 feet is dangerously far apart and 352 feet is obviously worse. Improvising on the spot, they decide on the only alternative. Joe, last on the rope, will break the four-foot wands into two-foot halves and place alternating flagged wands and bare sticks approximately every rope length, or 150 feet.

It's all he can do, but it's not an ideal solution. Though cheap and flimsy, these wands, like the proverbial horseshoe nail, assume an importance here out of all proportion to their earthly value. In the Alaska Range, serious whiteout means you can't see your boots. Going blindly through such soup, there are plenty of ways to die. You can stumble off the west side of Denali Pass and slide to your death down that 45-degree wall, as a number of climbers have. You can walk off either edge of the summit ridge and fall thousands of feet. You can step onto a cornice that will collapse and send you plunging 7,000 feet to one of the glaciers below. For an end less dramatic but still unpleasant, you can just wander off the route, get lost, and disappear.

These mini-wands will stick up out of the snow only twelve inches at most, giving 50 percent less visible surface than a four-foot wand inserted one foot into snow. A typical McKinley snowstorm could bury them in an hour. And half of the mini-wands will have no flags.

Joe tells Howard to lead off, adding that he'll bring up the rear, placing wands as they go. It's a superfluous order. Howard has already made himself rope leader, having tied in up front and instructed Jerry Lewis and Paul to tie in behind him, in that order.

Finally, at 12:03 p.m., Jerry bellows a hearty "Hi ho!" and they step off toward the summit. Joe feels "neither overly tired nor ill," and if the weather holds they will almost surely make it to the top. He has to know that he is roped up for a summit assault and descent—the climb's single most dangerous day—with three men who don't much like him. He has no ill feelings for Jerry Lewis and Paul; in fact, he has come to like both of them for their quiet, competent ways. But Howard, with what strikes Joe as his niggling criticisms and poorly concealed air of superiority, is something else.

Joe has known most of the men in his own crew just a month, having climbed previously only with Steve Taylor. But under the stress of conditions not unlike frontline combat, he has come to like and admire them. He will later conclude slide shows about the tragedy with photos of the seven victims and the statement, "These were my friends." When I saw the show, his declaration had the ring of truth, and our talks about the dead men during our time together reinforced that impression.

Joe's own team members may be less skilled and fit and not as well equipped as the Colorado trio, but those facts heighten his paternal affection for them. Their struggle has been greater and their discoveries more painful, yet they are still in there punching. Yes, he would rather be sharing *their* rope.

But things are what they are, and Joe has been climbing mountains long enough to know that you take what they give or you get nothing at all. As the men leave camp, all probably glance over their shoulder for a last look at the bright little cluster of yellow and blue and orange tents.

Joe AND THE Coloradoans are not the only climbers taking happy advantage of this weather. Bill Babcock and his five-member MCA team are on the trail in the good early light of 3 a.m., passing the Muldrow's Lower Icefall, skirting the Hill of Cracks, and occupying the Wilcox team's old Camp III, at 8,100 feet, still littered with broken plastic snowshoes.

Four men in their twenties, and a woman twice their age, Grace Jansen-Hoeman, MD, make up Babcock's MCA team. Bill, their leader, is already an experienced Alaskan mountaineer and will go on to direct the University of Alaska's prestigious Outdoor Adventures Program for more than twenty years. Bill's younger brother Jeff, twenty-two, is on his first serious expedition. He has climbed New Hampshire's 6,288-foot Mount Washington, but nothing higher. Chet Hackney, twenty-nine, is a tough, blond-bearded 200-pounder. A dental technician in real life, Chet is, as Bill recalls today, "a terrific worker, always willing to make the extra relay, make snow walls, and carry heavy loads." Gayle Nienheuser, twenty-five, is six feet two, thin but exceptionally strong. Bearded and already balding, he is a diesel mechanic on the U.S. Army base in Anchorage. His wife, Helen, led the first Alaskan climb that Bill ever undertook; the Nienheusers and Babcocks remain friends today. Full-blooded Native American John Ireton is a twenty-three-year old student at Anchorage Community College and an extremely strong climber. He and burly Chet make many extra relays when the other members of their group are exhausted. After their party is high on the mountain, John risks his own life (as does Chet), racing an approaching storm to search for survivors beneath Archdeacon's Tower. And it will be empathetic John Ireton, more than any other person—civilian or NPS employee—who "demonstrated incredible sensitivity and patience while talking with parents of the deceased climbers. John was the perfect person to do this respectfully," Joe would write later in White Winds.

Grace Jansen-Hoeman is the only female member of Bill Babcock's team. Married to Vin Hoeman, leader of the ambitious South Face Expedition described earlier, she is a strong and determined climber consistently hampered by poor acclimatization. Several years after her husband is killed by an avalanche on Dhaulagiri, she pushes her own luck too far in Alaska and dies in an avalanche herself. Some who knew her well believe that after losing Vin she went to the mountains seeking not to avoid death but to find it.

John Ireton, who has been suffering a cold or altitude ills (or perhaps both) improves dramatically this morning, regaining good health and humor. As the morning wears on down at Camp III, it becomes a hot and lovely day, cloudless, with almost no wind. The sun loosens consolidated snowpack, sending avalanches crashing all day long down the cliffs of Pioneer Ridge, to the group's right, and Mount Tatum, to their left. The climbers are close enough to feel wind generated by some of the bigger slides, but distant enough to enjoy the ongoing spectacle.

There are no avalanches to distract Joe and the Coloradoans while they climb the easy half-mile grade toward Denali Pass. Nevertheless, Howard finds the breakable crust surface difficult going. As they approach Denali Pass, the surface improves: hard, windblown expanses of snow. Looking down-mountain, they can see broken cloud cover at about 12,000 feet, but nothing disturbing. Above them stretches the glistening, shallow parabola of Denali Pass, the 18,200-foot saddle between 19,500-foot North Peak, to their right, and the ridge leading to McKinley's 20,320-foot South Peak, to their left. There's little wind. The temperature is a few degrees above zero.

Everything is different up here, of course, but the men are particularly aware—they could not fail to be—how strange the air itself is. It has an odd electric smell and feels so light and thin that it's like water compared to rich, thick cream, which is how air feels at sea level after you've been at altitude for any length of time. You breathe it down there and can't believe that you never noticed before how incredibly beautiful it is, how *nourishing*.

The first glints of pain will flicker in thigh and back muscles, and Howard, knowing that his friend Jerry Lewis has not been feeling strong, keeps a moderate pace. Back at the rope's end, it appears to Joe that they are all moving in slow motion. Even so, after about forty-five minutes Jerry calls for a break.

They rest at Denali Pass at 18,200 feet. Here on the Muldrow Glacier side of the pass, the terrain is not terribly steep. Just over on the West Buttress side, though, is that 45-degree face, which can be sheer ice, wind crust, sastrugi (frozen, wind-sculpted waves), loose powder, or some maddening combination of all those. More climbing falls occur there than on all of McKinley's other routes combined, and long plunges over steep ice and rock have predictably unpleasant consequences. In *Surviving Denali*, Jonathan Waterman described a 1983 accident where Charlie Sassara, one member of a two-man team, traces his friend and partner Robert Frank's fatal 4,500-foot drop down the West Rib: "Sassara descended, badly shaken, finding blood, pieces of equipment, and several pieces of Frank's bones with flesh attached."

At Denali Pass they find several caches left by previous expeditions, including a stack of gray-weathered wooden boxes that may have been from one of Washburn's early climbs. Some of the boxes have been broken open, perhaps by the 1967 Winter Climb members stranded up here back in February. Those men—Art Davidson, Ray Genet, and Dave Johnston—recorded a true temperature (without windchill) of almost minus 60 degrees Fahrenheit near this very spot. Shortly after that, a storm attacked with winds of up to 130 miles per hour, dropping the windchill factor off the bottom of the scale, which read minus 148 degrees Fahrenheit. That led to the title of Davidson's book about the ordeal: *Minus 148*. The three survived the storm by digging an ice cave and staying in it for four days and nights—horrible days and nights, to be sure. Lacking pots, they drank water from their urinal can and defecated into their sleeping bags—but they survived.

At 1 p.m., Joe retrieves the Dyna-Com five-watt CB radio from his pack, pulls up the three-foot antenna, and tries to raise seasonal ranger Gordon Haber down at Eielson Visitor Center. There's no response. These radios require line-of-sight contact to broadcast, and here they don't have that.

In unbelievably still air, they linger right on the saddle, Howard and Paul standing, Joe and Jerry sitting on the snow. Imposing Mount Foraker, at 17,400 feet the second-highest peak in the Alaska Range and now a thousand feet below them, is a magnificent black-and-white pyramid shining in the fierce sunlight.

At 1:13 p.m. (these times are from Howard's precise pocket log), they start moving again. They had been heading northeast to reach Denali Pass; now they turn left and begin climbing almost due south along the gradually steepening ridge. They are about a mile and a quarter from and 2,120 feet below the summit of South Peak.

At 1:55 p.m., at 18,400 feet, finally with line-of-sight contact, Joe tries Eielson again, and this time Gordon Haber comes on the air. In later life Gordon will go on to become a wildlife biologist and one of Alaska's most prominent activists for the protection of wolves. But he is not a climber and has no mountaineering experience, and his job as seasonal ranger mostly involves dealing with tourists' complaints about bug bites and smelly outhouses. To be in radio contact with a major mountaineering expedition is the most exciting thing that has happened to him here.

Haber and the other rangers at Eielson kept logs of their radio communications. Those transcripts still exist, so we can "hear" their conversations with the McKinley climbers, word for word. Gordon says enviously, "I'd really like to be up there with you guys."

Joe, who *is* up there three and a half miles above sea level with the Coloradoans, replies, "Frankly, I would just as soon be relaxing on a sunny beach. Gordy, we'll try to make radio contact every two hours from now on."

"Roger that," Haber says. "I'll monitor."

"Also, Paul Schlichter wants to set off an orange smoke bomb on the summit. Can we have permission to do that?"

There's no scientific value to the smoke bomb. In fact, after a few hours' surveying work down on the Muldrow Glacier, the Wilcox expedition abandoned all scientific pretense and have been climbing for the sake of climbing. As for the smoke bomb, they just think it will be a hoot if people all the way down at sea level can see their orange eruption.

"Let me check with headquarters. I'll let you know."

"Thanks. By the way, Clark and McLaughlin may try for the North Summit today from Camp VII. I don't see anyone moving up now, but they mentioned it before we left." This is further affirmation that Jerry Clark and Mark were feeling strong and healthy.

"Roger that." Haber signs off. It is about two o'clock. The most important thing about this conversation is what it does not contain: There is no mention of a storm on the sixteenth. If one were incoming, Gordon surely would have reminded the summit team of that fact. And Joe, unless he were completely delirious, would surely have asked for a weather update.

Howard leads them on up the ridge toward the summit. He and Paul are amazed at how strong and fit they both continue to feel:

> There was no wind. Although the world seemed to hold its breath, we did not hold ours. Lewis, just behind me on the rope, was breathing heavily. I could hear Wilcox at the end of the rope, puffing like a steam locomotive. Lewis started to feel the effects of altitude, and began calling for short rest stops.

Joe's "puffing like a steam engine" isn't necessarily a bad sign. Given researchers' findings about the relation of HVR to performance at altitude, Joe's robust breathing may signal that he, like Howard and Paul, is a superior acclimatizer. Jerry Lewis, on the other hand, is starting to falter. Given his size, and the fact that he was having difficulty lower down, this isn't surprising. Jerry has by far the most body mass to haul up this cruel hill, and at altitude. Up here the Rule of Fights is stood on its head: a good big man will not beat a good little man every time. In fact, there have been few, if any, mountaineers both big and great. Everyone who meets Reinhold Messner, the first man to solo Mount Everest without oxygen and unquestionably the greatest mountaineer of all time, is astonished at his almost frail-looking physique. McKinley expert Jonathan Waterman ran into Messner on the Kahiltna and discovered that "he looked emaciated. I wanted to fix our hollow-cheeked, anorexic hero a fattening meal."

The climbers move on again, taking about three hours to ascend the next thousand feet—about six vertical feet each minute, or about one foot every ten seconds. To experience this pace, climb an average staircase, spending ten seconds bent over and panting on each step. Realize, also, that this is not overly slow at this altitude. Even at this snail's pace, thigh muscles, polluted with lactic acid, begin to burn. Shoulders and back ache from the chafing weight of a loaded pack. A climber's neck hurts from continually looking up the mountain. Cracked lips bleed and sting. Feet, even if not yet frostbitten, are sore from the prodding of crampon bars and straps. The chest aches from panting and coughing. The mind is foggy, thoughts are thick and syrupy, mired in dangerous hypoxia. What does it actually feel like to be laboring in such a place? Jon Krakauer, of *Into Thin Air* fame, wrote a vivid description of how he felt on Everest in 1996:

> I felt drugged, disengaged, thoroughly insulated from external stim-
> uli. I had to remind myself over and over that there was 7,000 feet
> of sky on either side, that everything was at stake here, that I would
> pay for a single bungled step with my life.

Krakauer was at about 28,000 feet, so you might think that the effects of altitude on him would be far more severe than on men 8,000 feet lower. That would indeed be true but for the fact that Krakauer was using oxygen. As high-altitude physiologist and Everest summiter Brownie Schoene told *Outside* magazine, "Climbing Everest (or K2 or any other 8,000-meter peak) with oxygen brings the peak down to around 20,000 feet at rest and 24,000 feet while climbing." In addition, as Peter Hackett and other McKinley experts have noted, McKinley's proximity to the North Pole, where the atmosphere is much thinner, makes 20,000 feet on McKinley equal 23,000 on Everest.

At 4:06 p.m., the climbers reach 19,550 feet, atop the low ridge (an easy grade up, only about fifty feet high) behind Archdeacon's Tower. The single most prominent feature on the summit route, Archdeacon's Tower is named for Episcopal archdeacon Hudson Stuck, leader of the expedition that first climbed McKinley's true summit. The jagged rock tower pokes a hundred feet or so up off the ridge above Denali Pass. The men rest here for sixteen minutes (Howard's pocket log again). The trail ahead is visible, leading down the gentle ridge, then across the quarter-mile area so flat that climbers call it the Football Field. "The trail stood out because it was a discordant line in this world of streamlined snow, its surface slightly higher or slightly lower than the surrounding slope," Howard says in his book.

At this point, to lighten his pack Joe caches thirty-five (by his count) remaining wands among some rocks sticking up from the snow on the Archdeacon's Tower ridge. That would mean he placed thirty half wands on the preceding one and a quarter miles of trail, or one wand about every 220 feet.

Leaving the ridge, they can look down to Camp VII and see the colored dots of their tents.

The summit team crosses the Football Field, then starts to climb the steep 500 feet of Kahiltna Spur, one of three ridges that lead to the summit from different directions. Here they have to wade for the first time through loose snow up to two feet deep. Joe notes that "the upslope convinced me again of our greater altitude." Before long the surface hardens and their crampons bite well again, but Jerry is flagging, now calling for rest stops every few minutes. Thankfully, the eerily perfect weather continues. Howard and Paul actually have shed their parkas and are climbing in shirtsleeves, so warm is the sunshine and still the air. McKinley treats few climbers so well.

At about six that evening, they step onto the summit ridge. One of Howard's photographs in *The Hall of the Mountain King* shows the ridge exactly as they saw it, a long, gradual upslope curving to the right. The foreground of the photo shows where the prevailing wind has cut grooves into the surface, which rises up from left to right at an angle of about 15 degrees. The wind has sculpted the ridge's edge into a series of clearly visible cornices; beneath them, the mountain face drops off steeply. At the end of the long curve stands the summit, and in the photo you can see it stabbed with what look like wands and ski poles.

Howard warns the others to stay well to the left on this ridge because of the cornices on the right. These deceptively fragile, hair-trigger trapdoors can drop a careless climber 7,500 feet to the Kahiltna Glacier. For a few minutes the curving ridge blocks their view of the summit, but then Howard shouts, "Hey! I can see it! *I can see the summit!*" It is barely more than a football field away. For Howard, it is a moment of almost inexpressible elation. In his book he writes, "This moment was the climax of ten years of dreams and two years of planning and preparation."

Joe's recollection is remarkably different, subdued, grim even, evoking images of blood and death:

> Less than 200 yards away and 150 vertical feet above us was the object of our quest. Littered with brightly colored pickets and wands protruding at various angles, it resembled the tired, banderilla-pricked shoulders of a bullfight beast.

They ascend a brief, easy upslope, then a final section steep enough that it forces Joe to draw three gasping breaths between each step. He keeps the radio transmitter button pressed during the entire walk up the summit ridge, about ten minutes, so that the rangers at Eielson and the climbers at Camp VI (who have the other radio) can share the experience. This makes the ever-vigilant Howard uncomfortable. He worries about wasting batteries but says nothing, not wanting another squabble to spoil the pure joy of this once-in-a-lifetime moment.

At 6:29 p.m., on Saturday, July 15, 1967, Howard steps onto one of the most coveted summits in the world. He and the others have done this the hard way, with no air support, man-hauling everything all the way up from McGonagall Pass, and they are entitled to feel supremely proud of themselves.

"Howard's on the summit now," Joe radios to Eielson. "Set to reel Jerry Lewis in. Real steep ridge up here. Now Paul's going in."

It has taken the men, according to the unfailingly precise Howard, six hours and twenty-six minutes to reach the summit. The skies above them are clear, the wind light from the south, the temperature six degrees Fahrenheit. A more perfect day McKinley does not deliver.

The Coloradoans are jubilant. They dance around, as successful summiters are wont to do, hugging one another, slapping backs, shouting congratulations. For Joe, alone, cold, tired, the experience is a bittersweet ending to his own years of dreaming, planning, and organizing, twenty-seven days of climbing, thirty-nine miles of route finding, and three and a half vertical miles of ascent.

His mood is dampened further by knowing that most accidents happen during descents. Excluded from the hugs and backslaps, he finds all

the celebrating grating and premature. There is still a lot of downclimbing to do, and it will be more difficult and dangerous than any climbing
they've done so far.

Nevertheless, Joe calls in the good news to Gordon Haber down at
Eielson and, through a funky radio patch, to Wayne Merry at Wonder
Lake Ranger Station.

"This is Joe Wilcox of the Wilcox-McKinley Expedition. We're on the
summit of the mountain now. With me are Howard Snyder of the Colorado group, Paul Schlichter of the Colorado group, and Jerry Lewis of
the Colorado group. The weather's just fine. Some clouds at about seven
thousand—ah, high cirrus. We've been in the clear all day. Light breezes
from the—ah, south, I guess. It's quite an exhilarating experience. We've
all been planning this for years . . . we're all glad to be on top."

"Well, congratulations, Joe," Wayne says. And then, giving an indication of just how primitive communications are in 1967: "It's real good to
hear you from up there. *It's the first time we've talked to anybody on top of
the mountain.*" [Emphasis added]

Joe passes the radio to Howard, who says, "This is Howard Snyder. I
want to say thanks very much for the assistance you gave us, and the
advice. It's a beautiful day up here and we're sure glad to be here."

Taking the radio back, Joe continues, "I don't know if any of these guys
have a few more words to say. We're not going to really do much up here;
take a few pictures. I think we have a few banners. I have banners from
all five of the universities I've been to, and one from my hometown at
Neodesha, Kansas, and one from the State of Kansas, since I think I'm
the first Kansan to climb Mount McKinley. And that's all I have to say. I
send my greetings to everyone there."

After a few minutes getting ready to set off the flare that Paul has carried up, Howard takes the radio and narrates: ". . . two, one—the flare
ignited its generating smoke. Now it's starting to generate enough smoke
to be seen. There it goes. Now it's off. Can you see us? Over." One of
Howard's photos captures this moment—Paul Schlichter standing on
the summit, back arched, arm and flare punched into the sky, smoke bil-
lowing up. It's a beautiful image, powerfully conveying victory and defi-
ance and elation.

Gordon Haber exclaims, "Yeah, we see you. Ten-four. We can see it! We can see it! Ten-four." A bit later, he asks, "How's your temperature and wind and so on and so forth up there?"

"The wind is about ah—fifteen or twenty, with gusts up to twenty-five," Howard replies.

"Well, that doesn't sound too bad—ah, pretty cool up there?"

"The temperature we just checked is six degrees. Actually it's pretty comfortable. I've got my heavy down gear in my pack."

"Well, that isn't too bad at all. Boy, you guys really got the beautiful weather."

"Sure did. We're glad we started out today. It started out a little overcast and blowing snow, and we wanted to go anyway, but it sure turned into a beautiful day. If you want a little description from the summit here, Foraker is completely out of the clouds, the clouds are down about eleven thousand feet, and it looks beautiful. All the peaks off to the southeast are visible, the clouds are lying low in the valleys, and it's just a beautiful view up here."

It's a detailed enough description that if mare's tails (high, wispy cirrus clouds with curling ends) or other storm signs were visible, Howard would have mentioned them. And because they were talking of weather, Haber would certainly have made at least passing reference to updated information about any approaching storm. Even if Haber did not mention it, Joe or Howard would have asked for such an update. Still further evidence that there was no July 13 storm warning.

Jerry Lewis next takes the radio and chats with a woman named Ethyl Worthington—his next-door neighbor in Colorado who by sheer coincidence happens to be at the Eielson Visitor Center. Then Joe asks Gordon to send a postcard to his wife, Cheryl, letting her know that they are okay and he will be home in two weeks.

"Okay, we got that and we'll sure send this postcard off. Ah, glad to do it, and again I say—congratulations!"

"Ah, thanks a lot," Joe acknowledges. "This is KHD6990 Unit One on the summit of Mount McKinley."

Before leaving, they take summit photos. Exhausted Jerry Lewis gets down on one knee, half his face in shadow. He ties an American flag to his ice ax and holds it out for the camera. Something between a grin and a grimace squeezes his eyes tightly shut. He is feeling weak and sick. Posing next, Paul gets down on one knee, too, and also unfurls an American flag. He smiles—calm, happy, clearly feeling on top of the world, or at least North America. Howard squats down on his heels, pulls out yet another American flag, and looks positively jubilant, overflowing with a sense of fruition and accomplishment. Leading every step of the way on this, the climb's key day, has been very sweet indeed, adequate recompense for all the preceding hassles and frustrations.

In his choice of pose, as in other things, Joe is the odd man out. When Howard and I look at this slide together forty years later, he says only, "The Invisible Man." Joe remains standing erect and holds out not Old Glory but a Kansas State College pennant. He leaves his parka hood pulled up, and it completely covers his face with shadow, rendering it as invisible and mysterious as a monk's under a cowl. The image is an accurate reflection of Joe's feelings:

> I had expected to be elated at this momentous moment; yet as the summit approached and the skylines receded on all sides, I felt strangely disappointed—not in the summit itself, for I felt a deep respect for the mountain, but in the relative insignificance of the day's climb. The summit stood nearly four vertical miles above sea level, halfway through the earth's troposphere, yet the fulfillment of my elusive reasons for climbing the mountain were not here; they were hidden in the mental sweat of pre-trip planning, the pounding dust of the Alcan, the mosquitoes and river of the tundra, the storms and crevasses of the Muldrow, the wind and deep snow of Karstens Ridge, and the cold thin air of the Harper. The fulfillment was in the shared struggle of twelve men matching their intelligent might against the unknown. I fully appreciated now why those at high camp were waiting for their friends. [Emphasis added]

They linger about an hour and a half there, a relative eternity in McKinley summit stays. Before departing, Howard buries a book of matches in the snow. Inside the matchbook, he has written a memorial message to honor a beloved Boulder employer and friend who had recently died: "In memory of Walter E. Hickenbottom. The finest boss ever . . ."

Just before eight that evening, as they are readying to leave, Joe says that he will take the lead going down, which will require them to switch ends of the rope. Howard makes no objection. Leading the *descent* is meaningless. In fact, the end of the rope is more important than the front on descent, because in case of falls, it is the last man standing who will save or doom those ahead.

Joe is first off the summit. Proving just how quickly weather can change this high on McKinley, the wind has freshened to a steady 25 to 30 miles per hour and has blown in drifts of new snow deep enough to obliterate the distinct trench dug by the upward passage of four big men in boots and crampons. Many of the half wands are also gone—buried or blown away. Both bode ill for any subsequent summit climbers who might encounter fog or storm. The men are too tired, cold, hungry, and intent on their own safe descent to take much notice. As if those were not distractions enough, Jerry is beginning to have serious difficulty. He's exhausted and weak, and calls for ever more frequent rest stops.

Even descending, breaking trail through this thick, dense windpack is exhausting. Joe, also tiring, hands the lead back to Howard at Denali Pass. Paul is tooling along just fine, but Howard is worried about Jerry and Joe.

It's almost astonishing that any of them are still walking at all, given what they have just accomplished. After twenty-seven days of exhausting load hauling, dehydration, radically altered diets, poor sleep, altitude sickness, and killing stress levels, they have just climbed up the vertical equivalent of two and a half Empire State Buildings with thirty-pound packs on their backs and five pounds on each foot, in air that has 50 percent less oxygen than that at sea level. And now they are climbing *down* those two and a half Empire State Buildings. Have you ever tried, or even imagined, walking up and down the Empire State building's stairs with a pack on your back and heavy boots on your feet—*five times?*

They left the summit at 7:53 p.m. and reach Archdeacon's Tower thirty-nine minutes later, passing the wands cached there. "[M]ore out of rest than reason," as Joe recalls, they do not retrieve them. Nor, as they descend, do they replace any wands blown away or add any to make them more frequent. They make Denali Pass at 9:30 p.m. and walk into Camp VII at 9:53 p.m., precisely two hours after leaving the summit. Six and a half hours going up, an hour and a half on the summit, two hours coming down: a ten-hour round trip.

As they approach Camp VII, they are astonished to see the other team of four, who have been climbing up from Camp VI for ten hours, just arriving. A hundred yards downhill from Camp VII, Anshel, John, Steve, and Walt are moving in slow motion. Their nearly immobile forms are silhouetted against a backdrop of thick, dirty-gray scudding clouds that, to Joe, gives the scene an eerie Gothic flavor. Joe, Howard, and the other summiters drop their own loads and hurry down to help.

Steve waves them off. He's still going strong under a mountainous pack and has been moving slowly just to stay with the others. Walt and Anshel are also in good shape. The only one really hurting is the expedition's Incredible Hulk, John Russell. During the day he began to suffer so severely that Steve and Walt divided half his load between them, bringing the weight of their own packs to more than eighty pounds each, considerably more than the thirty-pound packs that Joe and the other summiters were hauling.

During the last two days, these four men have worked much harder than anyone else, including the summit climbers. They bring with them another 150 wands and thirty more man-days of food, enough to feed the entire twelve-person party for about three days. Each of the four men, then, began their haul under about fifty to sixty pounds, because their loads also included tents, sleeping bags, clothing, stoves, and all the other personal summit gear. They brought this, plus another eighty pounds of food, from Camp V yesterday, and then did this haul to Camp VII today. These have been easily the most grueling two days of the entire expedition.

A photograph taken by Anshel on July 15, as he and the others were leaving Camp VI for their last carry to Camp VII, shows John leading and Steve Taylor coming behind him. A bundle of wands is visible, tied to John's pack. It's impossible to tell how many wands are in the bundle. There do not appear to be any wands tied to Steve's pack. The wands that had been left in Camp VI earlier were wrapped into three separate bundles, however, so to judge from the photo, Anshel (who does not recall now) may be carrying one of the remaining two bundles, and Walt Taylor the other.

The men dump their packs. Joe's summit team, and the team that just arrived from Camp VI, settle in to recover from their respective climbs of the day. Camp VII is now fully occupied. Joe is glad to see that Dennis's day of rest seems to have done him good; he appears stronger, can keep food down, has his color back. But John Russell, weak and nauseated, quickly throws up most of the cheese and hamburger dinner he tries to eat.

No one objects to turning in early. When they cinch their tent doors and wriggle into sleeping bags, the sky is spattered with stars and the wind is light. But at some point during the night, the wind begins to roar. That bodes ill for the morrow, when eight climbers, all tired and at least one sick, will try to find the summit of the meanest mountain in North America on a poorly marked route in steadily worsening weather.

PART THREE

ACCIDENT

I am afraid it was all inevitable. We were as wise as anyone can be before the event.

— APSLEY CHERRY-GARRARD
The Worst Journey in the World

15

MONDAY, JULY 17
Just One More Wand

On the morning of Sunday, July 16, it is very clear that nobody is going anywhere, thanks to sustained 50-mile-per-hour winds. At some point, Joe thinks of digging a snow cave, but ". . . the secure marginality of the present shelter beckoned me back inside for a period of peace." At one point, to relieve frustration, Dennis begins howling like an old dog. Before long, everyone else in camp is howling right along with him. Being tentbound does things like that to you.

Sunday crawls by, and then Sunday night, and mid-morning on Monday brings weather as clear and beautiful as that enjoyed by the first summit team. Nevertheless, cautious Jerry Clark tells Joe he'll wait a bit more to see what might develop. Anshel is tired and wants to descend with Joe and the Coloradoans. Steve Taylor is sick, and may not go to the summit, but all the others will. Joe plans to stay in Camp VII to await the second summit team's safe return.

On Monday morning, the mantle of leadership floats from Joe's shoulders and settles onto Jerry's, who tells Joe, authoritatively, to go down. He reminds Joe that he, Jerry, has the majority of the strongest climbers with him, and adds that Joe's descent will conserve fuel and food at Camp VII. Dennis seconds Jerry's request for Joe to descend.

Joe doesn't agree immediately. One of the cardinal rules of expedition leadership is that you stay with the team. But—what if there are *two* teams? And complicating things even more, each "sub-team" will have its own leader (Jerry Clark and Howard) with or without Joe. Yesterday's climb has left him sluggish in body and mind; sorting these things out with half a brain, or less, is extremely difficult. But usually deferent Jerry is firm. Excepting Steve Taylor, all the other climbers are *Jerry's* people, and the logic of conserving food and fuel is indisputable. Acceding to the weight of evidence, Joe agrees that it makes better sense for him to descend than to remain and starts packing his gear.

Howard, already packed, asks ailing Steve Taylor and John Russell if they want to descend with his group. Both decline, Steve politely and John angrily, as though Howard's invitation were an insult. Howard then reviews the summit route with Mark, who predicts they will make the top today and then descend tomorrow from Camp VII all the way down to the Muldrow Glacier. If nothing else, Mark's statement suggests how good he and the others must be feeling, but Howard remains skeptical. He's not sure his own team could have done that after their summit push.

At 11:59 a.m., Howard, Paul, Jerry, Anshel, and Joe, tied in that order into one 270-foot rope, leave Camp VII for the last time. They all cast long glances back in the direction of Mount McKinley's summit, the small white spot they have risked so much to gain and will most likely never see again. When almost out of shouting range, they call a last, hurried farewell to the men remaining at Camp VII:

See ya tomorrow!

THE DESCENT TO Camp VI at 15,000 feet is actually more difficult than their climb to the summit on July 15. Only Howard and Paul are completely healthy. Even on the initial flat area, between Camp VII and the dropoffs beside the Harper Icefall, Jerry and Anshel call for frequent rest stops. After an hour of downclimbing, they get a brief glimpse of Camp VII. Howard is surprised to see Jerry Clark and his party still milling around the camp, despite this rare good weather.

Three hours later, they reach Camp VI, pitch tents, and feast. With bellies full, there is nothing to do but huddle in sleeping bags and wait for the 8 p.m. radio call from Camp VII.

It is about noon when the four summiters and Anshel leave Camp VII and drop out of sight around the corner of the Harper Icefall, the remaining seven men no doubt look around at the camp, at one another, silent for a few moments. It's impossible to know for sure what each is feeling, but they're probably all relieved. At last they are on the mountain as *their* team, without the expedition's tension generators, and back under the genial direction of Jerry Clark. Before long, Walt would be as likely as anyone to break the silence.

We gonna climb this mothah or what?

Yeah, but let's give it a bit more time, Jerry says. He is probably even more cautious than he would have been when ultimate responsibility for their fate rested on Joe's shoulders. His "better safe than sorry" response would be to wait for some kind of weather report from Eielson, which no doubt prompts some grousing at least from Walt and John, but also grudging acceptance that Jerry is right to wait just a bit to see if this weather holds. Dennis, in particular, would be happy to stand by a bit longer. He's feeling better, but not really *good,* and still carrying that feeling that has stuck with him like a blister that will not heal, all the way from Rainier.

It's not cold, really—a few degrees above zero. The wind is blowing only about twenty miles per hour and the sky is painfully bright. Jerry knows that two important changes almost always precede big McKinley storms. First, whiteout signals the onset of a lenticular cloud cap, which in turn means that one of McKinley's localized storms is brewing up and can strike full force within an hour or less. The other is the appearance of mare's tails—high, wispy cirrus clouds that precede the onset of storms coming from beyond. At this point, Jerry isn't seeing any of those signs, but he would dearly like to know what's beyond the sky he *can* see.

A half hour passes. A couple of the climbers would go back into their tents, snuggle into sleeping bags, and doze off. Others might read, make notes, snack. Jerry fiddles with the radio. One thirty comes and goes.

It could be Walt, or even John Russell, who finally runs out of patience and proclaims, Come on you slackers, it's time to get up this mountain, goddamnit! Bodies start flying around and the camp is bustling in moments.

Amidst the hustle, Jerry, ever the populist, asks one more time whether everybody is feeling good about this. Everyone is, now that push has come almost to shove-off time, except Steve Taylor. He's not violently ill, but just doesn't feel well enough to try for the summit. He's probably more worried about holding them back than about endangering himself, but in any case he says he'll just wait here while they do their summit thing.

That could prompt some heated debate. Not one of them is comfortable leaving Steve alone. Someone—Hank Janes, perhaps, or Dennis—still feeling slightly off—volunteers to stay with Steve. This ignites such a furious refusal from the normally mild-mannered Steve Taylor that the others have to suppress grins.

Staying above the fray, Jerry would be weighing options. Expedition protocol says you do not leave one man, especially a sick man, alone on a mountain. But Jerry knows it's a rule often broken when a summit is in the offing. And Steve is not truly sick—just not feeling up to the grueling 4,800-vertical-foot trip to the summit and back. He's eating and drinking normally, not vomiting, thinking clearly—or as clearly as you can at almost 18,000 feet. He has good shelter and plenty of food and fuel, and his insistence that the others go remains unshakable. After weighing all the factors, and having heard Steve's adamant urgings to *get going, guys!* Jerry agrees and tells the others to finish getting ready, because an hour has already slipped by. It's after two o'clock.

But the innumerable little "getting ready" tasks that six men must accomplish before they actually start climbing to the summit of a 20,320-foot mountain would consume another hour at least. Adjusting and lacing on crampons. Filling water bottles. Stuffing pockets with trail food. Lashing snow shovels to summit packs. Putting on lip cream. Wiping goggle lenses. Urinating. Defecating. Finding a lost ice ax, the right down jacket, goggles. Shoving sleeping bags into stuff sacks. And doing every extra thing to make Steve as comfortable as possible and allay their own anxieties at leaving him here.

Finally all are set to go. Jerry takes one last look at the two rope teams standing in their puffy down parkas the colors of autumn leaves, waiting for his word. The others are looking not at him but up toward the summit they can't yet actually see. Their Golden Fleece at last within reach, the dream about to be realized. An ecstatic moment, surely, but Jerry is older than all of them, old enough to know the other half of that equation: once achieved, the summit will turn from dream to memory. Dreams, like Christmas presents yet unopened, make you happy. Memories, like all things lost forever, make you sad. So, it is with excitement, but also a tinge of regret, when shortly after three in the afternoon on Monday, July 17, 1967, Jerry Clark yells some exhortation—*Hey you mothahs! We gung ho and ready to go?*—and they step off, one by one, on the way to the end of their dream.

So now we come at last back to where we began, watching Jerry Clark and his team march up the gentle slope toward Denali Pass and, beyond that, into the dark annals of mountaineering tragedy.

Walt Taylor, good acclimatizer, the strong, wry young doctor-to-be, is leading the first rope of three men. He had written his autobiography like a poem in free verse:

> *I am twenty-four years old.*
> *I weigh one hundred fifty-five pounds.*
> *I am five feet eight inches tall.*
> *I have flat feet.*
> *I grew up in Indiana.*
> *I went to high school in Indiana.*
> *I have a burial plot reserved in Indiana.*
> *I plan to die elsewhere . . .*
> *I first learned to climb with Jerry Clark.*
> *I first learned to water ski with Jerry Clark.*
> *I first learned to snow ski with Jerry Clark.*
> *I first learned spelunking with Jerry Clark.*
> *I first learned scuba diving with Jerry Clark.*
> *I learned to smoke and drink on my own . . .*
>
> *I used to climb mountains to tell people I climbed mountains.*
> *I used to climb mountains to get to the top.*
> *I used to climb mountains to test my courage.*
> *I fell thirty-five feet two years ago and landed on my head.*
> *I climb mountains to look at the climbers and the sky and the rock and*
> *the snow and the flowers.*

He was also the one who wrote this, in a subsequent letter to Jerry Clark: "Perhaps our party is a lot weaker than I've guessed."

Dennis Luchterhand would probably have led the other rope but for the fact that he had begun to suffer appreciably from altitude the last couple of days. John Russell wasn't feeling well, either, so he would not be up front. Hank Janes had not led a single rope team to that date, and Mark McLaughlin had done only one short lead, so it's not likely that either man would have been tasked with taking one to the summit. Jerry Clark had led more advance team miles (five) than anyone except Joe Wilcox (eight), and he was now this team's official leader, so he would have been first on the second rope. They would have put the two climbers who'd been ill—Dennis and John—in the middle position of each rope, with two healthy men last. That leaves Mark McLaughlin last on one rope and Hank Janes last on the other. Early in the expedition, John had argued with Jerry and Mark, and had refused to rope up with both of them thereafter. It's not likely he would have tied in with either now, on the crucial summit climb, given the care that he and everyone else had exercised thus far in choosing rope mates. Mark and Jerry were close friends who had climbed together a lot, and Walt and John had become close on the climb. Hank just seemed to get along with everybody. So it's safe to assume that the first rope would have been Walt Taylor, John Russell, and Hank Janes. Jerry leads the second rope, with Dennis in the middle and Mark last.

Back in camp, Steve Taylor watches them go. Skinny when he began this climb, he now could pass for a POW. Steve's emaciated state has a more ominous implication than just looking skeletal. With his already low percentage of body fat reduced to almost nothing, Steve is more susceptible than ever to hypothermia.

He is devoutly religious, playful, and gentle minded, no wave maker. After helping to pull Jerry Lewis out of the crevasse, in fact, Steve is mentioned rarely in Howard's and Joe's accounts of the climb. The least experienced man on this trip save one, Steve still knows enough to understand that he has reached his limit on this mountain. He's exhausted from the month of hauling seventy-pound loads up the mountain and, if not incapacitated, is still queasy and weak from the altitude. Though his reasoning power has been cut sharply, his mind is still functioning well enough that summit fever doesn't burn out his instinct for self-preservation. He won't make the top this time. Lord's will, and so be it. He knows the saying about old climbers and bold climbers. He'll be around to climb another day.

Steve Taylor is genuinely happy for the others, but if he's not the loneliest man on Earth just now, he isn't far from it. He crawls back into his tent, wriggles into his sleeping bag, and likely does what many lonely mountaineers do to ward off fear and depression. He writes in his journal. That document was never found, but it's not hard to imagine what he's putting down just now. Hopes for the other guys' summit chances, reflections on how hard this climb has been, and perhaps disappointment that the expedition has not been a happier one.

It doesn't take much to tire him out, so before long he sets aside the journal, snuggles deep into his down mummy bag, and, doubtless, asks God to keep the others safe, to protect Joe and his team, and to keep his own faith strong.

Prayers said, he tries to sleep. But a spark of dread, deep down, must flare in the back of his mind like a match in a black cave. It's his brain asking the "what if?" question that can't be escaped at times like this. What if my parachute fails? What if my regulator malfunctions? *What if they don't come back in twelve hours? Or two days? Or at all? What if . . .*

THE MEN CLIMBING behind Walt and Jerry—most especially Dennis and John—now may actually be feeling better, as sometimes happens if you can make yourself get moving when suffering from altitude. At 4:40 p.m., Jerry radios a report to Gordon Haber down at Eielson. He says that there are six climbers on the way to the summit. They are now just above Denali Pass, which would put them at about 18,300 feet, with an estimated time of arrival (ETA) at the summit, Jerry says, between eight and nine o'clock that evening. He adds that the weather is fine: temperature about five degrees, wind just fifteen miles per hour.

Jerry's summit ETA is odd and unrealistic. He and his team have taken about an hour to gain 400 feet of elevation climbing a gentle slope in fine weather. The summit is still another 2,020 vertical feet above them. To meet Jerry's timetable they will have to climb at almost 500 feet per hour, over more difficult terrain, at ever-higher altitude to make the summit by nine o'clock. The other team, which reached McKinley's summit two days earlier, climbed from this point to the top at a rate of 500 feet per hour. But that team had only four men, and they were among the strongest and most experienced climbers in the whole group. It's true that Jerry Lewis slowed Joe's summit group, but John (and perhaps Dennis) is slowing Jerry Clark's team.

At 8:00 p.m., Jerry raises Gordon on the radio again. They have climbed into cream-thick whiteout, cannot see any wands, don't know where they are. He says that they *may* be on the summit ridge (which they would have had to climb at 625 feet per hour to reach by then) and asks Gordon to find out from Joe if the summit is corniced.

Because this was before the days of microwave relay towers and satellite phones for civilian communications, Jerry and Joe, who are not within line of sight with each other, must communicate through Gordon, at Eielson, 18,000 feet below Jerry. It works like this: Jerry calls Gordon with his question; Gordon relays the question to Joe; Joe gets the answer and radios back to Gordon; Gordon relays the information to Jerry.

Based on Joe's answer, Jerry estimates that they are only an hour from the top, another miscalculation. It was 4:40 p.m. when they radioed from about 18,300 feet. Roughly three hours later, they are projecting that his team will reach the summit in an hour. It's hard to understand how Jerry could have believed that they were climbing 25 percent faster than the first summit team. Altitude befuddlement could have been the culprit. Or perhaps he didn't know how long Howard's rope took to reach various points on the route. One thing, however, is certain: At this point, neither Joe nor Howard nor the rangers nor the climbers themselves in Jerry's party know where they are.

Ninety minutes later, at 9:30 p.m., Jerry raises Gordon yet again.

"Gordy, this is a real problem up here. Ah, do you have any arrangements to contact Unit Two [Joe, in Camp VI, at 15,000 feet]?"

"I tried to call him just a little while ago and I couldn't get an answer," Gordon responds. "Why don't you let me try it again—stand by. KHD-six-nine-nine-zero Unit Two, Unit Two, this is KHD-six-nine-nine-zero Eielson Base. I don't get an answer from Unit One, Jerry. I originally had told them we'd—you'd—probably be calling about a quarter to nine and so they said they'd be listening in. I imagine they had their radio on and shut it off. But they might—they might turn it on periodically—ah, although I don't know when. I don't imagine they'll leave it on the whole time 'cause of the batteries. What's the problem?"

Jerry's response suggests that the problem is serious but not a crisis. Visibility is poor and they're unsure of their location, but the weather is not threatening. "We don't know; it's not well wanded at all. We've lost the wands. We're just floundering around. We don't know whether we're on the summit ridge or not. We don't know whether the summit ridge is supposed to be wanded or not—and, ah, we just thought we'd check it out. We've been getting pretty close to the summit but—ah, we can't tell. We're just floundering around on the flat here. Visibility is about four hundred feet."

The transmission breaks up for the next few exchanges, but then Jerry starts to come in clearly again. "Roger, we're at the summit ridge. We have followed the wands to what we think may be the summit ridge. I'll say that over again. We have followed the wands to what we think may be the summit ridge. And if we find one more wand . . . one more wand, it'll probably be enough to tell us which way we have to go on the ridge. That would be enough for—to tell us which way to go on the ridge." At that point, the batteries in Jerry's radio weaken and his voice fades out.

Growing concerned, and using a different radio, Gordon calls his boss, Wayne Merry, at the Wonder Lake Ranger Station.

"I just got a call from Unit One and they're having problems up there right now. I don't know what's going on yet. But their batteries are cold and I told 'em to warm 'em up a bit so I could understand more what they're saying. But it appears as though they're—they're kind of lost or something . . . I want to get back to the radio right now . . . just wanted to let you know what was happening. Seven-zero-two, clear."

"Ten-four. I'll be outdoors about five minutes but I'll be back after that. . . . Thanks a lot."

Gordon waits and waits for another call. He has no direct experience of what it's like to be up where Jerry and his friends are, but Jerry did not seem panicked or even afraid—just lost. Gordon decides there's no reason to call Wayne back yet.

Finally, at 10:45 p.m., Gordon's radio crackles and he grabs for it. "This is KHD-six-nine-nine-zero Eielson. Go ahead, Unit One."

"Eielson, I read you too—over." It's Jerry Clark's voice.

"Ah, say again. Go ahead Unit One—this is Eielson."

There is a long silence. Gordon repeats his request for Jerry to go ahead. There is no answer.

Jerry's reports, though fragmentary, provide important information. The scarcity of wands between Camp VII and the summit, which in good weather would have been inconsequential, has caused Jerry's team to become lost. To quote from R. J. Secor's authoritative *Denali Climbing Guide*, "At least 100 wands, placed 100 feet apart, are needed to mark the route from Denali Pass to the summit. . . ." There is no way that the first team, with their "mini-wands," could have adequately wanded the route, and as a result Jerry and his team are "floundering around on the flat."

Using important clues contained in Jerry's broadcasts, we can try to establish his position. One: they are close to, or on, a ridge that they believe may be the summit ridge. Two: they have been wandering around on a large, flat area. Three: visibility is about 400 feet. Four: they cannot see any more wands. With these clues, and a good estimation of the distance they have traveled, we can fix their location somewhat accurately.

Distance first. We know that it took Jerry's team an hour to climb 400 vertical feet from Camp VII to 18,300 feet, just above Denali Pass. If after 4:40 p.m. they climb somewhat more slowly, say 300 feet per hour (a reasonable estimate, given fatigue, decreasing visibility, and increasing altitude), they would have been at about 19,500 feet when they made their 8 p.m. broadcast. During this call, relayed by Eielson to Joe at Camp VI, Jerry said that he thought they might be on the summit ridge and, to make a more definite determination, asked Joe whether it was corniced.

We know from a later radio broadcast that they were not at the summit ridge, so they had to be somewhere else below it. This is supported not only by that broadcast but by other facts. They had to be climbing more slowly than Joe's team, hindered as they were by inadequate wanding, the failing John Russell, and whiteout. The only other ridge that Jerry could be referring to would be the low (about fifty-foot elevation gain), relatively gentle one that runs southwest from Archdeacon's Tower and immediately precedes the quarter-mile-wide flat area (the Football Field) leading to the base of the actual summit ridge. Archdeacon's

Tower ridge is located at about 19,500 feet, right at the realistic limit of
Jerry's progress.

They have apparently been following wands but now cannot see any
("We've lost the wands"), despite having 400-foot visibility. Two sources
suggest that the route beyond the Archdeacon's Tower ridge and out
across the Football Field was not well wanded. Climbing on the fifteenth, Howard found it so: "Under our perfect weather conditions, the
route ahead was plainly visible, a fine white line running across the flat
area between the Archdeacon's Tower ridge and the base of the summit
slope. The trail stood out because it was a discordant line in this world
of streamlined snow." The trail stood out, in other words, not because it
was wanded, which Howard would have mentioned if that had been the
case, but because he could see it cutting through the undisturbed snow
of the Football Field.

The second bit of evidence of nonwanding comes from Joe himself.
After Howard's book came out, Joe self-published a small paperback
volume, *A Reader's Guide to the Hall of the Mountain King*, containing
corrections of many errors that Joe identified in Howard's book. In *A
Reader's Guide*, Joe included a photo taken by Howard during their
ascent on the fifteenth. Joe is trying to demonstrate that the route across
the Football Field was wanded, and includes the photo as support: "By
4:30 PM we had climbed to 19,550 feet and crested the low ridge behind
Archdeacon's Tower, a large rock outcropping. We took a long rest as we
looked at the wanded route ahead of us." The photo shows a distinct line
of tracks, as Howard described. But it also shows just one wand, which
is virtually impossible to see without magnification, "on the flat where
Howard claims that the wind had removed the wands." Oddly, though,
in *White Winds* Joe writes, "The high party was having difficulty following the route in the whiteout; apparently the storm of July 16 had blown
a lot of the wands away."

If we know where the visible line of wands ended, we have more evidence pinpointing where Jerry's team got lost and the spot from which
they made their radio broadcast. Joe does not claim that *he* wanded the
route across the Football Field. From *White Winds*: "On the ridge behind
Archdeacon's Tower we could see that the rest of the route to the summit was well wanded so we cached the rest of our wands." These wands,

like those they've already followed, must have been placed by earlier climbers from a West Buttress expedition. The point here is that, not having set wands himself, Joe would have no way of knowing how deeply and securely they had been inserted, or how long they had been there, all of which would have affected their ability to withstand the strong winds of July 16. It's also true that the Football Field, the single largest flat area above Denali Pass, would be the one place where strong winds blowing unimpeded would have been most likely to blow out wands.

Finally, there is this: The lower ridge extending south from Archdeacon's Tower is itself about a quarter mile long. There is no guarantee that Jerry Clark's team, befuddled by whiteout, struck the ridge at exactly the same place that Joe's team did earlier in perfect weather. Even if there *were* wands running out across the Football Field, which the weight of evidence renders unlikely, a few hundred feet one way or the other on the low ridge could have made them invisible.

The ridge behind Archdeacon's Tower, then, is almost certainly Jerry's location at the time of his 8:00 p.m. and 9:30 p.m. broadcasts. After the last broadcast is cut short by failing batteries, the men are left in dusky gloom, thick whiteout blurring everything in eerie mist. The temperature is probably about zero, the wind fifteen to twenty miles per hour. Visibility now is so bad, and getting worse as light fails, that it will be increasingly dangerous to continue up *or* down. They are lost, as Jerry admitted.

They would stand talking through their options. One is to keep going to try to relocate the route, but John is feeling lousy and probably would opt for descent. That's option two. They have been placing their own wands on the way up here, but downclimbing in conditions such as this is even more unpleasant than going up. And the wind, which has been wiggling some of the wands around for two days, could be blowing more out right now.

Hey, we're not in any danger, right? someone would point out. I can see Walt Taylor doing this. Nobody's really sick. That summit could be just right up there.

Some would nod assent; others, depending on how they feel, might stay on the fence. But what they would all do is turn to Jerry, their leader—not for his two cents but for a decision.

Until now, he has not had to do any real leading, if you discount route-finding leads. He has not had to make decisions sure to please some and anger others—decisions that can save them or kill them. Now, though, he has to. The realization must hit him as it could not have before: *I am responsible for these men, my friends, their lives.*

Jerry Clark has been in bad whiteout before, in the Pacific Northwest and the Antarctic. But this is different—higher, colder, more exposed, the margin for error blade-thin. They have only three choices: climb, descend, or stay put. Given such options, and the potential consequences of choosing the wrong door up here, a man of Jerry's makeup would take the most conservative option, especially if his decision can be grounded in doctrine. So he asks them,

What's the first rule of survival when you're lost?

They all know what it is: *Don't panic and stay put.*

That's right, and I think that's what we should do.

They have Dennis's shovel, and perhaps another. They all have ice axes and sleeping bags with covers, and they have a stove with fuel. Why not dig snow caves and bivouac?

There are concerns.

Is this a good idea so high? one of the more cautious men, Hank perhaps, would ask.

And we don't know what the weather's gonna do, someone else says.

There's no reason to believe that it'll get bad. But if it does, I'd rather be snug in a cave than out on the route, Jerry says.

Most accidents happen going down, someone else points out.

It'd be easy to get on the wrong side of Denali Pass, another ventures.

Heck, we're not that far from high camp.

And you know what? We're not *really* lost that bad.

Gradually they convince themselves, and not incorrectly, that staying put is the option of choice.

Jerry would put it to a vote. The decision, as we know from later radio communications, is to stay put. So at about ten o'clock in the evening on Monday, July 17, they start digging snow caves, taking turns with one or more shovels, pitching in with ice axes, hands, anything that lends itself to digging and scooping.

They probably dig two caves, one for each rope team of three men. Why two caves? Simple compatibility, for one thing. The rope teams were made up to keep together those men who worked best together. Hunkering down in snow caves brings you into much more intimate contact than roping together, so those who climbed together will sleep better together.

Architectural integrity, for another. Any snow cave big enough to accommodate six climbers side by side would have to be at least ten feet wide, or twelve to fourteen feet for any kind of comfort. That width greatly increases the likelihood of roof collapse. John Ireton, of the MCA expedition, recalls that the ceiling of the cave he dug at Camp VII, originally high enough for him to sit upright, had sagged to just above his chest when he awoke the next morning. In addition, a cave mouth that wide would also be more difficult to block with packs. You *could* dig one long straight cave with enough depth to accommodate six—three in back and three in front—but that would have been a much less comfortable arrangement. (What happens when the middle guy in the back row has to pee, poop, or puke?) Plus, three men are an ideal number for burrowing into a hillside: number one hacking out snow from inside and pushing it back and number two behind him pushing snow to the cave mouth, where number three clears it away.

Either way, it would take them about three hours to make their caves. Digging at that altitude is hard work, and they'd probably need to rest often. At about quarter to eleven, while taking a break, Jerry tries to raise Eielson to tell Gordon what they're doing. There's just enough juice left in the batteries to make contact, but they fade out before Jerry can tell him anything.

SNOW CAVES ARE always too small, so you're butted up against an icy wall or other human bodies. There's inevitably a lot of rustling and shifting, burping and farting, and at least one guy will chatter until someone tells him to shut up. You don't want to go outside to pee because it will disturb your cave mates and you'll have to move all the packs that have been shoved in place to seal the cave entrance. So everyone tries to lie as still as possible, thinking about girlfriends instead of burning bladders, reminding themselves that all things pass and morning *will* arrive.

Of course, you have all those discomforts in a tent, as well. No matter how good your $850 bombproof Rumdoodle-Tex dome, it is still only nylon and aluminum and *will* be destroyed by a big enough wind. So, disconcerting, free-floating anxiety always plagues climbers (at least it did this one) trapped by big storms in tents. It's impossible not to lie there reflecting on the fact that the nylon walls of your shelter are a fraction of a millimeter thick. So your brain, despite itself, begins calculating the probability factors involved in just one tent wall or seam having a weak point, which means that you don't sleep much. When it gets really bad, you do pray—let me personalize this: *I did*—whatever your sea-level agnostic pretensions.

A cave, on the other hand, evokes the safest place you have ever been or will ever be—the womb. It's quiet enough that the loudest sound you hear is often your own breathing. The light in a snow cave is a soft, muted blue. If not literally warm, a cave is protected from wind and precipitation and therefore is as warm, relatively speaking, as any environment you're likely to find on a mountain—much more so than any tent. And by the time you put on all your down clothing and slip into your mummy bag, as long as the bag stays dry, you stay warm.

So it's not unrealistic to imagine that the six climbers, once they've settled in, blocked off their caves with packs, munched snacks, and drunk water, may feel okay about their situation. They're tired, of course, but during their 9:30 p.m. radio broadcast, they reported no one suffering from altitude or anything else.

But are they feeling anything else as they lie there listening to one another breathe? Security in their togetherness, surely. With the exception of John, these young men have known one another for years, and even John will have become, in his irascible way, part of the pack after twenty-nine days of sweating together up this mountain. Trust in their leader too. Jerry is older, at thirty-one, and more experienced, with his extensive climbing record and Antarctic forays. He's been an instructor for the U.S. Army in mountaineering safety and cold weather survival. He's calm and easygoing and always thinks first of the group. He's a man they trust. They know, too, that the other guys made it to the top and back the day before yesterday so easily that it was almost a cakewalk.

But there would be something else: the knowledge that they are lost near the top of mythic McKinley, whose upper reaches are terra incognita to them, like those blank areas on the maps used by Columbus and

Magellan that cartographers, having nothing better to supply, filled with sea monsters and demons. No gorgons or krakens up here, of course, but the unknown is life's demon in chief. And, in the end, they, like Steve Taylor, will take it with them into sleep.

Down at eielson, Gordon waits a long time with the radio in hand after the aborted 10:45 p.m. broadcast. Eventually he puts the radio back on the desk and returns to paperwork.

It is about 850 miles from the McKinley summit to the center of the Bering Sea. A storm, much more serious than the one-day blow of July 16, was birthed out there on July 14 or 15 and has been moving westward, carrying hurricane winds and a snow load of several feet, losing little strength and likely catching an afterburner boost from the jetstream.

16

TUESDAY, JULY 18
Last Words

On Tuesday, July 18, Gordon Haber might well be staring out the window of the Eielson Visitor Center, wishing he could see the mountain, which is completely obscured by low-lying clouds and hard rain. His CB radio crackles. (Well, not exactly *his* radio. The NPS had to borrow the radio from a local man named George Robinson, because the park service had no other way to communicate with the Wilcox party).

"Eielson, this is Unit One. Eielson—"

"Jerry? This is Gordy. What's up? Where are you? What happened last night? You called about quarter to eleven I guess and I heard you call and I answered but you didn't, you didn't acknowledge. I thought maybe you had radio trouble."

"We're on top, Gordy. The summit. We probably didn't copy you, ah, we had some weak batteries. In fact they're still weak right now, we ended up bivouacking as a matter of fact. It got so fogged in that we couldn't go up or we couldn't go down."

"Well, you're coming in loud and clear right here now. Ah, how long do you plan on staying on top?"

"Oh, five or ten more minutes, Gordy. Kind of cold up here." Jerry tells Gordon that the temperature is about six degrees above zero, with a fifteen-mile-per-hour wind, but he doesn't say which direction it's coming from.

At this point, Mark McLaughlin takes over the radio. "Hey, Gordy, you still sending postcards from the summit?"

"Ah, yeah, go ahead."

"I'd like to send one to my parents. Have you got a pencil and paper there?"

"Go right ahead."

"Dear Mom and Dad. Radio from the summit. A-okay. See you in a week or two. Love, Mark."

"Okay, got that. How about giving us a little description of what you can see up there. Ah, tell us how the view is right now."

"The view consists of—ah, four other guys at the moment. That's all. It's completely whited out. The—we're sitting just below the summit. You can see the wands on the summit. That's all. Over."

"Well, you didn't luck out like the last four, I guess. They had a real good view when they were up there. Do you mind just naming off the people that are up there right now?"

"Ah, sitting on the summit: Jerry Clark, Hank Janes, Dennis Luchter-hand, Mark McLaughlin. Oh! And Walt Taylor. Wouldn't want to forget him—he led all the way up."

"Okay. Say, when I talked to Joe last night—Wilcox—ah, he was won-dering what had happened to the seventh man. He thought seven were going to try for the peak."

"Seventh man is Steve Taylor and he didn't feel good at all—so he stayed in camp at seventeen-nine. He's probably wondering where we are at the moment."

"Yeah, I imagine he is."

"Jerry wanted to say—all five of us got to the summit at exactly the same time."

Here Mark gives the address to put on his postcard, but the batteries are beginning to weaken.

"Ah, I didn't read that, but we can find your address somewhere else. I think someone else ought to have it here on record."

"Well, I guess that's about all the talkin' we can do, especially when you're not copying us," Mark says.

"Okay, thanks a lot for the call. Yeah, I can't read you very well at all anymore. You're . . . very indistinct. I think your batteries are going down. Ah, just before you do cut off, what time do you want us to stand by for the next call?"

"Just eight I guess, and that's all I have."

"Okay, eight p.m. Then we'll—we'll have someone here then. Be looking forward to talking to you, and congratulations again. Ah, if nothing further, then this is KHD-six-nine-nine-zero Eielson Base, clear."

"Thanks very much. KHD-six-nine-nine-zero. Unit One, clear."

It is about fifteen minutes before noon. According to their own report, the men are healthy and uninjured. Mark feels well enough to dictate that jaunty postcard to his parents, and to emphasize Walt Taylor's leading role, and to describe the way in which they all summited at the same time, symbolic of their unity.

Neither Jerry nor Mark mentions, and Gordon Haber does not ask about, the summit team's sixth man, fiery John Russell. He was with them when they left their 17,900-foot camp the day before, but he is not with them on the summit. Why not? Why John goes unmentioned during this broadcast from the summit has been one of the tragedy's great riddles.

Various theories, none very satisfying, have been advanced. One that has never surfaced before is worth examining, because its source is the man on the other end of the radio, Gordon Haber. In a letter to Howard, Gordon stated his belief that Jerry Clark and the other four summiters agreed to say nothing about John Russell because they did not want the world to know they left him behind—alone, sick, and weak. Their hope was that the great good news of their summiting would make irrelevant whatever happened en route.

Gordon felt no particular malice toward Jerry's team, but neither did he know any of them well. His theory, however, suggests that he may have had the same low opinion of the climbers shared by many others at the park, thanks at least in part to Brad Washburn's advance warnings.

Had Gordon known the men better, he would have understood that Jerry Clark was not the kind of man—none of them were the kind of men—who would have "abandoned" John if they thought he was in danger. And even if they intentionally omitted John's name from their summit broadcast, they would still have to account for his absence later, especially if John himself felt that he had been abandoned, so the price for this omission would have been permanent ignominy greater by an order of magnitude. John was not one to give others the benefit of any doubts, or to forgive and forget. If they had left him in dire straits, he would never have let them, or the world, forget it. Under scrutiny, that theory just won't wash.

Howard believes that John was too ill to go to the summit after the bivouac, so he waited there for the others to return. Joe agrees that John was probably too sick to go to the summit, but he believes that John would have descended immediately to Camp VII.

Joe and Howard are both right in assuming that John's altitude sickness kept him from going to the summit. He was just not one of those lucky people, like Walt, with the genetic blessing of handling altitude well. Some or all of the others doubtless offered to descend to Camp VII with him. But John, gruff and profane though he may have been, was not selfish. Joe noted how, on any number of occasions, John would have hot drinks and soup waiting for people returning to camp, even after a heavy workday of his own. So he would have pointed out, gruffly and profanely, that they had encountered no crevasses on the way up, that the route down was wanded, that the weather was now fine, and that he was perfectly capable, thank you, of getting his own goddamned ass down that goddamned hill, and he wasn't going to listen to anyone gripe later that big baby John Russell made them forfeit their own chance at the summit.

Thus while the others were climbing up, John would surely have been climbing down, and would have reached Camp VII and Steve Taylor before the remaining five climbers made the summit. Still: why would they not mention him in their broadcast? I believe they simply forgot. Reaching the top at last, they were jubilant, relieved, high not only physically but emotionally, about as close to orgasmic ecstasy as you can get this side of great sex. They were also fatigued physically and mentally, hypoxic, memories and reasoning power shaved to a fraction of their sea level facility. In the weird mental neverland created by exultation and exhaustion, brains awash in the strange brew of adrenaline, endorphins, and lactic acid, the one fact of John's absence simply got lost. *They were on the summit*, and the enormity of that realization shoved everything else aside.

THE SUMMIT BROADCASTS by Jerry and Mark tell important things, though. Perhaps most significant is that they are all in good enough shape for Mark McLaughlin to describe the team as "A-okay," and to dictate a cheery postcard note to his parents. Thus bivouacking in caves the previous night, a decision that will be criticized by every expert who commented on the expedition, clearly did not leave them so debilitated that they were in imminent peril, or apparently even uncomfortable. Had any one of them been really sick or incapacitated, or had they been seriously concerned about their ability to get down safely, they would have turned around. And once on top, they would surely have alerted Gordon to any problems. They did not.

Something else: "Jerry wanted to say—all five of us got to the summit at exactly the same time." Thus they waited for all to come abreast, linked arms or held mittened hands, and strode those last few steps together, literally comrades in arms. They arrived not as individuals but, as Tenzing Norgay and Edmund Hillary did on Everest, as a *team* achieving its long-sought goal together. They not only climbed this mountain—they mounted its summit with hearts untroubled, a gift that Joe did not receive.

Their radio communication from the summit lasts about ten minutes and contains a few more than 500 words. As Jerry said to Gordon, with no view to speak of they don't plan to linger. So at noon or shortly after, they sort themselves back into two separate ropes and start down. Very soon, a storm hits.

Where are they then? Recalling the first team's progress is helpful. After arriving on the summit at 6:29 p.m. and spending about an hour and a half there, Joe's team began downclimbing and reached Archdeacon's Tower exactly thirty-nine minutes later, at 8:32 p.m.

Even allowing forty-five minutes for Jerry's team to descend that same distance, they would arrive back at their bivouac site between 12:45 and 1:15 p.m.—about when the storm makes its grand entrance.

It would be a mistake to think, as some have suggested, that downclimbing the remaining route to Camp VII would have been easy, or even advisable at this point, primarily because of how this storm materialized. I wanted to know that myself, so during my time with Howard I asked him just that: "How quickly did the storm strike?"

Howard is a big, strong man who keeps himself in shape, and to answer my question he smacked one fist into his other palm so violently that it made me jump. "Like *THAT!*" he exclaimed. "That's how fast." And he was down at 15,000 feet when it arrived. At higher altitude, weather can change even more sharply and extremely.

Jerry Clark knows how difficult the descent became for Joe's summit team, and also knows that he and his own team are, if not exhausted, certainly tired. So when the weather turns ugly, I see him calling a halt and telling the men that he doesn't like the feel of this wind. It's getting stronger, and wands may be blowing out below them. Always solicitous, he will ask if anyone is having trouble with hands or feet. Given the relatively mild temperatures, probably no one is yet.

Again, they would talk options. They can move back into the caves and see what happens. They can all keep going down. Or they can split into two groups, some going on down, others remaining in the caves.

The group would veto that last one immediately. Splitting up would violate all the mountaineering rules they have learned; it is not an option. No one is anxious to downclimb in these conditions, which, though in daylight, are worse than the ones last night. The wind, especially, is a concern. It's growing stronger even as they stand there, hunched over, shouting to hear one another. It's not a hard decision, except for one thing. What about John?

They'll have to assume he made it back down to Camp VII. He should have had ample time and weather good enough to do that. Reassured by having settled that logically, they get to work. It would take about half an hour to clear fresh snow out of the caves. The wind grows steadily stronger, snow begins to fall more heavily, and the whiteout remains impenetrable. The men crawl into their caves, then pull packs across the openings and secure them to ice axes embedded in the snow. It is about three in the afternoon on Tuesday, July 18. Jerry tries to call Eielson, but there is no answer.

Down at camp vi, early in the morning Joe and the others are basking in the same fine weather that allows Jerry Clark and his friends to see the summit after their bivouac. But by ten o'clock an ominous lenticular cloud cap, sure harbinger of a storm, has shrouded the summit, and more clouds can be seen slithering down the mountain toward their own camp. By noon, heavy snow is falling, driven by wind strong enough to make the men feel as though their faces are being whipped.

There is still no real crisis to manage, so Wayne Merry's July 18 entry in his record of communications with the expedition is a single paragraph saying that Jerry's party made the summit safely and in decent weather—0 degrees Fahrenheit, fifteen-mile-per-hour winds, whiteout. "Seemed to be in good spirits and mentioned no difficulty other than getting lost the previous day."

Yet without anyone on the ground or the mountain noticing, the situation has changed dramatically. Until July 17, a single party of twelve men was climbing the mountain. On that day, however, they split into separate parties of five (descending to Camp VI) and seven (remaining at Camp VII). The next day, the party of seven split again, becoming two parties of six and one (Steve Taylor). The day after that, the party of six becomes two parties of five and one (John Russell). When John descends to Camp VII, he turns Steve's party of one into a party of two.

So on July 18, there are, in descending order, Jerry and four companions at Archdeacon's Tower ridge at about 19,500 feet, Steve and John in Camp VII at 17,900 feet, and Joe's group of five in Camp VI at 15,000 feet. In addition, there is Bill Babcock's MCA Expedition of six down on the Muldrow at 10,000 feet. At the mountain's base, park service officials are occupying three different offices separated by a hundred miles; and the Alaska Rescue Group is in Anchorage, 180 miles to the south.

Tough bill babcock and his team spend this Tuesday, before the storm hits, down on the Muldrow, ferrying eighty-five-pound loads from 8,600 feet to 10,000 feet, making the round-trip in an incredible two hours. The weather is pleasant, the temperature about 25 degrees Fahrenheit, though whiteout blankets their route most of the day.

While they're doing that, at some point during the morning, perhaps even while the summit climbers are radioing their good news to Gordon Haber, Steve Taylor hears footsteps crunching toward the tent. The weather is still clear. He scrambles out and is astonished to see John Russell, alone, trudging toward him.

Even in his weakened state, John reaches Camp VII during this spell of mild weather. But the descent has left him spent, shoulders slumped, head down, moving slowly. His beard and mustache are clotted with snotsicles, and he almost falls over shucking out of his pack.

Sucking air, John flops down on the snow in front of Steve's tent. He is pale and can't seem to catch his breath. Steve removes John's crampons, pulls him inside, and gives him a drink, perhaps warm Tang or grape Kool-Aid, two of the expedition's powdered drinks of choice. For the first time on the mountain, John isn't growling and grousing. He accepts the help and drink gratefully and explains what happened in a dialogue probably similar to this.

Got good and fucking lost last night.

Where are the others?

Ahhhh, they went for the summit this morning when it got clear.

They just left you?

Hell, no. I told 'em to get their asses up that mountain, buddy.

And you couldn't make it?

I'm a beat dog, Stevo. Altitude's got me down.

So how did you all get lost yesterday?

Some *asshole* broke the fucking wands in half and stuck 'em in like that. You couldn't see 'em for shit. I couldn't believe it.

Steve and John would certainly discuss trying to go back down to Camp VI, where Joe and the others are, but John says, no way. It's too windy, he's too tired, and they need to wait for Jerry Clark and the other guys. The memory of his own struggling descent would still be fresh in his mind, and it was probably scary. Being alone on that mountain was enough by itself. But he was also tired and ill, and may have had to keep sitting down, and when he sat down he wanted to go to sleep, and he knew that if he did, he'd probably never wake up, so he had grabbed handfuls of snow and slapped them hard into his face.

Steve and John don't talk for a while after that. John drinks endless cups of liquid and munches snacks—fudge, peanut butter cups, Logan bread. Finally Steve says he should try to go out and find the other cans of Blazo, but the wind has kicked up and he doesn't move right away. John doesn't move either; he just lies in his bag, panting softly, eyes closed.

After a time, Steve would call up the energy to dress and go outside on a fuel hunt. Just before crawling through the tent's tunnel entrance, he might glance back at John—big, red-bearded, piratical John, the strongest man he's ever known and maybe the roughest—now curled up small in his sleeping bag, hands under his chin, snoring, groaning softly every now and again like a child in a troubled dream.

Down at camp vi, Joe hears the news from Eielson: Steve Taylor stayed in Camp VII. Jerry Clark's team, after bivouacking the night before, made the summit at 11:30 a.m. that morning, July 18. Joe is surprised to learn about the bivouac, but he is actually encouraged by the fact that the men holed up and then were able to continue climbing. This tells him that they must not have been bad off in the morning. He knows that Jerry is prudent in the extreme and feels certain that his deputy leader would never have taken up a team with serious problems.

But then the weather begins to deteriorate; 8 p.m. comes and goes with no radio contact. Joe eventually snuggles back down into his sleeping bag, with a small, sharp fear beginning to gnaw inside him as he drifts off. Much later he awakens with a start. Deep into the long night, Anshel suddenly exclaims, "Listen! I hear voices!"

They both sit up, straining to hear. Though the wind is so loud that Joe doesn't understand how Anshel could have heard anything, he unzips the tent and looks out. He listens for a long time, but there is only the wind wrapping their tent with ghostly shrouds of snow.

17

WEDNESDAY, JULY 19
We Will Live to Tell Stories

This morning, July 19, the storm is still raging over Jerry Clark and his cave mates, but their bladders are raging as well. They discuss how to deal with this, because the wind is blowing sixty to seventy miles per hour, with stronger gusts, producing a brutal windchill. They're not inexperienced at these things, of course, so someone produces a piss bottle, just a quart plastic bottle like their water bottles except for the important difference of bearing the word *piss* written in indelible ink, and they get to work. They've been in the caves only twelve hours or so at this point, so they probably still have the energy, and inclination, to joke a bit about yellow snow and don't mix up those bottles, boys, and—going to the next logical step—wondering what happens when it's time to take a crap.

Their sleeping bags will be a bit damp but still holding up okay, so nobody's hypothermic yet. Jerry and Mark, the only two men wearing leather boots, are almost certainly experiencing cold toes, but they can still keep blood flowing and their toes feeling alive by wriggling them conscientiously.

To produce drinking water, they will melt snow with the stove that Jerry, ever the cautious one, made sure to bring, fuel tank filled. They *will* be thinking about water now—how much they have and how much they can make. The standard recommendation for active climbers' liquid intake at their altitude is a gallon per person per day, or at least enough to keep urine gin-clear. Because they're just lying in snow caves, not exerting themselves, they can probably get by on three quarts a day each.

But for the five of them, that's still almost four gallons of water per day needed to stave off dehydration, which itself hastens the onset of frost-bite and altitude sickness, including that malady's two most dangerous killers, pulmonary and cerebral edema.

Assuming that their Optimus 111B's fuel tank is close to full (it uses a pressurized gas tank in operation, so the tank is never completely "topped off"), it will have a burn time of about three hours. It takes roughly twelve minutes to melt enough snow to produce a quart of water at their altitude, which means they'll be able to make about fifteen quarts, or almost four gallons. They will have enough to allow for 80 percent of the recommended fluid for one day, 40 percent for two, 20 percent for three, et cetera. It's a cruel calculus indeed, because the more water they need, the less they will have. If they plan to make the water last for two days, they'll each be able to drink about 1.6 quarts per day. Not great, but stranded climbers have survived for days on a lot less. Jerry would advise the others to drink only half of their water now; he knows that a McKinley storm could easily stretch out another day.

Down at camp VI, Wednesday brings higher winds and heavier snow all night and into the morning. But at about ten o'clock, the clouds part briefly and Joe can see North and South Peaks, though not Camp VII itself. No men are moving anywhere. *They're going to be stuck in high camp another day*, he realizes.

The men with Joe pass this long day dozing, munching snacks, reading paperbacks. At eight that evening, Joe unzips his tent door far enough to toss out the radio's dipole antenna—a long, T-shaped wire. The wind blows it out straight, like a streaming pennant. He switches on the radio, listening for a call from high camp. Nothing. He raises seasonal ranger George Perkins at Eielson, talks briefly, then signs off. It is at this moment that he knows for the first time, beyond doubt, that something is wrong. Later he will write, "A sinking emptiness gripped my emotions."

If they could call, they would call. If they don't call, it's because they can't.

That frightens him, but it also makes clear that there is only one option: he and the other healthy climbers at VI will have to go back up. *Now.* To Howard, who has been standing outside Joe's tent, he proposes that the two of them and Paul start back up at once. Howard, fully exposed to the 50-mile-per-hour winds, feels as though ice crystals are flaying his face, and suggests that this weather is no time to try a climb back to high camp. Joe, incensed, asks whether Howard, having made the summit, doesn't want to go up anymore. There is no little irony in the fact that they are having this conversation within arm's reach, but neither can actually see the other.

Fourteen years later, Joe will write in *White Winds,* "Realizing that I would not be able to budge Howard and Paul out of camp until morning, I reluctantly agreed to wait. I tried to contain my boiling temper in fitful sleep."

The storm blows on with a distinctive, if schizophrenic, character. For periods, winds lessen and snow falls so heavily that it accumulates faster than they can shovel it away from their tent. Then for a while high winds resume, blowing down-mountain, only to be displaced soon by heavier snow. The cycle repeats and repeats. It is the result of two storms fighting for possession of the mountain. Later analysis will show that the strong southwester that had blown in from the Bering Sea was bumping shoulders with an occluded front to the northeast. This opposition is a major reason for the storm's record-breaking length.

Up at camp vii, throughout Wednesday Steve and John will be battered in their tent by fiercer winds and heavier snow than those buffeting Camp VI. It's not easy to imagine what it's like being trapped in a tent in a windstorm of this magnitude, but here's a way to get an approximation. Lie down in the back of a friend's pickup truck on a winter night while it cruises along an interstate highway at about sixty miles per hour. To simulate sticking your head out of the tent every once in a while, stand up so that your head rises above the truck cab's roof. To simulate going outside to pee, in case you forgot your piss bottle . . . well, best not do that. In a truck in winter you'll experience the wind's power and roar, the violent bouncing and buffeting, the paralyzing cold—everything but the altitude. You can get some idea of that, too, by holding your breath for thirty seconds out of every minute, because air at their altitude has about 50 percent of the oxygen it contains at sea level.

Surely Steve and John cannot sleep, so they will lie awake, stiff with cold and fear, grabbing the tent's center pole every time a particularly vicious gust hits. At some point the wind becomes so fierce that they have to sit up and clutch the pole against their chests, bracing it with their whole bodies. They will have to do this in shifts. The pole is life. If it snaps, the tent will lose its structural integrity and the wind will tear it apart quickly. Without its protection, they will die.

They are both wondering, I imagine, just what happened here. Like most twenty-two year olds, they have not spent a great deal of time thinking about death in the abstract and even less time contemplating their own deaths, though it is true that the Vietnam war has young men their age thinking more about such things than any similar group since the 1940s.

But neither considered, in his wildest imaginings, that he might die on this trip. It's been a lot of little annoyances, they both understand that. But something else has finally dawned on them: Whoever said this climb would be easy was full of shit. At some point, if they talk about Dennis's premonition, John may be persuaded to tell Steve about the dream he had lower down, that big jet airliner landing on the Muldrow, those people opening the door and calling out, *Come on with us, we're going to heaven,* and how he told them, *Can't go with you now, I gotta climb Mount McKinley. . . .*

THINKING ABOUT THE seven men up high, I wonder when players in a tragedy realize that the story is about their own destruction. When that iceberg sliced open the *Titanic* like a beer can, did the passengers think they were going to die? They were frightened, surely. But didn't they just expect some uncomfortable time in open lifeboats, then a rescue, then telling the story for the rest of their lives?

A close friend of mine named Bob was diagnosed with pancreatic cancer, which is the Judge Roy Bean of cancers. Nobody gets out alive. Bob was brilliant, well read, nationally known in his field. He spent time online and in medical school libraries, so he knew about pancreatic tumors. But eighteen months later, hours from death, he swam up through the morphine fog and looked at me with shocked eyes and asked,

"What happened, Jim? What the hell *happened?*" All that time, he had never really thought he would die. We never really do.

Did the young Smokejumpers trying to outrun that blowup in Mann

Gulch think it was going to incinerate them? Apparently not, not even in the final seconds when the tidal wave of fire was about to wash over them. One man, Walter Rumsey, told investigators later that he was watching scenery as he sprinted up the hillside, trying to outrun the racing flames behind him. Another, David Navon, a 101st Airborne Division paratrooper who had survived the siege of Bastogne, stopped to take snapshots of the blaze running him down. Rumsey made it, seemingly for no reason other than luck; Navon did not. The fire burned him and twelve others to death.

Jerry Clark, Hank Janes, Dennis Luchterhand, Mark McLaughlin, and Walt Taylor, though still trapped in their snow caves on the evening of Wednesday July 19, and Steve and John in their tent at Camp VII, do not really think they are going to die. They are sore and stiff and starting to suffer from the cold as their damp down bags lose insulative power. Some certainly are enduring altitude-induced headaches, and they are all hungry and thirsty, but it has not yet begun to be truly bad.

They will be experiencing fear to varying degrees, and impatience with the storm, and will pass the time by dozing and daydreaming and worrying. They will certainly feel gratitude for the warmth and security of the other men's presence. But in the deep place where every one of us exists alone, they are all thinking the same thing that the *Titanic* passengers and my friend Bob and the Smokejumpers thought:

This will pass. My life will go on. I will live to tell stories about this.

18

THURSDAY, JULY 20
Where Is the Cavalry?

At five o'clock on Thursday morning, July 20, Joe is awakened not by screaming wind but by sudden silence. He recalls urging everybody into motion. Howard's recollection is that *he* got things going. Howard and Paul gobble Jell-O and dried fruit, hurriedly stuff their packs with clothes and sleeping bags, a Colorado stove, kerosene. Joe loads three gallons of Blazo into his pack, and they hit the trail by six-thirty.

The good weather window slams shut almost immediately. As they are snowshoeing out of camp, with Joe leading their three-man rope, the wind picks up and heavy snowfall resumes. Soon they are struggling straight into winds of forty miles per hour that only get stronger as they climb. The snow falls so thickly that Paul's tracks are filled in by the time Howard, just fifty feet back, reaches them seconds later.

By nine o'clock they have traveled only three-quarters of a mile, and conditions are worsening rapidly. Joe stops beside a small ice hump. Howard and Paul join him, and Joe tries Eielson on the radio. But Eielson has no weather information.

The three men stand there, assaulted by the wind, silently knowing that they will not be able to climb to Camp VII in these conditions. If the wands behind them blow out and the track is obscured, they may not even be able to find their way back to their own camp. But they are tortured by the knowledge that the other men are stranded up there.

Howard and Paul know the decision must be made, but they can't make it. That responsibility falls to Joe, the leader, so he makes the call.

They will leave the fuel there on the trail so that they can pick it up when they come back. Howard argues that that makes no sense, because it won't do anybody one bit of good there in the snow, but Joe has made his decision. They return to Camp VI without the fuel.

Later that day, Joe will print in ragged block letters in his small expedition diary,

> Wilcox, Paul, Howard start out from 15000' with fuel to check on high camp team at 530 AM. After 4 hours and only 3/4 mile in windy blizzard conditions we run out of wands and are forced to turn back.

It is the last entry he will make, because very soon he and the other four men at Camp VI will be fighting for their own lives.

At about the same time that Joe and the others turn around on the trail, Jerry Clark and his men would be talking about what to do, with the storm entering its third day. They had spent the night of Monday the seventeenth in their snow caves, then went to the summit on Tuesday the eighteenth, were trapped by a storm near their snow caves on the descent, spent Tuesday night in the snow caves while the storm kept blowing so hard that it seemed sometimes the mountain shook, remained trapped all day Wednesday, and then spent Wednesday night in the caves.

So by now, on Thursday morning, if they've been careful, they still may have half a quart of water each, but probably not more. They may have run out of food, having packed only enough to get them to the summit and back.

The men were too experienced to gobble all their food on the seventeenth, before heading to the summit. On the eighteenth they would have eaten a disciplined breakfast, then probably nibbled some more on the summit, as much to celebrate as from hunger. That afternoon, after digging out and reoccupying their snow caves, they would have eaten again, and probably a bit more later that evening.

The nineteenth would have been a long day, and they surely would have nibbled a lot. The longer a storm lasts, the greater becomes the need to believe that this is the last day, for sure. And that makes it easier to drain food and water supplies. Vince Lombardi said that fatigue makes cowards of us all, but it also makes it harder to do anything, even ration snacks, with discipline. So by Thursday morning, July 20, unless they had brought an unusually large amount of food for a summit bid, or were unusually disciplined in rationing themselves, they probably had little, if any, food left.

But everyone is still alive on Thursday morning. Unless altitude sickness has struck someone hard, which seems unlikely just now, they are not in mortal danger yet. The two men suffering most from altitude were John and Dennis. John has gone down to join Steve at Camp VII, and we know that Dennis will be one of the last men standing. The wind is terrible, but the temperature has not plunged, so Jerry Clark and his men would not yet be suffering seriously from hypothermia. But they are beginning to weaken, and this process will accelerate the longer they remain, and they all know that. It's time, once again, to talk options.

There are three, Jerry would say. We can stay put and wait for the cavalry. People will be wondering where we are. They'll get a plane up.

Planes can't fly in this weather, someone else would put in.

Well, *some* can, Jerry would correct, because from his Antarctic days he knows that specially equipped C-130s, the big four-engine prop-driven aircraft called Hercules, which still chase hurricanes today, might be able to get up in this weather, at least to orbit the summit.

So where the hell are they?

"They"—C-130s, jets, helicopters, army troops—had pulled out all the stops just six months earlier to rescue the Winter Expedition trio, and every one of these men would have known about it. The Winter Expedition and its rescue operation had made national news. It's true that helicopters couldn't fly until the storm was pretty much over, but the big planes could get up sooner.

Jerry doesn't know where they are. But it doesn't matter, he would say. We have to take care of ourselves. So we all go down together, or some of us can stay put and others go down.

We shouldn't break up the group, someone would caution, perhaps Mark, who's involved with search-and-rescue work with the Oregon outdoor and climbing organization called the Obsidians and knows the inviolability of that rule.

They decide that the best option is to sit tight but be ready to make a run for it when the weather breaks. All for one and one for all. For the time being, they will stay put, stay together, wait it out.

Even with hindsight, it's hard to argue with the logic of that decision, frustrating though it must have been for them. And there is something else. Feelings of helplessness are one of the hardest things about being trapped this way, because helplessness breeds hopelessness. Crammed into their caves, hungry and thirsty and groggy, they have felt helpless. But now, this semblance of a plan has rekindled enough hope to hold its evil twin, desperation, at bay.

After the storm sends Joe, Howard, and Paul packing back to Camp VI, Joe raises Eielson, with Howard standing by to overhear the communication. Now convinced beyond a doubt that the men up high are in trouble, Joe makes his first overflight request, instructing Gordon to tell the Alaska Rescue Group (ARG) this: If there is no radio contact with Jerry's team at 8:00 p.m., he wants an overflight of Camp VII, with an airdrop of fuel and radios and batteries, and a count of men in that camp. Gordon assures Joe that he will make the call.

Shortly after, the old black dial telephone, heavy as a rock, rings on Wayne Merry's gray desk. He expects that the call will be yet another report about damage that this storm is doing to roads, bridges, buildings, tents, and vehicles. It already washed out several sections of road between Wonder Lake and park headquarters, and it shows no sign of letting up. It looks to be one of the worst and longest storms he's seen up here.

But the call is from Gordon, who has had a disturbing conversation with Joe Wilcox. He and four of his people are down at 15,000 feet, but the other seven haven't been heard from since Tuesday at 11:30 a.m., when they radioed that they had made the summit and all were okay. Wilcox said that the men up high have food but are probably out of fuel, or very low, and he asked that the ARG be notified for an overflight and an airdrop of fuel and radios if there's no contact with Jerry's party at 8 p.m.

Wayne acknowledges the request. Be sure, he tells Gordon, to talk to Wilcox at 4 and 8 p.m.

THE ARG, OR Alaska Rescue Group, is in 1967 a volunteer search-and-rescue organization in Anchorage. Joe and Howard signed a standard agreement in which the ARG guaranteed to come to the expedition's aid in an emergency, and Joe's expedition guaranteed to cover costs. The National Park Service then required all expeditions attempting McKinley to sign a contract for emergency support service with some such organization. Because the ARG is in Anchorage, and enjoys a kind of unofficial "favored nation" status with the NPS, most expeditions use it.

This NPS policy is not a bad idea in theory, but, as Wayne Merry confirmed, "in those days it was pretty much pro forma." In addition, Anchorage is about 180 miles as the crow flies from McKinley, and in 1967 Alaska, that's a long way. More importantly, it is about 20,000 vertical feet lower. The ARG does not own any aircraft, so it must subcontract with private air services or, in extreme cases, get help from the U.S. Air Force. Procuring assistance from the first group is unbelievably expensive; from the second, unbelievably complicated.

After talking with Gordon, Wayne calls *his* boss, Chief Ranger Art Hayes, to notify him of the developing situation. Art, in turn, calls the ARG's Gary Hansen in Anchorage. The ARG log kept by Hansen from that point on indicates that Art spoke with or left a message for him at 2:15 p.m. that day, alerting him "there may be trouble."

When Wayne hangs up after talking with Gordon, he is concerned but still not terribly alarmed. From his review of the climbers' autobiographies, he knows that Jerry Clark is one of the most experienced members of the expedition, a man who has mountaineered all over the Northwest and in the Antarctic. He knows that Mark McLaughlin, Dennis Luchterhand, Hank Janes, and Walt Taylor had solid lower 48 climbing experience as well. Steve Taylor was one of the rookies, but Wayne knows that he didn't go for the summit. And he knows that the other rookie, Anshel Schiff, headed down to Camp VI on July 17. Still, on July 20, Wayne begins keeping a written record of conversations and events.

Gordon Haber, the last man to speak with Jerry Clark and his team, recalled Wayne Merry and his capabilities; his admiration for the man remains sharp. Every person I spoke with who was familiar with the tragedy, in fact, seconded Gordon's assessment of Wayne.

"He was my direct supervisor," Gordon told me, "and I can tell you that he did a remarkable job with what he had to work with. Wayne was the competent professional on the scene and he did everything he could." Here Gordon paused before adding, "But he was greatly thwarted by the people in the headquarters office."

At camp VI, as Joe, Anshel, Howard, and Paul stand outside their tents at a bit after noon, the sky begins clearing. Before long they can see the sun and the whole upper mountain: South Peak, Farthing Horn, Archdeacon's Tower, Denali Pass. They are not in line of sight with the high camp, but they will be able to see anyone descending as soon as they come over the lip of the Upper Icefall. It's impossible to imagine how relieved Joe Wilcox must feel at this moment, knowing that those up high, even led by as conservative a man as Jerry Clark, will seize this good weather to get down.

We don't know for sure what happens next. But here's what I believe is the most reasonable and likely scenario. Almost a vertical mile above Joe, at about fifteen minutes before one, Jerry Clark stands outside the snow caves with the other four climbers. The sky is beautifully, blessedly clear, whiteout dissipated, temperature a few degrees above zero, wind down to a niggling twenty miles per hour. In other words, virtually perfect downclimbing weather.

This is the break they've been waiting for. There's not much talk. They want to hurry, stuffing gear into packs, fumbling on crampons, mittens, goggles, finding their ice axes. They *try* to hurry, and probably feel as though they are moving quickly, but in fact they cannot be. Whether they realize it or not, they're in the same weird fog that Joe recognized while trying to put on crampons for his own summit day:

> Simple tasks like strapping on my crampons required great concentration and an unreasonable amount of time. The alarming revelation was that this functional slowing did not register mentally. I felt that I was performing at my accustomed speed. My watch seemed to be running fast!

In the bright sunlight, Jerry and his men are a colorful crew—orange and red and green parkas, orange and red wind pants, green and yellow gaiters, green and red Kelty packs. But they are stiff, sore, and tired from their long cave stay, hungry and thirsty and depleted, so when they do get moving their progress is slow and halting. It's a virtual certainty that they will not make it a hundred yards before having to stop. Someone's crampon will come loose, or goggles will fog, or perhaps, as was the case with Jerry Lewis, the worst off will nearly collapse after not very far at all, requiring all the rest to stop until he recovers and can continue.

When they do, some will be counting steps, the mountaineer's time-honored way of burrowing into the mind to hide from discomfort and impatience. All will certainly be working hard to keep from swinging wildly between ecstatic relief and debilitating fear, relief that they are finally moving, and fear of how far they must go.

Down at wonder Lake, still socked in, Wayne Merry reviews everything he has learned. Wilcox has said that the men up high are probably out of fuel, and must be running out of food as well. Wilcox has also requested an overflight to drop fuel and a radio, and to count the people in that camp. He said that he would pay for it. But what concerns Wayne most is that the men of Jerry Clark's team have not been heard from for two days. He knows that they have a radio, and that they were able to broadcast from the summit on July 18, at which time they sounded okay and reported no problems.

He sorts through scenarios. The radio batteries may have given out. The radio itself may have stopped working. They may not be in a line-of-sight position from which they can broadcast. They brought smoke flares to the high camp but may not have taken them to the summit. And if they have them, they may be reluctant to use them; if they're okay and send up orange smoke, it might be mistaken for a distress signal. If they are in distress, people down low seeing smoke might misinterpret that as a sign that the men are okay; the other team had set off an orange flare to celebrate. There's no set protocol for using the flares to signal.

Wayne is moving from a state of concern to a grimmer awareness. He knows two things. One is that there are too many possibilities to be able to sort through them and arrive at any kind of likely conclusion. The other is that he and his agency can afford to assume only one thing: the worst. Accordingly, he begins drafting plans for an all-out rescue operation that would be directed from his Wonder Lake Ranger Station.

WHEN THE WIND hits again, Jerry's group, thankfully, is still in the lee of rocky outcrops behind and north of Archdeacon's Tower. From this vantage point, they can see the orange and red tents of the high camp, but the wind is already frightening. So close, and yet so far.

Jerry knows that if the wind gets much stronger, it could literally blow them off the mountain. He estimates it as a steady seventy to eighty miles per hour. It would be insane to venture onto the exposed spine of Denali Pass. They could try going straight down the face below Archdeacon's Tower to Camp VII, but days ago he could see from Camp VII that there is a big ice cliff down there. They could try to go around the ice cliff, or rappel down it, but some of them will likely not have the strength to do that, just as Jerry Lewis could not have done that during his own, much less harrowing, descent.

This time, there's no huddle, no discussion. Jerry makes the decision, and it is the only one he can conceive that will not kill them.

We gotta go back! he yells over the wind. They hadn't bothered to rope up when they left the caves, because they had been over the route already and knew that it was safe. They also didn't want to take the time. So they all just turn around and start back up the way they had come.

It is harrowing, the most frightening and difficult thing that any of them have done in the mountains. The wind has become unreal. A couple of them are surfers, and this feels as though they are being smashed by a huge wave. During especially violent gusts, they drop to hands and knees and claw their way along, depending on their ice axes to keep them stuck to the mountain.

WHAT DID JOHN and Steve try to do during the three hours of good weather? It's possible to produce a likely reconstruction of their experience at Camp VII on this day, but it will be easier to do that after we know more about what Bill Babcock and his MCA team find there a week later.

Down at camp vi, the calm weather lasts a bit less than three hours, after which blanketing snowfall and fifty-mile-per-hour winds resume. All the men retreat to their respective tents. Because Joe and Anshel have pitched their tent broadside to the wind, they must keep shoveling it out. Between bouts of digging, they lie in their mummy bags and talk. Joe will say later that it was here, during the bad days at Camp VI, that he formed a relationship with Anshel that continues to this day.

They talk, of course, about the men up high, dissecting various theories of what might have happened to them. After a while, Joe realizes that the older man has changed. His face is leaner, angular, his eyes more confident. When he speaks, his voice is firmer and calmer than at any time in the expedition.

"You know," Anshel tells Joe, "I think to not try the summit with the second team was the most important decision I have ever made in my life."

In anchorage on Thursday, Gary Hansen, having been alerted in the early afternoon by Art Hayes, is working the phones. He first calls Captain Flanik of the Rescue Coordination Center (RCC) at 5 p.m., to inform him of the developing emergency, which may require support such as that provided to the Winter Expedition team. Then he calls back Art Hayes, leaving a message asking for more details about the Wilcox party's situation. About four hours later, at 9:15 p.m., Hayes returns Gary's call and tells him that the "Lower Party" (meaning Joe at Camp VI) has requested an overflight to count people at Camp VII and to airdrop supplies. Yes, Wilcox will reimburse ARG for the costs. Gary calls Paul Crews, another ARG official, but there's no answer. Then he calls pilot Lowell Thomas to ask what kind of plane could make an airdrop this high in this weather. Thomas tells him that a powerful turboprop airplane called a Turbo Beaver, owned by an area man named Ward Gay, will do the trick. Gary calls Gay. No answer. It's 9:50 p.m. He next tries to find some CB radios. Though it's long after closing hours, he calls a Mr. McFarland, who owns a company called Communications Engineering, to see if he can check out three sets that the ARG keeps on reserve there.

At 4 p.m. on Thursday, July 20, Wayne speaks directly with Joe to get more facts. What he learns prompts him to begin keeping a formal record of events and communications: "Log of Wilcox Expedition Rescue." His entry for this radio contact concludes,

> *Wilcox was told that under present conditions, his team was the best hope for assistance for the upper party if assistance was needed, as they were nearby, acclimatized, equipped, and feeling strong.* He understood this and planned to move up as soon as weather permitted. [Emphasis added]

Wayne also tells Joe that the ARG has been alerted and that if there is an overflight, he will be billed for it. Joe again okays that, and repeats, firmly, that he wants local pilot Don Sheldon alerted if the ARG cannot fly. This is his second request for an overflight. Wayne confirms that a go-ahead on the flight will be transmitted to ARG at 8 p.m. if the upper camp is not heard from then.

In 1967, Don Sheldon is already referred to so commonly as "legendary Don Sheldon" that you could be forgiven for thinking that the superlative is actually part of his legal name, "Legendary Don" Sheldon, as in former middleweight champion "Marvelous Marvin" Hagler. Sheldon has plucked climbers and other victims of the Alaskan wilderness from more harrowing places than anyone could remember, risking his own life countless times to save others. The Right Stuff, Alaskan version. Sheldon's unbelievable flying skills are exceeded only by his courage. To paraphrase F. Scott Fitzgerald, the very brave are different from you and me. In addition to his richly deserved fame as a pilot, Don is known as outspoken and feisty—an airborne equivalent of Brad Washburn, who happens to be one of his close friends.

At 8 p.m., fifty-six hours after the summit team was last heard from, Joe speaks on the radio to seasonal ranger George Perkins, who has relieved Gordon Haber at Eielson.

"Have you heard from Unit One?" asks Joe.

"Negative—we've heard nothing."

"Neither have we, and we have seen nothing all day . . . Go ahead with the air observation." It is Joe's third overflight request.

"Okay, little more information that Wayne wanted from you. First of all, how's your weather—temperature, wind, visibility?"

"Visibility is good. Temperature has been—never been below zero. The wind is . . . inconsistent from the southwest. The windchill factor is tremendous. I'd say it'd be the equivalent to forty below . . . shoveling out the camp." Joe estimates that the wind is blowing at least fifty miles per hour, and that they can see the top of the Lower Icefall.

George tells Joe, echoing Wayne's earlier statements, "*Well, at this time it looks like your team there is the best hope for the guys up at seventeen-nine. You're the closest and acclimatized. You should move out as soon as possible.*" [Emphasis added]

Joe repeats what he told Wayne during the 4 p.m. call: They will make another try to climb to Camp VII the next morning, weather permitting.

Howard, standing outside, hears Joe's end of the conversation and asks if he's planning to try for the high camp again. Joe replies that they don't have any choice—they must start up as soon as they have decent weather. All of Howard's experience in the mountains is still telling him that it is a bad idea, but he is unaware that Wayne and George didn't suggest or hint but *told* Joe to climb back to Camp VII as soon as possible. Thus Joe is now compelled not only by his own feelings of responsibility for the men trapped up high, but by the directives of two National Park Service officials who have placed primary responsibility for rescue squarely on his shoulders.

Down on the ground, no one calls Sheldon.

On THURSDAY MORNING, Bill Babcock and his MCA companions, 3,550 vertical feet below Joe's group and almost 8,000 feet below Jerry's, awake to several inches of new snow, with more falling and the visibility zero. Having wanded the route from the base of Karstens Ridge up to their camp at 11,550 feet, they keep bulling eighty-five-pound packs up the ridge's steep shoulder. With everything up, they even consider going all the way to Browne Tower, but (probably to everyone's relief) the wind kicks up, and the snowfall increases, dumping two feet of fresh, dangerous powder on the sharp ridge, so that's that.

The first thing they do on this exposed spine of rock and snow—after dropping those monster packs—is build an igloo. Only then, with safe refuge assured, do they pitch tents. The high winds and whiteout continue. They are now trapped by the same storm that has imprisoned Joe's team at Camp VI, the two men at Camp VII, and the five others up high.

On THURSDAY EVENING, in Camp VI, Howard, Jerry Lewis, and Paul settle into their sleeping bags. The wind outside sounds as though it is increasing. In his book, Howard recalled their last words of the evening.

Jerry says, "Now I lay me down to sleep."

"I pray the Lord my soul to keep," Howard adds.

"If I die before I wake," Paul intones.

"I pray the Lord my soul to take," Howard finishes their group prayer.

FRIDAY, JULY 21
A Most Unusual Storm

On Friday morning, the storm is growing worse, astonishing every climber on the mountain, including the experienced members of maverick stockbroker Boyd Everett's audacious South Face Expedition. Before coming to McKinley, Everett organized and led expeditions to Mount Logan and Mount Saint Elias and experienced bad weather on both. Even so, the 1967 July storm is unlike anything he previously encountered, and he makes a point of noting this in his expedition report: "The duration and violence of this storm seemed to be unusual even for Mount McKinley." And even with that, because many veteran McKinley climbers believe that weather is often worse on the mountain's high northern reaches than on its southern side, Everett may be experiencing a milder version of the storm that hit Joe's expedition.

At Camp VI, conditions are bearing out that theory. The Coloradoans' tent is stretched balloon-tight by unrelenting wind and could explode at any minute. If that happens, they will die. They are now in nothing less than an arctic hurricane, as Howard's description in *The Hall of the Mountain King* illustrates:

> It was not possible to stand outside the tents without being flattened by the wind. Breathing while outside was extremely difficult. If a man faced into the wind, he could not exhale. If he turned his back on the wind, a partial vacuum was created in front of his face, pumping out his lungs as though with a pulmotor, thus preventing

him from inhaling. A six-foot journey outside the tent was a major risk.

Six feet. Their world has shrunk to sixty square feet of safety, give or take, with sanctuary assured only by nylon walls no thicker than a tissue.

During the morning radio contact with Eielson, Joe estimates the wind to be blowing a steady fifty miles per hour, gusting to 65 miles per hour and higher. Howard thinks it's even worse: gusts approaching a hundred miles per hour.

Joe and Howard both know that if conditions are this bad at 15,000 feet, what they must be like up higher beggars the imagination. Nevertheless, later in the morning, Joe broaches the idea of mounting a rescue climb back to Camp VII. Howard's response, at least as perceived by Joe, is cool. What, Howard asks, could they accomplish by returning to Camp VII? Even if they reach it, which is probably unlikely, they won't be in any condition to help seven men who will be in even worse shape.

Worsening weather soon moots the issue. It becomes so bad that even Joe cannot see his way clear to a return trip, abandoning any hope of reascending and in fact growing more concerned whether he and the others at Camp VI will be able to get *themselves* down. Indeed, as the storm peaks on this day, life rapidly deteriorates into a struggle for survival at Camp VI. Later in the afternoon, Anshel goes outside to urinate, and when he returns from this brief excursion his hands are frozen white. Joe brings them back to life under his armpits, where they feel like bricks of ice.

A bit later Joe himself goes out to shovel the drifts off their tent. Before he can do anything, the wind picks him up and he is suddenly airborne, flying like Superman or, perhaps more accurately, a windblown bug. At the last moment he grabs a tent guy line and arrests his flight, but it is a terrifying experience. On the other, "milder" side of McKinley, members of the Western States Expedition, climbing the West Buttress route, will be blown forty feet through the air. Deposited by a moment's lull, they save themselves only by clinging to rocks, where they are whipped about like bedsheets on a clothesline.

In all his many days on mountains, nothing like this has ever happened to Joe, who weighs 195 pounds with all his climbing gear and clothing on. Snatching the shovel before it, too, blows away, Joe crawls back to the tent, hugging the ground like an infantryman under fire. Sky-diving simulators—big, padded wind tunnels positioned vertically like silos—must generate 120- to 140-mile-per-hour winds to keep a human body aloft. Wind that strong no longer behaves like a gas or even a fluid; skysurfers (skydivers with snowboards on their feet) speak of "standing" on the air column beneath their boards. The strongest sustained wind I ever experienced was about 70 miles per hour. Trying to move against it was like standing neck deep in a riptide.

As hours pass without the storm abating, Joe and Anshel cannot shovel fast enough to keep their tent from being buried. At about ten o'clock that night, they are forced to make a choice; risk the danger of staying put, or bail out of their own tent and seek shelter with the Coloradoans. Anshel dreads the move only slightly less than Joe. Anshel is worried that Howard and his two mates won't let him and Joe in.

"Don't ask them. Just tell them that we're moving in," Joe says, and Anshel does.

Howard and the others do make room ungrudgingly for the new arrivals, rearranging themselves so that the five men end up lying squeezed shoulder to shoulder. Each man has about eighteen inches of space, which is exactly the width of your computer keyboard. With two groups of big men who do not much like each other crammed tightly in a tent designed for two middling people who do, it is a very long night.

LATE ON THURSDAY afternoon, after being trapped above Denali Pass by the same resuming windstorm that has pinned climbers in place up and down the mountain, Jerry and his friends struggled back to their caves at the Archdeacon's Tower ridge. There they spend Thursday night, and there they remain trapped when the storm peaks all day Friday.

Things now began to edge from serious to desperate. At the very least, Mark and Jerry Clark, in their leather boots (and possibly some of the others), must have frostbitten feet, if a minute or two outside his tent had been enough to freeze Anshel's hands 3,000 feet lower on the mountain. Art Davidson, of the Winter Expedition, stuck in an ice cave back in February, also suffered frostbitten feet, adding to his ordeal's claustro-phobic agony: "A sharp, pulsating ache made both my feet feel as if they were about to explode."

Fatigue and altitude are dragging all of Jerry's men down. They have been without food and water probably for twenty-four hours now. Jerry may think vaguely of trying to take off his boots and massage his feet, but the effort required will seem insurmountable. His hands go numb, too, but he can warm those under his arms or in his crotch, so they still have some feeling.

Jerry will understand better than the others what is happening, having learned more about high-altitude and cold-weather physiology during his Antarctic training. He will not say this to his friends, because he doesn't want to frighten them, but Jerry must know that if the storm doesn't break soon, some of them will be unable to move and could die right here. Given the way he's feeling, he could well be one of them, which would make him a dangerous burden for the younger, stronger men.

A steady man, no panicker, Jerry Clark has been in enough situations on mountains to know fear and how to manage it. So he is afraid, cer-tainly, but not about to give up and surrender control to his animalian midbrain. In truth, he is likely being overtaken by something even fiercer than fear: guilt. He brought his friends here. He knew they didn't want to come with the Coloradoans, but finally did not annul that strained marriage. He led them to the summit after their bivouac, and now he knows he should have taken them down instead. Perhaps worst of all, he knows that if he gets sick and can't move, his men may not be willing to leave him.

Down at 11,550 feet, in their camp on the spine of Karstens Ridge, Bill Babcock, Chet Hackney, and Gayle Nienheuser get up at 1:30 a.m. on Friday, anxious to attack the ridge above. It is clear and very cold, but there is almost no wind. Bill boils up water for hot drinks, and urges the others into motion.

Two hours later, they are breaking trail up to the larger, safer 12,100-foot campsite. The fresh snow is waist deep and dangerously unstable, giving way underfoot as though they were walking on clouds. They stop, gasping for breath, fully aware that to continue in these conditions invites disaster. There's only one alternative, and they dread it almost as much as falling: shoveling off the ridge.

Bill, the veteran, has equipped his expedition with huge aluminum scoop shovels. About fifteen inches wide by twenty inches deep, with stout wooden handles and weighing about five pounds, they are the tools of choice for farmers who need to move tons of grain efficiently—and for Alaskan mountaineers. Working with these, the MCA climbers shovel in two-hour shifts; fifty feet is a good shift's work.

At noon, a storm blows down from the Harper and hits them suddenly, like a giant fist. In short order the wind is sweeping over them at fifty miles per hour and whiteout closes in. But these are hardy souls, and they keep at it, trenching all the way to 12,100 feet. By the time they've finished, the winds are even worse and visibility is literally zero. They retreat to the 11,550-foot camp, build thick snow walls around their tents, reinforce the igloo, and settle in.

Even down at Wonder Lake, Friday morning brings drenching rain and high winds from a storm that will turn out to be one of the worst in park history. Neither of Don Sheldon's light planes can fly in these conditions. An air force C-130 could conceivably fly, and, during even a brief lull, could make airdrops of fuel, food, radios, and dry sleeping bags, but this option isn't being considered seriously by anyone other than Wayne Merry.

Throughout the morning, he continues working on a detailed plan for a full-blown rescue operation. Though surprised that Joe has not requested one yet, he has no doubt that such a request could come at any moment.

At 2:45 p.m. on Friday, three days and nights since Jerry Clark's party was last heard from, Wayne informs Chief Ranger Art Hayes of what's required for an all-out rescue. This is something Wayne Merry clearly knows how to do—may in fact know how to do as well as anyone in North America at that time—his expertise honed by a decade of search-and-rescue work and, just five months earlier, by managing the Winter Expedition rescue. Wayne's plan calls for accommodating ten men here and twenty-five to fifty others in nearby camps, using the Kantishna airstrip twenty-eight miles away, acquiring a multiday supply of aviation gasoline for the Turbo Beaver aircraft, getting Handy Talky radios for climbers and base sets for the airstrip, and (lesson learned from the Winter Expedition experience) appointing a good press officer. Hayes listens but evinces no readiness to commit to such an ambitious, expensive operation, which surely would be splashed across the nation's newspapers. The Wilcox team is large and has a number of experienced men. What's the rush?

Wayne understands very well what the rush is, and his recollections remain vivid to this day:

There had been another SAR event with the Winter Expedition in January that year. I had been in Talkeetna when they were initially flown up to the Kahiltna Glacier by Don Sheldon. I especially remember helping to cram Jacques Batkin into the back of 42U [Sheldon's plane] he had managed to get his body in with all the gear, but could not find room for the last Korean-booted foot he dragged in. I managed to wedge it in for him. A day later he was dead in a crevasse. A great guy, and I felt it deeply. It was a pretty strong foreshadowing.

Then came the rescue, when the entire team was missing. I was sent over to Talkeetna to manage it. What a circus! We were working out of a motel. The Air Force was there with a Chinook and two Hueys on the ground, T-Birds [the Lockheed T-33 Shooting Star was a slow, sturdy jet used for pilot training and reconnaissance] flying low altitude recon on the mountain, and C-130s (or maybe it was 118s) occasionally at higher altitudes. There was a rescue team from Washington with the Whitakers [sic], and one from Anchorage. There were also ground troops, about fifty reporters—and one telephone. But beneath the confusion and inter-agency conflict there was a deep feeling of foreboding and even doom which affected most of us. We would be eating a good dinner at the table and feeling guilty, because we were sure the climbers were dying and we couldn't do a damn thing about it.

When the climbers were finally brought in, mostly intact, I got a good feeling for what they had been through. I talked with the whole gang later at Summit on their way home and got a graphic picture of a subzero wind so strong that it rumbled like a waterfall at the mouth of the ice cave. Shiro Nishimae described what it was like lying on his belly on the ice with the pick of his ice axe dug in and pivoting like a weathervane from the wind's force. . . . I also remembered what it was like once on Mount Rainier, having been knocked off my feet by the wind and having windblown crystalline snow sandblast my face so that it oozed for a week. The thought of being 8000 feet higher and 40 or 50 degrees colder was boggling. And as we did a lot of Park patrols in winter, sometimes when it was 35° or 40° below zero, I had a sincere appreciation of what cold could do to you. [The Wilcox Expedition] would have been a lot less stressful if I didn't have an idea of what they were going through. Maybe that lack of empathy [in other park officials] was a factor in the slow rescue reaction which traumatized me so much.

THROUGHOUT THE MORNING and afternoon, the storm blows on, dumping unprecedented amounts of rain, washing out roads, culverts, and bridges. Violent winds are disrupting radio and telephone services. In the midst of all this, Wayne is trying to orchestrate communications between himself, Art Hayes in the chief ranger's office, George Hall in the superintendent's office, Eldon Reyer in the chief district ranger's office, Gordon Haber and George Perkins at the Eielson Visitor Center, Gary Hansen of the Alaska Rescue Group in Anchorage, and Don and Roberta Sheldon in their planes and hangar.

Late that afternoon, having heard nothing from Hayes, Wayne contacts him again "to reiterate the importance of fuel in the proposed drop." Perhaps exasperated at this poking and prodding by a subordinate, Hayes says that the full message has been transmitted to Gary Hansen. *Somebody else's problem now* is the unspoken message.

Hansen, in Anchorage, has packed an emergency airdrop that includes stove fuel, batteries, CB and Voice Commander radios, and some food. He also readied a separate supply drop for the 15,000-foot camp. One not inconsequential problem: no plane is available to fly the supplies up to the mountain. The next best option, incredibly, is a bus that leaves Anchorage at 5:15 p.m. that day and will arrive in Talkeetna, theoretically anyway, at 9:30 p.m. This effectively rules out any possibility that the radios, batteries, white gas, and food could find their way to the stranded men this day.

No planes up also means no overflight to view the higher mountain, assess problems, and reassure men in trouble that help is, if not imminent, at least on the way.

20

SATURDAY, JULY 22
Where Death Has No Meaning

F irst thing Saturday morning, Wayne tells Eldon Reyer to have Art Hayes direct Don Sheldon (does that convoluted chain not give a strong taste of what Wayne Merry is dealing with?) to check on the locations of the Mountaineering Club of Alaska and Western States Expeditions, anticipating that one or both may be called upon to help with a rescue.

The Western States Expedition, which has been climbing the West Buttress route, has radios that communicate with stations in Anchorage 160 miles distant but not with Wayne just 28 miles away. Attacked by the same storm, this expedition has been dug in at 17,200 feet on the west side of Denali Pass, fully occupied by their own battle with the weather that also has the MCA team trapped at 11,550 feet.

Sheldon cannot fly because of a 4,000-foot cloud ceiling around the mountain. As Wayne knows, a four-engine C-130 Hercules could fly. But none are requested from the Rescue Coordination Center (RCC), and Chief Ranger Hayes has shown no inclination to call the air force into action. Increasingly desperate, Wayne vents some of his frustration in the rescue log: "It appears that there is little to do now except plan for a break in the weather."

On a whim, he tries Channel 7 on his radio, though he's been told that it doesn't work. In fact it does, allowing him to monitor Don Sheldon's radio broadcasts from his plane and to communicate directly, "5x5," with Roberta Sheldon at their hangar/office in Talkeetna. Later in the afternoon, clouds that have wrapped McKinley since July 18 appear to be breaking up, lifting the ceiling to 12,000 feet. Wayne asks that Sheldon drop a note to the Western States group, informing them of the situation and advising that their help may be needed. Thus the National Park Service, in 1967, resorts to communication methods used by pilots in World War I.

This "rock 'n relay" patchwork communication system is not what someone might wish for who is faced with mounting the greatest rescue operation in McKinley's history. Wayne asks that the 100-watt linear amplifier from Superintendent George Hall's own headquarters be installed at Eielson for the duration of the emergency. It never happens.

At 8:30 p.m., Wayne speaks with Joe at Camp VI. Anshel and Jerry Lewis are in bad shape, Jerry by far the worse. Wind has all but destroyed the camp. Their gear is soaked, the five men are jammed into one tent. Five days of food remain at Camp VI, but no fuel. The mountain is clear, wind about fifteen miles per hour, temperature hovering around zero.

Wayne asks whether any of the men can ascend to the high camp, and Joe replies that only one of them feels strong enough to climb back up, and then only if a dry sleeping bag can be airdropped. Joe, Howard, and Paul discussed the possibility of going back up earlier in the afternoon. Joe will write later that he was ready and willing to try an ascent, but Howard and Paul were not and that Howard, at least, was trying to undermine his leadership: "Howard was silently stalking my resolve, like a vulture waiting for my will to weaken."

With the value of hindsight, it appears that Howard's response— "Don't make more victims"—was correct. But saying that now fails to take into account a factor of immense importance then: the two directives that Joe received from NPS officials.

Howard insists to this day that Joe was in no shape to do any more climbing; Paul Schlichter and Jerry Lewis, and therefore the weight of evidence, agree. Howard believes that Joe's attempt to shift blame onto the two Coloradoans stems from some deep need to absolve himself in his own mind and those of others. Joe contends that he felt terrible responsibility for those up high. In addition—and this is a critically important fact that has been completely overlooked until now—he has been told not once but twice by NPS officials that his own team is the trapped men's best hope, and that he should get back up to them as soon as possible.

The idea is not pursued further, and plans are made for them all to descend at 11:00 p.m. They can leave food at Camp VI, but there is no more fuel. Joe believes that three days of food may be left at the high camp by now and adds that snow conditions at 17,900 feet would have allowed the upper group to dig in.

Assuming that Sheldon's overflight is imminent, Joe asks that the pilot waggle his wings at them if the upper team seems to be okay, but circle three times counterclockwise if it appears they need help. Sheldon, alas, has gone to Anchorage and will not be back until close to midnight.

A T LEAST SOME of the men stranded up high must now be in serious trouble. No diaries were ever recovered that would tell us what Jerry Clark and his friends were going through at this time, but some other mountaineers have been in similar straits and returned to tell their tales. The famed mountaineer and physician Thomas Hornbein, in his book *Everest: The West Ridge,* gave us what I consider the best such description ever written.

After summiting Mount Everest via the unclimbed West Ridge at 7:15 p.m. on May 22, 1963, Hornbein and three other climbers are caught by darkness while descending the South Col route and are forced to bivouac in the open at 28,000 feet. They have no tents or sleeping bags and cannot dig snow caves because they carry no shovels. With their ice axes they chip out little depressions in the steep, frozen slope and settle in for a night from which they know they may not wake. What Hornbein wrote about that night high on Everest tells us what life is like now for Jerry and his friends in their caves:

> Mostly there was nothing. We hung suspended in a timeless void. The wind died, and there was silence. Even without wind it was cold. I could reach back and touch Lute or Barrel lying head to toe above me. They seemed miles away. Unsignaled, unembellished, the hours passed. Intense cold penetrated, carrying with it the realization that each of us was completely alone. Nothing Willi could

do for me or I for him. No team now, just each of us, imprisoned with his own discomfort, his own thoughts, his own will to survive. Yet for me, survival was hardly a conscious thought. Nothing to plan, nothing to push for, nothing to do but shiver and wait for the sun to rise. I floated in a dreamlike eternity, devoid of plans, fears, regrets. The heat lightning, Lhotse, discomfort, my companions, all were there—yet not there. Death had no meaning nor, for that matter, did life. Survival was no concern, no issue. Only a dulled impatience for the sun to rise tied my formless thoughts to the future.

The sun did rise that next morning, and Hornbein and his friends climbed down into legend.

The sun does not rise on July 22 for the five men up high in their caves, nor on Steve and John in their tent, because the storm continues. Some may be near death already, others may be in relatively good shape. These things are hard to know. But we do know what is happening to their bodies as they lie in the caves day after day.

At some point, when their down clothing and sleeping bags have become wet and no longer provide much insulation, they begin shivering relentlessly. This is their bodies' autonomic attempt to work muscles and generate heat to combat dropping core temperature. Shivering will continue during the first two stages of hypothermia.

But shivering generates only about as much body heat as walking, which is far from enough to compensate for what they are losing. Their ability to think is eroding. Their speech becomes slurred; they are lethargic and sleepy, perhaps irrational. Eventually they stop shivering, but instead of signaling relief, this is an indication that death is closer.

At this point their core temperature becomes so low that the transmission of neurological impulses from brain to muscles and organs is impaired. As more and more heat is lost, their muscles stiffen. That in turn accelerates the decline in their core temperatures. Unable to walk, or even to stand, they lie, semiconscious, slipping toward coma.

After a time the muscles deepest inside their bodies—heart and diaphragm in particular—also begin to stiffen. Toward the end, movement is reduced to a few heartbeats and breaths per minute. Looking at them, you might think them dead already, so small and infrequent are their respirations. Even when they finally do draw breath, it is almost impossible to see, especially if they are swathed in thick layers of clothing.

Electrical activity in the brain, the body's biggest user of oxygen, begins to shut down, so that, close to the end, nerve impulses are random and infrequent, like fireflies flickering in the dark. The Alamo of vital life forces—that deep brain area commanding autonomic nervous system functions such as breath and heartbeat—begins to fall silent. They would now be unconscious, their skin waxy and pale. The chest rises and falls, rises and falls . . . and finally, at some point, does not rise again.

They will not all die at the same time, for reasons both physical and spiritual. Research has proven that in identical conditions some people live and others die; survival becomes an issue of mind rather than matter, hence the term *will to live*. Modern climbers understand this, and the best of them train their wills as assiduously as their bodies. Reinhold Messner is one of many great mountaineers who has written extensively about the importance of will. Swedish climber Goran Kropp soloed Everest without oxygen in 1996. Writing after the event in *Ultimate High: My Everest Odyssey*, he recalled that all the extreme training for his ordeal focused on one goal: "Did I have enough will power yet?" Beck Weathers's miraculous resurrection on Everest's South Col in 1996, after being left for dead by three rescuers on three separate occasions, may be the greatest recorded example of will defeating death.

In *Surviving Extremes*, climber and physician Ken Kamler examines the role of will in human survival. After twenty pages of sophisticated scientific explication, this is his conclusion:

> The true nature of will remains mysterious. Is it an electrobiochemical resource hidden deep within the brain or a force instilled from without by a higher power? The electrical spark generated by the cingulate may be the origin of will, or it may be the first detectable result of faith. The answer is within our bodies but beyond our grasp.

In what order will Jerry Clark and his partners succumb? That is impossible to say for sure, of course, but we can make informed suppositions about what happens to them. We know that at least two physical factors affect how the human body responds to hypothermia. Size is one. Bigger people, with more bodily surface area, lose body heat more rapidly than smaller people, given similar percentages of body fat. And body fat is the other factor. People with higher percentages of body fat—good natural insulation—retain body heat more efficiently. It's no accident that Eskimos' bodies have evolved to be short and round, and contain an unusually high percentage of body fat.

We know the men's physical characteristics when they began the climb. Steve Taylor, at six feet two inches and 155 pounds, was the most ectomorphic man in the group; Mark McLaughlin, at six feet and 150 pounds, was a close second. They both would have lost fifteen to twenty pounds by this time, and their bodies would have been vulnerable to hypothermia. John Russell, at five feet nine inches and 175 pounds; Hank Janes, at five feet five inches and 140 pounds; and Walt Taylor, at five feet eight inches and 155 pounds, were shorter and stouter than any of the others, and would likely have been the most efficient heat retainers, even assuming that they, too, had lost many pounds. Jerry Clark, at five feet seven inches and 145 pounds, and Dennis, at six feet four inches and 175 pounds, were somewhere in between the tall, thin men and the short, heavier ones.

The other thing we can say with some confidence is that their deaths will not be horribly painful. Accounts of dying this way have come to us from surprisingly varied sources. Tom Hornbein's near-death experience, noted above, is one. Another is that written by Robert Falcon Scott, who wrote almost to the very end as he lay freezing to death in his tent, assuring family members that his two already dead tent mates suffered little, and not once mentioning any pain that he himself was in. Many soldiers froze to death during World War II's Battle of the Bulge. In *June 6, 1944: The Voices of D-Day*, Gerald Astor cites the experience of one paratrooper with the marvelous name Raider Nelson, who almost joined their number. "I was caught in a blizzard, alone on outpost. My company moved out before daylight but sent two guys to find me. They pulled me from a snowdrift just in time, because the freezing pain had left me and I was enjoying the illusion of lying in the warm sun on some beach."

Tom Hornbein's account echoes this: "I floated in a dreamlike eternity, devoid of plans, fears, regrets. . . . Death had no meaning nor, for that matter, did life." None of us wants to die, given decent health and intact mentation, but when my own time comes I, for one, would be more than satisfied with dreamy freedom from pain, fear, and regret.

The STORM RAGES all Friday night at Bill Babcock's camp on Karstens Ridge. Bill, who seems to have a fondness for activity at 1:30 a.m., decides at that early hour on Saturday morning to reinforce their igloo, working in winds exceeding fifty miles per hour. At some point, the team members are diverted by the need to strike their tent, for fear it will be destroyed.

By five that morning the wind begins to die, but it is clear to Bill that Grace Jansen-Hoeman, the physician and only female member of their party, is declining rapidly. She seems unnaturally exhausted, has trouble carrying loads that earlier would not have fazed her, is increasingly moody, and will not eat. She and Jeff continue to have problems with freezing feet, and even Bill himself is suffering the first signs of altitude sickness: bad headache, chest pains, extreme fatigue.

They remain hunkered down, tantalized by a brief break in the weather at noon. Finally, at about half past two, despite continuing high winds and whiteout, they dig a path up to the 12,100-foot camp, relay all their supplies there, and settle into this more secure site.

When SATURDAY MORNING comes to Camp VI, Joe and the others have spent eleven days at 15,000 feet or higher and are beginning to suffer the consequences—lassitude, loss of appetite, decreased urination, extreme fatigue. The camp is in shambles, morale is at rock bottom. Joe's description of this nadir remains the most-quoted passage from *White Winds*:

> The wind had long since bared our weaknesses and was now crushing our strengths. It had been more than a day since I had eaten a warm meal and the crowded tent did not afford a safe opportunity to operate a stove. I sipped at my near empty water bottle in a vain attempt to keep pace with dehydration. Soon the dark urinations of

the past day ceased completely. Morale plummeted. An apathetic tangled mass of compressed humanity lay in the tent's pale blue glow, with little sleep or communication.

During the 8:30 p.m. radio contact on Saturday, Eielson had asked whether any of them could go back up if dry sleeping bags were supplied. Joe had indicated that he alone was willing to go. This had infuriated Howard, mostly because he felt that Joe's insinuation was that he and Paul could go but wouldn't, but also because Howard simply didn't believe that Joe was physically capable of making the climb himself. Willing, perhaps; able, no.

Assuming that they all will be heading down-mountain after the 11:00 p.m. radio report, Howard and Paul go outside and begin sorting food and gear. But both men are worried about Karstens Ridge, which can be treacherous for healthy expert climbers in good weather; it was here that Elton Thayer, the experienced climbing ranger, took his fatal fall in 1953. Some of the pitches approach 45 degrees. Going down slopes such as those is scarier and far more difficult than climbing up them, particularly if they're blue ice hidden by drifts of loose snow, as will almost certainly be the case now.

Outside the tent, where they can speak privately, Paul says that Joe, Anshel, and Jerry Lewis will not be able to downclimb Karstens Ridge this night. Howard agrees, and says that their best hope is to feed them well, get some sleep, and hope the weather holds for a morning start.

During the 11:00 p.m. radio contact, Howard asks Joe to report that they have sick men in the party and for that reason could not go back up to 17,900 feet. Joe says only, "We have a couple of people hampered and cannot travel tonight." Dissatisfied with this explanation, Howard demands the radio. He desperately wants to explain his belief that the sick people in the party include Joe and that it would be folly to attempt a reascent. After repeated tries, Eielson finally copies what Howard is saying: "We have three people pretty sick up here. This is why we could not go up. We have to get these people down." They plan for an 8:00 a.m. radio contact the next morning, and sign off.

Radio chores done for the night, Howard and Paul shovel out the yellow Mountaineer tent and crawl in, relishing the space and looking forward to their first good sleep in three days and nights. After being trapped with three other big men, the unaccustomed "luxury" of two men in a two-man tent feels wonderful. But it does not lessen their fear about tomorrow's descent, or their disappointment at how things have turned out.

From where they lie, the expedition has deteriorated into something worse than a debacle. McKinley has done nothing to diminish the instant dislike that flared between Howard and Joe at Rainier and has soured their "climb of a lifetime." Seven men are trapped high up. Some or all of them may be dead. Jerry Lewis is very sick and getting worse. Anshel is sick and weak. Though Joe believes himself to be strong and with faculties intact, Howard is worried about his physical and mental states. Perhaps more alarming than any other single thing, as yet there is not a whit of evidence to indicate that, excepting Wayne Merry, anyone down low understands how bad things are on the mountain.

In his book, Howard recalled his and Paul's grim conversation before falling asleep:

"You know what they are going to say?" he tells Paul. "They're going to say, 'That's a big group, bigger than most expeditions. They've got lots of equipment. We don't think anything too serious could have happened to them.'"

And that is exactly what "they" *are* saying, and will continue to say, even long after Jerry Clark and his friends are dead.

Howard is worried about something else, not without justification. An extraordinarily intelligent young man, he knows that history does not parse with delicacy or finesse. If their worst fears come to pass, and many men die here, he will not be remembered as Howard Snyder, who survived—and tried to stave off—one of the worst tragedies in mountaineering history. He will be remembered only as someone who had a role in it.

21

SUNDAY, JULY 23
Mixed Messages

E arly on Sunday morning, Eldon Reyer calls Wayne:
"I've been in contact with Sheldon. He's getting ready to take off, but he's doubtful of his chances of getting through because of turbulence." That part of the message doesn't surprise Wayne, who knows that the weather at Talkeetna has to be just as rotten as it is here. But the next part of the message does surprise him:

"Sheldon is very upset with Wilcox abandoning the upper group, and thinks he just wants publicity. I couldn't make him understand the proposed signals for the climbers."

This refusal to "understand the proposed signals" is an odd statement from a veteran pilot such as Don Sheldon. How could he fail to understand a request to waggle his wings or fly in counterclockwise circles? There is no evidence of problems with the radio transmission itself—Reyer and Sheldon understood each other clearly. And even novice pilots (I am one, so I speak from experience) can waggle wings and fly counterclockwise circles.

And why would Sheldon harbor the incorrect beliefs that Joe Wilcox "just wants publicity" and "abandoned" Jerry Clark's party? And even if Sheldon assumes, wrongly, that Joe Wilcox *is* a heartless publicity hound and *did* abandon the others, why should that make it any less urgent to rescue seven men trapped by a life-threatening storm?

Don Sheldon died of cancer in 1974, so I could not interview him for this book. (I did interview his widow, Roberta Sheldon, but she had no contact with the expedition and could shed no light.) Criticizing men who have achieved greatness in their field is always difficult. Doing so when, because of death or other reason, they cannot respond in their own defense is unpleasant enough to provoke a visceral reaction, at least in me. But the alternative—to ignore obvious and disturbing facts—is even more unsettling to contemplate, because it would be dishonest and cowardly. People of great accomplishment are still people, and people are fallible. To insist otherwise does neither them nor the pursuit of truth any great service.

I have unlimited admiration for Don Sheldon's courage and flying ability. There is no doubt that he was one of the greatest, bravest, and most talented civilian pilots of all time. But there is also no doubt that his actions throughout the July 1967 tragedy are hard to understand or explain, especially when viewed in light of all his other transcendent heroics.

Wayne senses that, for whatever reasons, all is not right with Sheldon and tells Reyer to ask for a big Rescue Coordination Center (RCC) plane to fly over the mountain because "it appears that Sheldon may not be effective." At 10:00 a.m., Wayne learns from Art Hayes that no RCC plane has been requested. Wayne's boss, park superintendent George Hall, probably still smarting from having been publicly flogged for the Winter Expedition rescue's huge expense, and no doubt leery of triggering an even bigger response so soon after, wants to wait for the result of Sheldon's flight.

An hour later, Wayne gets on the phone and urges Hall to directly authorize a high-altitude flight by one of the large military aircraft. Then he calls the Sheldon hangar. Don, it turns out, is flying on the other side of the mountain, ferrying supplies and personnel for Boyd Everett's South Face Expedition, which makes an RCC flight even more urgent. But headquarters won't budge. Nothing will happen until Sheldon can make his overflight. Hayes and Gary Hansen feel that relying on the civilian climbers already on the mountain is a better option than RCC airdrops, despite the fact that it will take Bill Babcock's MCA group five days, minimum, to reach Camp VII, and a C-130 could be orbiting the peak in five *hours*. Undeterred, Wayne keeps punching away until finally he is told that Superintendent Hall is "standing by" and "in favor of" a high-altitude flight. Wayne is relieved but wary. If eight years in the bureaucracy have taught him anything, it's that "is in favor of" can be a long way from "is ordering."

MORNING BRINGS CLEAR skies and light wind to Camp VI. The men there can see all the way to the summit, but Joe's excitement is quickly offset by something terrifying and inexplicable: He can't feel or move his hands. At first he thinks they're frostbitten, but they're not cold to the touch. He has no idea what's causing the paralysis, and that makes it all the more frightening.

It's likely that Joe's condition is the result of hypoxia rather than hypothermia, though, when the two occur together, each magnifies—*potentiates* is the word physicians use—the other with unfortunate results for the sufferer. Whatever the cause, this paralysis, on top of everything else that has happened, is the proverbial backbreaking straw for Joe.

"I sat huddled in the middle of the tent—defeated," Joe wrote in *White Winds.* "I had matched my will and strength against Denali's wrath—and was now but a child, humiliated before a stern master."

As Howard and Paul are digging out packs and gear from snowdrifts, Anshel steps out of his tent and promptly collapses.

Hey—are you okay? Howard asks, alarmed.

Just dizzy, Anshel reassures him. But it's a struggle getting to one knee. Not long after, Jerry Lewis drags himself out and is, if anything, in worse shape, so depleted that he can't pack his gear.

Howard enters the tent while Joe is still sitting on its floor, unable to move his hands. Assuming they're frozen, Howard tries to warm them by placing them against his belly, but the treatment doesn't work, so he goes back out to continue packing for the descent. Anshel comes in, and Joe asks him to strap on his crampons. It is a moment of ultimate role reversal both sad and ironic, the expedition's least experienced member now taking care of its Super-Alpha leader.

"I'm going to rope you up second behind me. I want a strong man there to belay," Howard tells Joe a short while later "in a tone that told me he had assumed command," as Joe wrote later in *White Winds.* If the expedition has an emotional crux for Joe, this is it. "I would be going down the ridge with the others. I had joined the deserters."

It's understandable why Joe would feel ashamed. But he is being too hard on himself, not to mention Howard and Paul, by calling himself and them "deserters." A nearly identical situation prevailed just five months earlier during the Winter Expedition emergency. With Art Davidson, Ray Genet, and Dave Johnston trapped in an ice cave at Denali Pass, four others—leader Gregg Blomberg, Shiro Nishimae, John Edwards, and George Wichman—huddled in an igloo at 17,200 feet, just 700 feet lower down. Throughout the storm, these four repeatedly considered trying to climb to their partners' aid. In the end, they made the agonizing decision that adding more victims to the emergency would have hurt rather than helped. And no one then or thereafter ever accused them of "abandoning" or "deserting" their three friends.

Another analogous situation occurred during the 1996 disaster on Everest. With people missing, dying, and dead at 26,000 feet, three climbers at 24,000 were apprised of the situation by radio. Two of them, Todd Burleson and Pete Athans, were expert professional climbers. The other was talented amateur Ken Kamler, author of the aforementioned *Surviving Extremes,* back for a second shot at Everest. Athans and Burleson started up immediately. Kamler stayed behind. "Not only would I not be able to keep up, I'd more than likely end up as one of the casualties."

Many readers undoubtedly are familiar with the ultimate example of partner separation—the saga of Joe Simpson and Simon Yates, brilliantly told in Simpson's book *Touching the Void.* In 1985, after summiting 21,000-foot Siula Grande in the Peruvian Andes, Simpson and Yates got in trouble while descending in a storm. Simpson fell, shattering a leg and kneecap, which disabled him. Yates began lowering his partner down their steep route, pitch by pitch. On one particularly treacherous section, Simpson began sliding out of control; he plunged over the lip of a cliff and was left dangling from the climbing rope tied into his harness. Only Yates's frantic belay, far above, saved them both from certain death. The men could not see or hear each other, the raging storm was worsening, and night had fallen. Simpson's swinging weight was beginning to pull Yates, inch by agonizing inch, from his own insecure belay stance in powdery snow on the steep face. It was the kind of inconceivable horror that only visits us in nightmares, but it was real. In minutes, Yates knew that he would come off and they would both fall, smashing to their deaths on whatever lay beneath the precipice over which Simpson had slid. Faced with an unimaginably difficult choice, Yates cut the rope, dropping his partner to certain death—or so he thought. Amazingly, both men survived without serious lasting damage to their bodies.

No one found fault with the Winter Expedition men, or with Ken Kamler. Although a few did condemn Simon Yates, the man in the best position to complain, Joe Simpson, did not. Simpson remained Yates's friend and staunchest defender. Everyone involved in these crises was following the primary rule of emergency response: *don't make more victims.* All of which is to say that although it might have been horribly painful for Joe Wilcox to descend with the others, no man among them was a deserter.

Finally, all five men are packed and tied into a single 270-foot rope created by joining two shorter ones. Howard leads, Joe comes next, then Jerry, Anshel, and Paul. They start down a few minutes before nine o'clock on Sunday, July 23, and from the first step their descent is, as Howard expected, nightmarish. In the first 150 yards of easy terrain, Jerry falls three times and takes longer to get up from each fall. Whenever Jerry goes down, Joe and Anshel, both tired themselves, also plop down in the snow. Watching all this from his last position on the rope, Paul thinks, *This is it. We might as well go back and call in the helicopter.*

But they struggle on and eventually come to the end of this easy section. From here they must traverse the much steeper slope beneath Browne Tower. They can see the high camp from here, and the lower slopes beneath Archdeacon's Tower. Howard stops and looks back up. He sees neither tents nor people there, nor any evidence of color or motion. But they are more than two miles away by now, and they have no binoculars, and the storm has been blowing at peak intensity for days, so it's not likely that he would have spotted anything even if men were moving up there. Yet he is coming to accept that an unimaginable calamity has occurred.

After another five to ten minutes of descent, Howard pulls up short before traversing onto the steep face beneath Browne Tower. He has been stopped by something so terrifying that every one of the survivors remembers it vividly to this day.

The slope itself, steeper than any expert ski run, has been blown clean of snow. Its surface is like polished white marble. When Howard gingerly steps onto it with one foot, his dagger-sharp crampon points barely scratch the impenetrable surface. Bizarrely, the snow that had been packed down by their ascent is still there, stuck precariously to the slanting ice face, creating a fragile, foot-tall catwalk no wider than two snowshoes. It looks like an invitation to suicide.

Feeling almost certain that venturing onto this face—especially with the faltering Jerry Lewis—will be fatal, Howard suggests returning to Camp VI and starting their descent again, making a new route lower down. Paul and Joe object, pointing out that crevasses threaten down there. There is no other choice but this steep slope. If they want to go down, they have to risk the crumbling snow ledge. Before moving out, Howard rearranges the men on the rope. He wants to have the strongest possible belay for Jerry Lewis, so he puts Paul right behind him, with Anshel next and Joe last.

"Step only on the uphill edge of the snow trail," Howard warns the others. Where hard-packed snow meets slope, the surface will be strongest. Taking a deep breath, concentrating like a wire walker, Howard eases out onto the precarious footing. It feels to him "like walking on a window ledge across the face of a building," except that the window ledge is made of crumbly snow.

Howard has done enough serious climbing to be comfortable with exposure on small ledges thousands of feet in the air. But before this, he's been up there with healthy partners, solid protection, and levels of risk that are thrilling rather than terrifying. Now he is on the same kind of terrain that killed Elton Thayer, performing a traverse so hazardous that, ultimately, only luck will determine whether they live or die. To get across something like this is as much a mental challenge as a physical one. Howard must shove his brain's eons-old survival urges into a little mental box and keep them stuffed there while they kick and scream, *"Go back, you idiot, you're going to die!"*

Before he has gone twenty feet, a small section of the snow ledge breaks off beneath his left crampon and tumbles down the ice face, exploding as it falls. It happens again a bit farther on, and then, unbelievably, one of his crampons breaks. He can't stop, and he can't go back, so he goes on, clanking "like Jacob Marley in his chains."

Unbelievably, Howard makes it across. Even more incredibly, the others do, too. Possibly the snow ledge was firmer than they had any right to believe. Maybe it just was not their day to die. Whichever, they surely must know that surviving this traverse is nothing short of a miracle.

At 11:00 a.m., they reach Parker Pass. Descending from Camp VI to this point earlier in the expedition required thirty minutes. This day the same distance has taken two hours.

While the men are resting at Parker Pass, it becomes clear that Jerry Lewis may not be able to go much farther. There's nothing else for it: Before they tackle the steeps of Karstens Ridge, Howard gives Jerry one of the orange, heart-shaped five-milligram Dexedrine tablets they have brought for just such an emergency. Known to pharmacologists as dextro-amphetamine sulfate (and on the street as "Dex"), the drug is a central nervous system stimulant developed in the 1920s and first used to treat depression and obesity. Taking it in any appreciable dose makes you feel as though you have just chugged a pint of double-strength espresso heavily laced with sugar. (At least that's how it made me feel many years ago after a misguided doctor prescribed some to help me lose weight.)

The recommended dose is from five to sixty milligrams, and there are long- and short-acting formulations. The orange tablet that Jerry swallows is the short-acting variety, but in actuality that means he will not experience the drug's peak effect for two hours. A much larger dose would have been appropriate, given his huge body mass. In any event, Jerry seems to derive little benefit. In *White Winds*, Joe wrote that even after swallowing the tablet, Jerry "periodically collapsed precariously to the snow, which made me very thankful for the fixed line. An unchecked fall here would not stop for at least 3,000 feet."

At 14,000 feet, they pause briefly atop the precipitous Coxcomb, a rounded formation, protruding up and out from the main ridge, which presents the steepest gradients of the entire route. Standing there, they can see bright orange tents far below at the 12,100-foot camp—Bill Babcock's MCA Expedition. In other circumstances it would have been a moment for rejoicing, but they are too exhausted to do anything but plod on. Before they have gone twenty steps, Jerry Lewis, the team's biggest man, falls on the route's steepest pitch.

Sunday morning brings another tantalizing but ultimately treacherous period of good weather to the MCA team. Very early, they start making the route to Browne Tower at 14,500 feet. Chet Hackney leads, until he takes the kind of fall from the knife-edged ridge that pulled Elton Thayer's friends off it and killed him. The consequences this time are frightening but not catastrophic. Belayed by the others, Chet regains the ridge where, shaken, he hands the lead off to Bill Babcock. It's not their morning. Before they go much farther, Jeff Babcock has crampon problems. Then the wind becomes intolerable. Finally, they end up making a cache at 12,800 feet and struggling back down to their camp at 12,100 feet.

There they wait for another break in the weather. At about noon, Bill Babcock and the others are standing outside their tents when a brief clearing reveals a sight that will change all their lives. Bill's expedition diary:

> [F]ive men were seen descending from the coxcomb. Three of the men were stumbling along having great difficulty.
>
> We filled thermos bottles had lunch & started our second relay. We met them at top of 12,800 steep pitch. Helped belay them down. All returned our camp at 12,100. We were told seven men remained on the Harper. Probably without food or fuel for the past 7 days. I encouraged Wilcox to order an all out rescue over radio.
>
> Weather very bad heavy snow gusty winds. Grace looking worse morale very low thinks she might be sick. Carried very little loads.
>
> Jerry Lewis Colorado group very sick. Wilcox in shock hard to communicate with. . . .
>
> Evidently Howard & Paul had to dress, put on crampons & fold tents and pack gear of Jerry Lewis, Eshol, [Anshel] and Wilcox who could no longer help themselves. Food cached at Browns Tower— fuel one mile above and more food and snow shoes at 16,500.
>
> Evidently second team went for summit on 17th at 2 p.m. afternoon. Bivouacked on the way but finally arrived on summit. They

had trouble returning. Evidently lost their way because of lack of wands. One person remained at the tent on the 17th, six went on to the summit.

Evidently during a fierce snow storm at 17,900 some food and fuel were lost. On the 18th, 19, 20, 21, 22, 23, high winds prevailed and despite several efforts the 5 climbers at 15,400 couldn't return to aid the seven, believed to be at the 17,900 foot camp.

One Colorado climber mentioned at one time the tents could be seen but at a later date they could not be seen. Evidently at least 2 perhaps more of the 6 remaining at the high altitude camp were having altitude conditioning problem. All were well equipped despite loss of tent due to refueling while stove was lit. . . .

Wilcox told me that they were deceived by the good weather and made only one relay from 15,400 to 17,900 and the bulk of their food and fuel were left at 15,400 while the whole party was at 17,900. Despite urging by the Colorado group and Wilcox 7 of Wilcox's members chose to wait a day for their summit bid and consequently the group split up. The 5 who climbed the peak on the 15 or 16 then left camp 17,900 to leave more food and fuel for the remaining seven.

Bill wrote those sentences within hours of his first meeting with the descending five men. They are an invaluable record of statements made by Joe, Howard, and the others closest in time to the events they were describing. Here are the most important descriptions to come out of that diary:

"five men were seen descending from the coxcomb. Three of the men were stumbling along having great difficulty."
Three men, not two. Anshel, Jerry, and Joe, according to disinterested eyewitnesses.

"We were told seven men remained on the Harper."
On the Harper. Thus Joe and the other four believe that Jerry Clark and his team had made it back to Camp VII. At this point, no one is thinking that the men are languishing in ice caves.

"I encouraged Wilcox to order an all out rescue over radio."
Bill Babcock is not suffering—at least not as much as Joe—from fatigue and altitude. Bill's judgment is the least impaired. That, plus his greater Alaskan experience, makes his estimation of the need for and timing of an all-out rescue reliable.

"Weather very bad heavy snow gusty winds."
Bad weather still prevails down at 12,100 feet on Sunday, July 23—seven days after Jerry's team started for the summit, six days after they were caught while descending by the storm that continues undiminished.

"Wilcox in shock hard to communicate with."
As described by a knowledgeable and impartial observer, down as low as 12,100 feet.

"despite several efforts the 5 climbers at 15,400 couldn't return to aid the seven, believed to be at the 17,900 foot camp."
There was only one effort to reascend—Joe, Howard, and Paul's attempt early on the morning of July 20, and it was short-lived. But the belief that all seven men are trapped at Camp VII, and not higher on the mountain, is important.

"Despite urging by the Colorado group and Wilcox 7 of Wilcox's members chose to wait a day for their summit bid and consequently the group split up."
Later critics will suggest that responsibility for the party-splitting is Joe's. But Bill's entry reveals that Joe *and* the Coloradoans "urged" the others not to waste the good day. It's hard to imagine what else Joe could have done. Ordering men to climb to the summit would hardly have been wise or appropriate.

"The 5 who climbed the peak on the 15 or 16 then left camp 17,900 to leave more food and fuel for the remaining seven."
A good reason for doing so, about which Bill records no criticism.

Bill babcock, like Joe and Howard, has spent the previous year or more planning and organizing his own Mount McKinley expedition. He and his team have had their own share of earlier travails—getting lost on the way in, internecine feuding that led to three members abandoning the climb, rotten weather lower down and fierce storms higher. Worst of all, their oldest climber and team physician, Grace Jansen-Hoeman, is already suffering seriously from altitude way down here at 12,000 feet. That she is now in real danger Bill Babcock has no doubt, even though the probable cause, cerebral edema (a potentially lethal accumulation of fluid in and around the brain), is not well known to mountaineers at the time.

Of the five new climbers in his camp, Howard appears coherent, Paul "semi," Joe and the others "hanging on by a thread." Joe appears to be "in shock." Even before they reach the tents, Howard launches a bitter indictment of an expedition gone very bad. He was, Bill recalls, "very hostile toward Wilcox," commenting on "how slow the Wilcox group was during the climb and in his opinion how poorly organized."

After returning to camp, Bill puts Jerry into one of two MCA orange Logan tents joined at their doors. Paul, Jeff Babcock, and Howard also occupy this tent, while Bill, Joe, and other expedition members cook in the adjoining tent, passing food and drink through to Jerry, who is being treated like royalty with hot drinks, smoked salmon, moose jerky, and other goodies to speed his recovery.

At this point, Howard simply cannot contain himself any longer. As Jeff says today,

> Howard spoke of the problems with logistics, decision-making, and the frustrations of the descent and trying to get across Parker Pass and back down the Coxcomb after the storm. I do not want to misquote Howard, but suspect much of what he related to me was very similar to the commentary in his book. What I recall more distinctly than his monologue (since at that point in the climb, I had no idea what he was talking about) was his over-all "low key" frustration and anger.
>
> His bias toward Joe came through loud and clear, even though his demeanor and verbalizations were very soft spoken. I do recall

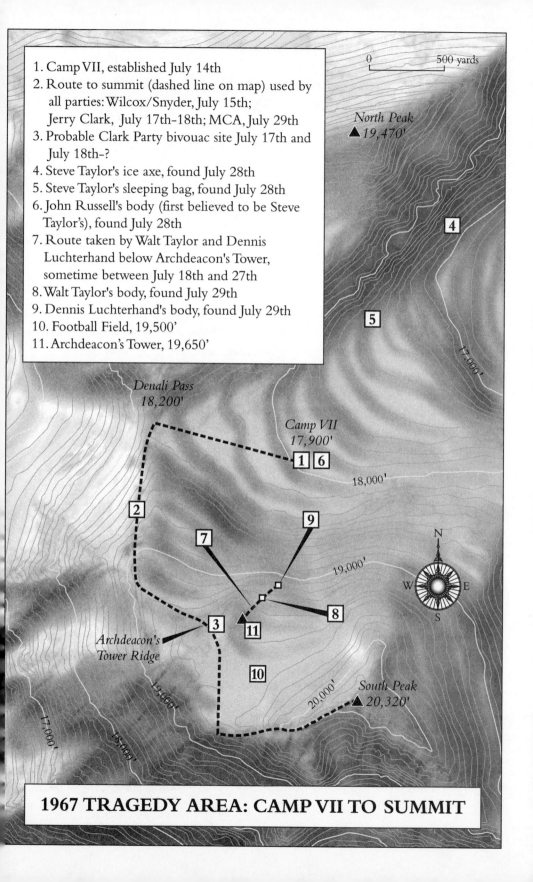

1. Camp VII, established July 14th
2. Route to summit (dashed line on map) used by all parties: Wilcox/Snyder, July 15th; Jerry Clark, July 17th-18th; MCA, July 29th
3. Probable Clark Party bivouac site July 17th and July 18th-?
4. Steve Taylor's ice axe, found July 28th
5. Steve Taylor's sleeping bag, found July 28th
6. John Russell's body (first believed to be Steve Taylor's), found July 28th
7. Route taken by Walt Taylor and Dennis Luchterhand below Archdeacon's Tower, sometime between July 18th and 27th
8. Walt Taylor's body, found July 29th
9. Dennis Luchterhand's body, found July 29th
10. Football Field, 19,500'
11. Archdeacon's Tower, 19,650'

1967 TRAGEDY AREA: CAMP VII TO SUMMIT

Howard uttering one or two very derogatory comments that were directed toward the tunnel entrances that connected both tents. I do not recall what the word or words were specifically. I remember that underneath this very understandable emotional display, tears began to trickle down Howard's face.

Howard was certainly in control, but his facade was crumbling before my eyes. He was greatly upset, saddened, and angered by the situation in which he and his teammates (Paul and Jerry) had become enmeshed.

Howard also recalls the incident. In an e-mail to me, he wrote,

Joe was in a state of denial from the time we left Camp VII on the 17th. He denied he was weak and sick; denied (or more likely was oblivious to) the sickness of John and Steve; denied that we had weak, sick people (including him) in Camp VI.

Upon reaching Camp V and the MCA, he refused to call a rescue, thereby denying the overwhelming evidence for a tragedy at and above Camp VII. That would be the basis of the frustration, helplessness and grief that you mention, and the genesis of the comments that I would have made to Jeff as we heard Joe in the next tent, refusing rescue for the second summit team.

While others are reviving Jerry in the tent, Joe is being revived just by the descent to this lower altitude. At 2:00 p.m. he radios Gordon Haber, who asks whether Joe wants to call for an all-out rescue. Joe says that he does not wish to do so now, but wants to wait for the results of Sheldon's overflight scheduled for the next morning—his fourth overflight request. Gordon asks Joe twice more whether he wants to call for an all-out rescue, and twice more Joe says no. He ends the conversation with Gordon by repeating, "I would like a rescue pending Sheldon's flight. From information based on Sheldon's flight should a rescue be decided." Request number five.

Bill suggests that Joe may be worrying too much about public reaction to the cost of a helicopter rescue, in light of outcries over the use of expensive military aircraft to aid the Winter Expedition in March. Joe recalled in *White Winds*:

Bill Babcock seemed amazed that I had not yet called an all-out rescue. Apparently the helicopter rescue of three climbers on the Winter Expedition had been very expensive (the helicopter had been brought in from Seattle) resulting in a lot of criticism from the public. "There are critics who will claim that people should not be allowed to climb mountains to just get in trouble and waste the taxpayer's money," Bill said, "but you can't worry too much about that—you might have seven stiffs up there."

(An aside about costs of such rescues—flying a helicopter 2,400 miles from Seattle to Talkeetna would have cost, bare minimum, about $2,500 then and about $12,000 now.)

Bill and Joe go back and forth for a while, but finally Bill is able to win Joe over.

Joe wrote later, "I decided that, if necessary, to increase the tempo of the support operations, I would give the go-ahead on a rescue."

But he does not. From *White Winds*: "The MCA climbers offered us the use of their snow shovel and ice saw to level our tent platform. Their hefty tools made ours look like toys. In a few minutes the job was complete, and I proceeded to get better acquainted with the MCA group."

Also from *White Winds*: As afternoon moves toward evening, Joe writes, "It didn't seem that enough was being done toward getting aid to the high party. . . . I paced the camp in restless anxiety and pondered the feasibility of going back up with the MCA group."

During that evening's radio contact with Eielson, Joe repeats the earlier instructions that an all-out rescue effort is contingent on Don Sheldon's overflight: "I then clarified my request from the previous radio contact. I wanted rescue operations to be ready to go into effect immediately following Sheldon's overflight of the high camp."

Anshel, hearing this at 8:30 p.m., believes that Joe has indeed given an unqualified go-ahead for the all-out rescue and proclaims to the camp that this has happened. But the truth is not so clear-cut. For one thing, Joe says in *White Winds* that he knows "high winds could keep Sheldon's light plane from flying for days. . . ."

In addition, it is not clear to NPS people that Joe is okaying the all-out rescue. Wayne Merry's entry in the rescue log reads, "Wilcox

wishes to wait for calling the rescue until Sheldon has flown, however
he emphasizes that rescue should be ready to go immediately if flight
shows trouble."

"Those were early times," Wayne Merry recalls, and the protocol for
triggering an all-out rescue was unclear, if only because so few *had* been
triggered—the John Day epic in 1960, and the more recent Winter Expedition rescue. The NPS clearly had exclusive jurisdiction, including
statutory responsibility for law enforcement, rescue, and other adminis-
trative duties. The only person who could initiate an all-out rescue
involving other agencies or nonpark resources would have been the park
superintendent, or someone acting at his behest—the chief ranger, for
example. But it's more than likely that the superintendent would seek
some kind of approval from the NPS regional office in Anchorage before
doing anything as drastic as calling in the air force.

With all that said, the expedition leader (if available) was certainly the
person who would have the best idea of conditions on the mountain, so
it's extremely unlikely that any NPS official would call an all-out rescue
involving other agencies without first getting the opinion of the expedition leader and arriving at some kind of agreement.

As far as the Alaska Rescue Group was concerned, even if they
believed that a rescue should be initiated, they would have had to involve
the superintendent first. Similarly, the Rescue Coordination Center
would not make a move without being officially invited, and that could
bring its own complications. When the military did arrive on the scene
during the Winter Expedition, they assumed they were in control.
"That took a little ironing out before we all got on the same page,"
Wayne recalls.

Joe was the titular leader of the expedition, but could he have been
the only one to make an all-out rescue call? He would have been the logical first choice, certainly. But the previous day Howard, after observing
Joe's incapacitation, assumed de facto leadership of the team, directing
preparations for their descent from Camp VI and leading the rope team
down. With a clearer head and stronger body, he could have taken over
the radio and simply on his own authorized an all-out rescue.

Alternatively, because Howard and Bill Babcock agreed that Wilcox
was "in shock," they could have joined forces to demand immediate

launch of an all-out rescue. Failing that dramatic an action, they might have at least stated their firm belief that delay of an all-out rescue would endanger the men higher up.

They did neither. Perhaps expecting them to do so, from our vantage point four decades later, is simply expecting too much. It was 1967, remember, on the cusp between the Age of Conformity and the Age of Aquarius, when crew cuts still ruled, blue jeans were prohibited from public schools, and "Question Authority" stickers were as rare as seat belts. Bill Babcock was just twenty-nine years old and Howard only twenty-two. Both were undoubtedly aware of the recent ugly uproar over tax dollars being squandered to rescue lunatic climbers, and the fact that they themselves might be personally billed for rescue expenses. Finally, to experienced mountaineers, the role of expedition leader carried authority akin to that of a captain on his ship. To usurp that authority would have been a drastic action—perhaps not as serious as maritime mutiny, but virtually unprecedented.

Having said all that, and examined all accounts of events at Camp V, we return to the unavoidable question: Why did Joe not authorize an all-out rescue then and there? There is every reason to expect the worst, and little if any reason for optimism. In *White Winds*, Joe explained his inaction this way.

Eielson then asked if I wanted an all-out rescue called for the upper camp. The question was quite perplexing. Airdrops had already been cleared and according to Park Service policy these could only be authorized (except for scientific groups) in an emergency situation. Weren't we already in a rescue? Our backup, the Alaska Rescue Group, had already been notified and were likely riding their bags pending the overflight. I could not imagine them ignoring the serious findings of an overflight or waiting for a formal request in an obviously grim situation. Airplaines had not been able to fly near the mountain in over a week without risking having their wings ripped off in the turbulence. Even if they could, the mountain was not about to be stormed by paratroopers and helicopter landings would be unlikely at extreme elevations. The MCA party was not only the best positioned and acclimated, but the only feasible rescue team unless another expedition was higher. And this possibility was already being checked out. I could not see how more could be accomplished by calling an all-out rescue.

The answer to the question "Weren't we already in a rescue?" is so clearly *no* that it's hard to imagine how Joe could have been confused. But it's important to note that we know things Joe cannot and does not at that moment. Despite his reassuring image of the Alaska Rescue Group as a platoon of intrepid hearties sitting on duffel bags beside an idling C-130, the Alaska Rescue Group is at that point one lone man, Gary Hansen, doubtless with good intentions but so far riding only a desk in an office rather than a duffel bag beside a runway.

Regarding helicopters, given how hard it was to get to just 17,000 feet, it's not at all likely that a helicopter of that era could make it safely to 17,900 feet or higher, and that was probably the focus of Joe's thought about helicopters. (Of course, helicopters *could* fly much closer than 12,100 feet at a time when days, indeed hours, could make the difference between men living and dying.)

On the other hand, how realistic was Joe's dismissal of paratroopers and military assistance? He mentions them only as hyperbole to indicate how ludicrous it is even to imagine such a show of force. But only four months earlier, the immense Winter Expedition rescue effort included the famed Whittaker brothers, Jim and Lou; an entire team from Anchorage; helicopters, C-130s, T-33 jets; and a sizable detachment of soldiers all "chafing at the bit," as Wayne Merry recalls it.

So in the end, although some reasons for reticence existed, others gave cause for action, and it remains difficult to understand how Joe could *not* see that more might be accomplished by calling an all-out rescue. He was an extraordinarily intelligent man, and a mathematician at that, and his mind would normally have distilled all the variables down to a simple, undeniable risk/benefit analysis in minutes, if not seconds: Calling an all-out rescue *might* help, and *cannot* hurt. Therefore, it *must* be done.

But he did not. Why not? Partly, it is the weight of those various misapprehensions noted above. Partly, too, it is altitude and exhaustion.

But there is another powerful force at work here—one not mentioned in any of the other accounts of this tragedy. Elisabeth Kubler-Ross pioneered research that identified the ways in which people react upon learning that they will soon die or will suffer the deaths of loved ones. The first stage of reaction to death by the victim, and those closest to them, is described as numb, unfeeling, and disconnected—all symptoms of deep denial. The imminence of our own deaths, or of those we are close to, is so devastating that our immediate response is to deny their reality. As Kubler-Ross and others have demonstrated, the denial response is as universal and autonomic as the tendency of blood to clot. Combined with youth, exhaustion, confusion, fatigue, altitude, and ignorance of actual rescue preparations, denial conspired to create a barrier that would have been difficult for any normal person to surmount, let alone one in Joe's debilitated condition.

WAYNE MERRY'S AFTERNOON has been even more frustrating than his morning, so frustrating that it pushes him over a dangerous professional edge. At first, interference from local radios in cars and trucks makes it impossible to communicate with anyone. Finally reaching Roberta Sheldon at 3 p.m., he learns that her husband has not flown after all—too much wind.

Wayne hangs up and calls Eldon Reyer, who repeats that the decision has been made to wait for the results of Sheldon's flight, whenever it may take place, rather than request a big military plane.

Wayne can bear it no longer. In a different tone, he *directs* Reyer to "pass on my recommendation to Art that an RCC plane make a run if it appears at all possible, rather than waiting on Sheldon's small airplane. He's excellent for close-in support if conditions are right, but larger craft could give a look from a few thousand feet when Sheldon can't fly."

They need a look *right now,* Wayne emphasizes, to see what the story is at 17,900 feet. He adds that it would be even better if supplies could be carried aloft, ready to be dropped. Finally, Wayne wants to make sure that the RCC is alerted to the possible need not only for observation craft but for Hueys, military helicopters like those that were doing such yeoman service in Vietnam.

Wayne knows that Reyer can only pass his demands up the chain of command, an ascent whose every stop along the way will strip off some of his requests' urgency. So now Wayne can only pace around his office and watch the weather disintegrate—again. Later in the afternoon, he makes a bitter entry in his log: "Weather now entirely obscuring mountain—any chance of flying anything is probably gone for today."

The day finally whimpers to an end at 8:00 p.m., when Joe radios a request that families of his party of five be called collect to report their sons' safe retreat from McKinley. Wayne relays the request to park headquarters. It is never done.

If Wayne felt alone and impotent before, events conspire throughout the night to make him even more so—literally. Torrential rains wash out roads linking him to the outside, isolating him physically as well as philosophically from the immovable bureaucracy at park headquarters.

By the end of this day, for all the reasons noted above and perhaps still others (we have no records of any communications between George Hall and the NPS regional office, for example), no all-out rescue is called for or launched. Thus with the oceanic resources of the National Park Service and the United States Air Force untapped, responsibility for trying to save Jerry Clark's team now falls squarely on the shoulders of Bill Babcock, a brave young Alaskan, and his four courageous friends whose climb has taken them not only up McKinley but into the Wilcox Expedition's epic tragedy as well. One person has never been above 6,200 feet, none has formal SAR training, and all are exhausted from fighting the mountain for weeks. But—and perhaps this is another trait of their generation—they take the job without hesitation or complaint. In one of the day's last communications to Eielson, Bill Babcock estimates that it will take four days of climbing in perfect conditions to reach the high camp.

22

MONDAY, JULY 24
Some Will Die

As if Bill Babcock does not have enough problems on his hands, Grace Jansen-Hoeman takes a sharp turn for the worse on Monday morning. She has been sharing a tent with him and Jeff. After a long and sleepless night, in behavior completely out of character, she begins berating Bill for his cooking, deriding his decisions, and calling him and Jeff "pigs." They are friends, and Bill is alarmed rather than offended. He keeps a close eye on her throughout the morning, but she does not improve, suffering dizziness, severe headaches, and continual vomiting. Bill finally asks Joe to take her down. An accident analysis later published by the American Alpine Club will state that the descending climbers were "strengthened" by Grace's addition to their party. Its author clearly had not taken time to ask Bill, Joe, or even Grace herself before committing that error to print.

Thus at about noon, two groups head down McKinley from the MCA camp. Howard, Jerry, and Paul as one group; Joe, Anshel, and Grace as the other. After about an hour, Joe yells over to Howard, asking where and when he wants to meet lower down to eat and camp. Howard's response, as recalled by Joe, was "a profane reply indicat[ing] that he was no longer interested in my opinions or suggestions, and so we continued the descent as two estranged groups operating independently." None of the others I interviewed remember such an exchange, but there's no question that the two groups were by now indeed estranged.

The descent is difficult for all of them, particularly for Howard and Jerry Lewis. Jerry has recovered some strength but has painfully frostbitten feet. Howard is carrying more than a hundred pounds and has aggravated an old injury to his left foot. And he's suffering from a fresh gash behind his right knee, made by one of his crampon points during a fall.

Now left in Camp V are only Bill Babcock and his brother Jeff; Chet Hackney; John Ireton; and Gayle Nienheuser. Not long after Joe and Howard's groups start down, forty-mile-per-hour winds and heavy snow blast the MCA camp anew and continue all day, adding to the previous snow accumulation of five feet or more. Moving around entails wading through shoulder-deep drifts. The snow doesn't let up until nine that evening, at which point the wind becomes so violent that their tents "all but blew away" and are saved from destruction only by the combined efforts of their occupants, who spend most of the night sitting up and bracing tent poles with their own bodies. Jeff Babcock, his feet already cold for several days, begins to have trouble with his freezing toes. Nevertheless, Bill tells Eielson that they will try to reach the stranded men up high as fast as possible, and will start climbing as soon as the wind allows.

If Monday, July 24, is little more than an exhausting, rainy slog for Joe and Howard's groups, at least they make some downward progress. Such is not the case at Wonder Lake. That morning, Wayne learns that Don Sheldon still has not flown. The Alaska Rescue Group has not assembled and dispatched an SAR team. The National Park Service officials have not requested an overflight by a C-130. In fact, the only decision that Art Hayes and George Hall have made is to not make any decisions. Jerry Clark and his companions have not been heard from since 11:45 a.m. on Tuesday, July 18—seven days and nights ago.

During the 8:00 a.m. radio contact on July 24, Joe asks whether Wayne believes a large plane could fly at high altitude for observation. Wayne assures him not only that one could, but that he has been urging such a flight for days—without success. Joe confirms that there have been windows during which such an overflight might have been made.

After breaking contact with Joe, Wayne tries to reach Art Hayes and George Hall. No answer. A half hour later, he tries again. No answer. For Wayne, the inaction is maddening. Bill Babcock's last estimate of his MCA group's condition this day is only "fair." Given the storm conditions at 12,100 feet, Wayne knows that the climbers will not be moving today. His one contact with Sheldon, at 3 p.m., reveals that the pilot earlier flew some people to the South Face Expedition base at 7,400 feet but is now grounded by winds.

Come Monday's end, only Gary Hansen of the Alaska Rescue Group has made a tangible contribution to the rescue effort. Earlier, Sheldon told him that they should have oxygen breathing cylinders, which might be needed for sick climbers or for him when flying near the summit in his unpressurized cockpit. On Sunday evening Gary finally located a supply source, and on Monday sent two cylinders to Don Sheldon on the 9 a.m. Alaska Railroad train to Talkeetna.

SLEEP THIS NIGHT comes hard for everyone on and off the mountain as they grapple with the realization that sooner or later dawns on every player in a tragedy. Some people are going to die, and that will be horrible. Others are going to survive, but they will be damaged in ways that passing time may scar over but will never, ever completely heal.

23

Hard Men Indeed

Tuesday brings hard labor scarcely less punishing for those going down the mountain than for those going up, though the rewards for those descending are greater. On Monday, Howard, Jerry, and Paul had climbed down past the Great Icefall, the Hill of Cracks, and the Lower Icefall—Howard and Paul under hundred-pound packs—camping eventually on the lower Muldrow. Tuesday brings them off the glacier, onto the moraine, and then, at 8:30 a.m., in bright sunshine, to McGonagall Pass, through which they had climbed so eagerly on June 23. To Howard, it "seems strangely quiet now, austere, even desolate."

They change from the filthy climbing clothes they have been wearing almost a month into clean gear for the tundra crossing. Howard discovers that he has *gained* ten pounds. He is the only man on the expedition to gain weight. Paul Schlichter holds his own, neither gaining nor losing, but all the others lose at least twenty pounds.

Howard attributes his weight gain, and Paul's holding steady, to the "huge, palatable, high-calorie meals" that his menu planning provided. That's not an exaggeration. Howard considered nutrition, palatability at altitude, and the appetites of big men working hard every day. He doubled manufacturers' recommended portions, and his final plan included 2.67 pounds of food per man per day. That's deceptive, however, because a lot of their food was freeze-dried, which weighs only a fraction of its reconstituted weight. Here's a typical supper:

Double-portion Swiss steak with gravy, mashed potatoes, and peas
Summer sausage or deviled ham

Edam or Gouda cheese

Snickers bar

1 quart Wyler's drink mix

1 roll sour fruit candies

1 cup freeze-dried prunes or apricots

1 slice Logan bread (3 inches × 2 inches × 1 inch)

THEY CONTINUE DOWN into the wide Cache Creek Valley, a new world, rich with colors and smells and sounds absent from their experience for a month: fire-red lichens, dusty purple monkshood, magenta campion, bright yellow tundra rose. The wet sedge grass and moss give off sweet scents, and even the land seems to be speaking, as Howard, moved to wax lyrical, writes: "The gossiping brook prattled in our ears."

At 2:17 p.m., after descending 8,000 vertical feet in twenty-five hours, they pitch a tent, eat dinner, and settle in for a long, long sleep, midnight sun be damned. During the night, Howard dreams of shadowy figures prowling through their camp, whispering rough things he can't understand. Come morning he will realize that they were not dream shapes but Joe, Anshel, and Grace on their way to Wonder Lake.

THE MCA'S CHET Hackney awakes first on Tuesday at about six in the morning and announces that the storm has blown itself out. It's a good thing. They had spent most of the night shoveling snow, bracing the tent frames with their bodies, getting almost no sleep. Their stay at 12,100 feet has been trying. Bill Babcock, who will spend twenty more years climbing in Alaska and will summit McKinley five times altogether, recalls the three days of storm in Camp V as "horrendous. The worst I've ever seen. Just horrible."

After breakfast, they bury the tents. From here on, they'll dig snow caves. This lightens each man's load by about ten pounds (which still leaves each man carrying about eighty pounds) but also means two hours or more of hard digging at the end of every day's climb.

At 8:00 a.m., Bill radios Eielson of his intention to make Browne Tower this day, and they hit the trail. Whiteout clamps down at 2 p.m. and snow begins to fall, light at first and then with real intent.

L IKE ALL THE others, Wayne's hopes are buoyed, then dashed, by McKinley's fickle Tuesday morning weather.

Bill Babcock's 8:00 a.m. report from 12,100 feet could not be better: no wind, clear sky, visibility excellent, weather in which a light plane could fly easily. More news: in this good weather, the Wilcox team is coming down in two separate groups, and Grace Jansen-Hoeman, sick from altitude, is coming down with one of them.

Wayne Merry tries to have park headquarters tell Sheldon about the good weather and get him up immediately. They can't get through. Wayne then calls Sheldon himself on another frequency and suggests that he fly *now*. Sheldon is loaded and ready; he should be up around the North Face in ninety minutes. Suddenly he asks an odd question:

"Why don't those MCA people at 12,100 go up and have a look?" The question echoes Eldon Reyer's report of the day before that Sheldon was "very upset with Wilcox."

It is a strange question from someone who knows as much about McKinley climbing as Don Sheldon. Bill Babcock and his party are camped at 12,100 feet. The climb from there to 17,900 feet could take fresh, fit climbers a week or more under normal conditions. Bill has estimated that his MCA group, climbing (relatively) light and fast, relying on airdropped supplies in clear weather, can *maybe* do it in four days, *if* the weather is perfect.

Wayne explains this to Sheldon. No reply is printed in the log, but Sheldon does fly.

Later that morning, flying with the radios and supplies that Gary Hansen bussed up from Anchorage, Sheldon radios to Wayne that he has Bill Babcock's party in sight. They're at about 12,300 feet and going up fast. That's the good news. The bad news is that there's a standing wave cloud covering everything down to about 17,000 feet.

Wayne asks Sheldon to drop radios and food to the MCA group where they are now. Sheldon refuses. He tells Wayne that he's going to drop them at 15,000 feet, almost a vertical half mile above the MCA team's present location. Sheldon's intent may be to save Bill and his team the effort of carrying supplies an additional 2,700 vertical feet. They are going well now from what he can see, and groups do make the climb from

Camp V, at 12,100 feet, to Camp VI, at 15,000 feet, in a single day—
although only if rested and blessed with perfect weather. Bill's team is
neither rested nor fresh, and any number of other things could still slow
them down: altitude sickness, fatigue, injury, equipment failure, and, of
course, bad weather.

Wayne asks, Why not just drop supplies to the MCA team where they
are? Or maybe part of the supplies?

I'm dropping everything at fifteen thousand, Sheldon snaps, and that's
that.

Sheldon makes the drop, tossing bags out of his plane's open door.
They land about a quarter mile west of the 15,000-foot camp, where they
will help the MCA team when—and if—they get to Camp VI, and only
then if the drops have not been buried beneath several feet of new snow.

With the drop complete, Sheldon reports that the standing wave cloud
is socking in McKinley quickly. One of these localized storms can attack
in an hour or two out of a perfectly clear sky. Not even Don Sheldon
could fly into one of these and expect to fly out again. He heads down to
check on the Western States people climbing the West Buttress route,
then flies gear and more people over to Boyd Everett's South Face crew
at 10,000 feet.

Another weather window has slammed shut. Wayne repeats to Art
Hayes what Sheldon has told him, then tells *him* to relay this information to Gary Hansen of the ARG. His frustration finally getting the better of him, Wayne adds pointedly,

"We need a sharper operation. Possibly high overflights as soon as the
weather clears again. And somebody needs to make a decision about an
all-out rescue."

Hayes says he'll discuss that and get back to Wayne.

He does, but only after six hours have passed. The likely between-the-
lines message: *Don't push too hard, Ranger Merry.* The report, in addition
to being so late, offers no help or reason to hope for any. Hayes says that
he tried unsuccessfully to call Gary Hansen, who wasn't available. Then
he called "someone else at ARG." Hayes thinks, but isn't positive, that
they're trying to arrange for an RCC plane. That's it. Six hours, two calls.

Wayne knows that the office-bound Hayes has never been high on
a big mountain in a severe storm—in fact, hasn't done any serious

mountaineering—and understands that this may contribute to the lack of urgency in the chief ranger's voice. That there *is* an absence of urgency, not only in Art Hayes's voice but everywhere else in the NPS except Wayne Merry's increasingly frantic mind, is sadly indisputable. Long after the event, Howard, Joe, Anshel, Wayne, the MCA team, and the parents of the climbers who die will decry the NPS officials' failure to comprehend that a life-threatening emergency was upon them.

Hoping for better news, Wayne raises Eielson in the afternoon and is finally rewarded. The MCA team has reached Browne Tower, at 14,500 feet, and hopes to make it to 15,500 feet the next day. As Wayne feared, Sheldon's airdrops will do no one any good. Bill Babcock reports that they're in "OK" condition. Wayne renews his efforts to get a big RCC C-130 up and orbiting the mountain, freighted with a supply-laden drop sled that can be off-loaded up high.

Time passes into gray evening. Wayne paces around his office, angry, frustrated, mind racing. What else can he do? He can't stop thinking about Bill Babcock and his men hunched under eighty-pound packs, fighting through waist-deep drifts, gasping like sprinters, muscles on fire, and young, green Jeff, who's never been above six grand and hurting who knows how badly. And far above them, seven more men entombed in shredded tents or snow caves, some almost certainly dead and others close but hanging on, faces ice white, hands and feet long gone, bodies eating themselves, minds dissolving.

Confined now by the storm and the tiny office and the vast but no less imprisoning government agency for which he works, Wayne stops, glares out at the thick gray funk, listening to rain tattooing the roof and the restless wind rubbing the building's walls.

He tries the radio again, and again, and raises no one.

Wayne Merry's life has been defined by action. Now, fed up, he takes one that, in the military, would be construed as flagrant insubordination at best and mutiny at worst. The NPS is less hierarchical than the army or the navy, of course, but if what Wayne is about to do will not end his life in front of a firing squad, it could well terminate his exemplary eight-year career.

He calls a local ham radio operator, Celia Hunter. He gives her phone numbers for Gary Hansen and two other ARG officials and asks her to call them at once.

"Tell them I want an RCC plane to orbit McKinley with a drop sled and to look for any activity at seventeen-nine. Tell them to fly as early as possible in the morning—that's when good weather will be. And tell them I will be responsible for all of this."

Celia Hunter tries for hours to get through to the ARG people. She calls again and again by radio and by phone—but cannot reach a single soul.

BILL BABCOCK AND his friends climb through the morning and into the afternoon, pitch after pitch, Sisyphean labor. They're not enjoying much about this mission handed them by fate. The scale of things on McKinley makes it important to think in small bites; otherwise, your brain starts a queasy *I can't do this* slide toward the slough of despond. So to stay focused and insulate themselves, they might count their steps, or stare at their snowshoes or cramponed boots, counting to fifty or one hundred, not looking up until they hit the appointed number, then starting the count all over again.

This ploy can induce a kind of numb trance, but sooner or later pain will intrude. There are just too many ways to hurt doing this. Under eighty pounds, the 1967 Kelty pack with its meanly padded straps cuts painfully into the tops of your shoulders the minute you heft that monster. You can shift some of the load by loosening straps and cinching your pack's unpadded waistband tighter, but that soon overloads hips and glutes, which then begin to squeal with pain. Big thigh muscles don't care where the pack load is centered—they just make an endless bass note of pain beneath all the other higher, sharper hurts. Throats get raw from sucking the thin, dry air; eyes hurt from squinting. Then there are some pains unique to each person—the odd knee injury, that "fixed" herniated disk, a stitch that won't quit.

Babcock and company are breaking trail not only through an endless succession of uphill pitches but through steadily worsening pain as well, and it takes hard men to keep doing that hour after hour after hour. These are hard men indeed, the Alaskans among them just a generation or two from the legendary Sourdoughs, whose unbelievable climb was chronicled earlier. They battle to Browne Tower, at 14,500 feet, and arrive at five that evening.

Sheldon was supposed to drop supplies and fuel for them along the route, but they find nothing and assume that the drop was lost in white-out. In fact, it's being buried under accumulating snow 500 vertical feet above them. They spend the next two hours digging the requisite snow cave, building an igloo, then melting snow and fixing dinner, which they are nearly too exhausted to eat. By the time they're ready for sleep at 11 p.m., heavy snow is falling again.

They're still almost a vertical mile away from Camp VII, which is good and bad. It's good because being that far away means they aren't yet thinking of what could be waiting for them up there. It's bad because, as seasoned climbers, they know what the trapped men are enduring, and this makes it impossible for them to rest completely even for a moment. Thus at day's end, Bill Babcock, so spent that he can barely hold a pencil, nevertheless forces himself to make a ragged entry in his expedition diary. The lament is not for himself or his hurting friends:

> VERY TIRED.
> Park has yet to declare emergency for 7 poor souls above us.

24

WEDNESDAY, JULY 26
Crossing the River

O n Wednesday morning, Joe, Anshel, and Grace break camp at 4 a.m. and hike through hard rain to flood-swollen Clearwater Creek, which has burgeoned into a raging river several hundred yards wide. Only Joe is able to cross it, and only then by using his pack as a lifesaving float. With Anshel and Grace sitting tight, Joe walks on alone until he reaches a hill overlooking the monstrously transformed McKinley River:

> A mile and a half away was not the many channeled, braided river of my recollection, but a single blackish mile-wide devastating force, gouging the earth with abandon. Not even the soft tundra could absorb the roar of the swirling water, the rumble of tumbling boulders, and the splintering snap of logs tossed about like twigs.

This is an excellent description, but nowadays we can go him one better. Think of those frequent Weather Channel clips of rolling, boiling flooded rivers you've seen, the kind that rip houses off their foundations, overturn trains, and pick up 18-wheelers as if they're toys. That's what Joe confronts.

His soaked pack won't float anymore. There's no point in going back across the Clearwater. But staying where he is, between the two flooding rivers, would be ludicrous. Joe doesn't think he could make it across this raging river even if he were fit, rested, and healthy, but he realizes that there is no choice. So in he goes, and is quickly plucked off his feet by the mile-wide maelstrom. He has survived an arctic hurricane and a climb to the summit of Mount McKinley and back—and now this river may kill him.

What had been the river's ankle-high rivulets are now chest-deep torrents. Formerly waist-deep channels are now roiling water many feet deep. It's like being churned in a giant grinding machine. At one point the violent water rips his wind pants down around his ankles, making it impossible for him to swim. Nearly unconscious, he gives himself over to the current, so exhausted and cold that he just has to take what comes.

Miraculously, Joe scrapes up on a submerged bar just shallow enough to snag him. If not for this bit of pure luck, he surely would have drowned. There he remains, vomiting filthy, silt-laden water, then finally launching himself back into the flow. At last he flops down on the opposite bank, soaked, hypothermic, exhausted, bleeding. It is as close to death as he has ever come, and he isn't sure, to this day, why he has survived.

WHILE JOE STRUGGLES with the McKinley River, Wayne Merry, in the Wonder Lake Ranger Station, continues his own struggle to breathe life into the stillborn rescue operation. At 8 a.m., he asks Art Hayes at park headquarters whether the ARG and the RCC have been alerted.

Not just yet. But don't worry, it will be taken care of at this end, Hayes tells Wayne, in a tone that suggests that his subordinate is overreacting.

Having not much faith that things *will* be taken care of at that end, Wayne makes the risky move of going over Hayes's head by telephoning the chief ranger's own boss, Superintendent Hall.

"George, I just want to make sure you're fully aware of everything that's happening."

"They've been keeping me informed of the situation," Hall says tersely.

Ten minutes later, Hayes calls back. According to Wayne's log, Hayes asks him, "What was the position of the seven men at seventeen-nine?" At this late date, it is an astonishing question from Mount McKinley National Park's chief ranger. This is the first thing he should have known, or learned, when a problem was reported.

Wayne explains that they were camped about a quarter mile from Denali Pass, on the Harper Glacier.

"Did they make it to the top?"

"We know that one man, Steve Taylor, stayed in camp because he was sick. The others made it. They radioed from the summit about noon on the eighteenth." *My God,* Wayne thinks, *that's nine days ago.*

Two hours pass. Wayne calls George Hall and asks for a summary of what's being done. He also tells Hall that they need to discuss a rescue.

The ARG council is in a meeting, Hall says. Sheldon flying low reconnaissance is probably the best way to learn how the climbers are doing. (The same refrain that Wayne has been hearing for days.) Those MCA people should be in the area before long—twenty-four to forty-eight hours, he'd guess. And this weather won't let Sheldon or helicopters get up to 17-9.

"What about the climbers coming up the south side?"

"It turns out they don't have a radio antenna so we can't talk to them."

"So what *has* been done so far?"

(Wayne takes careful notes as Hall speaks.)

"Sheldon dropped gear at 15,000. The rescue council has to determine whether a rescue can be made. And whether one is needed."

Whether one is needed?

"Remember that at least three of these people up there are experienced in mountain rescue. It's reasonable to assume that if anything was wrong, they would have been spotted coming down."

"These people haven't been heard from for *nine days*, George."

"The National Park Service can only coordinate here. Keep that in mind."

"So what do we do now?"

"The important thing, I think, is to locate those climbers up high and arrange a pickup—if necessary."

If necessary?

It is hard for Wayne to believe what he is hearing.

"The last we heard from them was on July 18th," he reminds Hall. "Since then, there have been several times when they could have come down to 15,000. We haven't seen any activity there, or any fresh tracks."

"Believe me that I'm very concerned about the safety of these men," Hall says. Then, in a puzzling non sequitur, he adds, "if the need arises, just about any sized airplane equipped for water landing could land on Wonder Lake. The Kantishna strip is inaccessible just now."

"So far, it seems to me that the only thing we've done is to ask Sheldon for an observation and drop flight," Wayne points out. "And that seems to be taking a backseat to other flights, like the South Face group. You know that C-130s could fly over the summit right now."

"Maybe. But right now you need to just sit tight pending further decisions, Wayne."

George Hall is not mean, not a martinet, does not dish out chicken-shit. But Wayne understands that right now Hall *has* just told him, boss to underling, to sit down and shut up.

And that's what he's doing—sitting tight, waiting, and fuming—when at noon the door bangs open and in walks Joe Wilcox, having swum the McKinley River, hiked six miles to the nearest road, and hitched a ride here to Wonder Lake.

Exclaiming congratulations, Wayne rounds the old desk, grabs Joe's hand, and starts pumping, but then he eases off. Joe looks even worse than most men coming off a long bout with McKinley. He's thin, hollow eyed, exhausted, as scuffed and bruised as if he had lost a street fight. No matter how bad climbers coming off McKinley look, though, if they have made the summit, they are almost always jubilant, heady with the joy of having made it up and down one of the world's most coveted peaks. Joe looks anything but jubilant, and his reply to Wayne has a bitter edge.

"Some conquest," he says, adding that his expedition is strung out in at least three different groups and has not communicated for more than a week, and the Clark party could even be dead.

Joe knows that Wayne means well, and he *is* glad to be back here, confident that rescue efforts are moving forward. Then he learns that his confidence is misplaced. The high-altitude reconnaissance flight he requested days ago has not been made. Don Sheldon has made no high overflights, and has dropped supplies in the wrong place. And George Hall has just told Wayne to sit tight and wait.

Joe cannot believe what Wayne is telling him, and says so. He asked for a high-altitude overflight *days* ago. And why did Sheldon drop the supplies at 15,000 feet that were supposed to go to Camp VII?

Wayne can only shake his head and admit that it has been frustrating for him too. He explains that even down here, this storm is one for the record books. It has interrupted radio communications between here and headquarters, knocked down telephone poles and lines, and washed out a number of roads and bridges.

Wayne wants to learn as much as he can from Joe, so they examine maps together, Joe pointing out camps and routes. As they're doing so, Wayne asks whether Joe needs frostbite treatment for his hands.

They're not frostbitten, Joe says.

"But Eielson got a radio message that you had frostbitten hands."

"That was Howard's opinion—not mine."

Wayne is struck by the anger in Joe's voice and asks, "How did the Colorado guys fit in with the expedition?"

"Not at all." And then: "If anything happens to the upper party, I will never forgive them."

"Forgive who?"

"Howard and Paul," Joe says. "They ran out on the upper group. They refused to go back up to the high camp."

"Oh! My impression was that they were well-conditioned, cool-headed mountaineers."

Wayne is taken aback by what Joe has told him. It is the first hint he's gotten that serious problems existed on the mountain throughout the expedition. When the whole group showed up for their briefing and equipment check, the three Colorado climbers looked fit, their equipment was impressive, and they seemed focused—more so than at least some of the other climbers in Joe's party. Wayne had overheard a couple of those young men, in fact, talking about what a "walk-up" this climb was going to be.

Now at wonder Lake, Joe must try to expedite rescue efforts for not one but two trapped parties. The seven men up high are still unaccounted for. Anshel, Grace Hoeman, and the three Coloradoans are trapped by two flooding rivers. Joe is particularly concerned about Jerry Lewis; Grace warned that walking any farther than necessary on his badly frostbitten feet would risk permanent injury to the damaged tissues.

No military helicopters are available, making a private craft the only other option. Joe requests that one be sent immediately. Even a low-altitude version will cost $125 per hour ($720 per hour in 2006 dollars), with a three-hour minimum fee, or \$375/\$2,160. To an impoverished, recently married graduate student living on a shoestring budget, it is a fortune, but Joe agrees to the payment without hesitation.

The chopper picks up Wayne Merry, then retrieves the remaining five stranded climbers from beside Clearwater Creek. Howard is initially reluctant to fly out in the helicopter, preferring to walk out the way he walked in. But once he is airborne and sees the McKinley River, he changes his tune:

"The braided channels had vanished, the river was filled from bank to bank. It was a mile wide; a cold-water Mississippi. I was suddenly very glad that we were crossing it in a helicopter."

On WEDNESDAY MORNING, after a quick breakfast, Bill Babcock's team sets out in two feet of fresh snow, plowing through nearly bottomless powder with gargantuan packs and depleted bodies. Gayle Nienheuser does a heroic job of breaking trail all the way up. Bill's diary:

"Very difficult going. Everyone tired too—to hard work of day before > after sleepless night. We were still very exhausted and spent some 2 hrs. looking for Sheldon's air drop . . . which was, incredibly enough, wrapped in a white pillow case!" [Emphasis in original]

Frustrated beyond measure, Bill radios a request for more food and fuel to be dropped. Even more than the words he's writing, the deteriorating appearance of Bill's diary gives the starkest indication how this forced-march climb is eating away at him and the others. Until now, every page in the little book has been filled with neat, legible script; sentences running straight and level from margin to margin; punctuation, spelling, and grammar correct. Wednesday's entry could have been scribbled by a drunk. The neat script has become ragged and irregular, well-composed sentences have given way to rough fragments littered with misspellings and write-overs. It is the writing not of a drunk but of a man in the far reaches of exhaustion. And frustration:

> Sheldon flew over early and dropped food fuel batteries etc. But 2 ft. new snow prohibits us from finding it. Park fails to contact Sheldon and when he flies the morning of the 27th he does not drop anything?! No sign of seven who are lost. Spend two hours looking for

Sheldon's air drop. With two feet of new snow this was a terrible waste of time and energy. Sheldon's reliability highly questionable and to the fact of pillow case drop, unwanted drop at 15,100 His uncertainty of exact location of first drop after it could not be found etc.! Never should have done it.

FUCKING PARK

25

THURSDAY, JULY 27
Far Too Little, Way Too Late

On Thursday, at 5:55 a.m., Jerry Lewis and Grace Jansen-Hoeman fly out on the helicopter to a town with the eerily appropriate name of Farewell. From there, Jerry can be transported by fixed-wing aircraft to Anchorage, where he will begin receiving treatment for serious frostbite. Return to lower altitude has restored Grace's health.

At 10:00 a.m., Wayne speaks with Howard and Paul about their availability, in case high-altitude helicopters are summoned to Camp VII. They, and Joe, are the only remaining climbers from the expedition who are fit and acclimatized to go that high that quickly. Paul already volunteered to fly with any air force C-130 that might take off, but, oddly, the Air Force Academy graduate was told by someone at the RCC that they wouldn't take "civilians."

"I asked [Howard and Paul] to be available, and they said they would be, in Anchorage, and that seemed quite reasonable to me," Wayne recalls. Howard and Paul drive away in Jerry Lewis's Power Wagon, the iron horse that got them—and Joe's overloaded trailer—up the punishing Alcan. Anshel rides with them as far as park headquarters, where he will catch a train to Anchorage. The two big Coloradoans pretty much fill up the truck's cab all by themselves.

On their way out, they stop at park headquarters, and Howard's description of their brief encounter with Art Hayes and George Hall confirms that even at this late date, the NPS officials are not convinced that a true emergency exists. Or, worse, they believe that, if one does, it's not their problem to deal with. So pronounced is their foot-dragging that even shy, reserved Anshel loses his composure:

> When we arrived at Park Headquarters, we went in to talk with Chief Park Ranger Arthur J. Hayes and Park Superintendent George A. Hall . . . Hall said, "We've checked over their application forms. They've got some experienced men, including a couple with rescue experience. We don't see how anything too serious could have happened to a party that large."
>
> Schiff exploded, "What do you mean, nothing could have happened to them? They haven't been heard from in ten days!"
>
> On the mountain, we had begun to worry on the night of the nineteenth. At the base of the mountain, men who understood mountains and climbing began to worry just slightly later. But in more distant places, some were still not convinced, because they could not imagine the irresistible power of a high mountain storm.

Recalling those moments when we met, Howard remained incredulous thirty-nine years later. Although readily admitting that Arthur Hayes seemed "a nice guy," Howard still laments that "he was not a climber and didn't know the situation on the mountain."

THE WEATHER THIS day is good, bringing at last a stir of rescue activity. Two high overflights are finally made. Don Sheldon flies to 18,000 feet at 4:30 a.m. and circles the peak, but he sees no sign of the Clark party. This is disturbing but does not guarantee that all the climbers are dead. People trapped by winter accidents have survived for incredible periods of time, as avalanche expert Jill Fredston notes in her excellent book on the subject, *Snowstruck*. In 1982, a twenty-two-year-old woman named Anna Conrad survived five days after an avalanche buried her in the ruins of a steel A-frame building at the bottom of Alpine Ski Meadows in northern California. The record, though, is held by two sisters and an eleven-year-old girl from the village of Bergemetto, in Northern Italy. In 1755, their home was buried beneath forty-five feet of snow by a monster avalanche that took twenty-two lives. They were entombed in what

Fredston describes as "a fetid, tar-black airspace roughly twelve feet long, eight feet wide, and five feet high." A young boy buried with them died, as did cows, chickens, and a donkey. The women and girl survived an almost unbelievable thirty-seven days. Serendipity was at work here: they could never have lived so long without the milk of two goats that were trapped with them and also survived. But, as Fredston points out, these are anomalies.

Reliable rules of thumb have evolved that predict the survival of buried avalanche victims. A person who remains entombed for thirty minutes has less than a 50 percent chance of getting out alive. Burial for an hour reduces the odds to 23 percent. But those grim statistics do not apply to people holed up in snow and ice caves. The three Winter Expedition climbers survived six days and seven nights in their ice cave up by Denali Pass, but only because they were lucky enough to have extra fuel and food from caches nearby. Jerry Clark and his men have been missing for two days longer, without extra fuel or food.

At about half past ten that morning, the ARG's Gary Hansen and Paul Crews fly over McKinley in the sleek, powerful Turbo Beaver from Anchorage. There is no ARG rescue team on the mountain, just Hansen and Crews flying above it. They observe the Western States party above Denali Pass, going strong for the summit, but see no sign of Jerry Clark or any of his team. Chief Ranger Hayes doesn't tell Wayne Merry about these flights until 6:55 p.m., fourteen hours after the first one took place.

Even later in the evening, Wayne learns from Hayes that Don Sheldon will drop more supplies, radios, and batteries to the MCA group. He will also drop a note from the NPS to the Western States Expedition (WSE), asking its members to join in the MCA's search effort. However, a handwritten entry in the rescue log states, "Note: neither the drop nor the message to WSE was made."

Still later, seasonal rangers Gordon Haber and George Perkins come over from Eielson to Wonder Lake, bringing tape recordings of the previous days' communications. With Wayne they listen to the tapes, examine maps, and talk through various locations where the seven trapped men might still be holed up and surviving. No one is optimistic. The day's last rescue log entry by Wayne reads,

If the party were weak, they would probably not be able to stand against high winds, and would elect to stay put hoping that a lower team would come to their aid, or that their absence would trigger an air drop. This would leave one man at 17,900, weak but well supplied with food and sleeping bags.

For JOE WILCOX, the evening ends badly. He lies on his bunk in a nearby trailer, to which he has moved from the cramped attic at Wonder Lake, listening to hard rain spattering on the metal roof. He is desperately tired, in pain from his many cuts and bruises, and more depressed than he can ever remember. But he cannot give up hope. Just before falling asleep, he thinks, *At least there is this: the weather is good up high and they finally got a rescue going.*

THROUGHOUT THURSDAY, July 27, Bill Babcock's MCA group continues its sprint up McKinley. At 8:00 a.m., Bill radios Eielson that they expect to reach 17,900 feet by seven that night. They report no wind and perfect visibility.

The team continues to be frustrated by Don Sheldon and the National Park Service. That morning, Sheldon inexplicably dropped a message asking whether Bill and his team had seen the missing climbers. His note also contained directions to help them find the supplies he tossed out of the plane the day before in white pillowcases.

Shortly after, an unidentified park service official calls Bill on the radio. Bill's diary:

> Park calls. Says little. Seems they have pretty much given up on 7 climbers. <u>They did not communicate with Sheldon so we are low on fuel if we find 7 alive up there.</u> [Emphasis in original]

Sheldon flew earlier that morning to 18,000 feet and saw no sign of life around Camp VII, Steve and John's last known location at 17,900 feet. Jerry and his four companions almost certainly bivouacked in snow caves at about 19,500 feet, but Sheldon apparently does not go higher than 18,000 feet. It's true that no one told him to search higher, but also true that a man of his experience might suspect it better to be safe than sorry. Neither he nor anyone in the NPS thinks to let the MCA team or Wayne Merry in on the results of his reconnaissance.

Bill Babcock and his men depart 15,100 feet at 10 a.m. Before long, they stumble on three radios wrapped in a white pillowcase. Bill's diary entry about this has a tone of resignation: "Sheldon dropped one he was supposed to keep. He was supposed to leave one of the other ones with the Western States group, however, he just dropped all 3 in a pillow case without bothering to read the note that was inside."

At about half past two, the weather turns foul again, with building winds and heavy snow. Ploughing on to 16,500 feet, they find the three gallons of fuel that Joe cached by the little ice hump where he, Howard, and Paul were turned back by the storm on July 20. The exhausted MCA men build roofless "semi-igloos" and cover them with tarps.

To their horror, they discover that one of their two stoves has suffered a broken safety seal (ironically, the same problem that caused the tent-destroying fire for Joe's team). This means that every chore requiring a stove will now take twice as long, so Jeff and Bill get no supper until 10 p.m. That's inconvenient, but having only one functioning stove means something much worse for all of them. Their safety margin has disappeared. If the last stove goes, they can climb no higher, and the putative rescuers' own survival will be threatened.

THEY HAVE REACHED the point of physical exhaustion where everything seems to be happening through a dull haze. It's quite easy to sit for fifteen minutes thinking about filling a pot with snow, just thinking and knowing that it isn't hard but waiting and waiting for the body to kick into gear. Buried somewhere beneath the fatigue and the generalized pain lies the knowledge that they are searching for other young men like themselves, some of whom may have already died. Following from that is the awareness, which also has to be kept down pretty deep, that if other young men are dead or dying on this mountain *right now*, something similar could happen to the MCA men themselves tomorrow or the next day. It's trite to say that bravery isn't the absence of fear but the ability to carry on despite its gutting presence. It's not trite to do it.

26

FRIDAY, JULY 28
We Cannot Look at Him

At 8:00 a.m., Wayne learns that Bill Babcock and his team are preparing to leave 16,500 feet and head for 17,900 feet. The snow surface is variable, the wind between 10 and 15 miles per hour. Bill reports that they finally did obtain batteries and three small ARG radios from Sheldon's July 25 drop, which, as Wayne feared, took them days to locate. They did not find the larger, more powerful Voice Commander radio that was supposedly dropped as well. Sheldon did not drop them anything last night, as they had expected he would, so the MCA team now has only ten days of food and fuel, including all drops and caches.

They certainly know, as at least Wayne does down deep, that this is a precious-thin margin for what they are about to undertake. They may make it to 17,900 feet this day, or may not. Probabilities are against them, given their exhaustion and McKinley's weather. Once there, they may accomplish their mission quickly and get down, or may not. Odds against them increase the higher they go. They could easily be stormed in for days, as has already happened to the Clark party that they are rushing to aid. If they locate any of those men alive, caring for them will quickly account for much of the remaining food and fuel, not to mention slowing their progress. It is clear that Bill and Jeff Babcock, Chet Hackney, John Ireton, and Gayle Nienheuser are voluntarily placing their own lives at risk, which grows more extreme with every upward step they take.

At 11:05 a.m., Wayne begins an extended radio transmission with Don Sheldon about airdrops to the MCA team, which has requested fifteen

263

days of food and fuel. The conversation with Sheldon is so remarkable that Wayne makes verbatim notes and, at 1:55 p.m., transmits them to Art Hayes with a directive that they be tape recorded. The dialogue begins at 11:05 a.m. with Sheldon's announcement:

"I'm dropping the last of a load of MCA gear at the 14,300-foot level."

Wayne is aghast. The MCA team is now somewhere between 16,500 and 17,900 feet and heading up fast. If Sheldon's earlier determination to drop supplies 2,700 feet above the rescue team was incomprehensible, this new plan is insanity: 14,300 feet is more than 2,000 feet below their present location and 3,600 feet below Camp VII. They will not be back at 14,300 feet for days—perhaps weeks. A drop at 14,300 feet will be absolutely useless to Bill, his four companions, and any survivors they may discover.

Wayne asks that Sheldon save at least some of the supplies for a higher drop. He points out that the MCA group is expecting a drop at 17,900 feet and that supplies dropped so much lower won't do them any good.

I'm dropping this stuff here, Sheldon snaps. He informs Wayne that this is as high as his plane can go. And he counters that the supplies will do them a lot of good down at 15,000 feet, because "they were only about a half mile up the glacier."

A *vertical* half mile up the glacier, maybe. But Jerry Clark and his men may be clinging to life by the slimmest of margins, frostbitten, comatose. At this late date, adequate food and fuel could well mean the difference between their survival and death. Bill Babcock knows that they cannot afford to squander many hours retrieving supplies dropped half a vertical mile below them.

Wayne has to wonder also about Sheldon's declaration that his plane can't fly as high as Camp VII. It had just done so at 4:30 a.m. on the previous day, without any untoward incidents. Sheldon has two planes, and it is possible that one may not be able to fly at 18,000 feet, but then the question becomes why he would use that aircraft knowing that overflying McKinley's summit area is his most important mission.

While Wayne is pondering that riddle, he accidentally overhears a conversation between Sheldon and his home station that only adds to the muddle. The pilot is landing at Mountain House (a shelter on a section of the nearby Ruth Glacier now named, ironically, the Don Sheldon

Amphitheater) to pick up a second load that Sheldon says is also to be dropped in the same place at 14,300 feet.

Wayne has now heard Sheldon's plans three times from the pilot himself, and still simply cannot believe them. The log records his consternation and incredulity:

> The altitudes quoted cannot be accurate; this would put the drop below Browne Tower . . . they will lose all the ground they gained yesterday, another day is lost, and they will have to relay loads higher to consolidate and be safe . . . especially if they wind up feeding 7 more men. If the party is not actually descending, this cuts their safety margin at the high camp.

At about half past noon, there is more conversation with Sheldon, still airborne. Wayne asks Sheldon if he passed the message about linking up with MCA to the WSE party on the other side of Denali Pass.

Sheldon reports that he has not.

Wayne asks whether he has been in contact with them.

Sheldon says no, because they are above 18,000 feet and he can't go that high.

Wayne wonders how Sheldon could know their location if he cannot fly that high. He asks the pilot whether he saw them up there.

Sheldon says no, he wasn't able to find them.

THAT PUZZLING TRANSMISSION concluded, Wayne monitors another between Sheldon and the pilot's base station, passing on a request from Gary Hansen to contact the Western States party and ask them to aid in the search. For reasons that remain unclear, it never happens.

Next, Wayne dictates for the record detailed rescue plans requested for immediate launch. This is the same plan that he has already communicated twice to Hayes and Hall. Among its highlights are:

> 1. Stop depending on Sheldon alone for high altitude operations or critical communication. His aircraft has limited capability, and communications . . . are a serious problem. He is not getting the job done up high.

2. I recommend that the Rescue Coordination Center, Major
Stevens, be asked to supply a rescue-type plane such as a C-130 or
C-118 and that they make a large airdrop of supplies just east of
Denali Pass. . . .

I recognize that this suggestion was not requested, but wish to
have it considered by those responsible for the operation.

Art Hayes acknowledges receipt of the entire transmission, and says
frostily that "it would be discussed."

At 2:45 p.m., George Hall radios back, not to inform Wayne that his
plan has been put into action but that it has been passed on for more discussion. The rescue log entry about this conversation vividly demonstrates what maddening vacillation Wayne has been dealing with for more
than a week now:

2:45 PM: Supt. Hall called to see if the above recommendations
had been made in consultation with Wilcox. (Indicated Hansen
was on the phone). Merry replied that they had grown out of discussions with Wilcox, and would immediately ask Wilcox to read
the message over for his thoughts. Wilcox read over the above and
concurred. Merry reported this to Hall. Hayes asked again the
details of the materials desired for the drop. Merry asked if part of
the message had not been taped, [which he had instructed Hayes
to do] and which should be re-read. Hall requested that only the
items for drop be reiterated. This was done, and reasons for each
briefly repeated.

2:55 PM: Hayes called Merry to ask when he wished the drop to
be made. Reply was that it probably should be as soon as possible,
in case the weather changed again, but that whoever was doing the
rescue planning probably had all the facts and would be in a position to make the decision. Hayes asked to talk to Wilcox, asked him
if he was definitely calling for this drop. Reply was yes. Hayes asked
that, if the drop was made, if it would not be two days before the
climbers reached it. Wilcox said it should be tonight if they were
going up. Hayes said he understood they were going *down*. Merry
clarified—quoted Sheldon as saying the group was descending to
pick it up; also suggested that the RCC establish radio contact with
the MCA to ask *them* where they would want it dropped. (as previ-

Mount McKinley, now more commonly known by its native name Denali, viewed from Wonder Lake. McKinley's storms, altitude, and latitude make Everest seem tropical by comparison. Because Earth's atmosphere is thinnest at its poles, 20,320 feet on McKinley is equivalent to about 23,000 feet in the Himalayas.

The expedition at Camp III, July 4, 1967. Left to right: Steve Taylor, leader Joe Wilcox, Colorado Expedition organizer Howard Snyder, Dennis Luchterhand, Mark McLaughlin, Paul Schlichter, Jerry Clark, Jerry Lewis, Hank Janes, Anshel Schiff, John Russell, and Walt Taylor. Dennis is looking down, perhaps preoccupied; he had reported premonitions before the climb.

MCA Expedition foods. The Wilcox team brought 1,900 pounds; Howard's trio, 415. Even eating 4,000–5,000 calories per day, McKinley climbers typically lose 15–25 pounds.

Colorado climber Jerry Lewis loaded for Camp V. Packs usually weighed 80 pounds, sometimes as much as 100.

A huge McKinley crevasse, terrifying but not deadly. Smaller crevasses covered by thin snow bridges are the killers on McKinley, and a danger even to expert climbers.

Jerry Lewis looking into the crevasse from which he has just been hauled. At the bottom, it was big enough for a basketball game.

Karstens Ridge, named for McKinley pioneer Harry Karstens. Muldrow Route's technical crux and site of McKinley's third fatality, the exposed ridge presents 45-degree pitches. The Wilcox and MCA Expeditions made Camp IV at its base.

Dennis Luchterhand on Walt Taylor's "Throne" at Camp III. Joe and Howard later competed for latrine-building honors at Camp VI, where Joe built matching MEN and WOMEN latrines—what Howard called "a monument to civilization."

Minutes after a faulty stove exploded at Camp VI. Mark McLaughlin, stunned, stands behind Walt Taylor, holding up his burned hand. John Russell looks on from the right. Only floor remains of the tent, which burned in seconds. It was one of three stove accidents that would prompt Howard Snyder to comment on the Wilcox group's "pyromanic tendencies."

Camp VII, 17,900 feet. Howard Snyder took this picture just before noon on July 15 as he and (left to right) Schlichter, Lewis, and Wilcox readied for their summit attempt.

Joe on the summit, 20,320 feet. He remembers feeling "strangely disappointed . . . the fulfillment of my elusive reasons for climbing the mountain were not here."

Launched in twelve hours in March 1967, the Winter Expedition rescue effort included three helicopters, T-33 reconnaissance jets, C-130s, rescue teams from Washington State and Anchorage, and more than fifty military personnel. Ranger Wayne Merry's involvement in this massive effort made the difficulty of arranging a rescue for the Wilcox Expedition all the more frustrating for him.

In contrast, the Wilcox Expedition rescue effort. Leader Bill Babcock (third from left) and his four MCA team members voluntarily risked everything attempting to save Jerry Clark's stranded party of seven. Left to right, Chet Hackney, Gayle Nienheuser, Bill Babcock, and Jeff Babcock.

MCA snowcave at 17,900 feet. Chet Hackney cooks; Gayle Nienheuser sleeps, exhausted from the previous day's summit climb. During their descent, a sudden storm nearly trapped the team while Chet and John Ireton were investigating two bodies (later identified as Dennis Luchterhand and Walt Taylor) below Archdeacon's Tower. The men regained their snowcaves just in time. Jerry Clark and his party probably sheltered for days in similar caves near Archdeacon's Tower ridge.

"We cannot look at him. He's decomposed greatly," radioed Bill Babcock, on finding John Russell's body (assumed at the time to be Steve Taylor's) wrapped in this torn Logan tent at Camp VII on July 28. The body faces away from the camera. His head is the large, round shape on the right. Beneath it, his right arm extends down into the snow. In the foreground, a tarp covers a buried supply dump.

Close-up of the body at Camp VII. Having found this corpse, no one thought to search the tent's buried area, which could have contained another body. Gayle Nienheuser did search Mark McLaughlin's red tent nearby but found only wind-driven snow.

ously suggested.) Also that possibly a T33 could drop the small radios as they had done during the winter operation.

The phone conversation ends without Hall or Hayes committing to any of Wayne's recommendations. Listening, Joe simply cannot believe what he has heard. Recalling his frustration in *White Winds*, he wrote,

"If Sheldon can't fly high on the mountain, how did the ARG expect him to drop supplies at 17,900 feet? What kind of guy is Sheldon, anyway?"

"He's a strange guy to meet," Wayne admits. "You don't know if he's a genius or crazy. He has his own ideas and is hard to talk to, but the guy can fly. He can put that plane down where no one else can."

Joe acknowledges to Wayne that Sheldon's reputation for fearless flying is well deserved. "But I can't believe how slowly the rescue operation is going," he adds.

"You're not the only one," Wayne says, hesitates for a moment, then pulls several typewritten pages out of a desk drawer. "Read these."

Joe does; it is Wayne's letter resigning from the National Park Service, for which he has worked eight years. "That's how frustrated I am."

Wayne does not resign from the National Park Service, at least not right away. Ten years later, researching *White Winds*, Joe reconnects with Wayne. In a 1977 letter to Joe, he explains what happens next in his life:

> *Personal history: despite the tremendous frustration of being unable to convince anybody at Park HQ that there simply had to be something wrong on the mountain, I became convinced that I would have to leave the NPS. However, I thought that if I could obtain the Chief Ranger job I could do some good, and so applied for it as a last-ditch measure. Much to my surprise, I got the position. I accepted it with reservations, but in the following year found that I was unable to accomplish anything of substance within the bureaucracy and so resigned in April of 1969 after ten years of service.*

There's nothing Joe *can* say, having seen Wayne's letter. But at least reading the letter helps him understand that he has not been alone in feeling frustrated and angry with what has shaped up to be one nightmare on top of another, endless days of discussion and dithering without any action other than the selfless efforts of an independent climbing party that was already on the mountain. Four decades have done nothing to dispel Joe's frustration with Don Sheldon, but he does believe that he knows at least part of the reason for the great pilot's strange behavior: "I do think the disposition of Don Sheldon, who as far as I remember had no contact with any member of the expedition, was effected [*sic*] by Washburn's attitude." There is no written evidence to confirm this suspicion. But certain facts, such as Sheldon's assertion on the radio that Joe was climbing McKinley only for publicity, echo Washburn's criticisms that preceded Joe's expedition to the park. What's more, Washburn would likely have shared his thoughts about Joe and his team with Sheldon, a close friend.

With nothing else to do, Joe goes back to his trailer, sits down on the bed, gets up, sits down again. They'll come and get him if anything happens. He lies down, closes his eyes, mind humming like a motor with no off switch, spinning out thought after thought about the men on the mountain, Jerry and Hank and Walt and Dennis and Steve and John and Mark, seeing their faces, hearing their voices, remembering John's rough humor, Jerry's corny quips, Walt's steadiness, Mark's joking.

In Anchorage, at 3:10 p.m., the ARG's Gary Hansen speaks to Chief Ranger Art Hayes, who passes on Wayne's detailed recommendations for launching an all-out rescue. Hayes adds something that Wayne did not. "Since communication has been difficult with the McKinley Park Hotel, in the event that confidential information would need to be transmitted from the park to Hansen or the other way, the following number should be used. . . ."

"Confidential information" is bureauspeak for death.

Hansen immediately calls the RCC's commander, Major Stevens, who is "not optimistic" about the chances of launching such a complex and expensive operation. At 4:30 p.m., Stevens calls back with a question: "Can this be accomplished commercially?" Only after much more discussion does the RCC commit to flying a mission the next morning.

WHILE GARY HANSEN is haggling with the RCC, and Bill Babcock's team is getting closer to 17,900 feet, Wayne Merry sits alone in his office reviewing the rescue plans he has repeatedly recommended, looking over the maps and camp locations that Joe had pointed out. He flips through the stack of bureaucracy paperwork—this has nothing to do with the crisis now in progress—that grows fatter on his desk every week. But his eyes bounce off the forms and copies, so he just restacks the sheets and shoves them aside.

He sits there in his gray GS-9-level chair with its cracked plastic armrests and broken springs, his arms folded across his chest, staring out the window, turning over and over in his mind the fact that he, one of North America's leading SAR experts, is planted squarely at ground zero of the worst tragedy in North American mountaineering history and cannot do one goddamned thing about it.

FRIDAY MORNING, AFTER spending a frigid night in their igloos at 16,500 feet, Bill's team crawls out and finds, amazingly, decent climbing weather. It is bitter cold, but the wind is down, they can see the sun, and only a few high clouds stripe the sky overhead.

This is good news, but one brief and troubled night's sleep high on the mountain has done little to help them recover from recent days and nights. Thus they are exhausted even before stepping onto the route, and all are suffering to varying degrees from the altitude—headaches, nausea, lassitude, lack of appetite, muddled thoughts.

On top of which, with one of their two stoves dead, melting snow for the day's water and cooking breakfast take twice as long as usual. They will be kneeling inside the igloo in their blue and red and green down parkas, hands clamped under armpits, listening to the one stove's tiny roar, enduring the always endless wait for steam to issue from their battered pressure cooker.

It is an incredible effort just to talk, but someone doubtless says,

Sure is good to have some decent weather, eh?

And just as certainly someone else says,

Sure as hell won't last long either now, will it?

They're all a bit dazed, not only from the altitude but because their minds still haven't been able to fully digest the fact that somehow this climb of a lifetime, the biggest adventure that any one of them ever imagined, has suddenly become something very different.

After some time their hot drinks are drunk, breakfast glop spooned down, latrine visited. Roping up, they look toward Denali Pass, the sky so bright that it stings even through glacier goggles. Today they will surely reach 17,900 feet and whatever Camp VII has to show them.

At about nine in the morning, Gayle Nienheuser, Chet Hackney, and John Ireton start up from 16,500 feet as a three-man rope. They get the head start because Gayle has come down with a cold and can't match the pace they set yesterday, so it's anticipated that Bill and Jeff, on the trail a half hour or so later, will catch up to the other three.

If you could watch them now, they would appear to be moving very slowly, climbing at much less than their usual 500 feet per hour. The pace seems glacial to the climbers themselves, tormented as they are by the knowledge that seven other men up higher have suffered through one of the worst McKinley storms on record and have not been heard from since July 18, ten days ago. It's like a reverse version of that dream where you run and run as fast as you can but can't escape the monsters. Here they're climbing and climbing as fast as they can, but they never seem to get closer to men who may be within hours or even minutes of dying.

Bill's diary:

> We have no faith in air drops > too fouled up communications
> Park say one thing Sheldon does another. Steep slope takes from 10
> am until 5 pm to reach every one tired John & Chet put Gayle on
> our rope as our pace is slower

That "steep slope" is the Upper Harper Icefall's headwall, which rises 800 feet from where they were camped—to about 17,300 feet. It takes the men seven hours, or about 114 feet per hour, to surmount this obstacle. That gives some idea of their condition; they would normally complete this section in about two hours or less. We've used sea-level demonstrations to give some idea of what this kind of climbing is like, so here's a final one. Go up the stairs in your home one step at a time, pausing for thirty-two seconds on each step. That's as fast as these tough men were able to climb at this point.

About a mile from Camp VII, their first discovery: an ice ax abandoned on the snow next to the trail. Short of a body, it is about as disturbing a find as they could make. Most mountaineers this high would rather part with toes than ice axes. During Joe's entire struggle across the McKinley River, where he nearly drowns, he does not let go of his ice ax. It's reflexive, like a trained diver keeping the regulator in his mouth, no matter what. With your ice ax you keep gravity at bay. Without it, you become its prey. John, first on the lead rope, picks up the ax. The others quickly climb forward to join him.

It is a standard Stubai ice ax, commonly used then, about three feet long with an oval oak shaft, steel head with a straight pick at one end, serrated adze at the other end, sharp steel point at the bottom, wrist loop attached to a ring on the upper shaft. A label at midshaft displays Stubai's red, white, and blue logo of the day, with the words *Qualitatserszeugvisse STUBAI* TYROL AUSTRIA. They find no one's name or other identifying information on the ax, so they don't know that it belongs to Steve Taylor, a fact that Joe later confirms with painstaking examination of expedition photos. The ax indicates that Steve almost surely descended to this point, or one nearby before inexplicably losing the ax.

What does it mean? Should they carry it along or leave it here?

It could be evidence, someone says.

Evidence of what?

They're not sure of what, nor does anybody want to think in terms of *evidence* and *findings* just yet, so John drives the ax shaft deep into the snow and they march on.

After another few minutes, they are stopped in their tracks by an even more disturbing discovery: a red sleeping bag wrapped around a green-painted bamboo pole that is driven firmly into the snow. It is John Russell's pole, about eight feet long, the one that he carried all the way up the mountain, would have taken to the summit, and must have brought back down with him after the July 17 bivouac.

Up close now, they see that the sleeping bag is actually a blue Co-Op McKinley model in a red Alpine Hut shell. Two strips of blue nylon flagging, each about an inch wide and two feet long, are tied to the pole's top and flutter in the wind like pennants. The pole isn't perfectly vertical but angles back up toward Denali Pass, as though whoever stuck it there might have been leaning into the wind at that angle himself, or at least knew that the pole would need to lean into the wind blowing down out of the pass if it were to have any chance of remaining in place. Looking inside the sleeping bag, they find a pair of socks and a pair of down booties. They will not learn until later that the sleeping bag, like the ice ax, belonged to Steve Taylor.

This is eerie indeed. You may not be able to move without your ice ax, but you can't *live* without your mummy bag. Not one of them can imagine why any sane climber would leave his bag wrapped around a pole, in the open, exposed to snow and winds like those that have been blowing for the last week or more. In the final delirium of exhaustion and death, when a short-circuiting brain flushes blood from the body core out to the extremities, producing a brief feeling of warmth, men have been known to do strange things—in particular remove some or all of their clothes. At the end Robert Scott did just that, throwing open his clothing, as though he were too hot rather than freezing to death. Raider Nelson, imagining himself basking on a sunny beach instead of freezing to death during the Battle of the Bulge, might have done the same thing.

But this does not appear to have been the work of a man deranged. The bag has been placed here with intention. The wind could not have picked up this bag someplace else, whipped it around like a giant leaf, and then against near-infinite odds centered it perfectly on this pole, in this particular spot. It would be as unlikely as the pole, propelled by the wind, happening to stab itself into the mountain at this particular point. All the men know that neither of these items arrived here by chance.

Somebody put the pole and the bag *here* like this, but why? A signal perhaps? But to whom, and meaning what? Or maybe whoever did this was simply unable to carry the bag and pole any farther. But a good down sleeping bag with cover weighs just six to seven pounds. One more thing that, as far as I could tell, has not been noted before: The hundred-mile-per-hour winds that prevailed on July 21 would have blasted the bag and pole out of here, or at least stripped the bag off the pole and sent it flying. Thus both were probably put here after that date by Steve Taylor, who must have kept on going with only his ice ax.

Why would he leave his sleeping bag here? It's probable that winds of up to 150 miles per hour would have blown Steve's pack clean out of Camp VII, no matter how well he had secured it outside the tent. This is exactly what happened to Ray Genet's pack during the Winter Expedition's stay in their ice cave, as Art Davidson recounted in *Minus 148*:

Pirate refused to believe what the wind had done during the night. On going to sleep, he had fixed a rope to the pack which closed the cave's entrance, then tied that rope to his arm to keep the pack from being blown away if a gust dislodged it. He woke to find both the rope and the pack gone.

This occurred during the night of March 4, well after the worst of their storm had passed.

Without a pack to stuff it in, Steve would have been carrying his sleeping bag some other way, probably draped like a shawl over his shoulders. But in the high winds that continued to buffet the summit area until July 27, the sleeping bag carried thus would have been like a sail or, worse, like a wind sock. Walking with it would have proved dangerous. By the time Steve discovered this, he could have been too far below camp to climb even the few hundred yards back up. Rather than simply abandon the bag to the wind, he wrapped it carefully around John's bamboo pole and went on his way.

But how did the pole get there? Only three possibilities exist. John put it there, then returned to the tent. Or Steve put it there before his final descent attempt, then returned to the tent after he did so. Or Steve carried it with him on that last try, leaving the pole and the sleeping bag at the same spot. Steve was well enough to attempt a descent, and it seems unlikely that John would have carried Steve's bag down. If anyone made that round-trip, it would have been Steve, but it does not seem likely that he would have expended precious energy in such an effort. The remaining scenario has Steve beginning his descent with both pole and sleeping bag. He could have brought the pole for use as a crevasse probe, or he might have intended to place it just where it was found, inclined into the wind for security, because there it would have been visible to men at Camp VI, especially if they used binoculars. What would he have been trying to signal with the pole? Perhaps only that John was alive and remaining in Camp VII.

Having placed the pole, Steve would have continued his downhill struggle until at some point the wind lifted him up, as it did much heavier Joe Wilcox down at the less exposed Camp VI, and blew him off the mountain.

BILL BABCOCK AND his team, exhausted and dazed by altitude, are not theorizing like this as they finally look up to Camp VII itself, another 400 yards distant. They know that only two tents were left up here—Mark McLaughlin's homemade red Mountaineer tent with its external aluminum frame, and one of the Wilcox party's tall orange Logan tents pitched around a center pole. Bill and his team also know that a food cache and three quarts of fuel are buried somewhere near the tents, but they have no idea where these might be.

Nearing the site and looking left to right, this is what they see. The front half of a red plastic snowshoe protrudes from the snow. To its right, only the very top of Mark's red tent is intact and visible; the rest is completely buried. A few wands sprout, in no apparent pattern, from the snow around the snowshoe and the tent. Twenty feet to the right of Mark's tent, and uphill toward Denali Pass, one of Dennis Luchterhand's long wooden snowshoes protrudes vertically from the snow. Six feet to its right is an orange mass of frozen tent fabric, the remains of the Wilcox Logan tent, apparently blown down in the storm. About ten to fifteen feet behind the orange jumble, Dennis's other long snowshoe sticks out of the snow, next to a pile of something they can't quite make out. The two snowshoes anchor tent guy lines.

They see no evidence of Steve Taylor or anyone else. But as they approach, Bill Babcock notices the smell first, carried downglacier to him by the wind. Though he has never encountered this odor before, he knows instinctively what it is. They walk to within fifteen feet, the smell growing stronger with every step, then closer, then around to the uphill side of the frozen tent remains. Bill's diary:

"a ghastly sight, a man sitting upright, alongside a logan tent. His face and hands are blue green white, frozen yet decomposing. The smell almost makes me vomit."

Bareheaded and barehanded, the dead man is holding the wind-torn remains of his tent in a literal death grip. His longish hair and beard are frozen and matted. His face and hands are discolored, cracked, and blistered. It seems possible that he was hanging onto the tent's center pole while the wind ripped the tent apart around him. Then, exposed, he froze to death. Or perhaps he froze to death before the tent shredded.

Except that he appears to have wrapped the tent around himself, which he could have done only if it had been blown apart before he died. And why is he wearing neither hat nor gloves?

He has sat here for days, sometimes exposed to the grilling sun, refreezing at other times, swelling and splitting as the forces of decomposition did their work, his face now the bluish green of steak gone bad. His eyes, the worst thing about any corpse, are open and staring, though cloudy. Normally they would be the first thing eaten by McKinley's voracious ravens, which peck holes through the toughest pack fabric, but 17,900 feet is too high even for them. The eyes seem to follow Bill Babcock as he circles the body, not looking for clues so much as just looking. It is the most horrible thing he has ever seen, or ever will see, and this is true for the others as well.

They all know that someone else may be in the red tent. Indomitable Gayle slices it open. He finds a tremendous amount of snow inside, deposited by wind strong enough to force it through closed zippers, but nothing else.

To Bill it feels like death is literally with them here, a presence so powerful and unsettling that the urge to get away from this dead man and this fatal plain is almost irresistible. Illogically, Bill also feels a glowing rage inside him, and only after he is off the mountain will he understand it.

No one wants to touch the corpse, or even stay close to it. There is nothing remotely poignant or elegant about this poor man. He is not like George Leigh Mallory, for instance, found on Everest in 1999, transformed by dry cold and altitude into something resembling a white marble sculpture. There is only stench and decay about this corpse, frozen in its orange shroud on this evil-feeling plateau.

The weather is holding—clear sky, ten- to fifteen-mile-per-hour winds, the temperature a few degrees above zero. But they understand what a lethal spot this is, given its position in the giant gunsight of Denali Pass. So before doing anything else, they dig snow caves, upwind of the dead man.

Then they search the camp's remaining area, glad for a reason to move away from the body and for tasks to focus on. They find a lot of food sitting in the snow outside the tents, along with a brown sleeping bag cover and some odds and ends of equipment, but not the three quarts of fuel.

It does not occur to them, nor has it to anyone else in the ensuing forty years, that the orange Logan tent may contain another body, or even bodies. The Logan is a big tent, almost seven feet high at its peak, roomy enough to accommodate three men comfortably, five in an emergency. The segment they have seen wrapped partially around the dead man is only a fraction of the tent's total fabric; the rest of it lies buried under the same snow that has covered almost Mark's entire tent. It is certainly possible that another body is down there, wrapped or tangled in more of the Logan tent's fabric. It could be one of six men: Jerry Clark, Hank Janes, Mark McLaughlin, Dennis Luchterhand, Walt Taylor, or even, though this is a remote possibility given their earlier finds, Steve Taylor.

But they can't be faulted for not thinking of this, or for failing to excavate the entire tent. They have climbed from 12,100 feet to 17,900 feet, under killing loads, in abominable conditions, with no tents and only one functioning stove, in three and a half days. Joe's team, climbing in good weather, carrying lighter loads and using tents that were much less taxing to erect than snow caves are to dig, required seven days to cover the same distance before occupying Camp VII. And *that* was fast enough to bring complaints from some of his team. The MCA men are confronting horror like none have ever seen, at almost 18,000 feet, where their brains would have trouble repeating nursery rhymes accurately, let alone sorting through all the possible ways in which men at this camp might have met their ends.

After their canvass of the area, Bill, gritting his teeth and holding his breath, tries to investigate the corpse further, knowing that it may bear a wallet, a diary, or a camera. But the dead man's tent and clothes are a frozen carapace. Hacking away at them with his knife is simply more than he can endure.

At 8:00 P.M., Bill Babcock radios Eielson that they are at Camp VII.

"We read you faintly on that," Gordon Haber says. "Are any members of the seven—are any of the seven members alive?"

"We found one body . . . one body. Over."

"I read you to say you have—you have found one body. Is that correct?"

"Roger, roger, in the tent. In the tent. Over."

"Have you seen anything of the other six?"

"Negative—negative. Over."

Static breaks the rest of Bill's transmission. Gordon asks, "Repeat, please—repeat."

"Tomorrow. Over."

"Please repeat again."

"We'll try for the summit tomorrow. Over."

"Ah, repeat your sentence three times slowly please."

"Five going to try to go to the summit tomorrow." Bill repeats it twice more.

Gordon tells George Perkins, who is there with him, "They're going for the summit tomorrow." George, taking the mike, asks, "I read that as you are trying for the summit tomorrow. Is that correct?"

"Roger, roger. We will search on the way. We will search on the way. Over."

Gordon, to George: "Find out who that guy . . . is."

"Do—is the—body Steve Taylor?"

"Do not know. Over. Do not know. Over," Bill says.

"You do not know, okay. Ah, we will be continuously monitoring the radio, ah, through the day tomorrow. Ah, anytime you wish to make a call—there will be someone here. Do you read?"

"Roger, roger . . . a weather report . . ."

"You would—do you want a weather report?"

"Roger, roger, roger."

"Fine, ah, what time?"

"Three AM—three AM. Over."

"Ah, did you say three AM?"

"Roger . . . our climb. Over."

George Perkins: "Stand by one. Ah, one question—was the body at the location of the seventeen-nine camp?"

"Roger, in the tent."

"Ah, stand by one."

Gordon Haber then calls Wayne Merry on a second radio set. "Seven-zero-one, this is Seven-zero-two."

"Seven-zero-one."

"Wayne, they're at the seventeen-nine camp right now and there's one body up there. They don't know who it is yet. Ah, ah, stand by one."

"Okay, I read that, ah, there were no . . . this again—there's only the one at the seventeen-nine camp. Is that right?"

"Ten-four. He's right at the camp. Ah, they're still on the line right here. Do you have anything else?"

"Okay, ask 'em to try and get identification, ah, and tomorrow, ask 'em to tend to look for breaks in the wanding pattern—that might have confused them coming down in a, ah, whiteout. And, ah, that would probably be the general vicinity where they dug in."

"Ah, roger on that."

George Perkins, who now has the radio contact with Bill: "As you go up—look for breaks in the wanding pattern. The rest may be dug in. Do you read me?"

"Roger—we read you loud and clear."

"Ah, what are your present weather conditions?"

"Twenty-five-mile-per-hour wind—gusting higher. Over."

"Roger. Ah, do you have other information for us at this time?"

"Not at this time. Temperature's just above zero. Over."

"If you can possibly make identification, ah, please do so."

"We cannot look at him. He's decomposed greatly. . . . Over."

I N HIS TRAILER, Joe looks at magazines, killing time, unable to focus on much but the covers. *Sports Illustrated* has basketball's Lew Alcindor dunking a shot. It is a month after the Six Day War, between Israel and the Arab states of Egypt, Jordan, and Syria. That major conflict was shorter by three weeks than Joe's time on the mountain. Jordan's King Hussein ("The Least Unreasonable Arab") graces *Time*'s cover. The new *Playboy* features a pretty strawberry blonde giggling at the reader, her bikini top having just been unsnapped by invisible fingers.

A knock on the door. Wayne opens it, steps inside.

"They found one body at the seventeen-nine camp," he says. They just look at each other while the news penetrates. "There's no sign of the other six. I'm sorry, Joe."

Joe drops the magazine, takes a deep breath, stands up. The pain and grief he's been holding at bay come flooding out. Wayne steps over, touches him gently on the shoulder. "I have to get back to the radio. Come on over when you feel like it."

Joe assumes that the dead man is Steve Taylor, because Steve is the only one who stayed behind when Jerry and the others went up. It occurs to Joe that there is cruel irony in the fact that he has learned first of the death of the only man he really knew well. Images keep flashing through his head: Steve, like a little kid on Christmas Eve, when they first talked about climbing McKinley. His near-desperate work convincing the park service that he was up to this climb. The endless hours packing supplies in Provo, smiling all the while.

The tiny trailer becomes unbearable. Joe wanders around the Wonder Lake campground, his mind roiling. Other strolling campers give a wide berth to the grungy, beat-up figure walking aimlessly, eyes downcast, lips moving in conversations that only he can hear.

Steve was by himself in that tent. The others were together. Maybe they dug in and survived. There's a chance. . . .

After leaving joe in the trailer, Wayne telephones George Hall with word that the MCA group has found one body at 17-9. No others yet. Depending on the weather, they plan to start for the summit tomorrow at 3 a.m. and will search all along the way. Wayne wants an immediate airdrop of food and fuel for them. It's possible, he explains, that they will find survivors dug in higher up, so this could turn into an even longer siege.

Hall's resistance has been softened—though not dissolved entirely—by the discovery of a body. They didn't actually say "corpse." A body, after all, *might* be alive. So just to be sure, he asks Wayne if "body" indicates that the man they found is, well, definitely dead. Wayne assures him that yes, in this case "body" means *dead*.

Ten minutes later, Hall calls back. An approaching front will sock everything in above 3,500 feet by tomorrow. No wind prediction available. Wayne tells Hall that they need to get up a big, slow Rescue Coordination Center (RCC) plane orbiting the summit *immediately* with an experienced mountaineer-observer aboard. They should look over the entire route from Denali Pass to the summit. Jerry Clark's party had a snow shovel, so they could have dug in.

Dug in? Do you mean they would have dug a hole? George Hall asks.

Yes, that's what I mean, Wayne says.

Why would they do *that?*

It's common practice for mountaineers to use shovels and ice axes to carve out snow caves in bad weather. They're more secure than tents.

Oh.

Shortly after, Hall calls back to tell Wayne that the RCC is dropping supplies to the MCA group. Then, minutes later, he calls back yet again to say that they're *not.* After an inexplicable delay, he calls a third time to report that now the RCC people don't think they can hit the Denali Pass area with a drop because it will be in shadow.

Wayne can't believe it. *There is plenty of light up there at this time of year,* he replies. *Shadows should not be a problem.* Hall does not volunteer to tell the U.S. Air Force its own business, and there the conversation ends.

At 11:30 p.m., in his last transmission of that evening, Wayne calls George Perkins at the Eielson Visitor Center and asks him to find out how many sleeping bags are still at the 17,900-foot camp. This might give some idea of the remaining men's chances for survival. He asks George also to find out how much food the MCA men have.

As midnight passes and Friday, July 28, becomes Saturday, July 29, Wayne has no thought of catching sleep. He monitors phones and radios, trying to think through many scenarios except the last, worst possibility. If that one turns out to be the right one, there's not much left to be done.

Up at camp vii, Bill Babcock and his crew, having searched the camp area and found nothing more, occupy their snow caves. Bill makes radio contact with the park. Gayle's cold is worse; everyone is exhausted.

Can you stay on and continue to search for the other climbers? the Eielson ranger asks.

Bill is aware how quickly authorities mounted the huge Winter Expedition rescue. So far, he has seen no evidence of anything even approximating such support despite the fact that more than twice as many men have been missing and for a longer time. The NPS and the RCC, in fact, have seemed perfectly content to let him and his four friends take the whole thing on themselves, and that's beginning to not sit right.

We're going to try for the summit tomorrow and we'll search as we go. Nobody wants to make a long stay up here.

The last entry for the day in Bill's handwritten diary reads, "Bill angry with Park as Sheldon flies, but drops nothing." In the more detailed expedition narrative written once he's off the mountain, Bill expands on that: "It seems very odd that our request made four days ago could not have been transmitted to Sheldon by now so that we would have had the emergency rations left with him." Bill is referring to fifteen days of MCA fuel and rations left sitting in Sheldon's own hangar.

JOE, AFTER MEANDERING around the Wonder Lake campground in a daze, goes back to the ranger station and sits on the porch. Wayne comes out and offers him a drink.

Joe, having accepted the Mormon faith to marry Cheryl, doesn't imbibe. But today he does. Wayne hands him a glass of lemonade laced with Lemon Hart Rum (the same bracing grog served to British sailors). Down it goes, and so does a generous refill.

Wayne is one of those men you just feel good talking to, and Joe needs to talk, especially about Steve Taylor. "Steve was a close friend. He had really blossomed into a strong, confident mountaineer."

"It's too bad that a man gets cut down just as he's coming into his prime," says Wayne. They drink in silence for a while. Then Wayne says something that has been on his mind for some time.

"You probably already know that, regardless of the circumstances, a tragedy is always accompanied by a great deal of criticism. As leader, much of that criticism will be directed toward you."

This is Joe's first inkling that a tragedy does not end when the bodies are found.

27

SATURDAY, JULY 29
And Two Make Three

A t 3 a.m. Art Hayes at park headquarters calls Wayne with news that would have been welcome days ago. An airdrop will be made in about five hours, and he wants Joe Wilcox at park headquarters immediately.

Joe heads out in Hank Janes's van, accompanied by seasonal ranger Dick Shields in a four-wheel-drive truck. The storm has washed out so many roads and bridges that they fear the van may get stuck.

Shortly after, George Perkins at Eielson calls to say that the MCA group reports no sleeping bags at Camp VII except the one wrapped around the green bamboo pole. This, to Wayne, is good news, because it means that all the others took their sleeping bags. Wayne notifies Art Hayes that there's still a chance that the others survived because they had sleeping bags, warm down clothes, and shovels to dig snow caves. Rations could be stretched, and they might have found other food sources, as the Winter Expedition survivors did. Even if some have died, others could use their gear and food.

Wayne knows, but does not say, that the Winter Expedition climbers holed up for six days. It has now been twelve days since Jerry Clark's party disappeared. In the expedition log, he writes, "the situation would probably be very critical now; they would be in the last stages of death from exposure. If they are dug in, it is very likely that they are on the east or lee side of the summit ridge, where the wind is less and the snow softer for digging in."

During the same conversation with Hayes, Wayne makes detailed suggestions for aerial observations, airdrops of medical supplies, use of high-altitude helicopters, mobilizing Alaska Rescue Group (ARG) physicians, readying supply-filled drop sleds, obtaining walk-around oxygen bottles, and various other preparations in case survivors are found. Then he asks pointedly,

"Did you copy those down, Art?"

"I copied down your comments on survival and search areas, but not the other suggestions. They've already been discussed and covered."

AT PARK HEADQUARTERS, George Hall wants to know whether Joe is certain that the body in Camp VII is Steve Taylor.

"Fairly certain."

"We need to be as certain as we can before calling his parents, and we need to do that soon, as news reports are already out that there is a rescue in progress."

"Considering the circumstances, I have just assumed that it is Steve, but I guess conceivably it could be any one of the seven. If the MCA gives a description of the body, I can probably make positive identification. . . ."

A bit later, the RCC's Major Stevens reports that a C-130 took off from Elmendorf Air Force Base at 7:06 a.m. that morning with Gary Hansen and Winter Expedition survivor Dave Johnston aboard as observers. They flew over Denali Pass, from east to west, at 7:40 a.m. They made nine more passes all told. During the eighth and ninth passes the C-130 dropped forty-six cases of C rations with 180 man-days of food, twelve double sleeping bags, five jerry cans containing 170 pounds of white gas, and nine two-man tents. All items dropped landed on the west side of Denali Pass in a line extending 100 to 300 yards from the top of the pass. It's not a bad drop, except for the fact that the supplies land on the wrong side of Denali Pass.

The C-130 circled the entire mountain once, observing the Western States Expedition already down to 12,000 feet on the West Buttress side, then returned to Elmendorf, landing at 9:23 a.m. Its entire flight, from takeoff to touchdown, including drops, took two hours and seventeen minutes. The calm period on July 20 had lasted three hours.

Sharing George Hall's concern about imminent media and family inquiries, Joe writes a series of questions, to be passed on to Bill's team, that he hopes will help determine whether the body is in fact Steve Taylor:

Was the body found in a red or an orange tent? Was he over six feet tall? Wearing beige down underwear and blue wool air force pants?

Was the sleeping bag a Co-Op McKinley, in a red Alpine Hut shell?

Were there any articles, such as pack, boots, water bottle, et cetera, bearing the initials S.A.T.? Was a red Expedition Cruiser pack and frame in camp? Was an Alpine Hut "Polar" down parka and a large pair of K boots in camp? What about an Alpine Hut pullover, red wind parka, and orange wind pants?

That done, Joe and George Hall decide that they cannot wait any longer. Hall places a person-to-person call to Perry Taylor, Steve's father. After a brief greeting, Hall gets to the point: "It is my unfortunate duty to inform you that your son, Steve, is believed to be dead. . . ." Hall passes on what they know and what they don't, then Joe takes the phone. The first question Steve's father asks is,

"Are you absolutely sure it is Steve?"

"We will have to wait for another radio contact to get a description. We might even have to wait for photographs to be certain."

To Joe's immense relief, the Taylors receive this awful news calmly, though they are doubtless secretly believing—*hoping*—that the man found was not their son. It is the same reflexive denial that Joe himself has been feeling for days.

Up at 17,900 feet, John Ireton rouses everyone at 2:30 a.m. for their summit attempt. Surprisingly, the weather is decent: temperature about five degrees below zero, wind steady at fifteen to twenty miles per hour. Each man packs all his down gear, four pairs of mitts, two extra pairs of socks, a sleeping bag cover, an insulated foam pad, a full thermos bottle, and other oddments that bring their summit pack weights, Bill recalls, to about forty pounds per man. Distributed among the team are the one working stove with three days of fuel, one big snow shovel, two heavy-duty ice saws, medical equipment, and emergency food.

Gayle is still sick with a cold but, thankfully, free of altitude illness. It takes them two and a half hours to get ready; they don't hit the trail until

5 a.m. It's important to remember this fact in light of criticism that will later be leveled at Jerry Clark's party for "wasting" three hours of good weather on July 17. More likely, that party was six men doing what it took to get ready, as Howard's team was on July 15 and Bill's team has been this morning. Jerry's party also took time, no doubt, to make sure that Steve Taylor was as safe and comfortable as they could make him.

This preparation time is also important in relation to the three-hour window of good weather that opened on July 20, while Jerry's team was trapped up higher. Though Bill's people are tired and degraded by altitude, they are doubtless in better shape than Jerry Clark's party or Steve Taylor would have been on that day. Thus it's easily conceivable that Jerry's team, and Steve, used up much of those three hours getting themselves ready, leaving just enough time to hike dangerously far from their caves and the tent before the storm blew back in.

Bill's two rope teams leave camp, sharing trailbreaking chores through half a foot of new snow up to Denali Pass. There Gayle, slowed by sickness, joins Bill and Jeff on their rope. Chet and John take the lead, climbing fast, breaking trail all the way to the summit. Gayle falters near Archdeacon's Tower, but warming weather, snacks, and Bill's encouragement keep him going. There are few wands, but the route is easy to follow in this clear weather, which also makes it easier for them to watch for caves or other evidence of bivouacs. They see neither, but given the last ten days of prodigious snowfall and driving winds, that's not surprising.

The previous days' grinding work has taken its toll. Bill's rope does not reach the crest of Archdeacon's Tower ridge until 12:30 p.m., seven and a half hours after leaving camp. It took Joe and Howard's team just three hours and thirty-six minutes to make the same climb on July 15. At their current pace, Bill knows it is unlikely that they will reach the summit before evening. A storm may blow in before then, but they decide to keep going.

During a subsequent radio call, George Hall wants the MCA team and the Western States Expedition (WSE) group to join forces and keep looking for missing bodies. The WSE is already far down the mountain, as Hall should know. And it feels to Bill that the superintendent is trying to order him and his team to take even greater risks than they have already.

"This was a serious blunder," Bill recalls. Bill's team is having enough trouble keeping themselves alive after their accelerated burst of rescue climbing at altitude. "I told him something rude."

John and chet keep moving well, but the route from Archdeacon's Tower on up becomes a freezing ordeal for Bill, Jeff, and Gayle. John and Chet reach the top at about two o'clock. On their way down about half an hour later, in deteriorating weather, they pass Bill's rope, which has just surmounted the summit ridge above the Football Field.

Bill, Jeff, and Gayle reach the summit, finally, at 3:15 p.m., and the experience is as frightening as it is rewarding. It's not terribly cold, but the wind is building and bad signals are everywhere. From below, ominous thunderhead cumulus clouds are boiling up the North Peak and West Buttress. Farther off, a major storm is moving in from the southwest, one of those Bering Sea monsters like the one that attacked Jerry Clark's team. And judging from the warming temperatures and whiteout now beginning to envelop them, there's evidence that McKinley is brewing up one of its own localized tempests. Thus they may be hit—as was Jerry Clark's party—by several malignant weather events at one time.

John and Chet, carrying the fuel and the stove, wait for the other three by Archdeacon's Tower. Just as Bill, Jeff, and Gayle return, Don Sheldon calls. He has spotted a body below Archdeacon's Tower, right on the line where desperate climbers might try to make a straight run down to Camp VII. Apparently the body is far enough down and blocked by a terrain feature that Bill and the others were prevented from seeing it on their way up.

It's important to understand what happens next. The MCA team members, possibly excepting Jeff, are experienced enough to know what kind of weather is stalking them now. In an hour, this summit area could become a killing ground blasted by hundred-mile-per-hour winds, cloaked in impenetrable whiteout, buried beneath smothering dumps of snow—the same conditions that killed the man at Camp VII and, presumably, the man beneath Archdeacon's Tower.

None of the men with Bill have brought sleeping bags. After so many days of unrelenting labor at high altitude, all are nearing the limits of their endurance. Nevertheless, without hesitation or a word of com-

plaint, John Ireton and Chet Hackney start down the treacherous
55-degree slopes beneath Archdeacon's Tower. Downclimbing this in
good weather would be harrowing, given the pitch, hidden crevasses, and
fresh snow. In the building wind and whiteout, it is far worse.

Moving beyond the lip of the steepening slope, John and Chet finally
see the man about 300 feet below them. Cramponing gingerly down the
untested face, they pass a wand still in place, obviously stuck there by
the man they're approaching. The only reason a climber would wand a
route he's descending is to help guide men coming behind him, either
then or later.

John and Chet reach the dead man. They brace against growing wind
that threatens to shove them off the steep slope and regard the second
corpse they have found in as many days. Wearing orange wind pants, a
reddish-orange wind parka, and overboots, he is sitting in the snow with
his left leg thrust out to brace himself. He is slumped forward, as though
hunched to protect himself from wind. Unable to go on, he froze to
death where he sat.

The wind is roaring, the whiteout thickening. But now they can see
another body a few hundred feet farther down, so they descend to this
one too. Sitting in the snow like the first man, he's wrapped in a green
cloth–covered Eddie Bauer sleeping bag and is wearing blue wind pants.
This man also has one leg extended forward, no doubt to keep himself
from sliding on down. But unlike the first body, this man is leaning back
against the mountainside. More snow covers him than the first man they
located. Does that mean he's been there longer, or just that this particular spot on the face accumulates more snow? There is no way to know
for sure.

Chet and John find no packs, ropes, ice axes, or other equipment.
Both men are situated along the straight line between Archdeacon's
Tower and Camp VII. They obviously expired trying to make that line-of-
sight descent that Bill imagined on his way up. They just as obviously
didn't know, or were desperate enough not to care, that an impassable,
fifty-foot ice cliff barred their way a few hundred yards farther down.

One more thing seems clear. They placed at least the one wand, and
probably more, as they descended. It would have made little sense to
place a single wand on a difficult route of this length. The wind could

easily have blown away the other wands. In addition, they were descending on a logical line, with a rational purpose—reaching Camp VII—governing their movements. Their positions in death indicate that they were in control of their faculties until they slipped into hypothermic coma. Thus their final hours and moments did not devolve into blind panic, as might have been expected.

Psychologist and author David Grossman has extensively studied human responses to extreme situations. In his book *On Killing*, he notes: "When people become angry, or frightened, they stop thinking with their forebrain (the mind of a human being) and start thinking with their midbrain (which is indistinguishable from the mind of an animal). *They are literally scared out of their wits.*" [Emphasis in original] Judging from all the available information, it's safe to say that this did not happen to the two men below Archdeacon's Tower.

There is nothing the MCA men can do for either of the two dead climbers. John and Chet do consider searching the bodies for documents and cameras, but their own situation is becoming more serious by the minute. It is not lost on them how exposed this face is, or that the two men died here in conditions almost identical to those that are developing at this very moment. The time it would take to search even one body could make the difference between living and dying themselves. They make the tough decision to climb back up the steep slope to Archdeacon's Tower, where the others have been waiting for them.

The weather is bad enough now that Bill and his four friends know they are racing the storm for their own survival. Moving as fast as safety and drained bodies will allow, they climb back down to Denali Pass and make short work of the easier descent to Camp VII and their caves. They dive in minutes before the attack of a storm that will last eighteen hours without letup and, had they been caught in the open on that face beneath Archdeacon's Tower, would have killed them as surely as the two men they found.

28

SUNDAY, JULY 30
One Hell of a Good Story

On Sunday morning, it takes Bill's team a half hour just to dig through the three feet of fresh snow blocking their cave entrance. Alerted by radio to an approaching window of good weather, they pack up and flee Camp VII at noon. Once again they're forced to plow through fresh, deep snow, but at least now they're going downhill, relieved beyond measure to leave the horrors of Camp VII behind. Bill and Jeff lead down to 16,500 feet. They stop, eat, drink, and continue, now with Chet and John leading. Chet promptly falls into a crevasse hard enough to break his Kelty pack—legendary for their indestructibility. Bill takes over the lead and soon drops into a crevasse himself.

At 3 p.m. they arrive at Camp VI, at 15,100 feet. The diary: "Unfortunately, we find that Sheldon has dropped our personal food and fuel some six or seven days after we requested it at 15,100 instead of 17,800 where we could have utilized it. Also three days ago we had told the park to tell Sheldon if he has not dropped our gear not to drop it. Communications certainly are fouled up. . . ."

After a long rest break, the men continue down, reaching the site of Camp V, at 12,100 feet, by 9 p.m. Sunday evening. During the subsequent radio contact, George Hall asks Bill,

"Would you fellows consider going back up?"

Once again, Bill declines. His diary does not contain the specific response, but when we met, he could only shake his head, still astonished at how little the park superintendent understood and how much he was willing to ask for.

The diary does contain other reactions. Bill and Jeff have always been close, and now they start talking about the dead men up high. Bill's diary records their sharing, and his own reactions, with extraordinary honesty:

> We had no feeling toward him as we did not know him. I looked at him the first day. He was unreal, frozen, discolored and horribly cracked and swollen. I disliked him particularly on the summit day and led a route 75 ft. wide of where he sat watching us. I felt no compassion until I was at 12,100 and 8,100 when I was greatly disturbed by his plight and the other six, 2 of whom we saw at a distance. At that altitude it is all one can do to meet his own needs. This poor fellow and his six companions made demands upon me and I resented it. It made me angry with my team, the park, Sheldon, anyone. Jeff discusses the situation with me, and has similar feelings.
>
> Gayle said he wished we had dug a hole and buried "him." Chet said he wanted nothing to do with any of them once he saw that they were dead.

They spend Tuesday, Wednesday, and Thursday climbing down off the glacier, through McGonagall Pass, and across the tundra to the McKinley River. It has receded since Joe's crossing, but it is still two deep, swift, freezing channels. All of the men fall while crossing. Jeff has to rescue first Gayle, then Bill.

On Thursday afternoon they finally reach the road to Wonder Lake, where they are picked up and trucked six miles to the Merrys' cabin. Cindy treats them all to a huge dinner. Barely able to stay awake, they sit through a taped debriefing with Wayne, then head for bed.

Before Bill falls asleep, one image from the last three days keeps coming back to him. Just after the team walked through McGonagall Pass and started hiking down into the lush, green Cache Creek drainage, they discovered lying close to the trail a beautiful eagle, struck to earth by a death for which they could find no reason.

WORD OF THE disaster is out by Sunday, while the MCA team is still four days away from Wonder Lake. That morning, a chartered plane from

Anchorage disgorges reporters. Their primary target is Joe, but George Hall keeps them at bay. Brad Washburn calls to reassure Joe that, despite their pre-trip feud, he "doesn't have an I-told-you-so attitude." Local newspapers carry the headline, "One Body Found On McKinley." Joe remains sequestered in park headquarters, loathing the thought of being grilled by reporters. Families of the missing climbers will not begin arriving until the next day, so he has at least twenty-four hours to prepare himself for the ordeal of having their grief added to his own.

Sometime during the afternoon, Joe learns that the MCA team is climbing down Karstens Ridge, having seen nothing more than already reported. Later, Joe and others will question their decision to leave Camp VII without conducting a more exhaustive search for victims and, just possibly, survivors. Joe reasons that the RCC airdrop provided them with food, fuel, and supplies for another month on the mountain, although it is true that the RCC dropped some of those supplies on the wrong side of Denali Pass, hundreds of feet down the treacherous face where more climbers fall than any other place on McKinley.

Wayne knows what an astonishing bit of climbing Bill Babcock's team has done, stretching themselves to the absolute limits of their endurance, slicing their margin of safety terrifyingly thin. But he also knows how terrible it would be if, much later, bodies were found in an ice cave with diary entries dated July 30 or even later.

Still, there can be no criticism, nothing in fact but the highest praise, for Bill, Jeff, John, Chet, and Gayle, who climbed to 17,900 feet through terrible weather, in an astonishingly short time, risking their lives every day and night for a full week, as part of a mission they had never planned on, and for which they received neither compensation nor recognition, while the resources of the Alaska Rescue Group, the Rescue Coordination Center, the United States Air Force, and the National Park Service languished in hangars and warm offices.

On SUNDAY, JOE greets Paul Janes, the Luchterhands, and Steve's parents. Between wrenching conversations with all of them, Joe finds George Hall and makes the revealing (because it reflects the strength of Joe's denial even at this late date) declaration that he will not believe that the remaining men are dead until a final aerial survey of all the tundra surrounding McKinley had been completed. Hall dismisses out of hand the idea of such a search.

The families are troubled that none of the three bodies found have been positively identified. They remain without any closure until Friday when Bill's team, having come off the mountain the previous day, meets with them. Elmer Luchterhand leads the questioning, John Ireton the answering.

Eventually, as John and others recall details, it becomes evident that the first man on the slope below Archdeacon's Tower was Walt Taylor and the man below him was Dennis Luchterhand. This is confirmed by their clothing and supported by the fact that, as the two strongest climbers in the group, they probably would have been able to descend farthest before expiring.

Identifying the first man they found, the one frozen into the Logan tent's folds, proves harder. The initial assumption was that he had to be Steve Taylor, the only man who stayed behind in Camp VII. But the assumption is questionable because Steve's sleeping bag was wrapped around the bamboo pole several hundred yards from camp, and his ice ax was found even farther down the trail. Despite these strong indications that Steve had started down to Camp VI, subsequent reports— including the American Alpine Club's analysis and the later description in Howard's book—maintain that the man in Camp VII is Steve.

But there is a more convincing argument that John Russell was the man found at Camp VII, although that argument will not surface until Joe's book is published in 1981. Joe reasons, persuasively, that Steve was a student at conservative Brigham Young University, where short hair was not just custom but school policy. Joe, who knew him best, believes that Steve's hair and beard were too short to have been "frozen and matted," as Bill Babcock described the corpse. John Russell's long, curly hair and ample beard would have fit this description more closely. Coupled with the even more compelling evidence of Steve's sleeping bag and ice ax on the trail, it seems virtually certain that John, not Steve, died inside the tent.

On Tuesday, finally unable to put off the experience any longer, Joe sits down for interviews with journalists. The longest of these is a meeting with *Time* magazine's reporter. Joe recalls, and so wrote in *White Winds*, that even before they begin, the man says,

"This may be a disaster for you, but it's going to make one hell of a good story."

Joe spends the next few days tying up loose ends, returning personal effects to families, making arrangements for the Hankmobile, giving away bits and pieces of expedition equipment that he doesn't want to bring home. On Friday, Joe, the MCA team, and some families take the train back to Anchorage. Steve Taylor's parents loan Joe money for his plane ticket to Seattle. Gary Hansen meets them at the Anchorage airport to talk about the disaster and report that Jerry Lewis is improving and will lose, thankfully, not toes but toenails.

This is the second time that Joe has made the flight from Anchorage to Seattle. The last time was in late August 1966, returning from the summer he had spent surveying for the U.S. Forest Service in rain-drenched southeast Alaska. He never saw Mount McKinley during that stint, but he would recall that "Denali's unseen presence invaded my subconscious thought with an elusive premonition. The following summer I would return to climb the most imposing mountain in North America."

Now, almost exactly a year later, Joe is once again leaving Alaska. He has realized his dream, and it has nearly destroyed him. He is impoverished, exhausted, emaciated, and physically beaten. Of course the worst wounds are deep inside, their only hint his eyes—once bright and blue as the pure Alaskan sky—dulled now by horror such as he never could have imagined.

He cannot know that worse is yet to come.

PART FOUR

AFTERMATH

The old adage claims that those who do not know history are cursed to repeat it. In a lesser-known corollary, some who do know history first-hand are cursed to re-live it in memory ever after.

— HOWARD SNYDER
e-mail to the author

29

Hanging Jury

C heryl meets Joe at Seattle-Tacoma International Airport and takes him to her parents' home in Puyallup, scene of the earlier backyard conference between Joe's team and the Coloradoans. Joe recuperates there for a week, getting treatment for his frostbitten toes, then returns to Provo. On the way he visits Mark McLaughlin's grieving parents. They tell him about a ghoulish Anchorage funeral director who pestered them for the contract to ship Mark's body. Mark's parents are friendly and understanding with Joe, empathizing completely with his own pain and sense of loss. The McLaughlins' response to Joe is typical; none of the parents ever blame him for what happened. In fact, when others unaffected by the tragedy do blame Joe, parents who have lost so much become his staunchest allies.

At some point during his first two weeks off the mountain, Joe learns that Grace's husband, Vin Hoeman, is planning to lead a "Humanitarian Climb" to find and bury the dead men, as well as locate any diaries, cameras, or anything that would help explain their deaths. Three of Hoeman's group are Seattle Rescue Council members. Lou Whittaker, who earlier complained to George Hall that rescue and recovery efforts had been inadequate, is also a member of this group, though he does not make the climb. Three other Humanitarian Climb team members, including Vin and the game Grace Jansen-Hoeman, back for another try, are from the Alaska Rescue Group. Vin will say later that he purposely included members of both organizations because of a need "for better liaison," which possibly means smoothing feathers ruffled by Whittaker's complaint to George Hall.

Sheldon flies all six climbers to 9,800 feet on the West Buttress route on Saturday, August 19. Grace, once again struck by altitude sickness, gets no higher than 12,800 feet. Sheldon evacuates her. On Saturday, August 26, Vin Hoeman and two others climb over Denali Pass from the West Buttress side and descend to the site of Camp VII. They search this campsite, find nothing, then climb down to the green bamboo pole. On July 28, Bill Babcock's team found at least six feet of this pole sticking up out of the snow. Hoeman finds six inches. They decide that excavating around the pole will be futile and return to 18,200 feet, where they spend a minus-25-degree night in snow caves.

The next day, one man is too sick to climb. Vin and four others leave him alone at the 18,200 feet caves (so much for the theory that responsible expeditions never leave men alone at high camps) and go for the summit. Along the way they search for evidence of the July expedition's victims. Hoeman and Ray Genet find three wands at the top of the steep face beneath Archdeacon's Tower "where no party would go if they could see to do better."

They find neither bodies nor evidence of snow caves, but that's not surprising considering that snowfall has almost completely buried the six-foot bamboo pole. Hoeman concludes that Jerry Clark's party probably spent the night of July 17 somewhere on the flatter shelf atop this face and on their way down from the summit as well.

After summiting and returning to this same area, Genet and Hoeman belay each other down the steep Archdeacon's Tower face, but they find no evidence of Walt's or Dennis's bodies.

The Humanitarian Climb team descends without incident, and Sheldon flies them back to Talkeetna on August 31. Vin Hoeman was understandably disappointed that his effort did not produce new evidence or answers about what happened to Jerry Clark's party. In his report he wrote, "Little was added to what is known of the fate of those who died in July, the deep new snow prevented accomplishment of the most important part of the mission."

His report's concluding statement hints at the emotion that moved him:

McKinley has cleansed herself and the immaculate shroud that conceals the remains of F. Jerry Clark, Henry Janes, Dennis Luchterhand, R. Mark McLaughlin, John R. Russell, Stephen A. Taylor, and Walter W. Taylor will soon harden into ice and move, in centuries' time, back to the lowland. We who remember will revere them along with their grand monument.

Joe is in Provo with Cheryl when *Time*'s August 11 issue hits the stands. Its article about the disaster appears on page 19:

ALASKA
Denali Strikes Back

Two columns of reportage frame a group picture taken at Camp III on July 4. John Russell, the man missing from everyone's reckoning, is missing from the picture as well, so it had to have been taken after he grumped back to his tent. No byline is attached to the article, which contains the kinds of errors produced by weekly deadlines and nonclimbing writers. The author states that McKinley "does not pose the classic technical challenges of the great Himalayan and Andean peaks," which veterans of the Cassin Ridge and Wickersham Wall ascents would doubtless dispute. The writer also errs describing Jerry Clark's second summit party: "Seven others, including the expedition's strongest climbers, opted to assault the pinnacle." Most of Jerry's team were experienced and skilled climbers to be sure, but not the expedition's strongest.

The article's bomb, however, is dropped not by the reporter but by the only source he quotes for attribution. It detonates in the last, verdict-issuing paragraph.

> Blaming serious tactical blunders and "fiendish" weather for what he calls U.S. mountaineering's worst disaster, Expert Alpinist Bradford Washburn added, "It's amazing more people haven't been killed on McKinley when you consider 400 are killed in the Alps every summer."

Washburn's insults private and public have already cut Joe deeply, of course. Now the iconic Mr. McKinley rubs salt—nay, *acid*—in the wounds by suggesting in the world's most widely read and highly respected news magazine that he, Joe Wilcox, is to blame for the tragedy. There is no mistaking that the phrase "serious tactical blunders" is aimed at Joe. Organizations do not make blunders. Leaders do.

Beyond shock and anger, Joe is fully aware of the damage that a statement like this by a source like Washburn in a publication like *Time* will do, so he fires off a response, which is published in the magazine's next issue:

> *In reading "Denali Strikes Back" [August 11 issue] I was amazed that Bradford Washburn blamed "serious tactical blunders" for the mountaineering disaster. This statement seems to indicate that the expedition made some mistakes that most mountaineers would routinely have avoided and that these mistakes were largely responsible for the tragedy. In talking with Mr. Washburn, I find that he had only sketchy information and did not at first understand why the expedition split into two groups. He certainly did not mean to imply that the tactics were responsible for the tragedy.*
>
> *It is difficult to determine why the disaster happened without knowing first what happened. . . . To suggest that this recent disaster could have been foreseen would not only discredit the victims but also be unfair to future expeditions.*
> *Joseph F. Wilcox*
> *Leader*

So the epistolary battle with Washburn, begun much earlier and interrupted by the expedition, is rejoined. Joe's *Time* rejoinder has Mr. McKinley seeing red yet again. This latest letter adds insult to the injury of Wilcox's crew rolling into McKinley Park with his name taken in vain in big dirty letters on the Hankmobile, a sacrilege he likely heard about quickly, given how well the grapevine between Boston and McKinley was working.

Washburn writes Joe a curt letter on October 2 defending his assertion that "serious tactical errors" caused the disaster, then dropping the curtain on their dialogue with a patrician declaration: "I simply don't care to debate this matter further." His feeling about Joe at this time is revealed in a letter that Washburn wrote later to Howard Snyder: "If you get in a pissing match with a skunk, you end up smelling like a skunk."

However, on August 25, more than two weeks after telling *Time* unequivocally that "serious tactical blunders" caused the tragedy, Washburn admits in a letter to George Hall that in fact he really *doesn't* know what happened: "I am eager to sit down with someone, in fact <u>anyone!</u>, who can give me a clear picture of what transpired."

For a variety of reasons, some more obvious than others, tragedies demand investigation. One is simply basic understanding—just figuring out what actually happened. Another is determining causation—understanding why such a terrible thing happened, hopefully to reduce the likelihood of its repetition. A third is determining who contributed—assigning responsibility. When tragedy involves the same entity responsible for its investigation, a fourth goal intervenes with depressing frequency: ensuring that somebody—*anybody*—else made this terrible thing happen.

After the 1949 Mann Gulch fire killed thirteen young Smokejumpers, "The Forest Service knew right away it was in for big trouble," wrote Norman Maclean in his book about the disaster. So great (and justified) was the forest service's fear that it convened an Initial Committee of Investigation on August 7, just two days after the fire. This crew overflew the disaster, walked the site, then ginned up a hasty report. With public outrage flaring, the forest service conducted a Formal Board of Review in late September. After performing its own overflights and site investigations, reviewing reams of documents, and interviewing "all key witnesses," the review board took only three days to issue a report. The verdict: "It is the overall conclusion of the Board that there is no evidence of disregard by those responsible for the jumper crew of the elements of risk which they are expected to take into account in placing jumper crews on fires." In other words, the United States Forest Service worked as its own investigator, served as its own judge and jury, and voted itself not guilty on all counts.

Cries of *Whitewash!* arose quickly. Disagreeing with the report, most of the dead young men's parents filed lawsuits "alleging negligence on the part of Forest Service officials." It certainly stoked media suspicions of bureaucratic ignorance, ineptitude, and cover-up.

Eighteen years later, the National Park Service apparently knew right away that it, too, was in for big trouble in the wake of the July 1967 tragedy. It was right to be concerned. Mountaineering accidents with higher death tolls have happened since, but at that point the McKinley event was the third worst such disaster of all time and the worst in North American history. It was a disaster of historic magnitude.

Seven exceptional young Americans were dead. Anybody who bothered to look closely could see that the chain of events leading to their deaths began when park service policy squeezed two individually cohesive but radically different teams into one larger, fractious, and unhappy mob. (Even Wilcox nemesis Howard Snyder's accident report, filed with the American Alpine Association, cited "Party Size Too Large" as a contributory cause.) You did not even have to look closely to understand that, having thus written a script for tragedy, the park service's mismanagement of later events increased the likelihood that its last act would leave bodies scattered about the mountain.

In September 1967, Wayne Merry has known all of this for many days, of course, and has already begun making ready to fall on his sword. For the time being, though, his dismay remains unannounced. But early on, other experts as knowledgeable as Wayne are looking closely at what happened on Mount McKinley in July and are not happy with what they are seeing. On August 3, world-famous mountaineer Lou Whittaker, a leading member of Seattle's Rescue Council and himself the victim of that serious accident on McKinley in 1960, chews George Hall a new earhole by telephone. The upshot of their conversation is Whittaker's belief that not enough was done to rescue survivors or to find bodies.

Mortified, Hall tries to lateral this hot potato to ARG's Gary Hansen, who whips it right back in an indignant letter written the same day they speak:

> *This letter is in response to a conversation by telephone between Gary Hansen, ARG, and yourself representing the Mt. McKinley Park Service, at 9:35 am, this morning. You mentioned that you had received*

*a telephone call from Mr. Lou Whittaker of Tacoma, Washington
(Member of the Mountain Rescue Council) expressing the belief that
the search effort for the missing party on Mt. McKinley had not been
taken far enough.*

*Members of the Board of Directors of the Alaska Rescue Group Inc.
have met to consider this comment and it is the consensus of the board
that Mr. Whittaker's statement is not true. . . .*

*We feel jointly that every possible effort has been made to put eyes
on the mountain and that . . . the five man Mountaineering Club of
Alaska ground search party did in fact make a very thorough search.*

The ARG (now known as AMRG, for Alaska Mountain Rescue
Group) did their best to help during the research for this book, but they
did not know where Gary Hansen is now, nor was I able to locate him.
So I could not interview him about the letter quoted above, which leaves
important questions unanswered. For example, having read that letter, it's
impossible not to imagine Jerry Clark sitting in a snow cave up at 19,500
feet on July 21 or 22, saying to his buddies, "Listen, guys, everything's
gonna be okay. Those Alaska Rescue Group fellows know their business."

The ARG did give written warning to expeditions that retained its
services that Alaskan climbing is harder and more hazardous than anything found in the lower 48: "The possibility of prolonged storms requiring many days holed-up in tents or snow caves is continual." The same
documents offer this assurance about what climbers in trouble could
expect from the ARG:

> The Alaska Rescue Group stands ready to help in any mountain res-
> cue. It is on call through the Rescue Coordination Center (Elmen-
> dorf Air Force Base, Anchorage) 24 hours a day. Whenever needed,
> A R G members will provide their unique skills and abilities to help
> save lives.

It's also hard not to be struck by the fact that in his letter of self-
defense, Gary Hansen points not to the National Park Service, the Rescue Coordination Center, or the ARG's own efforts but to those of Bill
Babcock's civilian MCA team.

The point here is not to flay the ARG or Gary Hansen. Until the very end, he may not have been provided with enough information about the dire urgency of the situation. In addition, he clearly tried to do the best he could with limited resources at his disposal. It *is* to say that the best defense that the ARG could find to counter Lou Whittaker's accusations was that "the five man Mountaineering Club of Alaska ground search party did in fact make a very thorough search."

If the park service bureaucracy proves incapable in July of launching a big, fast rescue operation such as the one sent in March to aid the Winter Expedition, it is anxious indeed to rescue the agency's image—and that is not all. By the end of July, talk of parental lawsuits is already in the wind; if they go forward, careers may end up twisting there as well.

So on or about July 31, with Bill Babcock's MCA team still on the mountain and Joe Wilcox still in the park, George Hall makes contact— probably by telegram and possibly by phone—with none other than Bradford Washburn, asking for his help. Washburn responds on August 2 with a four-page letter.

> Dear Mr. Hall:
> I was simply sick not to be able to come up this week and give you a hand—and just to help in anyway I possibly could in this infinitely sad and complicated time of anguish. If an out and out rescue operation had been involved, and I could have helped in saving lives, I would have just plain dropped everything and come anyway.

Oddly, Brad never asks why no "out and out rescue operation had been involved." But more striking is the acknowledgment that, by Washburn's reckoning, there never *was* an all-out rescue declaration by anyone on or off the mountain, and even Brad Washburn, way back in Boston, knows it.

Next, Washburn gets to the help that George Hall wants.

> I would be very happy, however, if you wish, to come up to Anchorage around September 12–13–14 for a conference and intensive study of the facts of this disaster with a view to weighing the problems that it presents to the National Park Service. [Emphasis added]

A bit further along, Washburn expands on suggested meeting dates:

I have given this a great deal of thought in the last two days [presumably since receiving Hall's telegram] and come to the conclusion that a meeting of this sort could almost certainly be handled more effectively in a month or six weeks rather than do it now with the families of the dead boys there, a party just coming off the mountain, and the *intense spotlight of the press focused on everything everyone says and does. [Emphasis added]*

A source close to these events (not Wayne Merry, for the record) remembers what was happening at the time. This person, who requested anonymity, confirmed that Washburn was summoned to lead a critique "to defend the park service" and that "there was a lot of friction going on at that time." This source added, "they made it kind of difficult for [Washburn] to say no."

The conference convenes at about one in the afternoon on Tuesday, September 12, in the Port Room of the Westward Hotel (now the Anchorage Hilton) in Anchorage. Washburn flies in from Boston, his expenses as an "NPS consultant" paid by the government. His wife, Barbara, comes along. The list of twenty-four attendees who show up Thursday morning reads like a Who's Who of Alaskan mountaineering. George Hall, Art Hayes, and Wayne Merry are there. Representatives from the Mountaineering Club of Alaska and the Alaska Rescue Group, including Gary Hansen, attend. Don Sheldon has flown down from Talkeetna. Art Davidson, Ray Genet, and Dave Johnston of Winter Expedition fame show up. All of the MCA McKinley Expedition/Rescue Team members except Jeff appear: Bill Babcock, John Ireton, Gayle Nienheuser, and Chet Hackney. Lou Whittaker, who earlier criticized the ARG/NPS effort, is not present.

From the outset, there is something strange about this conference. Star witnesses at the U.S. Forest Service Formal Board of Review following the Mann Gulch fire were Wag Dodge, Walter Rumsey, and Robert Sallee, the only three survivors of and eyewitnesses to the tragedy. The review board got at least this much right: Those who were there at the fire could provide more useful insights about what happened than those who were not. Organizers of the NPS "Anchorage Conference" apparently do not share this belief. The Wilcox tragedy's five survivors are conspicuous not for their illuminating testimony but for their absence.

Brad Washburn kicks off the conference by announcing this a priori assumption, recorded by the meeting's secretary: "Tactical errors assumed." A veteran mountaineer who was familiar with Alaskan climbing, the tragedy, and the National Park Service (but who was not an NPS employee) and who was present at the conference says today that its real purpose was clear from the outset:

"That was a 'get Wilcox' meeting . . . you had people trying to come up with blaming someone or something for all this. . . . There was all hell breaking loose from the parents. There was talk about legal action. Gross irresponsibility, etc."

Because George Hall is the superintendent of Mount McKinley National Park, and George Hartzog, a political appointee, is the director of the National Park Service, Hall has to know, and know that Hartzog knows, that forgiveness is not one of the government's saving graces. In Washington, D.C., George Hall's value and a Foggy Bottom mosquito's are about equal, Art Hayes's even less.

But some people care a lot about George Hartzog, most important among them the Lyndon Johnson administration people who got him appointed. These are not LBJ's finest hours, given "Veet Nam," as LBJ called it, and all its attendant miseries. There could not be a worse time for the National Park Service, led by an LBJ appointee, to be guilty of creating or even contributing to the worst tragedy in North American mountaineering history. Such a scenario could conceivably end with Hartzog's neck in the noose—unless someone else's can be inserted there.

Something else may be at work here—Brad Washburn's pride. Washburn's letters reveal the fury kindled by Joe's scathing and impertinent responses. In fairness to Washburn, it takes two to feud. Without each other, the Hatfields and the McCoys would have remained just two more families hardscrabbling in the Kentucky backwoods. Regardless, someone close to the situation at that time recalls, "Washburn, who was a god, was kind of hurt with the stuff that Wilcox had pulled, maybe took it a little too personally. *No one's* supposed to criticize Washburn, right?"

With the conference's "tactical errors" leitmotif established, the ARG's Gary Hansen, in his own opening remarks, says that the Wilcox Expedition was plagued from day one by "built-in problems." These included being a "composite group" and having a "lack of leaders" and inadequate "expedition experience."

After the ice has been broken by several hours of relatively polite discussion, Wayne Merry finally throws on the table ugly stuff that others have not wanted to touch. He says that Wilcox repeatedly "asked for overflights" as a prelude to calling for an all-out rescue, but he never got them. In light of that failure, how fair or realistic can it be to blame him for this disaster? Wayne asserts that such overflights could have been made, or at least attempted, at various times during the crisis, and the people who could have made them are in this room, and he wants to know why those overflights were not made despite Joe's and Wayne Merry's multiple requests.

Gary Hansen protests that weather factors prevented such flights, but Paul Crews, contradicting his own companion, asserts (wrongly) that numerous overflights were made. Wayne holds his ground, criticizing the air search response, sparking more heated rebuttals. In the end, as one attendee remembers, Wayne simply "got outshouted."

After the dinner break, working to summarize the day, Washburn makes two important statements. One is an apologia for the National Park Service: no major rescue such as that required by the July 1967 tragedy can be mounted "inside of a week regardless of time of a call-out." Having lifted blame from the agency's shoulders, he then drops it squarely on Joe's, declaring that the "competence of a leader to react" is the most important consideration in reviewing this tragedy.

The first statement is patently false, because the massive March 1967 Winter Expedition rescue effort got under way in a matter of *hours*. The second statement keeps the spotlight on Joe, while other parties slip quietly off the stage.

JONATHAN WATERMAN IS one of a number of experts who have noted that the 1960s "marked the end of an era on Denali," one called variously the "Pioneer Era" and "McKinley's Golden Age." By whatever name, it began centuries ago when Native Americans gazed at the mountain's summit, entranced, wondering what it would be like to stand so close to heaven. It ended when seven men found that out in July 1967.

Tragedies often end eras by forcing irrevocable change, and the July 1967 disaster did both. The eternal, essential hardships of climbing McKinley remained unaltered, but government administration of the mountain would never be the same, nor would the margin for error ever again be as thin and as keen as it was for Jerry Clark and his party.

Now is a good time to point out that today's National Park Service management of Denali National Park and Preserve is very different. It was very different as far back as 1981, in fact, during my brief sojourn there. Radios were everywhere. Kahiltna Base was superbly managed by Frances Randall. Expert climbing rangers roamed the mountain and staffed base facilities.

In George Hall's day, the entire park staff may have been fewer than twenty. In 2006, 266 men and women worked at the park, which operated with a budget of about $11 million. An all-time record 1,340 climbers attempted Denali by various routes; 775 of them, or about 58 percent, made the top. The NPS conducted thirteen rescues with nary a mishap, and only two climbers, or 0.1 percent of the total, died. In addition, some of the world's most important high-altitude research has been conducted at the 14,300-foot station. But perhaps the most revealing indicator of change for the better is that if you asked any international symposium to name the world's top five mountaineering search-and-rescue experts, chances are good that Chief District Ranger Daryl Miller and Chief Climbing Ranger Roger Robinson would make the list.

Somewhat surprisingly, not all climbers think those changes have been for the better. Jonathan Waterman, in a superb position to know, looked back from 1991 and wrote in *Surviving Denali* that after 1967, "Perhaps climbers were lulled into a false sense of security . . . self sufficiency was superseded by radios, helicopters, and dependence on other climbers. All of these factors had an adverse effect. . . ."

The Anchorage conferees, including leader Brad Washburn, inaugurate the new era by scrutinizing, if not the rescue response, many other aspects of McKinley climbing. How valuable are the medical exam and climbing application forms currently in use? How should "expedition experience" be defined? Who judges what qualifies as expedition experience? Can it really be measured? What provisions must be made for foreign climbers—Japanese and Germans in particular—with little command of English? Wind aloft data, currently available only from Anchorage and Fairbanks, should be more localized. With radio communications admittedly poor, what can be done to improve them? When, how, and by whom should an all-out rescue be initiated? If one is called, who pays? Should bonds be required for climbing groups? Would that increase the number of clandestine climbs without permits? Who pays for false alarms and for flights such as Sheldon's?

The Anchorage Conference produces a highly ironic denouement, a chain of events that its organizers could not have foreseen. George Hall learns to his dismay that once you let a stallion out of the barn, it is hard to corral him again. On September 22, with the bit firmly in his teeth, Brad Washburn writes directly to National Park Service director George Hartzog to report on the Anchorage Conference. George Hall and Wayne Merry, Washburn assures, "did everything that they could have done . . . nor could we see that they did anything they should not have done." At least one of those men, Wayne Merry, would argue with that. Later, Washburn identifies what he sees as the tragedy's root cause: "Their leadership simply was not sufficiently experienced to cope with the conditions that led to this tragedy."

Because Washburn did not give George Hall a copy of the Hartzog letter, the Director has one sent and requests Hall's opinion of Washburn's comments. Hall's response, which he apparently typed himself, is extremely odd. He begins by assuring National Park Service headquarters that *both* Washburns' presence was essential to the meeting's success because "Many points made at the meeting could not have been presented so clearly *with their experienced viewpoint*." [Emphasis added] Hall may be trying to justify the expenses incurred in bringing the Washburns to Alaska. But he is so discomfited that he mistakenly writes "with" instead of what he really means—"*without* their experienced viewpoint." To make such an error in a letter to his ultimate boss suggests how disturbed George Hall was.

In the same letter, Hall is forced to do some fast backtracking because of the vehemence of Washburn's attacks on Joe Wilcox. The superintendent warns, "Dr. Washburn is very strongly of the opinion that the Wilcox tragedy befell the group largely due to the inadequacy on the part of the leader." Nevertheless, the meeting "should lead in a year or two to the use of the Anchorage based rescue group for rescues."

You cannot help but wonder how Joe, Jerry Clark, and his friends—or even Gary Hansen and Paul Crews, for that matter—would have felt reading that NPS bosses believe that the ARG is still a year or two away from having any real rescue capability.

The letter contains another amazing statement, this about radios, which Hall admits are a good idea but confesses that "the park has no set to monitor them. Last year we stayed in touch with them [the climbers] by means of a system borrowed from our plumber."

In late September, back from his Alaska sortie, Washburn, still charging hard with that bit in his teeth (but without any direction of sanction from the NPS), requests weather records for most of July from the National Weather Service's Alaska Region director. This man, with a bureaucrat's uncanny ability to sniff out trouble across a continent, writes to his boss in National Oceanic and Atmospheric Administration (NOAA) headquarters.

> We have contacted the local office of the National Park Service to determine whether Dr. Washburn has an official status. As far as can be determined . . . he has not. Mr. George Hall, the local Field Director, indicated the situation is a touchy one and there is the possibility of some legal action.

On October 26, George Hall sends a Blue Envelope communication to George Hartzog in Washington, D.C. Blue Envelope, according to the United States Postal Service (USPS) *Domestic Mail Manual*, is the bureaucracy's closest approximation to the "Top Secret For Your Eyes Only" classification used by military and intelligence agencies:

> B. Blue Envelopes. Blue envelopes marked "SPECIAL ATTENTION MAIL to be opened only by ———," are to be used only to send official Government business materials subject to the Privacy Act and other materials of a sensitive nature. . . . Blue envelopes are to be opened only by the individual or office addressed.

Washburn's freelancing has begun to alarm Hall, especially now that
Brad is ranging out to other agencies.

> *In a letter to the Weather Bureau, he [Washburn] requests a detailed*
> *analysis of the area weather for the period of the tragedy, seemingly to*
> *support a conclusion at which he has already arrived. He believes*
> *[that] Joe Wilcox made serious tactical blunders and is fully responsi-*
> *ble for the tragedy. . . .* I feel we must use caution over Dr. Wash-
> burn's overwhelming treatment of Joe Wilcox. *This could eventually*
> *result in Wilcox seeking legal help.*
>
> *I was not aware that his visit here was designed to make a depth*
> *study of this tragedy, however we do have a problem separating him*
> *from this matter since, from the letters attached,* you will see he has
> a distinct personal involvement, *as well as our contact. [Emphasis*
> *added]*

WE WILL NOW be leaving Mount McKinley National Park and Alaska,
which is as good a time as any for the unpleasant but necessary assessment of the actions and inaction of park superintendent George Hall and
Chief Ranger Arthur Hayes. Both passed away before I could interview
them. They have been described by people who knew them as decent,
responsible men, not hard to get along with, conscientious about doing
their jobs to the best of their abilities.

But given all that they did *not* do, and given the fact that they were
bureaucrats, and given the utterly clear view from way up here in 2006
of how badly they screwed things up, it is tempting and easy to paint
them as the lead villains of this tragedy. We do not need to list again the
results of all the days they spent sitting on their hands and passing bucks,
which have presented themselves starkly and sadly throughout much of
this book. But all that must not obscure the fact that, in the end, just as
Steve Taylor could not be faulted for his inability to match the Coloradoans' pace on the tundra, Hall and Hayes cannot be faulted for not
doing a job they did not know how to do.

The National Park Service put them both in place and gave them
responsibility for administering Mount McKinley National Park, home
to titanic mountains and infernal weather and an iconic, lethal peak that
was, and is, the object of many climbers' lifelong dreams. The National

Park Service did not give them training in glacier travel, ice ax and cram-pon use, altitude, crevasses, avalanches, and search and rescue, or even radios to communicate with climbers on Mount McKinley. By George Hall's own admission, they borrowed a radio from their plumber.

So Hall and Hayes are not villains in the classic sense of knowingly committing evil acts for the petty purpose of protecting careers. They did not have the skills, experience, or knowledge to properly do the part of their jobs that required emergency mountain search and rescue. Thus they cannot be called guilty of not doing those jobs when dying men des-perately needed them to.

But they *are* guilty of this: They had under their command one man who may have been the best-equipped expert in North America to do such a job. Again and again and again and again, they not only ignored but sometimes frustrated Wayne Merry's increasingly desperate attempts to do the right things. Of *this* they are guilty indeed.

I've wondered how Hall and Hayes lived with that. I know how much smaller guilts over unrightable wrongs have stayed with me throughout the years, cutting like inextricable splinters. These were not stupid men. They had to know how badly they had failed, and what the price of their failure had been. They had to live the rest of their lives with that knowl-edge, keeping it trapped down so far that it might escape to torment them only deep into long, black, sleepless nights.

Neither were they men without hearts and souls, as evidenced in the one instance I found of either man speaking afterward about the tragedy. In 1991, as part of a much longer taped interview, George Hall finally came around to July 1967:

"We had crank phones in the area, somebody cranked and said they, you know, they spotted a body or found a body, and of course there were two of them. My question was, are they alive? I can hear myself say it, and I knew damn well they weren't alive. *I just wished they'd be alive.*"

They say you can hear a smile in someone's voice. On that tape, you could hear the tears in George Hall's.

30

Memorable Quotes

I t is clear that Howard Snyder's frustration has been building since long before he actually gets off Mount McKinley. His anger ignited at the spontaneous Super-Alpha clash between him and Joe Wilcox during their first meeting in the Mount Rainier base area. It was fueled by the harsh public upbraiding that Joe delivered, while still on the tundra near McGonagall Pass, for the Coloradoans' separation from Steve Taylor during the hike in. Continuing up the mountain, it was exacerbated by altitude, fatigue, and stress, devolving into a Mexican standoff much like the one that undermined the first winter attempt on the Cassin Ridge in 1982, described with excruciating honesty by Jonathan Waterman in his book *In the Shadow of Denali*.

Howard's anger and frustration had become so intense by late July, during the descent from Camp VI, that they erupted spontaneously during the first minutes of his encounter with Bill Babcock. It broke out again in the tent with Jeff, Paul, and Jerry Lewis, flaring into what Jeff Babcock would later describe as a "breakdown."

Howard begins thinking about writing a book about the disaster before the expedition ends, and starts to lay the groundwork for it as soon as he is off the mountain. While staying at Grace Hoeman's house in Anchorage, he records "Jerryisms" that will help re-create Jerry Clark's character and memorable quotes:

Jerryisms:

Gunsight Pass—"Gunsmoke Pass"
Clearwater River—"Crystal River"
Hill of Cracks—"House of Cracks"

Memorable quotes:

"Damn it, slow down. I can go all the way to the summit today if you want to, if we just go slow." Jerry Clark, as we reached site of camp VII at 17,900'. I was leading, breaking trail in 8–12 inch snow. Clark was last on the rope and yet he couldn't maintain the pace I was setting while breaking trail.

Dialogue between Howard Snyder and Jerry Clark on carry from Camp II to Camp III when on level stretch between top of lower Icefall and base of Hill of Cracks, 3 July, Jerry Clark kept telling me to slow down and McLaughlin and S. Taylor concurred, while I was setting the slowest pace I could without stopping.

Howard goes on to make more extensive preliminary notes:

Possible Chapter Titles:
The Importance of a leader
The reasons why
Book title: Expedition
Or: Expedition Log

Possible Chapter Titles:
Safety Last
Role Call of the Doomed
    2nd party's summit + down
Slow down and Die
Quick and the Dead
No Safety in Numbers
Arctic Hurricane (4 day storm)
Cakewalk—our summit climb
Death March their " "

Into the Hall of the Mtn. King
The Mountain King (weather)

Possible Book Titles:
Killer McKinley
Nightmare in the land of the Midnight Sun
Inferno of Snow—trapped on Mt. McKinley
Frozen Hell or Inferno
Only Five Returned
Death Rode the Wind
(In The) Hall of the Mtn. King
The Story of the tragic Wilcox McKinley Expedition

I ASKED HOWARD when he decided to write a book about the disaster, and when he began making notes. He replied,

> The Jerryisms and other quotes were written while we were at Grace Jansen-Hoeman's house in Anchorage. The possible chapter titles were written after our unspoken fears about the fate of the missing seven were confirmed, and sometime after leaving Alaska (there is a note citing Prince Rupert, B.C. which was written before the chapter titles). The chapter titles were written after I joined my parents in Vancouver, and might have been written in Monterrey, [sic] California. . . .
>   It is possible that the chapter titles were not written until I had read Joe's letter to Time Magazine, as that is the moment I decided that I had to write the complete account.

On October 16, Howard begins an exchange of letters with Brad Washburn that renews previous communication initiated when Howard was planning his own expedition two years earlier. After reminding Washburn of that and giving the background of his association with the Wilcox group, Howard advises that

> On the very slow and boring equipment relays . . . I occupied my mind at times by composing a letter to you in which I was going to thank you

for your counsel and inform you of some of the factors about the
Wilcox group. Some of the things which I was going to tell you at that
time cannot be related so freely now. . . .

Howard writes that the Wilcox group ignored Washburn's expertise
and advice, with disastrous results. For instance, the Wilcox group dis-
dained the admonition to "climb with the utmost speed on good days,"
which "led to their entrapment in a storm which gave ample warning of
its approach." Howard goes on to say that Brad's article in *Mountain*
World was "required reading" for Howard's team, and asks that Washburn
be sure to let him know when the Muldrow route guide is published.

On OCTOBER 23, Brad writes back.

I took a very dim view of the Wilcox party from the start. . . . I was
later so disgusted by his letter to TIME and its inference that no mis-
takes had been made that I concluded my brief correspondence with
him by sending the enclosed letter on October 2. A fellow who was
fundamentally responsible for the tactics that led to such a ghastly
tragedy should be meek and apologetic for his part in what happened,
rather than aggressive in his protestations that it was all the fault of
happenstance. . . . It is a real shame that the tragedy of that broken
hand forced your group into this unfortunate partnership.

Washburn also alerts Howard to something else:

I imagine that a rather thorough report and appraisal of the Wilcox
operation will probably be prepared, as a part of the standard AAC
Accident Report for 1967 . . . . . . [ellipsis in original] and you will
doubtless be asked many questions, not necessarily to indict anyone,
but rather to provide a full understanding of what happened. . . .

Finally, Washburn writes that he is still angry over Joe's slights:
"Wilcox and his crew chose to belittle the power of McKinley, and apparently deliberately tried to make fun of those of us who know it well. . . ."

 A FTER WASHBURN'S REFERENCE to the *Time* letter, and his warning about the AAC's upcoming accident report publication, Howard replies on March 7, 1968. With the letter he encloses a copy of the accident report that he has filed with the American Alpine Club:

> *Joe Wilcox's letter to <u>TIME</u> disturbed me but it did not surprise me. It was typical. Of course, there <u>were</u> very "serious tactical blunders" made, and they <u>did</u> lead to the tragedy. The mistakes which were made should have been routinely avoided.*

On April 1, Washburn concludes his correspondence with Howard, thanking him for a long telephone conversation. He also refers, in a way that strongly suggests but does not prove beyond doubt (only because writers of that era loved the passive voice much more than the active), that he has finished writing the report that will appear shortly in *Accidents in North American Mountaineering (ANAM)*:

> *Thank you very much for your additional letter of March 22 and for all the time that you gave me on the telephone last week.*
> *The AAC report on last summer's tragedy has now been completed and I hope that it will present what happened accurately and without bias.*

Unfortunately, the *ANAM* report, published soon after, did neither.

31

Summit and ANAM

onths before the American Alpine Club's report appears, Helen Kilness, an editor at *Summit Magazine*, asks Wayne Merry to write an article about the tragedy for her publication. *Summit* was then one of the world's most highly respected magazines devoted to climbing and mountaineering. Wayne has written for them before, and delivers his piece, "Analysis of the McKinley Tragedy," on September 9. The article appears as the December issue's cover story.

As a courtesy, Wayne writes to Joe Wilcox on December 11, just before the issue comes out, assuring him that, "It is a straight, brief narrative of events with a theoretical reconstruction of the actual tragedy. No analysis. No judgment. Object: to increase awareness of the tremendous potential of the mountain. . . . I hear you are still feuding with Washburn . . . ?"

Wayne is true to his word; his article points no fingers, lays no blame, makes not a single critical judgment. Readers at the time would not necessarily find anything surprising about this. Anyone privy to Wayne's twelve-day battle with the bureaucracy certainly would.

There is good reason for the article's "straight, brief narrative" quality. Wayne has known from the start that National Park Service officials all the way up to Director Hartzog himself in Washington, D.C., will read it. Wayne telephones George Hall on December 12 to tell him that *Summit Magazine*, with his article about the tragedy, has hit the newsstands, and he is planning to write a follow-up.

Wayne assures Hall that the article is "non-controversial to the point of being insipid," giving some indication of the restraint that Wayne maintained while writing.

Hall is furious—so mad, in fact, that he does not reply to Wayne until December 18, and only then in a Blue Envelope. Hall has spent some of the intervening time cooling off, and more time sounding out his bosses on how best to deal with this loose cannon.

Hall's memo is too long to reproduce here, but some excerpts are illustrative. First, he chides Wayne for publishing a reconstruction of the tragedy: "I prefer to squelch attempts to reconstruct the affair until we are sure the bodies will not show up next spring." The desire to squelch almost certainly grows from Hall's fear that bodies *will* be found with diaries written by dying men whose last thoughts were curses hurled at the NPS. Because Bill Babcock's diary directed similar rage at the NPS, and he survived the climb, it seems likely that men who were dying would have been even angrier and had even nastier things to say. More disturbing still would be evidence that some or all of the men survived after the "rescue" operation ended, or even lived for, say, ten days.

Hall then scolds Wayne for telling him on such short notice and waves the rule book under Wayne's nose: "Had this article appeared suddenly over your name, it would have been a rude shock to me. If this is a lecture, accept it as such . . . there are controlling regulations on conduct of an employee's outside work. . . ." The memo goes on to quote chapter and verse.

In the same note to Hall, Wayne has said that the next article will not mention his position as a ranger with the National Park Service, which oddly also upsets Hall, given that he's just been chewing Wayne out for writing the first article. Says Hall: "It is not particularly complimentary that you wish to divorce yourself from all references to the National Park Service."

There is an interesting coda to this episode. As part of his research for the follow-up article in *Summit*, Wayne wants to review the NPS Mount McKinley National Park headquarters log, which contains its own narrative of the July tragedy. But by the time he asks for it, the log is nowhere to be found.

THE HEART OF Wayne's article is his reconstruction of the Clark party's final days. He suggests that after summiting, the five men descended as they had come, but then "something happened to delay them. Perhaps it was the whiteout; perhaps a fall on the summit pitch; perhaps simply exhaustion. Before they reached Archdeacon Tower a strong wind from the northwest had arisen and was hurling snow directly into their faces with increasing violence. . . . There was no choice; they must bivouac and pray that the storm would be short."

Wayne sees their efforts to dig a snow cave thwarted by winds that quickly rose to a hundred miles per hour. The wind ripped away Jerry's pack, with the radio in it. They could only huddle in their bags in the meager shelter of rocks near Archdeacon's Tower, exposure draining their will and strength.

During some period of clearing in the next few days, they made a dash straight down the slope beneath Archdeacon's Tower toward Camp VII, which they could see about 1,500 vertical feet lower and a mile away. At least one of them carried his sleeping bag. Downward progress was pitifully slow, given their weakness and the steep, unfamiliar terrain. Well before they reached the 50-foot ice cliff that would have barred further progress, whiteout enveloped them and the weather turned vicious once again. Unable to see the route or even one another, they sat down on the steep face to wait for a break in the weather—which never came.

Wayne does not try to account for missing Jerry Clark, Hank Janes, and Mark McLaughlin, or to explain why Dennis and Walt were found sitting on the slope while the others were not. He does not speculate on the identity of the body found at Camp VII.

I AGREE WITH all the important parts of Wayne's reconstruction. The one point on which we differ is my belief that the Clark party, having carried at least one and possibly two shovels to the summit, would have dug secure snow caves for their bivouac of July 17 and thus would have returned to the caves the next day. The Winter Expedition survivors had dug caves into solid ice in similar winds in the dark. Jerry had taught cold-weather survival in Antarctica, and most of the others had spent more than enough time in mountains in winter to know the importance of snow caves and how to dig them. Dennis Luchterhand dug a twelve-man snow cave farther down on the mountain. To imagine them shivering helplessly near Archdeacon's Tower, where the snow surface lent itself to cave digging, while shovels lay unused a few feet away is just not reasonable.

Wayne's article ends with this offering: "any climber who sets foot on Mount McKinley enters the realm of enormous natural forces which no human strength can overcome, but which awareness can help to avoid."

This is unquestionably true, but it is like saying that the *Titanic* victims drowned because the ocean is full of deep water, or that the thirteen young Smokejumpers burned to death in Mann Gulch because forest fires are huge and hot. It does not move closer to an answer for the question How did it happen?

Many expected that this question would be answered by the next report, which appeared in the annual compendium of the American Alpine Club (AAC), *Accidents in North American Mountaineering* (*ANAM*). Though this analogy is far from exact, it is close enough to be helpful: The AAC is to climbing as the National Transportation Safety Board (NTSB) is to transportation. The AAC describes itself as "the country's premier mountaineering association," and that reputation is well deserved. Its multifaceted mission includes, among other things, "the promotion and dissemination of knowledge about the mountains and mountaineering through its meetings, publications and libraries; the cultivation of mountain craft, and the promotion of good fellowship among climbers." It is impossible to overestimate the number and importance of the American Alpine Club's positive contributions to American and international mountaineering. One of these is the Henry S. Hall, Jr., American Alpine Club Library, in Golden, Colorado, where, helped in every possible way by library director Bridget Burke, I conducted some of the research for this book. Another is the annual *Accidents in North American Mountaineering* (*ANAM*).

All of which makes the errors in *ANAM*'s analysis of the July 1967 McKinley tragedy so unusual. *ANAM* was, and is, the benchmark for investigation and analysis of mountaineering mishaps. Reports in this publication are models of objectivity and accuracy. The McKinley tragedy report, however, was an exception.

The report's first major error—and it is a huge one—occurs in its second sentence: "*radio report received from Park Service warning of big storm around July 16–17.*" Those italics appear in the original published version of this report, giving some idea of how critically important the report's author believes this to be. Unfortunately, it is simply wrong. In an earlier chapter of this book, I set out evidence regarding this claim. Every bit of credible evidence suggests that no such report was broadcast or received. Why its author would make this claim so early, and go out of his way to emphasize it typographically, is another question.

The second error comes in the second paragraph, in the report's account of the stove explosion that destroyed a tent. "W. Taylor loosened gas-tank valve of bad stove, releasing fumes which promptly exploded." An earlier chapter examines this claim, like the one mentioned above. The stove in question did not explode because Walt opened the gas-tank valve. It exploded because the stove's seal malfunctioned. Howard and Joe produced explanations of the stove fire. Joe's was that of an eyewitness who owned the stove and was familiar with its strengths and weaknesses. Howard, who used a different kind of stove, was not present. Yet the report writer repeated the explanation favored by Howard.

Writing about July 17, the author claims, wrongly, "it was the plan of the 7 men remaining there [Camp VII] to set out for the summit shortly and bivouac enroute, if necessary." Not true. The Clark party never intended to or planned a bivouac. Joe could have explained that easily, had the author bothered to interview him.

And "The leader of the group, Jerry Clark, although determined to reach the top, was reportedly in poor shape." Not true. Jerry had grown progressively stronger the longer he climbed, and at Camp VII he was in perfectly good shape, as evidenced by his statement to Joe (repeated by Joe in a radio broadcast to Eielson) that he and Mark might try to climb the North Peak before attempting the southern one. His new tone of command, *telling* Joe to go down the mountain on July 17, reflected this. So does his jaunty radio broadcast from the summit on July 18, which revealed that he felt fine even after the (unplanned) bivouac and summit climb.

On July 18, says the report, "At 11 A.M. the 6-man party reported that it had reached the summit of south peak. . . ." The summit party, however, reported that only *five* of them had reached the summit, and Mark McLaughlin read all five names for the record. This would have been revealed by even a quick review of the radio log—surely one of the most important documents available to a conscientious accident investigator. This omission is not by itself earthshaking. But such an egregious, offhand mistake does suggest that the report's author was less concerned with facts and accuracy than he should have been.

It goes on: "Except for typical lulls, the fury of this storm did not abate for 4 days." In fact, the storm began in earnest on July 18. The weather did not improve enough to allow summit overflights until July 27—ten days. This is important, because based on this misinformation the writer will draw comparisons between the Clark party and the Winter Expedition, intended to show the Clark party's ineptitude.

Writing of July 24, the report's author claims "the battered Wilcox party, strengthened by the addition of Dr. Grace Jensen [*sic*] of the MCA party, descended." Vin Hoeman's wife, Dr. Grace Jansen-Hoeman, was, if anything, sicker than all the other Wilcox group members with the possible exception of Jerry Lewis. An addition of strength she certainly was not.

Thus ended the report's narrative portion. Next came three pages of analysis, as distressingly shot through with error as were the preceding four pages.

The analysis begins with a statement as incorrect as it is prejudicial: "Wilcox, as leader, has received probably far more than his fair share of the blame for what transpired." That is simply untrue. So far, no one inside or outside the climbing community other than Brad Washburn and Howard Snyder has blamed Joe Wilcox for what transpired. Many, in fact, have praised Joe's organization, preparation, leadership, courage, and conduct on the mountain. Not the least important of those issuing such praise have been many of the dead men's parents.

The analysis continues: "The large unwieldy group had a generally low level of experience for this sort of enterprise. It did not have even one *highly*-experienced climber as a member." This is so patently false, and easily disproved, that it is not worth dwelling on. Readers who wish to can refer to earlier discussions about this.

After a general introduction, the report divides into a series of subsections. In *(1) Experience and Leadership*, it claims, "No member of this group was really experienced in this sort of an expedition on a huge, sub-arctic peak." It is obviously true that none of the twelve had climbed McKinley, but they had as much or more experience than most climbers making a first attempt on the mountain.

In *(2) Size of the Party*, the Wilcox group is criticized because it "was not a single homogeneous group. . . . The decision was unwise, as the mere concentration of 12 persons in a single weakly knit group created a situation potentially fraught with danger in the event of trouble." That is true, but the reason given for such a flawed team's creation—"The balance of this group [Howard's team] decided to combine forces with the Wilcox group at the last minute"—shifts responsibility for this catastrophic decision away from where it belongs and puts it squarely on the shoulders of Howard Snyder.

We have seen already what really happened. Howard and his team never "decided to combine forces with the Wilcox group at the last minute." As Howard puts it in his book, "After two years of painstaking and expensive planning and preparations our expedition was ground to a halt within twelve hours of our intended departure for Alaska." The NPS presented Howard and his two friends with a Hobson's choice: climb with the Wilcox team, or do not climb at all.

In *(3) Errors in Judgment*, the report repeats its earlier mistake about weather forecasting: "this party was warned about it [the storm] 3 days in advance (July 13) by radio at the 15,000 foot camp." That is demonstrably false, as we have seen, and it leads the author to this conclusion: "An evening climb by a battered party with an impending storm was suicidal." Wrong on all counts. It was not an evening climb, nor was the party battered, nor did they know anything about an impending storm.

DESPITE THESE ERRORS, *ANAM*'s report presents some findings and recommendations of genuine value. It suggests that the park service should have had radios, and good ones, and that a skilled climbing ranger, instead of unskilled seasonals, should have managed communications—the same recommendations made by the Washburn-led Anchorage Conference.

But those suggestions did not erase the errors. Because it was so unusual to find so many errors in *ANAM*, I realized early on that it was crucial to identify and interview the report writer. The report itself provided enough clues to get started:

> *Sources of this factual data*: Joseph Wilcox, Howard Snyder, Wayne Merry (District Ranger, N.P.S.) and Vin Hoeman.
>
> *Analysis*: In collaboration with Bradford Washburn and Wayne Merry. (Washburn was asked to appraise this disaster by the Director of the National Park Service)

I first contacted the current *ANAM* editor, a respected mountaineer named Jed Williamson, and asked if he knew who authored the report. He did not: "Sounds like Vin Hoeman, but I don't know for sure. He is dead, so is Ben Ferris—who was editor at the time. Maybe Wayne Merry knows."

Benjamin Ferris died in 1988. Wayne, very much alive up in remote British Columbia, also thought Vin Hoeman might have written the report. I doubted that, because in the tragedy's aftermath Vin became one of Joe Wilcox's staunchest defenders. Whoever wrote the *ANAM* report was not favorably inclined toward Joe Wilcox.

This made it logical to ask Joe Wilcox who he thought wrote the report. He responded in an e-mail:

> I don't know who wrote the *ANAM* report. I recall getting some sort of form report to fill out. I do know that Vin Hoeman did not write it. Vin (and wife Grace who climbed down the mountain with me) were among the few supporters that I had at the time and would not have written the one sided report. It's doubtful that the writer (who appeared to have no first hand knowledge of the tragedy) talked to people like Gordon Haber . . . whose radio logs do not show any storm warning relayed to the climbing party (I would think that

such a warning, if it occurred, would have been mentioned in
the radio log). As I point out in *White Winds,* the research meteorologists claim that the data at the time did not merit a storm warning. Lastly, Snyder did not talk on the radio at all at high camp (or
before). Obviously . . . Snyder got a bigger audience with the writer.

I asked Howard whether he had, in fact, had a big audience with the
report writer and might therefore know who it was.

"I have no idea who wrote the report. There was no consultation
with me."

Just four people were listed as having had any kind of input, authorial
or otherwise: "*Sources of this factual data:* Joseph Wilcox, Howard Snyder, Wayne Merry (District Ranger, N.P.S.) and Vin Hoeman."

The analysis itself was attributed this way: "*Analysis:* In collaboration
with Bradford Washburn and Wayne Merry. (Washburn was asked to
appraise this disaster by the Director of the National Park Service)."

Because no single author's byline appeared with the *ANAM* article,
and because the editor of that *ANAM* is dead, and because today Brad
Washburn understandably cannot recall much about his involvement
with the July 1967 tragedy, it is not possible to say with absolute certainty
who wrote the *ANAM* report. But after all the wild geese had been
chased, it was possible to say that it appeared likely that Brad Washburn
had written the report himself or, if not, had strongly influenced the person who did.

32

Just a Publicity Stunt

few mountaineers are forever associated with one peak: Edmund Hillary with Everest, Maurice Herzog with Annapurna, Hermann Buhl with K2. First ascents are almost always the source of such linkage. Ten climbers in two separate expeditions preceded Brad Washburn to McKinley's summit before his first ascent in 1942, but he is connected as intimately to McKinley as Hillary, Herzog, and Buhl are to their mountains.

Washburn's relationship with McKinley springs not from having been the first to climb it, or for pioneering a perilous new route, which subsequent ascenders of major mountains are wont to do. His second ascent of McKinley in 1947 took the same Muldrow Glacier route and ostensibly had cosmic ray research as an objective. His stunning wife, Barbara Teel Polk Washburn, accompanied him. Barbara Washburn had no mountaineering experience, told me that she did nothing to get in shape except "pushing a baby carriage," and lived harmoniously with a large, all-male team for ninety days before finally setting foot on the summit. In so doing, she became the first woman to climb Mount McKinley, and was one major reason why her husband's second ascent generated more notoriety than his first.

Brad Washburn eventually did pioneer a new way up the mountain. An accomplished pilot, he first spent many hours in the air reconnoitering a route on the west side that he had long thought "would go," as climbers say. In 1951 he and three friends went, climbing to the summit via what has since become known as the West Buttress route, named for the huge rocky ridge that is the crux of this long and grueling but non-technical way up. This was, by his own admission, the easiest, fastest, and safest way up McKinley. It still is; in 1995, a typical year, of 1,340 climbers attempting the mountain, 1,208, or 90 percent, used the West Buttress route.

The legendary English climber George Leigh Mallory was never able to completely explain to others, or really even to himself, his obsession with Everest. Brad Washburn had no such difficulty talking about McKinley. In the foreword to *Mount McKinley: The Conquest of Denali*, he wrote,

> My love affair with Mount McKinley can be traced to a single moment. In January 1936, Dr. Gilbert Grosvenor, then president of the national Geographic Society, asked if I knew of any unusually interesting bit of geographical exploration that could be pulled off at "not-too-great-expense." . . . I proposed a microexpedition to make the first large format photographic flights over and around Mount McKinley. . . . [Since then] I've come to hold this great peak and its beautiful but rugged approaches in deep affection—and, at the same time, in profound respect.

Washburn's "love affair" with McKinley was no less impassioned or compulsive than George Mallory's long and ultimately deadly courtship of Mount Everest. *Mountains of the Mind* author Robert Macfarlane is fascinated by George Mallory's fatal attraction:

> To read Mallory's letters and journals from the three Everest expeditions, as I have done, is to eavesdrop on a burgeoning love affair— a love affair with a mountain. It was a deeply selfish love affair, which Mallory could and should have broken off, but which instead destroyed the lives of his wife and his children—as well as his own.

Mallory died in his twenties on Everest, achieving in death the status of legend. Brad Washburn has devoted much of his long life to extolling Mount McKinley, but despite his extraordinary accomplishments as photographer and writer (he authored or collaborated on more than thirty books), he is largely unrecognized outside the mountaineering world's limited confines. The Boston photo dealer who sells Washburn's work summed it up best: "Mountaineers knew about Brad, but outside of that sphere he was almost unknown."

Sadly, BRAD WASHBURN died at ninety-six in January 2007, leaving a rich legacy of mountaineering, mapping, photography, writing, and, certainly not least, the Museum of Science in Boston. In 2005, though, he was alive and well, and because of his deep involvement with this story, I knew it was important to speak with him directly. I was concerned that, at ninety-five, he might not be able to recall details about the 1967 tragedy, but on the phone in the spring of 2005 he sounded lucid and, to be honest, cranky. That came as no surprise, because many people have described him as "cranky," "ornery," "a curmudgeon," and the like. After several calls, though, he agreed to a visit.

On a chilly, rainy day in May of that year, I traveled to Lexington, Massachusetts, to interview him and his wife, Barbara. Red geraniums and purple petunias were blooming in the white window boxes of their one-floor town house in an upscale retirement community. Brad answered the door in crisply pressed gray slacks, a red plaid shirt, brown walking shoes, and a preppy green belt emblazoned with blue whales. His wispy white hair was neatly combed. He was slightly stooped and appeared a bit frail, but the massive Jay Leno chin and hawkish blue eyes I had seen in many photographs were still in evidence.

He led us past a dining room table covered with letters, images, and other evidence of work still in progress. Bright Oriental rugs graced the floors, and Brad's framed photos filled up much of the wall space. Their home had a comfortable and lived-in, rather than elegant, feel.

If there was elegance in the room, Barbara Washburn, still striking despite her ninety years, provided it. She was casually dressed in blue slacks, a white sweater, and white sneakers (she was going to exercise classes three times a day then). Her cool, exquisitely polite poise and bearing were those of a Boston Brahmin. We settled into the living room's big, comfortable easy chairs for the duration of the interview.

I began by asking Brad to tell me what he remembered about the Wilcox Expedition. He said that he hadn't had anything to do with it and did not remember anything about it other than some people dying. Brad did not remember speaking with George Hall, who had called or telegraphed to tell him that his help was needed after seven men had died on the mountain, or anything about the Anchorage Conference.

At that point, Barbara broke in so smoothly that it was obvious she had grown accustomed to serving as interlocutor.

"He knew those details at one time, but I think he has forgotten them," she explained. Brad, to my surprise, sat still for that. Barbara's own memories were clear. "I remember we went up there [to Alaska], we were asked by the superintendent to come up and have a big conference."

Brad, somewhat adrift, said, "I have a vivid recollection, and I cannot find this anywhere in our stuff," and that moved us onto another track. He did have a vivid recollection, but it was of a different expedition and a different emergency. Barbara eased him back onto the right track.

"Brad, they came down the shortcut, straight down, I think. You know, from the top where we went along up that big ridge." Barbara was exactly right, referring to the fatal shortcut that Dennis and Walt and perhaps others tried to take straight from Archdeacon's Tower to Camp VII. "What year was this?"

"1947," Brad said.

"1967," I said.

"1967," Barbara said.

"1947," Brad corrected, because he was still confusing the Wilcox Expedition with the Washburns' 1947 climb. Barbara smiled and waved her hand politely but dismissively. I asked Brad if he remembered the sharply worded letter that he had written to Joe Wilcox before the expedition. Again, Barbara answered:

"That nasty letter? Oh yes, that was a pretty spicy one. I remember that one."

I handed a copy of the letter to Brad, and he read the last part of it aloud:

For your information according to our records McKinley has not yet been climbed blindfold or backwards nor has any party of nine fallen simultaneously into the same crevasse. We hope you may wish to rise to one of these compelling challenges.

Brad regarded the letter silently for a moment, then broke into a grin and chuckled.

"This seems an unusually sharp letter," I said. "It seems you were very upset when you wrote it. I'd like to know what Joe Wilcox did to tick you off so much."

"Well, I just simply said that it didn't matter if it had been climbed backward or forward—"

"Yes, but why were you so mad, Brad?" Barbara interjected.

"I wasn't mad. I was just disgusted. Because they were doing a *publicity stunt*," Brad said, his leathery face crinkling up in distaste.

"That *was* what it was all about," Barbara added. So there would be no stunning new discovery here. The sharp letter was simply prompted by disgust at the idea of using McKinley as part of a publicity stunt.

They both said that they had not read *The Hall of the Mountain King* or *White Winds*, and that they had had no contact with Howard or Joe after the expedition. That was not strictly correct, because Howard and Brad exchanged a number of letters after the expedition, all focused on Joe Wilcox's flawed leadership, and I have copies of those letters. They also joined in a long phone conversation, cited by Brad in one of his letters. But Brad certainly can be forgiven for not remembering a few letters and one phone call out of thousands of both in his long and busy life.

The discussion wandered for a while. Brad eventually brought it back to the 1947 expedition, which obviously had been on his mind since we first sat down. This was the ninety-day epic that culminated with Barbara becoming the first female McKinley summiter. I asked how they had come up with the idea of her going along.

"I wouldn't have ever done it if the movie company [RKO Radio Pictures] hadn't asked him to make a movie and said if you could get your wife to go it would make a better movie to have a girl in it. I had no ambition to climb Mount McKinley. It just happened. I had three little children at this point."

Barbara smiled beguilingly, then delivered *the* line of the interview: "And anyway, it wasn't that hard, you know."

I had never heard of the film, much less seen it, so I asked her to tell me more. "It was a short subject, a twenty-minute movie, and that was in the days when they had a twenty-minute short and then the feature film. And they came to us and said, you remember the book *The White Tower* about mountain climbing? By [James Ramsey] Ullman? The movie company said we are going to do a movie of that book but we don't think that the American public is at all interested in mountain climbing and we have to stir up a little interest for them to buy the book."

"And they gave us twenty-five thousand bucks for the trip!" Brad said, chuckling even more heartily than he had upon rereading his letter to Wilcox, the memory of $25,000 very clear, as well it might be. That comes to about $240,000 in 2006 terms. The studio also hired a full-time nanny to care for the three Washburn children back in Boston for however long the expedition took.

Barbara continued her recollections, which now became hilarious. "We had to have a newsman come along . . . he was a fat, cigar-smoking Hollywood type. And he hated every minute. Finally, on his own he apparently wired, called on the radio, and got help to come in and rescue him. And we didn't know what he was doing until the plane landed and he said good-bye I'm going. And he turned to me and said, 'Barbara, when I get back to Hollywood I'm going into the darkest nightclub I can find and smoke cigars and I am never going to look at another flake of snow in my life.'

"He was a fat, pudgy guy who couldn't have climbed anywhere. Totally out of shape. Then RKO sent a substitute guy in who had a wife who was a movie star. . . ."

Brad remembered that too. He said, "Very nice guy. I remember they had a plastic model." I looked at him.

"That is right," Barbara affirmed, remembering. "They had a model of, not Marilyn Monroe, but another famous actress. A full-sized body of her made in rubber like that and they wanted us to drop it off on the summit. We thought it was too cheap and didn't let them do it."

"A full-sized rubber body?" I wanted to make sure I heard that right.

"Yes," Barbara affirmed, "to us up there and we were going to take a picture of us [with it] on the summit. This big statue of the famous actress. You would know the name right off, she was lovely and I liked her very much."

The "fat, cigar-smoking Hollywood type" guy was an RKO publicist named Len Shannon. The movie star whose rubber dummy they were supposed to plant on the summit was buxom Rita Hayworth dressed in what Barbara referred to as a "very small bathing suit."

Whatever else can be said about that part of the expedition, this much is true: Barbara Washburn climbed to the summit of the highest mountain in North America with primitive, 1947 gear, three children left behind, no mountaineering experience, not a day of conditioning other than "pushing a baby carriage," and having to live for three months with a tribe of men. For that she deserves all the credit and acclaim it is possible to give.

But this is also clear: the 1947 climb was bankrolled by a classic Hollywood caper to the tune of $240,000 in today's dollars, complete with a fat, cigar-smoking Tinseltown P.R. Guy and a life-size rubber doll of Rita Hayworth in a skimpy bathing suit. It was, in other words, a grand publicity stunt.

33

Crossing the Line

The Anchorage Conference and the exchange of letters in *Time* magazine do not go unnoticed by families of the July tragedy's victims. On September 12, Paul Janes writes to Joe, "My wife and I enjoyed reading the letter you wrote to TIME Magazine and, of course, we support your position 100 per cent." The next day brings a letter from Walt Taylor's father: "We are indeed grateful for the excellent leadership that you gave to this tremendous team of mountain climbers. We read your response in the TIME magazine with interest and certainly with approval."

The McLaughlins' response to Brad's *Time* accusations is more pointed. "Read your reply to the editors of Time and it was very well done. It is too bad that when such a disaster happens, be it climbing, fire, wreck, or what have you, there is always some 'expert' sounding off with an opinion as to exactly what happened and why it has happened, when if he would look back or perhaps review the background of those involved, he would perhaps learn to shut up."

Nancy Clark Strong, Jerry's younger sister, is the most incensed of all. "I wouldn't let Bradford Washburn worry me if I were you. After reading some of the material in Jerry's papers that were sent from Alaska and noticing [Brad's] choice comment about wishing you would all fall in a crevasse, I would think that he would have had enough common decency to keep his big nose out of the expedition entirely. He strikes me as a very disagreeable, narrow-minded egotist, and it seems to me that we should consider the source in viewing any-thing he has to say!"

Last, but not least, in the group lining up to support Joe is Vin Hoe-man, who writes on October 26, "don't let Brad get under your skin, not as many people kowtow to him as he might have you believe. Certainly I've had, and still have my differences with him, nor have I kept such dif-ferences under my hat."

The most wrenching letter that Joe receives is from Ann Crosby, Hank Janes's fiancée:

> *I loved Hank very much. I applied to school in Portland, planning to be there with Hank this year. Well, I will be there anyway—that has to be done. . . . If there is anything you know that would mean a lot to me—about Hank, what he said, what he did, I would really, really appreciate it if you would pass it on to me. And if, in the future, if any-thing comes up, anything develops, that is related to all this, and to Hank, I would really like to know about it. The radio has been a mer-ciless messenger to me . . .*

THE TRAGEDY LEADS to even graver consequences. In late September 1967, Hank Janes's mother dies of a massive heart attack that is precip-itated by the stress of grief. On April 13, 1975, Walt Taylor's younger brother, Karl, commits suicide after battling severe depression for years. Walt's mother, Mildred Taylor, confirms for Joe that "Walt's tragic death played a part in his depression."

JOE WILCOX'S OWN ordeal will not end anytime soon. Though post-traumatic stress disorder (PTSD) would not be diagnosed and named until after the Vietnam War, following an accident such as the one that occurred in July 1967 Joe may well have experienced PTSD to some degree, and there is evidence of it in the years after the disaster. He returns to graduate school, pursuing an advanced degree in math and physics, but finds it almost impossible to focus on book work. He is sad-dled with debt for the various "rescue" expenses—Sheldon's flights and the helicopter for Grace and the Coloradoans chief among them. A contentious debate among various parents and the NPS over creation of a permanent memorial to the dead climbers keeps their memories from fading. Overshadowing everything is Brad Washburn's effort to paint Joe as the Iago of this tragedy.

The accident takes its toll on Joe's marriage as well. Through the spring and summer of 1968, their relationship declines steadily. "It was the beginning of the end of our marriage," Cheryl says. "It put such a stress on us both. Joe, he went into counseling. . . . I'll just put it this way. We no longer met each other's expectations." By July 1968, one year after the expedition's catastrophic conclusion, they are divorced.

Not surprisingly, Joe goes through periods of depression. Long before antidepressants had come into use, and when even visiting a psychiatrist— "head shrinker," in the parlance of the day—was stigmatized, this must have been an extraordinarily difficult time for him. Joe never takes to drink or drugs, prescription or otherwise, but love may be the best antidepressant of all. That same summer he meets a coed named Helen Carey, who is not only beautiful but a skilled climber as well. They are married that winter, honeymoon at a ski resort, and return to a vigorous regime of winter climbing.

Late in the season, with ten friends, they attempt a new route on the West Ridge of Utah's Mount Timpanogos. The route's final pitches winnow out everyone but Joe and Helen, who climb the last several hundred yards alone. Helen leads out along a sawtooth ridge with cornices overhanging a thousand-foot drop. She takes a safe line, at least twenty feet from the cornices' sculpted edges, and has covered about half the distance to the summit when, as Joe recalls, "there was a sharp crack like a bolt of lightning." A huge slab of snow, fifty feet long by twenty feet wide, breaks away. The fracture line is right in front of Joe's crampon points.

A mountain spine such as this is called a "jump ridge," because if your rope partner falls down one side, you jump off the other in the hope that your weights will counterbalance. Helen falls to the right; Joe leaps off to the left. But there isn't much rope between them, and he falls only a few feet before hitting the snow. He digs his ice ax into a self-arrest and waits for her falling body to snap the rope tight.

It never happens. He lies there, paralyzed with fear, waiting, but the rope remains slack. He is horrified, because this means one of two things:

some sharp edge of rock cut the rope, and Helen is taking that thousand-foot fall, or she somehow slipped out of the rope and is taking the same fall. He starts hauling in rope, frantic, panting, snow flying around him, certain that climbing has plunged him into another horrible tragedy.

"Hello there!" He looks up to see Helen, smiling brightly, peering down at him. She fell only a few feet before self-arresting and has been climbing back up on her own, creating the slack in the rope that terrified Joe.

They get off the mountain safely. But in the weeks that follow, Joe can't shake the horrible déjà vu that gripped him while he was lying there with slack rope on one side of the ridge and, as he believed, his new wife falling to her death on the other.

Just a few months later, he learns that an avalanche on Dhaulagiri, in the Nepalese Himalaya, has killed two of America's finest climbers, both of whom were also supporting players in the story of Joe's expedition: Boyd Everett and his good friend Vin Hoeman.

The news brings Joe, finally, to the line that divides old climbers from bold climbers. "How many more chances could I give the mountains before the odds caught up with me? Mountaineering had lost a great deal of luster for me. Now it seemed more like a game of Russian roulette."

In June, he and Helen lead some college friends up an easy route on Mount Rainier. At the summit, as he signs the register, Joe recalls that Steve Taylor had not done so after their pre-McKinley warmup climb. He signs Steve's name, then writes a simple tribute to his friendship with Steve and his love of mountains. It is the coda to Joe's own mountain climbing career.

34

Remaking History

In 1991, Brad Washburn coauthors the aforementioned *Mount McKinley: The Conquest of Denali*. A full chapter is devoted to the July 1967 tragedy. It repeats many of the errors contained in the 1968 *ANAM* report. The Wilcox team is described as having "marginal previous experience," which undervalues their climbing histories; mistakenly writes that the park service "suggested that the two parties join forces"; and claims that "when all twelve men arrived at McKinley Park Headquarters, they were finally persuaded to climb as a single team . . . ," though that decision had been made days earlier in the backyard of Cheryl Kehr's parents' home in Puyallup, Washington. The chapter claims that the tragedy was "well documented by Howard Snyder in his *Hall of the Mountain King.*"

Thus the chapter, rife with the same kinds of errors that undermined *ANAM*'s analysis, reaches essentially the same conclusion: The July 1967 tragedy occurred because of "the extraordinary combination of serious tactical errors" and because of the lack of "a single leader who was familiar with the ways of high-mountain weather."

In 1993, the eminent climber and writer Fred Beckey publishes *Mount McKinley: Icy Crown of North America*. He, too, devotes a chapter to the July 1967 accident, and provides harsher judgment yet: "the tragedy is a case study in inadequate leadership, inexperience, ineptitude, impatience, tactical errors, and lack of human consideration."

In 1994, McKinley veteran Jonathan Waterman devotes a chapter of his book, *In the Shadow of Denali*, to the July 1967 disaster. Waterman does make a sincere effort to get at the truth of what happened on the mountain and afterward, conducting research that includes three-hour interviews with Joe and Howard in their homes. But the starting point for his chapter is this: "Ask any Denali devotee why the tragedy happened and they will answer: because of Wilcox."

These excerpts reveal how posterity's view of the July 1967 tragedy, seeded by Brad Washburn's pronouncements and fertilized by the 1968 *ANAM* report, crystallizes over the years. Another important influence is Howard's first-person account, published in 1973, six years after the tragedy: *The Hall of the Mountain King.*

In 182 pages of text, the book contained about eighty separate criticisms of Joe Wilcox and other members of his expedition. You could not read two or three pages on average without encountering criticisms ranging in length from a few sentences to a full page. It is not exaggerating to say that these criticisms form the book's main theme. Here is a representative sampling:

> The ranger at the Information Center told us that Wilcox made himself out to be 'God's gift to Mt. McKinley.' . . .

> Wilcox called a meeting in the driving snow, to discuss the use of skis by McLaughlin and Clark. This donnybrook made our confrontation with Wilcox three days earlier look mild by comparison.

> When the last rope arrived in Camp II, they were told by Russell that, "Our Fearless Leader" tried to burn down the tent.

> Aside from Wilcox, none of the men in the expedition shared his ideas about publicity. They found the name of the expedition quite humorous and had long been referring to it as the "Wilcox Memorial Expedition."

And there was this, the cruelest cut of all: "Had it not been for Wilcox's illness, ensuing events might have been different." A reader is left with the assumption that by "ensuing events," Howard means the deaths of seven men.

A READER COMES away with the unmistakable impression that Joe
Wilcox's bungling, egotistical leadership, exacerbated by the men's own
inexperience and ineptitude, caused the deaths of Jerry Clark, Hank
Janes, Dennis Luchterhand, Mark McLaughlin, John Russell, Steve
Taylor, and Walt Taylor. At the book's end, after 176 critical pages,
Howard sums things up with a damning bit of faint praise:

> Both before and since the Wilcox Expedition, other expeditions on
> Mt. McKinley have made mistakes as bad, had personnel as inex-
> perienced, or had accidents.

Howard's final verdict is this: "The Wilcox Expedition had tragically
bad luck. But life's hold is much too tenuous in the mountains to trust it
to luck." And the book's raison d'etre is this: "The misfortune will never
be forgotten; therefore the contributing factors should be fully understood, so that they may be avoided by future expeditions."

Like the Anchorage Conference that preceded it, Howard's book contained no responses from Joe Wilcox or Anshel Schiff, the only two survivors of Joe's team.

The Hall of the Mountain King's approach is unmistakable. Not so
clear is why Howard felt compelled to write it that way. A partial explanation might have been that some or all of the seven dead men had been
his close friends, but that was not the case. His two Colorado buddies
and rope mates were Jerry Lewis and Paul Schlichter; he and they had
survived. And although Howard had never laid eyes on Joe or any of his
eight-man team before the two groups met at Mount Rainier National
Park on June 11, 1967, Howard held them all in low esteem. His treatment of them was so severe that family members of the fallen climbers
roundly condemned *The Hall of the Mountain King*.

The reaction of Steve Taylor's parents, Beth and Perry Taylor, was typical. They expressed their thoughts about Howard's book in a letter to Joe:

> *[W]e were devastated by it. Especially in view of a letter from Howard
> that had come as a request from us for any of his remembrances of the
> climb that concerned Stephen. [The Taylors sent Joe a copy of this let-*

ter.] As you can see, he expressed only admiration for Steve's character
if not his climbing ability or lack of it. His book, however, seemed full
of contempt for Steve.

IF PARENTS ARE disturbed by Howard's treatment of their sons, his
book also troubles knowledgeable climbers. Arlene Blum, author of *K2:*
A Woman's Place and the most successful and articulate woman mountaineer of her generation, reviews *The Hall of the Mountain King* in the
1974 *American Alpine Journal.*

Although acknowledging that "the events and personalities that contributed to this tragedy are vividly described in Snyder's book," Blum says
at the outset: "As leader of the Colorado party, Snyder shows some bias
in his impressions.

"Snyder is to be commended for lucidly describing his feelings toward
the Wilcox party, rather than suppressing unpleasant details to avoid
offending anyone," Blum states, but adds, "Still, one cannot help wondering if his superior attitude aided party harmony."

After weighing everything in the book, Blum finds it wanting:

> *The Hall of the Mountain King* is not a work of mountaineering
> literature of the first rank. Snyder is a bit too overanxious to prove
> his own blamelessness for the catastrophe. Consequently, we
> are treated to an abundance of quibbling details about both the
> extreme competence of the Colorado party, and the Wilcox group's
> lack thereof.

"Too overanxious to prove his own blamelessness for the catastrophe."
But *no one had blamed Howard Snyder for the catastrophe.* He did not
need to write a book proving his own innocence—at least not to the
world at large. He was not the expedition's leader, seemingly did nothing
to imperil the lost summit party, and even joined Joe's attempt to climb
back to Camp VII on July 20. On the face of it, he would seem to be due
praise, not blame, and in fact no one accused Howard Snyder of any cul-
pability, at least not until Blum's two oblique suggestions—one about his
impact on team unity, the other about striving for "blamelessness."

Arlene Blum was not the only distinguished American climber and writer to focus on the flaws of Howard's book. Dee Molenaar, a member of the fabled 1953 American K2 Expedition described above and also a brilliant artist and writer, described his feelings about *The Hall of the Mountain King* in a 1982 letter to Joe Wilcox after *White Winds* appeared. Molenaar had been asked to review Joe's book for the *American Alpine Journal*. "I enjoyed your book very much," he wrote. "I think you did a pretty thorough job in presenting your side of the story of that unfortunate tragedy and a very professional job of researching." Molenaar was less impressed with Howard's book.

> Doubtless [your] book will help ease the pain of those who lost sons and friends on this expedition. I don't think Howard Snyder's account helped very much in that regard. In comparing the two accounts, I must commend you for your restraint in responding to his version. I think he did an unnecessary amount of nit-picking criticism of your team, particularly you, throughout the book. He must have been an inhibiting feature in the party, the way he was continually looking with disapproval at every move you made, the way you stood, or breathed, or panted.

When repeated requests for an interview had gone unacknowledged, I told Howard that the reviews I had read of his book were critical and asked him, by e-mail, why he had written his book the way he did. Howard replied,

> Apparently I have led a sheltered life. In the nearly 40 years since the climb, over 30 since the publication of my book, virtually the only negative criticism I have heard about myself or my book has been from Joe Wilcox or his associates. . . .
>
> I wrote the book as a recollection of a major event in my life, one of some interest to the general public and more specifically to the mountaineering public. I wrote it while a student at the University of Colorado and McGill University, writing at night, seated in a chair in my living room, wearing a down filled jacket. Why a down filled jacket? Because the emotion of recounting those crucial days and their catastrophic consequences made me shiver as though I was standing in an icy gale on Mount McKinley rather than sitting in a warm living room.

The single greatest impetus to write the account was Joe Wilcox's public statements to the effect that no mistakes had been made, that the disaster was an unforeseeable result of what he characterized as the worst high altitude storm ever to hit any expedition in the history of mountaineering.

35

Twisting in the Wind

E very story has at least two sides. The other side of this tale is presented by *White Winds*, Joe Wilcox's own account of the tragedy.
It is not published until 1981—fourteen years after the disaster
on McKinley and eight years after Howard Snyder's book. Though clearly
intended to refute Howard's indictments, *White Winds* rarely mentions
him by name. At 150,000 words (compared to 50,000 in *The Hall of the
Mountain King*), it is a magnum opus of data—journals, meteorological records, radio logs, food and equipment lists, correspondence—all to
support one central theory: the seven climbers were killed not by bad
leadership or their own ineptitude but by a catastrophic McKinley "perfect storm":

> The ominous reality is so overwhelmingly compelling that its mere
> statement seems inadequate: Jerry Clark's summit party, without
> the slightest doubt, encountered the most severe, high altitude
> windstorm in all the previous history of McKinley mountaineering.
> Mount McKinley's prominent role as host to the most treacherous
> mountain weather in the world suggests a sobering conjecture: it
> may well be that Clark's group was caught in the most severe, high
> altitude windstorm in the entire history of mountaineering.

The apparent chink in Joe's book is the fact that three members of the
1967 Winter Expedition survived a horrific storm on the West Buttress
side of Denali Pass at 18,200 feet. To review a comparison of storms and

climbers: the March 1967 storm lasted about four days, the July storm eight. The March storm did inflict much colder temperatures, literally off the charts at minus 148 degrees Fahrenheit, with windchill factored in, compared to an estimated low of about minus 25 degrees Fahrenheit during the July storm. Both storms brought hurricane-strength winds, which most likely topped out at 150 miles per hour.

Criticisms first put forward by Brad Washburn and echoed by later analysts, including Howard, Fred Beckey, and Jonathan Waterman, cited inexperience as the July 1967 accident's prime mover. All of the men in Jerry Clark's team had at least some winter mountaineering experience, and several—Jerry, Mark, Dennis, and John in particular—had a lot. Steve Taylor was an experienced and skilled ice climber and mountain rescue veteran. Not even Anshel Schiff was a complete novice, as was Ray Genet, one of the three Winter Expedition survivors, who had never been on a mountain higher than 7,000 feet and could not even tie himself into a climbing rope. On closer inspection, as we've seen throughout this book, the "inexperience" argument is not supported by facts. Thus the storm does begin to assume tremendous importance.

Joe's exhaustive analysis of the July 1967 storm is the heart of *White Winds*. To conduct the analysis, he retains the services of Robert Kinzebach, a retired air force colonel and professional meteorologist with thirty-five years of experience in weather forecasting, a number of publications to his credit, and an impeccable reputation as a scientist. Poring over the reams of data, they begin to see a number of things unique to this storm.

First, it was not one storm but two. The storm on July 16 that kept the whole team tent-bound in Camp VII lasted a single day. Clearing followed on July 17, when Jerry Clark and his companions began their summit climb. Kinzebach's interpretation of weather data indicated that the second storm came in from the northwest, above Point Barrow, rather than from the southwest, as Brad Washburn stated.

Ultimately, though, the storm's origin is unimportant. What matters is the storm itself, and it was indeed a monster. It apparently produced more precipitation than any other since weather record keeping began. The average rainfall in July for Mount McKinley National Park to that time was 2.59 inches. The total rainfall for July 1967 was 7.39 inches, with 6.14 inches falling during the July 18 to 26 period and 3.28 inches on July 24 alone. Rainfall down low equates to massive snowfall higher on the mountain.

In 1967, meteorologists did not obtain weather-aloft data directly from instruments on McKinley. Instead, they sent unmanned balloons aloft every day at midnight and noon (Greenwich mean time, or GMT) from three stations that form a rough triangle, with McKinley at its center: McGrath, 147 miles to the west; Fairbanks, 160 miles northeast; and Anchorage, 140 miles south.

These balloon probes are called radiosondes, because their white shoebox-size instrument packs record dew point, temperature, pressure, and wind speed and direction, and transmit these by radio back to their launch stations. The U.S. Weather Bureau first used them in 1936, so the methodology by 1967 was proven.

Of the three stations, McGrath was the most important and most accurate predictor of actual weather conditions on McKinley. Weather moves from west to east, and McGrath was about 150 miles due west. The balloons sent up from McGrath twice daily reported data similar to, but less extreme than, what would have prevailed on McKinley at about 18,200 feet. This data showed that the temperature averaged about 2 degrees Fahrenheit during the storm's eight days. Humidity was very high on the night of July 17, producing the foggy whiteout that confused Jerry Clark and his team.

But wind is the killer up high. During the shorter, July 16 storm, the radiosondes recorded wind speeds of fifty-five miles per hour at 18,000 feet. The winds dropped to about twenty-five miles per hour on July 17. On July 18 and 19, they rose sharply to about seventy-five miles per hour, then dropped to thirty miles per hour during the morning of July 20—the same morning that Joe and the others at Camp VI experienced a three-hour clearing. That afternoon the winds began to build again, peaking at about eighty-five miles per hour on July 21, then gradually declining through July 26.

In his book, Joe cites three reasons why the winds on the mountain were actually even stronger than those recorded by the radiosondes. First, he cites the "airplane wing" effect: air moving over or around a mountain must flow faster than air traveling on an uninterrupted straight path.

Second is the Venturi effect, which occurs when a gas or a fluid is forced to flow through an area of reduced volume—the area between McKinley's North and South Peaks, for instance, or Denali Pass—which increases its velocity. Third is turbulence, which could result in wind speed increases on the lee sides of peaks, ridges, and passes. These three working in combination, Joe asserts, resulted in wind speeds that were 150 to 200 percent higher than the unaffected airflow recorded by the radiosondes. Thus he theorizes that winds on McKinley at 18,000 feet probably averaged 80 to 110 miles per hour from July 18 to 26, with peaks of 150 miles per hour or higher. Meteorologist Kinzebach's research supported these assertions.

Curious about how this storm compared with other McKinley weather events, Joe and Kinzebach collected similar radiosonde data for 105 months from 1946 through 1979. Their finding:

> The results of my investigation were startling enough to provoke my disbelief and cause me to recheck the data. The evidence was undeniable. There were no July windstorms even remotely comparable to the July 1967 storm. In 33 years of July observations (about 2,000 wind measurements) McGrath did not record a single July wind velocity aloft as high as the 1967 storm (82.8 mils per hour). In fact, of the eight highest McGrath July readings over a 33-year period, four occurred during the 1967 storm.

Joe's review of meteorological records leads him to conclude that the July 1967 storm was unique for length as well as intensity. The second-place storm on this list—ironically, the one that trapped the three Winter Expedition climbers in March 1967—was half as long.

All of which brings Joe to this: "Jerry Clark's summit party, without the slightest doubt, encountered the most severe, high altitude windstorm in all the previous history of McKinley mountaineering."

That may well be true, but Joe *is* trying to disprove accusations that his bungled leadership led to the deaths of seven climbers. What is unquestionably true is that Joe did the hard work of digging out this esoteric data and hiring Robert Kinzebach, an unbiased, professional meteorologist, to analyze it. None of the other writers who ventured opinions about this tragedy took similar pains before making pronouncements that impacted the life of the expedition's leader and the memories of its victims.

At MY REQUEST, Dr. Martha Shulski, Alaska state climatologist, retrieved July 1967 meteorological records and sent them to me. The FedEx box contained about ten pounds of 11×17 copies—hundreds of pages. Getting all that information was only half the battle, because I had no more idea of how to read those glyphic synoptic charts than Aramaic. National Weather Service (NWS) experts in the East did, however, and one, Scott Whittier, a handsome, strapping fellow who looks as though he could have played linebacker for Penn State, had spent some years in Alaska and so was particularly helpful.

The NWS documents show that on July 16 a storm hit the mountain, but it was short. It was followed by mild wind and mild temperatures on July 17 that lasted at least until midday on July 18. That is consistent with the findings of Wilcox and Kinzebach.

The July 16 storm, however, was on- and offstage so quickly that its only importance is the timing that it imposed on events that followed. At some point on the afternoon of July 18, adverse conditions returned and stayed put for what Scott determined to be an "unusually long storm." Its length was partly due to the size of the disturbance, but also to the blocking effect of weather immediately to the west and north, which held the storm more or less stationary over McKinley.

The NWS scientists explained, as well, that whatever wind speeds the McGrath radiosondes recorded would surely have been much higher on the mountain itself. The meteorologists cited the same reasons Joe pointed to in *White Winds*, and added two others. They agreed that the "airplane wing" and Venturi effects and turbulence would accelerate the winds, but thought that another phenomenon, "downsloping," would also have been at work. A river flows faster when the gradient of its downslope steepens, and moving air does the same thing. This is especially true when the moving air mass accumulates energy as it climbs a mountain's windward side, then suddenly drops down the lee slopes, which is where Jerry Clark and his team were huddling in their caves. (The most extreme examples of this are the infamous williwaws of Cape

Horn. These occur when cold, heavy air accumulates on the windward side of a mountain. Sooner or later, the air overflows the mountain's peak and screams down the other side, not infrequently with hurricane force.)

One more thing probably helped produce the unprecedented wind speeds during the July 1967 storm. The modern NWS calls them "jet streaks." At that time of year and at that latitude, the jet stream flows at about 23,000 to 25,000 feet. But when an already violent storm strikes a mountain such as McKinley, extreme turbulence can be thrust up into the jet stream itself. Think of waves rolling in off the ocean, striking rocky coast, and shooting spume hundreds of feet into the air. When the atmospheric equivalent of that happens, the jet stream can be inter-rupted and deflected, bringing its energy and velocity down to McKin-ley's summit area.

Finally, for still another objective review of the data, I sought out foren-sic meteorologist Greg MacMasters, who specializes in the reconstruc-tion of historic weather events. After examining the available records, he agreed with the conclusions of Kinzebach and Whittier.

All of which is to say that independent review validates Wilcox's and Kinzebach's analysis.

36

Survivors

One of my reasons for writing this book was to learn how the survivors of such a tragedy lived the rest of their lives. Survivorship was important to me personally. My father, one of the few Americans who served in the army during both world wars and Korea, had experiences he could not deal with. After Korea, his drinking went around the bend and he died in 1956, when I was eight.

Until now, this book has been about the '67 men. It seems best to end it with who they are now and how they made it to 2006.

Anshel Schiff

Anshel Schiff gave up serious climbing after July 1967, though he remained an avid skier and hiker. He has done seminal work in engineering seismology at Stanford University, so if you happen to be in a building that survives an earthquake, you may have Anshel Schiff to thank.

Because Anshel was experiencing recurring medical problems that required surgery while I was researching this book, we did not meet in person, but communicated by telephone and e-mail.

"I really don't know if I want to go dredging up all that old painful stuff," he said during our first phone interview. After that, some calls and e-mails went unreturned for weeks. I recognized that Anshel's health issues were working against our communication, but I sensed that something else might be in play here.

As it turned out, I was right. Anshel did not open up until after I had visited Joe, who passed on his belief that I was a serious writer trying to do an honest job. Reading *The Hall of the Mountain King* had made Anshel chary of authors wanting to write about the tragedy, even forty years later. When I asked him what he thought of Howard's book, he bristled, said that he found it difficult to finish, and spoke of its bias and inaccuracy. Anshel was particularly unhappy with the book's portrayal of him as a weak, unfit tyro who could not carry a heavy pack.

Anshel recalled being in good shape, contrary to Howard's description of him. He spoke of training by carrying a hundred-pound pack up many flights of stairs. In fact, looking back, Anshel feels that for the McKinley climb he may have been in the best shape of his life. But he found that during those early, grueling carries up the Muldrow, he could not eat much of anything except the excellent fudge that Joe and Steve had made. Even with that, he lost twenty pounds and could circle his upper arm with his thumb and forefinger.

But other than those memories, sharpened no doubt by rebukes received on the mountain, Anshel did not recall much about the trip. He took some photographs but kept neither notes nor diary. When we talked on the phone or exchanged e-mails, he answered many questions with, "I just don't remember." He did not even recall, for instance, how he and his friends from the Purdue Outing Club hooked up with Joe Wilcox in the first place.

Paul Schlichter

After the expedition, Paul Schlichter spent two tours flying three hundred combat missions in Vietnam. He admits that the McKinley tragedy was terrible, but found it eclipsed in his own life by the tragedy of Vietnam, which caused more casualties in his graduating Air Force Academy class than any in the institution before or since.

He served eight years in the military all told, but ultimately found that "I was just too independent for the air force." He resigned, earned an MBA at the University of California, Berkeley, and went into private enterprise, serving as the CEO of several major corporations.

Paul is still six feet four, and has friendly blue eyes and thinning sandy hair. He keeps his weight down to about 220 pounds with 150-mile bike rides and long mountain hikes, making sure to do one or two "fourteen-ers" every year. Clad in a red polo shirt, khaki shorts, and running shoes, he took me hiking through a state park not far from his house, an experience that left me breathless and convinced of his fitness level.

Now retired from the corporate world's high stress, he owns a small group of Colorado-based franchise businesses (not fast food) and lives in a lovely home in a beautiful town in Colorado whose main street, in one of several weird coincidences that attended this book's writing, is named Wilcox Avenue. His first and only wife, Beverly, is a trim, vivacious woman with a brilliant smile and musical voice. Their town is, like Paul and Beverly themselves, unfailingly sunny and perfectly turned out, one of those places where many of the women in supermarkets look as though they stepped out of *Town & Country* magazine covers.

I spent several days there with Paul. He struck me as a good man, content with his life and the way he has lived it, surprisingly modest and unassuming given the nature of his accomplishments. His well-appointed study is hung with pictures from his Air Force Academy days and models of the C-130s and C-5s he flew. There is also a framed shot of him on McKinley's summit. About the expedition he answered endless hours of questions and narrated a showing of his slides with compassion but without the visible, visceral pain I would soon encounter in other survivors.

When I asked him to tell me about the expedition, he started with the conflict between Joe and Howard. "From my standpoint, Joe was hard to like. . . . I think he had an overglorified view of what we were actually attempting to do. From a leadership standpoint, you know, of course we had two people, Howard Snyder and Wilcox." Paul felt that that was not good from the outset. Howard had more technical knowledge of the route from having studied Brad Washburn's pictures and climbing guide. And Joe, he said, just didn't take a strong leadership role. As proof of that, Paul cited his belief that Steve Taylor, Jerry Clark, and Anshel Schiff should never have been on the mountain in the first place.

"I think of the climb," he said. "I don't know if you ever saw that movie *Twelve Angry Men*. There were twelve men on the jury, and I think about the twelve people who were on the climb. . . . There was some informal coordination until we were forced to combine when the fourth guy in our group was in an accident and couldn't participate."

When I asked him for his final thoughts, Paul concluded neither with leaders nor conflict. He spoke, instead, of the storm. "I'm not sure even if the leadership had been ideal, even if everybody's conditioning had been terrific, I'm not sure with that storm on that mountain at that altitude near the Arctic Circle it would have made a huge difference."

Jerry Lewis

In another odd coincidence, it turned out that Jerry Lewis lived less than thirty minutes from Paul, and neither of them knew about the other until I told them. Thus it was an easy hop from Paul's place to Jerry's neighborhood in a Denver suburb. When I walked into his split-level home, two things struck me immediately. One was Jerry's size—six feet five, and at least 230 pretty fit pounds. The other was his silence. I arrived while he and his wife, Louisa, a fit, friendly woman with sensibly cut gray hair, were having dinner. One of the first things she said was, "Jerry isn't much of a talker."

He sure isn't. At dinner that evening, we sat around the table in complete silence as minutes ticked by and Jerry seemed completely comfortable not speaking. Few people are, especially in the company of new acquaintances. At one point later in my stay, we took a long hike up an 8,000-foot mountain not far from their home. Jerry said maybe six sentences going up, and a dozen more coming down.

I don't mean that he is recalcitrant or surly. Anything but. He answered questions willingly enough in his deep, rumbly voice, but casual conversation is not easy for him, and often many seconds lapsed between the end of a question from me and the beginning of an answer from him. I never did figure out what he was doing in his head during those lapses. He would sit in his chair staring into space, not exactly unfocused but not completely with us, either. It may be that he was praying silently. He and his wife are devout Mormons, and God is a real presence in their home. *Sweet* is an odd word to use about so huge a man, but there is an ursine sweetness about Jerry Lewis that makes you want to hug him, as you might want to hug a great bear if you only could, not so much because he needs it, but because of how much good it would do *you.*

Jerry had promised to show me his pictures from the expedition, so he dug them out and set up a projector in the living room of his house. I asked if he had shown these slides before.

"I've done it probably fifty times."

"Why?" I asked, thinking that it must not be a completely painless experience.

This answer came fast. "Because I owe it to everyone. To people who are going and should know what they're getting into." Then his eyes softened and took on that distant look again. From here on, he would sometimes answer my questions and sometimes seem to be answering questions that his brain was asking itself. For example, I didn't ask him if he thought anything else could have been done to help the men who died. But he spoke to the question anyway.

"If any one factor had been different, it would not have happened," he says, coming back to me and his living room. "It required a tremendous amount of bad luck."

Jerry hadn't seen the slides for quite a few years, so the images took him back through the expedition, freshening memories long buried.

"It was a disappointing reception at Rainier. Unfriendly atmosphere. I'd have backed out there at Rainier. I didn't understand it."

Jerry stopped, swallowed, breathed deeply. His cheeks took on a pink flush. Doing this was churning things up. He went on, speaking as though Joe and his crew were there in the room with us: "What have you got against us? I thought Joe would have pulled things together. When are we gonna be unified? Nothing was done to make us come together." He did not know at the time, nor did Paul or Howard, that Joe's team strongly opposed merging the two groups, and that this opposition, rather than any personal animosity, resulted in the frigid reception at Rainier.

Here Jerry had to stop again, longer this time. "This is welling up a lot of emotions I'm not used to." After a while we went on, viewing his exquisitely composed slides of fireweed, caribou, a rainbow over Kettle Pond during the hike in. He paused to reflect and voiced more memories.

"Joe was not a natural leader. He was a good person. But he never pulled us together. He'd say these things like about the skis that didn't matter a hoot on the Muldrow. I thought Walt Taylor was a natural leader. Jerry Clark could have been a natural leader, but he wasn't. He was friendly and spread good cheer. Walt was very strong and seemed to have good sense."

When we came to his pictures of Camp VI, at 15,000 feet, site of the infamous tent fire, he stopped again, staring at the screen with sadness and incredulity. "They were always cursing and tossing their stoves. Hard on their stuff."

About July 17, before he and the other four descended. "I asked Steve Taylor if he wanted to go down, but he didn't want to. I do remember thinking they were making a big mistake. The Colorado group had decided to do our thinking low and do our acting up high. The others were trying to rest at 18,000 feet, but it doesn't work at 18,000." *Think low, act high.* Paul had said the same thing, using exactly those words.

About Joe, Jerry has mixed feelings still. "Joe hardly spoke to me." He also readily admits that he himself was not a skilled or enthusiastic communicator, which doubtless added to the distance between them. But not all his recollections of Joe are negative. "He didn't seem like a publicity seeker to me. Joe saved our bacon being a good swimmer. He did us a great service."

Jerry went on with his reminiscences, and a surprising theme began to emerge. "Joe and me and Anshel were the least capable of anyone at 15,000 of doing anyone any good. Or ourselves any good." Of the abortive attempt to climb back to Camp VII, "When I was in the tent, I wondered, what do they hope to accomplish?" But he can empathize with Joe's dilemma. "He was feeling the weight of leadership. He was riled because he was feeling helpless."

At some points during the interview, remembering what happened brought Jerry (and Joe and Howard, for that matter) back to pain that couldn't be contained. This was another one of those moments. He said hoarsely,

"This is hard for me. I didn't realize I had these feelings still in me. They surprise me. Certain amount of grief. They boil up inside and I don't know how to deal with them or tell you about them." Then he said, "For the most part I don't feel responsible, but maybe another person could have done more." A bit later he added, "There was a time when I thought I should have done more." Survivor guilt, even now, after forty years.

After a while I asked Jerry how the events of July 1967 have compared to others in his life. "The climb itself is kind of a big thing compared to others. I don't rank it with marriage, having kids, and so on, but . . . There was a time which I could have walked away from it. And should have."

Then Jerry was quiet an unusually long time even for him. When he spoke, it was not of the McKinley disaster but about something that happened to him while he was in the army. "I'll tell you a story to show what it was like. We were up in Alaska and were supposed to fly some-place. I was already on the plane, but they told me to get off because I was too big. They put a smaller man on. The plane crashed and was never seen again."

Jerry began to cry, holding his bowed head in his hands. After a while he stopped, rubbed his face, looked around, regaining his bearings.

"Was he your friend?" I asked.

"Sure he was."

What was apparent to me then, and has grown in significance since, is that Jerry did not speak directly about the deaths of seven young men who were strangers originally but to whom the experience of climbing McKinley bonded him. Instead, he came up on the subject from the side, relating the story of one friend who died after taking Jerry's seat on a doomed airplane. He doesn't tell me the story of what happened on McKinley. Instead, "I'll tell you a story to show what it was like."

Not how it actually was, but what something similar to it was like. After forty years, that's as close as Jerry wants to come.

Howard Snyder

Of all the survivors, Howard was the easiest to find, because he is the director of one of Canada's most popular museums. Conversely, he was the hardest to interview. If Anshel was chary, Howard was downright avoidant. It took more than a year of requests by phone and e-mail to gain a personal interview with him.

When Howard finally did consent to an interview, he would not meet in his own hometown in Alberta, Canada. He first suggested that I accompany him on his twenty-fourth annual backpacking trip into the Grand Canyon, and I would have done so had my wife not suffered an accident shortly before the trip was to begin. (Another weird coincidence—this timing of the accident echoing the one suffered by Jerry Lewis's brother seven hours before the Colorado team was to depart for McKinley).

With the Grand Canyon trip out, Howard insisted on convening at his brother's home in Kalispell, Montana. The meeting, which lasted several days, produced a number of surprises. They began when Howard met me at my Kalispell hotel: the 2005 Howard looked more like his 1967 version than any of the other survivors resembled their earlier selves. He was bigger and beefier, but fit and not fat. For another, as he strode up glancing from me to his wristwatch, he announced apologetically,

"I'm fifteen seconds early," and he was only half-joking. Later, before dropping me off at a Staples where I would be copying documents, he said, "Let's synchronize watches" for the subsequent pickup, and we did.

I don't mean to imply that he was stiff and unfriendly—anything but, in fact. This was another surprise, because his phone manner and e-mails were a bit of both—characteristics noted by others including one of his daughters.

Howard had eyes the blue of deep, old ice, was clean-shaven, and was clad in black pants, a burgundy shirt, a blue jacket, and well-worn running shoes. A five-year-old skiing injury had curtailed his workouts somewhat, adding fifteen pounds to his waistline, but he wasn't overly disturbed. In fact, he laughed at the encroaching paunch and many other things, including himself. As I got to know him, I understood that he, like Paul, was supremely content with his life and the way he had lived it. His face showed the creases and furrows you would expect from sixty odd years, but the impression he made on first meeting was one of high energy and good humor, and neither of those faded as the days passed.

During my meeting with Paul, he noted that he and Howard almost always moved very fast when climbing. Paul's pace had moderated by 2005, but Howard's had not. He talked, walked, and thought fast (the diametric opposite of Joe Wilcox, who does nothing quickly and without serious forethought). About the only time Howard shifted out of overdrive was, thankfully, behind the wheel of his well-traveled van.

Howard's brother was away, so we had his yellow split-level home outside Kalispell to ourselves. Howard prepared with characteristic thoroughness for the interview, bringing a load of gear from the climb: ice ax, boots, crampons, summit pack, down mittens, Gold Line climbing rope, hundreds of slides, and stacks of documents. We looked over the old gear first, and I was struck at how much more everything weighed in 1967. For example, Howard's wooden-shafted Stubai ice ax was easily twice the weight of the Forrest Mountaineering model I carried in Alaska. To him it was a thing of Saarinen-like elegance, but to me it felt like a brick.

After we settled onto couches, Howard began at the beginning, when he, like many others living in the shadow of Boulder's Flatirons, became a climber young. "I had read every book about climbing in two libraries by the time I was twelve," he said. "I set four goals for myself, and one was to climb McKinley." The first attempt, in 1966, failed. Six men dropped out, one by one, and another—John Orenschall—got sick at the last minute. The trip was scrubbed just weeks before it was to start. Then the second trip was scrubbed seven hours before launch.

To demonstrate the care he put into planning, Howard brought voluminous documentation, including four legal pads with meticulous handwriting on every line of both sides of every page—menus, teams, equipment, schedules, routes, and much more.

I complimented the monumental care he took organizing and preparing. As a way of introducing the subject, I mentioned that it reminded me of Joe's own prodigious work. Howard's eyes flashed at the mention of Joe's name, and he said that the relationship between his group and Joe's was strained from the beginning. He cited a comment that Paul made after the abortive first meeting at Rainier: "Any stranger we met on the road would have been happier to see us than the Wilcox crew." Like Paul and Jerry, Howard had not known, until I explained it to him, how resistant Joe's group had been to joining the two teams. Even with that new knowledge, Howard's attitude toward Joe softened little. "Joe was not a decisive, effective leader. He was stiff, authoritarian, autocratic. But he did not really *lead*."

Speaking of himself and Joe, Howard noted that being an Alpha (or Super-Alpha) and being a leader are not necessarily synonymous. About Jerry Clark: "He was a fine gentleman, the pleasantest guy to be with. But *too* thoughtful and considerate to be a good leader." As proof, he cites his belief that John Russell and Steve Taylor should have been told to go down the mountain. "Both were asked to come down, and would not, so the two weakest and sickest men were both alone within hours." Joe or Jerry Clark, Howard believes, should have ordered those men down.

Like Paul, Howard believes that Walt Taylor may have been the best natural leader of the entire twelve. "Walt was too sassy to be a fine gentleman, but he was a natural leader." When Paul had spoken of John Russell, it was with distaste, but Howard's voice contained compassion. "John had had a rough life, and he was a rough guy. He needed a victory." But he acknowledged that John was too hard on equipment, and admitted that the stove explosion at Camp VI was damaging emotionally, if not physically. "It was not a morale builder. We were very lucky to have dodged a bullet."

As we talked about the stove explosion, I was struck by how much less critical Howard was of the Wilcox team now than he had been in his book, and this impression carried through the interview. For example, he wrote of the Wilcox group's "pyromanic tendencies," and suggested that incompetence caused the three stove accidents. But to me he pointed out that stoves were finicky, and even Brad Washburn had had a stove accident: "Washburn had a stove or pressure cooker explode on his U.S. Army trip," implying that if such a thing could happen to Brad, it could happen to anyone.

Howard retained mixed feelings about the National Park Service. Although acknowledging that the NPS, especially Wayne Merry, "did the best they could for us," a number of things about their effort left him dissatisfied. One was their use of radios. "They said, 'You have to have radios. And—oh yes—give *us* one too.'" George Hall's and Art Hayes's complete lack of mountaineering experience troubles him still, as did the paucity of weather information from the NPS: "the weather reporting was not emphasized."

Paul had surmised that even if everything else, including leadership and conditioning, had been perfect, the epic storm might still have taken seven lives. Somewhat to my surprise, because his book had not made such allowance, Howard agreed. "If we had been subjected to the same conditions those guys encountered, the same thing would have happened to us." Toward its end, his book had contained a similar apologia— that the storm was incredibly bad luck—but it ended with the assertion that mountain climbers who blame bad luck should look in the mirror. "The Wilcox Expedition had tragically bad luck. But life's hold is much too tenuous in the mountains to trust it to luck."

Shortly after, we were discussing implications of the fact that Joe actually knew only one man, Steve Taylor, of the eight he was leading. With surprising sympathy, Howard said, "Is that something a guy can be condemned for? No it is not. . . . That was just the way it worked out." And about the decision to leave Steve Taylor alone at Camp VII: "Now people just gasp at this guy being left alone at high camp. It is not that unusual and it's not that irresponsible. They did not think they were going to be away a whole day."

Still, Howard could go only so far in this direction, and returned to the crucial point that still divides him and Joe and probably always will. (Neither man expressed any enthusiasm at the suggestion of a forgive-and-forget reunion.) "Any men equipped as they were and subject to the same conditions, which they encountered, would almost certainly have met the same fate. However, the circumstances which entrapped the men were avoidable and gave ample warning of their approach."

When I brought us around to *The Hall of the Mountain King*, Howard repeated a variation of what he said to Steve Taylor's parents and what he has said to others: He did not think his book was terribly critical of Joe or the others in the first place and so, by implication, he did not see any great difference between his expressions then and now. But he also admitted that he had not read the book for more than twenty years. It occurred to me that, having been away from it for so long, he might genuinely not have recalled its true character. Another way to get at this was through motivation, so I asked him—again—why he wrote the book.

Howard loves rhetorical questions, and his conversation is peppered with them. "Why did I write *Hall of the Mountain King? The Time* magazine article [Joe's letter] was one big reason. To correct Joe's falsehoods." Later in the interview, but addressing the same letter, he elaborated, denigrating assertions that Joe made in it: " 'to suggest that this recent disaster could have been foreseen would not only discredit the victims but also be unfair to future expeditions.' Wrong, wrong, wrong. So here's misstatement of fact and an invalid conclusion that in fact does jeopardize future expeditions."

Having heard that before as well, I decided it was time to voice my own thoughts. I suggested that other things might have come into play.

"Here's a theory," I said. "You want to climb McKinley for ten years at least. It is a life goal. You invest an immense amount of time, energy, and money to organize and lead your own expedition. Fate kills the first attempt, but you press on. Then fate intervenes again and snatches away your dream of leading your own McKinley expedition. You salvage the climb, but only by joining a team which you consider, after some time on the mountain, to be badly led, dangerously unskilled, and physically unfit. Adding insult to injury, you take a gut dislike to Joe Wilcox the instant you two meet. Every day on the mountain only reinforces your reservations. Ultimately, your dream of a lifetime becomes a nightmare, one from which you can never fully escape."

In a very different context—police work—where I spent some years interviewing people who seriously did not want to be interviewed, I learned that listening to their words was good, but watching their bodies was better. For a moment Howard looked as though I had slapped him. He paled and stared, briefly (and perhaps the only time during our days together) at a loss for words. I still don't know whether he was angry, surprised, afraid, or some combination of those and other feelings. But he regained his composure quickly and said, without great force,

"No, it wasn't so much that."

He did not say, "That had nothing to do with it at all."

Our talk moved on. But one of the central questions of this whole inquiry was why Howard wrote his book the way he did, so whenever an opportunity arose during our time together I steered us back to the book. The next day, I told him: "I would be interested in hearing your thoughts if you were to re-read it now," and added that after three readings it still struck me as extremely critical of Joe and some of his team members.

He didn't deny that outright but was reflective. "I was pretty close to the event when I wrote it. And pretty passionate. Maybe I will re-read it sometime," he said without conviction, and I didn't really think he would. In the end, it was only on our last day together that he produced an answer that went beyond the "I want to help people" refrain. I don't mean to imply that helping others was not genuinely one of his motives. I believe that it surely was. But it did not seem to adequately explain the book's *personality,* for lack of a better word. The additional answer came, surprisingly, not in response to another direct question about the book but to one about how he coped with the tragedy once off the mountain.

Howard said that he needed no medication or counseling, because, in fact, *The Hall of the Mountain King* was his therapy. "In my life where I've been very, very angry I write down all my side of the thing and forget it. Put it away, don't look at it again. And so yes, there was a cathartic effect in writing the book. . . . Why else would I be so cold writing that book that I had to wear a down jacket? If it wasn't having that kind of emotional effect and therefore a purging?"

After a break for lunch at a nearby Wendy's restaurant, Howard presented his slide show about the expedition. He was going to show it not once, but twice.

"The first time I'm going to go through it exactly like I do for an audience," he said. "Then we'll do it again, and you can stop me and ask questions."

The show consisted of 145 color slides and included many taken by Paul and Jerry. Howard's narration was rhythmic and polished by many showings. It was factual, devoid of sarcasm, innuendo, and accusation.

Then we went through it again, and I did ask a lot of questions. Why, for instance, did he think that Jerry Clark's team did not return to Camp VII after becoming lost on July 17?

"That summit team may have had legitimate concerns," he said. "Maybe the decision was made because they couldn't go down. They may have elected to bivouac for the very good reason that the route was obscured by whiteout and decided it was safer to stay put. Which is what you're taught."

But even if he was now willing to give Jerry the benefit of the doubt about that particular action, Howard does believe that Jerry Clark's decisions, perhaps even more than Joe's, contributed to the tragedy.

"Wilcox made mistakes before the trip: organization of personnel.

During the climb: leadership and decisions. And after the climb: *Time*, letters, et cetera.

"However, it was Clark who originally got the men involved in the trip and recommended them, and it was Clark who was the decision maker when they did not go with us on the fifteenth of July. And when they went late and slow on the seventeenth. The decisions to go on or turn back and to bivouac or not were Clark's . . . the guy who was in charge of the decisions ultimately was Jerry Clark."

And where did he think they were lost? "I think they mistook the Archdeacon's Tower ridge for the summit ridge," he said, which matched my own belief. He added that the lack of wands was, in his view, a critical factor. Why, he asked, was John Russell, one of the least experienced men (in Howard's view), made responsible for carrying wands?

All perceptions, of course, depend on the position of the observer, as Einstein demonstrated. So from Howard's position, then and now, the decision to put John in charge of wands is indefensible. But from another vantage point, it's easy to see why Joe, as an expedition leader, might well have thought that John was the best possible candidate to bring up those wands. He had been the strongest load carrier by far and was still eminently healthy at Camp VI. If anyone were to be saddled with the extra weight of three hundred wands, John would have been the logical choice.

Then I asked Howard the same question I had asked everyone else: "How did the tragedy affect your life?"

A number of other things have ranked above it in import, he said— building his house in Alberta with his own hands, marrying, having children. But he also admits that the dead men revisited him for some time. "I had dreams about these guys coming back. Once they all came back except John Russell, who they had left behind because he was too slow. The other time only two came back and they were Walt Taylor and John Russell in a state of total collapse."

There was more to this answer. When visiting Joe, I found surprisingly visible evidence of the tragedy in his life even now, and it was there in Howard's life too—even more so. I wasn't in Howard's home, though he told me that in his dining room hangs a painting, which he commissioned, of Paul Schlichter releasing his orange flare on the summit of McKinley.

But that painting is far from the tragedy's most dramatic presence in

Howard's life. The events and people of July 1967 come alive in his slide show, and Howard estimates that he has given it almost three thousand times in the forty years since 1967. That averages to more than once a week that he has brought the '67 men to life not only for his audiences but for himself, resurrecting how they looked, the sounds of their voices, the ways they moved, the clothes they wore and foods they liked, the secrets they shared, as men will. How they lived, in other words, and how they died.

I found this extraordinary and pressed him to explain why he kept on doing the thing that must cause pain with every showing. He claimed that it hurt for a long time but didn't anymore (hard for me to imagine, but he said it). Regardless, his dedication to the presentation was—*is*—amazing, especially given the fact that he makes no money from it and, traveling far and wide, often pays his own expenses. He has given the show for large audiences in theaters in Montreal, Vancouver, Edmonton, Phoenix, and other cities. But it's not always like that. For a recent showing, he made a long drive in the dead of winter to a remote town. "It was bitterly cold and only three people showed up." Doubtless something like that must have happened fairly often during the forty years, but he never turns down a request to do the show.

"I've got lots of other presentations . . . but by far the most popular is McKinley. Almost everybody wants to see McKinley."

I still didn't understand. "But . . . why keep doing it?"

Jerry had told me a story. Now Howard told one. It rambled a bit, but here's the essence. "After showing people these presentations when they were kids, they come up to me later as adults, with their son in tow to see the presentation and I have had at least a half dozen tell me this, that it changed their life."

"How so?"

"They became very interested in the outdoors . . . in accepting very difficult physical challenges but also being aware that they do that wisely and safely because the consequences of doing it otherwise are too severe." I thought of *Catcher in the Rye*, Holden Caulfield in that field catching children before they run off a cliff.

Late in the evening of our last day together, we sat in Howard's van in front of my hotel, making wrap-up conversation. I felt that I knew him well enough by then to ask why he wouldn't meet me in his hometown.

"I wasn't going to let something into my house until I knew what it was." His caution still surprised me, because every one of the others I'd sought interviews with, including Joe Wilcox, had simply told me to come along whenever and offered me lodging in their own homes. But even this wariness was less surprising than his fear of letting "something into my house until I knew what it was." Not a person, or an author, but some *thing*. It made me feel a bit like the mutilated zombie son banging on his parents' door in *The Monkey's Paw.*

Perhaps sensing my surprise, or aware that the man who wrote *The Hall of the Mountain King* was a different man than the one who sat beside me, Howard added,

"Several people have said about me, 'He's a nice guy. He's just a real nice guy.' I really am just a nice guy." And, one might add, a real-life catcher in the rye.

Joe Wilcox

Joe was the first survivor I traveled to visit, but things have to end with him, just as they all began with him. For better or worse, the expedition and therefore the tragedy have come to bear his name, so it seemed that learning as much as possible from and about him would make the best platform for the interviews that followed.

Joe, like Howard, was initially cautious about an interview, but after several weeks he warmed to the idea, even inviting me to stay with him. His home is on the far north side of Seattle, and the college where he taught then is well to the south, so he kept a studio apartment near campus and stayed there occasionally after long and tiring teaching days.

"I don't know what your lodging budget is for the trip," he wrote, but "you are welcome to camp with me in the apartment (mattresses on the floor). . . ."

So that's what we did. Joe's studio apartment was about the size of a big expedition base camp tent. We slept like tentmates side by side on the living room floor, ate meals together, woke each other with our snoring, shared the bathroom, hung around campus. For getting to know someone pretty well quickly, it was almost as good as going on an actual climb together. We also spent time with his wife, Robin, in their home overlooking Puget Sound.

Joe is tall, lean, and still handsome. One of the first things I told him, on meeting, was how much he looks like the Western character actor Dennis Weaver.

"Yeah, a lot of people tell me that," he said with a chuckle. It's an appropriate linkage, because Joe hails from Kansas, that fountainhead of Western lore, home of Dodge City, Boot Hill, the sometime beat of Marshall Wyatt Earp. When Joe speaks, the twang and languid rhythms of Kansas are still in his voice.

He stays extremely fit by running marathons and shorter races, training with a discipline that even the best college and professional athletes often lose long before they reach Joe's age. Early every morning he would slip into his running togs and head out for five to six miles at seven to eight minutes a mile. On returning, he would sometimes pull a half gallon of ice cream from the freezer and have a bowl for his post-run breakfast, then put coffee on to brew. Along with running, sailing, his daughters, and his wife, ice cream and good coffee are two serious loves.

Joe is a fine example of the adage that "today's 60 is the new 40." A successful competitive runner, when he was over fifty he beat Frank Shorter in a 5K race (though he admits that Shorter "probably wasn't really trying"). He has set age-group records as well. He's also an expert blue-water sailor, currently completing a circumnavigation in stages, sailing legs during his college's vacations. He has been honored for his teaching, and chaired his college's applied mathematics department. In 1985, he was a NASA Teacher in Space finalist for Washington State. He has grown daughters who are happy and successful in their own endeavors and has been married for years to Robin, his third wife. She is an elegant, raven-haired woman with two master's degrees who once held a serious position at the U.S. embassy in Paris.

Brad Washburn once referred to Joe as "a bull with a built-in china shop," but if the Wilcox I met was a bull, he could only have been the gentle Ferdinand. Joe is a sensitive man, with eyes the dark blue of the deep ocean he loves to sail. He has by nature a more serious demeanor than the ebullient Howard Snyder and does not laugh as often or as easily, but neither is he gloomy or sour.

Writer Jonathan Waterman, on meeting Joe in 1992, wrote that he saw "great pain" in his face. When we met, it was fourteen years later and Joe was sixty-two. Life marks anyone who lives that long. Marriages fail—two in Joe's case. Parents die. Faculties and friendships fade along with dreams of fame, fortune, and glory. And we all have secrets deeply buried that cut like glass. You can see the years in Joe's face, but really the question was, did this Joe radiate more pain than the average sixty-two-year-old-Joe?

I did not see "great pain" in his face. But I did see sadness in his eyes, and an inordinate caution. It's easier to say what it reminded me of than to describe it directly. I once knew a man who, at twenty-four, had flown P-47s in the Pacific during World War II. He was a good pilot. He killed many enemy soldiers and pilots with his eight Browning machine guns and bombs. He was also very lucky—one of only five survivors of his twelve-man squadron. Young men pass from youth in many ways—marriage, achievements, parenthood. Living with death, and dealing it, had ended this man's youth.

Thereafter he lived his life fully, loved good food, played happily with his grandchildren, laughed easily. But you could see behind his eyes war damage that decades could not erase. He was an avid gardener, and more than once I found him standing knee-deep in red azaleas, trowel dangling from his hand as he gazed and gazed at the sky.

Joe is not active in the mountaineering community now, but, responding to an invitation, he attended a 1997 Denali Conference in Portland, Oregon. It was an updated version of the 1967 Anchorage Conference in that a veritable Who's Who of McKinley climbing convened: Daryl Miller, McKinley's chief climbing ranger; living legend Jim Bridwell; Dave Johnston of Winter Climb fame; guide Vern Tejas, who made the first solo winter ascent, to name only a few. And Brad and Barbara Washburn.

At the conference, Joe presented his slide show about the 1967 tragedy. It is not the kind of show that people applaud afterward, because it ends with pictures of seven dead young men and Joe's statement, "These were my friends."

After that last statement, no one moved or talked or even coughed. It was the silence that properly follows an elegy. But after a while, when people realized that that was it, there was a general shuffling and standing up. Part of it was Brad Washburn rising from his folding chair in the front row, walking up to Joe, shaking his hand, and saying softly, "You did everything as well as it could be done."

Washburn did not apologize then, or since, for any of his own actions. When Joe told me about Brad's 1997 gesture in Portland, he suggested that they had become, if not friends, at least not enemies. But it was also clear that a handshake and one sentence could not erase thirty years' worth of pain. During our time together, except for his description of the post-slide show gesture, Joe did not speak Washburn's name without heat.

Evidence of the tragedy was surprisingly present in Joe's life, even in 2005. When we got into his Jeep Wagoneer, I noticed copies of *White Winds* piled behind the front seat. Copies are also prominent in the bookshelves in his home and on his boat. Prints of the painting of McKinley that appeared in *White Winds* were stacked on the dining table of his apartment, where he was hand-numbering them for later distribution. The splendid painting itself, which Joe commissioned by Seattle artist Gus Swanberg, hangs over the fireplace in his home.

Evidence that is no less compelling for being less obvious finds expression in other areas of his life. When outfitting *Shepherd Moon*, his Island Packet 350, for blue-water cruising, he added 700 extra pounds of lead keel weight to compensate for topside equipment. All that keel weight, of course, is what makes sailboats sink like, well, lead once their hulls fill from capsize or holing. Both are relatively remote possibilities if a skipper watches the weather and sails conservatively, which Joe does. But the '05 Joe still worked very hard indeed—even harder than most blue water sailors—to cut the cancer of chance out of life. Thus he made *Shepherd Moon* positively buoyant, no small feat on a boat with 7,500 pounds of ballast. He meticulously carved 200 cubic feet of refrigeration-quality Styrofoam to fit in every available empty space, then installed two huge flotation bags besides.

On the Web site he maintains to chronicle his voyages, he has written: "Much of the expense of outfitting *Shepherd Moon* was in design and planning things that are not normally done on boats and without knowledge of what the benefits would be." Indeed. Even the boat's name bespeaks Joe's desire, or need, to avail himself of every possible advantage over fate. A shepherd maintains his flock and keeps it safe. A shepherd moon does the same sort of thing, on a much grander scale. "The name *Shepherd Moon* comes from space. They are the small moons that gravitationally shepherd the rings of planets."

After a while during my days in Seattle, I lost track of how many times Joe reassured me that now he was fine, loved his present life, relished the sailing and running and time with Robin, enjoyed teaching, cherished his daughters. "I hope I don't seem to you like a devastated man, because I'm not," he said again and again, with a smile that could have been ironic or beseeching, or a little of both. I had to admit to him, and to you, that, no, devastation wasn't the right word. But that refrain of reassurances made me think of how Muhammad Ali would grin when one of Joe Frazier's sledgehammer hooks caught him, as if to persuade us, and himself, that "Nah, didn't hurt a bit, ain't no big thing." It *was* a big thing when he got hit like that, of course, which was why Ali had to deny how much it hurt, lest his opponent, emboldened, swarm in for the kill.

Just as there had been an emotional crux to my meetings with Jerry and Howard, so was there one with Joe. And it came, as did the other two, unexpectedly. We were sitting in his apartment one afternoon, and I was asking questions and he was answering them. Finally I had no more to ask. At that point, he asked *me* one: "Do you think anybody will make a film from the book?"

I hadn't thought about it and said that I didn't know. He said that he had thought a lot about how a film might end, if one were ever made about the climb. Then he told me his thoughts. When he was finished, tears were shining in his eyes. And mine.

An older man is in his home, cutting ribbons of fabric out of the remains of an old tent. When he is finished, he folds the remaining fabric carefully and puts it away.

Then he is driving into Talkeetna. He parks at one of the flight service hangars. He gets out of his car, carrying a box, and a pilot comes out to meet him. They seem to know each other. They climb into the pilot's silver

Cessna, take off, fly through One Shot Pass, and soon are circling below McKinley's summit. It is a clear day in July, late, a huge orange sun balanced on the evening horizon.

The older man opens the box on his lap and takes out a wreath, to which he has tied the black ribbon he cut from the tent. He pushes the plane's door open, holds it against the slipstream, and carefully gives the wreath to the sky.

The wreath drops, borne and buoyed by the wind, turning over and over, ribbon streaming, floating, falling, falling into the dying sun.

Author's Note

M y research produced voluminous documentation that informs *Forever on the Mountain*. The foundation of this book was material from survivors: three other books, numerous journals, maps, old equipment and clothing, hundreds of photographs, and many hours of recorded interviews. These were augmented by hundreds of pages procured from National Park Service archives through Freedom of Information Act requests, scores more from other government agencies and several university archival collections, hours of radio communication transcripts, and countless interviews with experts in everything from abnormal psychology to forensic meteorology to mountain aviation.

However, no journals or cameras were recovered from the seven men who died high on Mount McKinley sometime between July 18 and 28, 1967, so presenting their last days, hours, and minutes was a challenge. One tempting approach was to fictionalize those events, but my editor wisely steered me elsewhere, asserting that to fictionalize even a small part of the narrative risked undermining its vastly greater factual parts.

I could render many of those final days' experiences realistically from my own time in mountains, which was enough to familiarize me with altitude sickness, avalanches, being lost, conflict, crevasses, exhaustion, frostbite, going hungry and thirsty, hypothermia, igloos, long storms, piss bottles, seventy-mile-per-hour winds, snow caves, and other realities of Alaskan mountain climbing. In addition, interviews with scientists and medical experts helped me understand and describe what was happening to the dying men's bodies and minds. Other sources provided valuable insight into what those men were thinking, feeling, saying, and doing as they slipped closer to death each day. *Minus 148*, Art Davidson's classic description of his near-death experience with the 1967 Winter Expedition, was illuminating. So were near-death accounts by two physician-mountaineers, Thomas Hornbein, of Mount Everest West Ridge legend, and 1996 Everest survivor Seaborne Beckwith Weathers. Other sources, too numerous to list here, were also helpful.

But for all that, some conjecture was inescapable, and the approach I chose was to try to involve readers in the process of deducing most-probable scenarios as I worked my own way to them through thickets of theory and conjecture. In so doing, I relied on a modified version of the probative legal concept of probable cause that I had been taught, and used often, many years ago: *a set of articulable facts, circumstances, and evidence which would lead a reasonable person to conclude that such a thing had happened, was happening, or was about to happen.*

A note about dialogue. Speech reproduced verbatim, in quotation marks, is supported by unimpeachable written source material. Other communications reported by multiple recollections or even by notes in writing, but made at some remove from the events, are shown without quotation marks.

Recommended Reading

Mount McKinley / Denali

First reads for those wishing to know more about the July 1967 tragedy on Denali must be books by the expedition's two leaders: Howard Snyder's *The Hall of the Mountain King* (1973) and Joe Wilcox's *White Winds* (1981). *A Reader's Guide to the Hall of the Mountain King* (1981) provides Wilcox's meticulous dissection of various errors he believes exist in *The Hall of the Mountain King*. (These books are out of print, but used copies can easily be found online.)

Three volumes about disaster were of inestimable help to me while writing this book, and are essential reading for anyone wanting to understand how best-laid plans become fatal tragedies: *Young Men and Fire* (1992) is Norman Maclean's brilliant investigation of the 1949 Mann Gulch fire that killed thirteen Smokejumpers; *The Perfect Storm* (2000) is Sebastian Junger's tale of terror on the high seas; and *the* classic story of a mountaineering expedition turned deadly, of course, is Jon Krakauer's *Into Thin Air* (1997), his first-person account of the 1996 disaster on Everest.

For details and photographs of the Muldrow Glacier route on Denali, there is no better source than Brad Washburn's splendid *Climbing Guide to the Muldrow Glacier Route* (1968).

Three comprehensive volumes containing everything from Denali's prehistoric geology to modern extreme climbing stand out. One is Fred Beckey's *Mount McKinley: Icy Crown of North America* (1993), which, despite errors in its report of the July 1967 tragedy, remains one of the best general introductions to Mount McKinley. A second is Bill Sherwonit's *Denali: The Complete Guide* (2002). Finally, David Roberts and Brad Washburn's *Mount McKinley: The Conquest of Denali*, is distinguished by Roberts's superb writing and Washburn's matchless photographs.

Two books in particular will be appreciated by those interested in learning more of Denali climbing's history: *The Ascent of Denali*, by Archdeacon Hudson Stuck (1914), and *Mount McKinley: The Pioneer Climbs,* by Terris Moore (1967).

For ordeal and survival on Denali, Art Davidson's *Minus 148* (1969) is already a legendary tome. Also essential reading for those interested in Denali's challenges and hazards are two books by Jonathan Waterman. *Surviving Denali* (1991) is an analysis of disasters on the mountain. *In the Shadow of Denali: Life and Death on Alaska's Mt. McKinley* (1998) is a collection of essays "about the emotional force of death." Both books go far beyond a quotidian compilation of facts and figures with writing as elegant and evocative as a brilliant lead on black ice.

Mountaineering and Extreme Survival

Four books about extreme survival were helpful. Peter Potterfield's *In The Zone* (1996), a powerfully written collection of climbers' near-death experiences (including his own) helped me better understand the McKinley tragedy. *Surviving Extremes* (2004), by the adventuring physician Ken Kamler, provided scientific and medical insights about humans in extremis that I found nowhere else. *Deep Survival* (2003), by Laurence Gonzales, brought systems-theory analysis to the examination of tragic events. That in turn led to Charles Perrow's classic treatise on the subject, *Normal Accidents* (1984).

The equally classic evocation of climbing as a breeder of fraternity, rather than fratricide, is *K2: The Savage Mountain* (1954), by 1953 American K2 Expedition members Charles S. Houston, MD, and Robert H. Bates.

The best reflection on the relationship between climbers and mountains that I have read is Robert Macfarlane's *Mountains of the Mind* (2003). For descriptions of harrowing expedition experiences at their best and worst, one cannot do better than *The Worst Journey in the World* (1922), Apsley Cherry-Garrard's account of his polar misadventures with Sir Robert Falcon Scott.

One author must receive special notice: David Roberts. His *True Summit* (2000), which revealed mountaineering icon Maurice Herzog's dark side, established for the climbing milieu what others have done for statesmen, artists, and soldiers—namely, that great men are not always good people. In a larger sense, Roberts is a writer who climbs, rather than the other way 'round. His work could legitimately be compared to that of novelist James Salter, America's greatest living prose stylist. As such, there is no better volume of work about climbing in all its glory and horror than David Roberts's articles in *Outside* magazine and his many books on the subject.

Photograph Credits

1. Courtesy of Gayle Nienheuser.
2. Dennis Luchterhand, reproduced courtesy of Joe Wilcox.
3. Courtesy of Gayle Nienheuser.
4. Howard Snyder.
5. Jeff Babcock, courtesy of Gayle Nienheuser.
6. Howard Snyder.
7. Jerry Lewis
8. Joe Wilcox.
9. Howard Snyder.
10. Howard Snyder, reproduced courtesy of Jerry Lewis.
11. Howard Snyder.
12–13. Wayne Merry.
14. Bill Babcock, courtesy of Gayle Nienheuser.
15. Courtesy of Gayle Nienheuser.
16. Jeff Babcock.

Index

Page numbers in *italics* refer to maps.

Schiff, Anshel (*continued*)
    helicopter rescue of, 255–56
    intestinal infection of, 97–101, 111
    loads carried by, 97–101, 131,
        159–60
    personality of, 99, 111, 350–51
    post-expedition life of, 97, 350–51
    in summit ascent, 132, 142, 201
    survival of, 97, 340, 350–51
    weight loss of, 98, 129, 351
    in Wilcox group, 90, 92
Schlichter, Beverly, 352
Schlichter, Paul:
    acclimatization of, 124, 142, 151,
        158, 164, 232, 244–45
    author's interview with, 351–53, 358
    Camp VI, 189–90, 193–94, 196,
        198, 204, 219–21, 224, 225
    climbing speed of, 103, 104, 110,
        138, 355
    in Colorado group, 53–54, 59–60,
        74, 78, 112, 146, 255, 355
    descent of, 164, 220–21, 224, 225,
        226–27, 229, 232, 234, 241,
        244–45
    as disaster participant, 189–90,
        193–94, 196, 198, 204, 219–21,
        224, 225, 226–27, 229, 232, 234,
        241, 244–45, 255, 258–59, 262
    as expedition member, 69, 74, 78,
        313
    flare released by, 150, 155–56, 199,
        363
    loads carried by, 99, 127
    with Mercer's horse teams, 77–83,
        102
    personality of, 59, 112, 136, 352, 357

physical appearance of, 52
post-expedition life of, 351–53
in summit ascent, 137, 142, 149,
    151, 153, 154, 155–56, 363
survival of, 340, 351–53
trailbreaking by, 58, 90
weight of, 244–45
at Wonder Lake, 258
Schoene, Brownie, 152
Schoening, Pete, 29, 116–17
Scott, Robert Falcon, 37, 57, 102, 218
Scrambles Amongst the Alps (Whymper),
    61
scuba divers, 51
Seattle Mountaineers' expedition (1964),
    115
Seattle Rescue Council, 297–98, 302
Secor, R. J., 172
self-arrests, 49, 89, 95, 96, 225–26, 229,
    298, 336–37
Shannon, Len, 332–33
Sheldon, Don, 30, 46, 116, 201, 203,
    209, 210, 211, 213–14, 222–24,
    234, 235–36, 239, 242, 243,
    246–49, 253–64, 267–68, 270,
    281, 286, 289, 298, 305, 309,
    335
Sheldon, Roberta, 211, 213, 222–23, 239
Shelley, Percy Bysshe, 15
Shepherd Moon, 368–69
Shields, Dick, 282
Shorter, Frank, 366
Shulski, Martha, 348
siege-style climbing, 87
Simpson, Joe, 225–26
"single push" climbing, 20
Siula Grande, 225

ABOUT THE AUTHOR

James M. Tabor is a former contributing editor to *Outside* magazine and *SKI Magazine* as well as a senior editor at *Backpacker*. His writing has also appeared in *Smithsonian, Reader's Digest, Time,* and many other national magazines.

He hosted the popular national PBS series *The Great Outdoors,* and is currently writing and producing a History Channel special about caves.

He studied writing with novelist John Barth at Johns Hopkins University's writing seminars, and his first published short story was included in the O. Henry Awards collection.